The 21st-Century Voter

Who Votes, How They Vote, and Why They Vote

Volume 1: Introductory Essays and Entries A–L

Guido H. Stempel III and Thomas K. Hargrove, Editors

 ABC-CLIO™

An Imprint of ABC-CLIO, LLC
Santa Barbara, California • Denver, Colorado

Copyright © 2016 by ABC-CLIO, LLC

All rights reserved. No part of this publication may be reproduced, stored in a retrieval system, or transmitted, in any form or by any means, electronic, mechanical, photocopying, recording, or otherwise, except for the inclusion of brief quotations in a review, without prior permission in writing from the publisher.

Library of Congress Cataloging-in-Publication Data

The 21st-century voter : who votes, how they vote, and why they vote /
Guido H. Stempel III and Thomas K. Hargrove, editors.
   pages cm
  Includes bibliographical references.
  ISBN 978-1-61069-227-4 (hardback) — ISBN 978-1-61069-228-1 (e-book)
1. Voting—United States—History—21st century. I. Stempel, Guido H. (Guido Hermann), 1928- editor. II. Hargrove, Thomas K., editor.
  JK1967.A17 2016
  324.973—dc23   2015018195

ISBN: 978-1-61069-227-4
EISBN: 978-1-61069-228-1

20 19 18 17 16 1 2 3 4 5

This book is also available on the World Wide Web as an eBook.
Visit www.abc-clio.com for details.

ABC-CLIO
An Imprint of ABC-CLIO, LLC

ABC-CLIO, LLC
130 Cremona Drive, P.O. Box 1911
Santa Barbara, California 93116-1911

This book is printed on acid-free paper ∞

Manufactured in the United States of America

To our wives, both named Anne, who supported and loved us through the long hours of producing this work

Contents

List of Entries

Preface

Franklin Delano Roosevelt and Ronald Reagan agreed on very little when it came to their visions of the appropriate role of government in American life. Yet they were in virtual lockstep in their admiration for the democratic process that brought two such very different men to the pinnacle of power in the 20th century.

"Democracy is worth dying for, because it's the most deeply honorable form of government ever devised by man," Reagan concluded. Roosevelt, likewise, rejected any hint of cynicism when it came to the essential meaning of the American Republic. "Let us never forget that government is ourselves and not an alien power over us," Roosevelt urged. "The ultimate rulers of our democracy are not a president and senators and congressmen and government officials, but the voters of the country."

Americans never seem to tire of praising their democratic forms and institutions. The temptations to lambast corruption, ignorance, and even outright malice within the halls of power must have been as strong in the 20th century as they are in the 21st. Yet our nation's most enduring political heroes have been those who have kept the faith that America is still, to quote the Puritans of the Massachusetts Bay Colony, "a city upon a hill, the eyes of all people are upon us."

The aim of *The 21st-Century Voter: Who Votes, How They Vote, and Why They Vote* is to assemble many of the key concepts and issues that drive 21st-century politics. The introductory essays, which include numerous useful tables, clearly lay out the structure of the American electorate in this century, including the important questions of who participates in elections and how various demographic groups cast their ballots. Following the essays are 237 short entries covering important concepts or personalities that have molded the process by which power is apportioned. The essays and entries were written by the editors and by scholars drawn from various related disciplines. Finally, the most recent political platforms of the Democratic, Republican, Libertarian, and Green parties are reprinted to list the lengthy and often entirely contradictory visions that Americans have for their nation.

Most items in this two-volume work are cross-referenced with "See also" suggestions to related ideas presented in other essays and entries in the book. Every item has recommendations for further reading on the topic, both print and electronic. Also included is a bibliography of general information resources and electoral maps of the last five presidential elections as of this writing (1996–2012). Key concepts and historical references are indexed at the end of the volumes so that ideas and issues in the essays and entries can quickly be located.

Finally, it is the hope of the editors that this work will instill a deeper understanding of the complexities of American political power into its readers. Democracies, unlike all other forms of government, are as intricate and convoluted as the people who compose them. America in the 21st century has a host of countervailing themes and contradictions. Never has the political process been more susceptible to moneyed interests than at this time of unprecedented concentration of wealth in the hands of a shrinking elite. Yet at the same time, never has America's democratic process been more open and inclusive of people of every possible human characteristic.

The editors hope that this encyclopedia will assist readers in understanding the modern political process, in recognizing the flaws that challenge America's institutions, and in celebrating our collective democratic vision.

Who Votes? A Demographic Overview of the American Electorate

Guido H. Stempel III and Thomas K. Hargrove

We hear frequently that the outcome of any election depends on voter turnout. Since not everybody votes, the question of who does is a matter of enormous political consequence.

The U.S. Census Bureau has been tracking voter participation through the Current Population Survey since 1994, a series of studies that has documented significant shifts in the makeup of the American electorate during the first national elections of the 21st century. These shifts have been crucial in determining the balance of power between the Democratic and Republican parties as well as in setting an array of important public policies. They also are symbolic of the changing demographic makeup of the broader United States population, even if they are not exact mirrors of the actual population.

The turnout rate in major national elections in the United States has fluctuated significantly since 1960, when an estimated 64 percent of Americans of voting age went to the polls in the presidential race between John F. Kennedy and Richard Nixon. (This and similar estimates were made in an era before the Census Bureau began tracking election participation.) Turnout began a steady slide downward through the politically turbulent era of the 1960s and 1970s before leveling off in the early 1980s. Only about 50 percent of the voting-age population is judged to have cast ballots in the 1988 campaign that saw Republican Vice President George H.W. Bush elected to the White House for one term. His successful Democratic challenger, Bill Clinton and third party candidate Ross Perot helped raise the rate to about 55 percent in 1992, but turnout hit a new low of 49 percent in Clinton's re-election in 1996.

Voter concerns about terrorism, the wisdom of the U.S. military incursion into Iraq, and a major economic recession at home caused resurgence in voter participation in the 21st century to levels not seen in 40 years. The Census estimates that in the 2008 presidential election, 71 percent of U.S. citizens 18 years old or older were registered to vote and 63.8 percent voted. These registration and participation rates are among the highest ever reported, although not quite as high as the estimated rates in 1960. The turnout rate dropped in 2012—as often happens when an incumbent president seeks a second term—but still remained above other recent elections. The Census Bureau reports that while registration rates among people of eligible age have been relatively constant in recent election cycles, the rate at which people participate in presidential elections has generally increased.

Table 1 Reported Rates of Voting and Registration: 1996 to 2012

Year	Registration Rate among Citizens	Voting Rate among Citizens	Voting Rate among Registered
1996	70.9%	58.4%	82.3%
2000	69.5	59.5	85.5
2004	72.1	63.8	88.5
2008	71.0	63.6	89.6
2012	71.2	61.8	86.8

Source: U.S. Census Bureau. *Voting and Registration in the Election of November 2000, 2004, 2008, and 2012.* (Washington, D.C., Department of Commerce.)

Table 2 Reported Rates of Voting and Registration among Men and Women: 2000 to 2012

Year	Registration Rate among Citizens	Voting Rate among Citizens
Men in 2000	68.0	58.1
Men in 2004	70.5	62.1
Men in 2008	69.1	61.5
Men in 2012	69.3	59.7
Women in 2000	70.1	60.7
Women in 2004	73.6	65.4
Women in 2008	72.8	65.7
Women in 2012	72.9	63.7

Source: U.S. Census Bureau. *Voting and Registration in the Election of November 2000, 2004, and 2008.* (Washington, D.C., Department of Commerce, 2002, 2006, and 2012.)

But the broader question remains: Who votes? The Census Bureau has documented significant differences between demographic groups. People of varying sex, age, race, education, income, and even geography have had significantly different rates of participation in national elections.

Women consistently were more likely to register and more likely to vote than were men, as Table 2 shows. During most of U.S. history, men dominated electoral politics. Women were granted universal suffrage with the 1920 ratification of the Nineteenth Amendment to the U.S. Constitution, which prohibited any state or federal sex-based restrictions on voting. Female participation in the electoral process expanded slowly and steadily through the 20th century, corresponding to a rising educational attainment and labor force participation for women, both closely correlated to voting. Women's registration and participation rates finally surpassed those of men in the presidential election of 1984. In the 2008 presidential election, women voters outnumbered men by 70.4 million to 60.7 million, then the largest numerical gender gap in history.

Table 3 Rates of Voting and Registration among Racial and Ethnic Groups: 2000 to 2012

Group and Year	Registration Rate among Citizens	Voting Rate among Citizens
Non-Hispanic Whites in 2000	71.6	61.8
Non-Hispanic Whites in 2004	75.1	67.2
Non-Hispanic Whites in 2008	73.5	66.1
Non-Hispanic Whites in 2012	73.7	64.1
Blacks in 2000	67.5	56.8
Blacks in 2004	68.7	60.0
Blacks in 2008	69.7	64.7
Blacks in 2012	73.1	66.2
Hispanics (any race) in 2000	57.3	45.1
Hispanics (any race) in 2004	57.9	47.2
Hispanics (any race) in 2008	59.4	49.9
Hispanics (any race) in 2012	58.7	48.0
Asians in 2000	52.4	43.3
Asians in 2004	51.8	44.1
Asians in 2008	55.3	47.8
Asians in 2012	56.3	47.3

Source: U.S. Census Bureau. *Voting and Registration in the Election of November 2000, 2004, 2008, and 2012.* (Washington, D.C., Department of Commerce, 2002, 2006, 2010, and 2014.)

Another remarkable change in 21st-century voting has been the rising participation rates of racial and ethnic minority groups. This increase was a significant factor in the election in 2008 and re-election in 2012 of President Barack Obama, the nation's first black chief executive. Non-Hispanic white voters have historically participated in elections more than any other race or ethnicity, but the political rise of so-called "people of color" has transformed American politics. Participation from black voters in the political process approached parity with white voters in 2008. The percentage of blacks surpassed the percentage of whites voting for the first time in 2012.

Generational voting patterns have also undergone significant change, although it remains true that older citizens are much more likely to cast a ballot than are younger ones. Nevertheless, the age gap has closed significantly. Younger voters at the outset of the 21st century were part of the best-educated generation in history, a factor that usually increases voting participation. The Census estimates the number of voters 18 to 34 years old leaped from 24.9 million in 2000 to 32.0 million in 2008. There was a significant reduction in the turnout rate of young voters in 2012 compared to other recent elections, although their participation rate was still well above that of 2000.

Table 4 Rates of Voting and Registration by Age Group: 2000, 2004, 2008, and 2012

Group and Year	Registration Rate among Citizens	Voting Rate among Citizens
18–24 years in 2000	50.7	36.1
18–24 years in 2004	57.6	46.7
18–24 years in 2008	58.5	48.5
18–24 years in 2012	53.6	41.2
25–44 years in 2000	67.1	56.1
25–44 years in 2004	69.3	60.1
25–44 years in 2008	68.2	60.0
25–44 years in 2012	68.7	57.3
45–64 years in 2000	75.4	67.8
45–64 years in 2004	76.9	70.4
45–64 years in 2008	74.9	69.2
45–64 years in 2012	75.4	67.9
65–74 years in 2000	78.8	72.2
65–74 years in 2004	79.5	73.3
65–74 years in 2008	78.1	72.4
65–74 years in 2012	79.7	73.5
75 and older 2000	78.0	66.5
75 and older 2004	79.0	68.5
75 and older 2008	76.6	67.8
75 and older 2012	79.1	70.0

Source: U.S. Census Bureau. *Voting and Registration in the Election of November 2000, 2004, 2008, and 2012.* (Washington, D.C., Department of Commerce, 2002, 2006, 2010, and 2014.)

The participation rate among voters 65 and older has held steady in recent elections, but the graying of America has continued as the Baby Boom generation starts to retire, helping swell the ranks of elderly voters. The Census estimates there were 25.5 million voters 65 or older in the 2008 election, up from 22.1 million in 2000.

Married people were consistently more likely to vote than those who were widowed, divorced, living separately, or had never been married, but the U.S. electorate has become less homogenous when it comes to matrimony. Singleness—the tendency of Americans to live outside traditional matrimony—has generally increased to an all-time high in recent years. That certainly affected the marital patterns of the U.S. electorate. Americans who've never been married are among the fastest-growing segments of the electorate, increasing from 19.2 million voters in 2000 to 35.9 million in 2012.

Table 5 Rates of Voting and Registration by Marital Status: 2000 and 2012

Group and Year	Registration Rate among Citizens	Voting Rate among Citizens
Married in 2000	76.2	67.7
Married in 2012	77.1	69.3
Never Married in 2000	56.4	44.0
Never Married in 2012	61.3	50.0

Source: U.S. Census Bureau. *Voting and Registration in the Election of November 2000* and *Voting and Registration in the Election of November 2012.* (Washington, D.C., Department of Commerce, 2002 and 2012.)

Table 6 Rates of Voting and Registration by Education and Income: 2012

Education and Income	Registration Rate among Citizens	Voting Rate among Citizens
No high school	49.3	37.1
Some high school	50.1	38.3
High school grad	63.7	52.6
Some college	74.3	64.2
Bachelor's degree	81.7	75.0
Advanced degree	85.7	81.3
Less than $20,000	61.8	47.5
$20,000 to $29,999	67.7	55.8
$30,000 to $39,999	69.2	58.4
$40,000 to $48,999	73.8	63.0
$50,000 to $74,999	77.4	68.0
$75,000 to $99,999	81.7	73.8
$100,000 to $149,999	84.9	76.9
$150,000 and over	87.1	80.2

Source: U.S. Census Bureau. *Voting and Registration in the Election of November 2012.* (Washington, D.C., Department of Commerce, 2014.)

Voting increased consistently with education and income, a trend that has not changed much over recent years. Of those who had not completed high school, only 39.4 percent voted, while for those with an advanced degree, 82.7 percent voted. The biggest gap, 15.5 percent, was between those who had not completed high school and those who had a high school degree. Of those with an income of less than $20,000, only slightly more than half voted. Voting participation generally rises with income, hitting about three-quarters of Americans in households earning $75,000 or more.

Since these trends have not changed significantly in recent years, Table 6 shows the participation rates according to education and income for only the 2012 election.

Many other factors can influence the likelihood that Americans will vote. It's long been recognized that people become more likely to vote when they perceive they have a stake in the outcome of an election or realize that public policy will directly affect them. Such people generally own their homes in a community, have a sense of "rootedness" to their community, have an expectation for employment that can be influenced by public policy, or have already shown a commitment to defending the nation through current or previous military service.

Employment status consistently matters. Of those who were employed in 2012, 64.3 percent voted compared to just 51.9 percent among unemployed persons. There was an even wider gap between homeowners, of whom 66.9 percent voted, and renters, of whom 48.9 percent voted. Length of residence also affected voting, with 75.9 percent of those who had been in their present residence five years or more voting, while only 51.2 percent of those who had been in their current residence for less than a year voted. Again, since these trends rarely change much from election to election, presented here are the voting participation rates in the 2012 election.

Geography has, historically, also influenced the rate at which Americans vote, although the causes of this can be complex and controversial. Voting requires registration, and in 2012 only 71.2 percent of American citizens were registered. Registration rules are set by the states and vary considerably. It seems evident that it is easier to register in some states than others. There are at least 11 states and the District of Columbia that permit registration on Election Day. Three of the five highest turnout rates were in states that permit same-day registration. But the state with the highest registration and turnout rate in 2012 was Mississippi, which also has the nation's highest statewide concentration of black voters who were highly

Table 7 Rates of Voting and Registration by Housing Tenure, Employment Status, Duration of Residents, and Military Service: 2012

Nature of Household	Registration Rate among Citizens	Voting Rate among Citizens
Employed	73.5	64.3
Unemployed	64.1	51.9
Owner	75.0	66.9
Renter	61.3	48.9
Less than 1 year	66.8	51.2
1 to 2 years	73.3	60.6
3 to 4 years	77.3	66.4
5 years or longer	84.9	75.9
Veteran	75.3	68.0
Nonveteran	81.2	77.0

Source: U.S. Census Bureau. *Voting and Registration in the Election of November 2012.* (Washington, D.C., Department of Commerce, 2014.)

motivated to vote for the re-election of President Obama. Also leading the nation in voter participation in 2012 were Wisconsin, Minnesota, Massachusetts, and Colorado. Of these four, only Massachusetts does not allow registration on Election Day, although the proposal has been under consideration by the Massachusetts State Legislature for many years.

States with the worst voter participation rates were Texas, Arkansas, Oklahoma, Hawaii, and West Virginia—none of which allow same-day voter registration. It should be noted that turnout was so poor in West Virginia that in 2012 it was the only state in which voting rates dropped below 50 percent of eligible citizens.

Many other factors influence voting rates. Turnout generally was better in those states voting for governor in the same year as presidential elections than in states that hold gubernatorial contests in other years. However, states that hold U.S. Senate races during presidential election years generally do not experience increased turnout when compared to states with no senate races.

Having a "favorite son" on a presidential ticket does not necessarily reap dramatically increased voter participation in the candidate's home state. In the 2008 presidential election, state turnout was well below the national average both in Arizona, home of Republican nominee John McCain, and in Illinois, home of Democratic nominee Barack Obama. The turnout in Illinois also remained slightly below the national average for Obama's successful run for re-election in 2012.

Table 8 Percent of Population Registered to Vote and Reported Voting: 2012

State	Registration Rate among Citizens	Voting Rate among Citizens
United States	71.2	61.8
Alabama	73.5	61.9
Alaska	72.8	58.4
Arizona	65.2	55.9
Arkansas	65.3	53.3
California	65.6	57.5
Colorado	74.4	70.4
Connecticut	70.4	62.7
Delaware	73.3	67.3
District Of Columbia	83.4	75.9
Florida	68.3	60.8
Georgia	70.7	61.9
Hawaii	58.9	51.6
Idaho	70.0	63.9
Illinois	72.7	61.5
Indiana	69.2	59.3
Iowa	78.2	69.4
Kansas	74.4	63.3

(Continued)

Table 8 (*Continued*)

State	Registration Rate among Citizens	Voting Rate among Citizens
Kentucky	72.1	59.3
Louisiana	77.1	66.3
Maine	77.1	68.6
Maryland	72.1	65.1
Massachusetts	78.7	70.8
Michigan	77.8	66.8
Minnesota	79.0	73.2
Mississippi	84.2	74.5
Missouri	76.7	63.9
Montana	73.3	65.7
Nebraska	69.5	61.6
Nevada	65.0	57.9
New Hampshire	75.9	69.4
New Jersey	73.0	61.9
New Mexico	68.6	61.6
New York	67.9	58.7
North Carolina	78.9	68.9
North Dakota	74.5	63.9
Ohio	71.1	63.1
Oklahoma	66.1	52.4
Oregon	74.3	67.6
Pennsylvania	71.9	61.6
Rhode Island	73.5	62.5
South Carolina	73.3	64.7
South Dakota	74.8	61.0
Tennessee	68.6	55.7
Texas	66.9	53.8
Utah	63.5	57.0
Vermont	73.4	63.3
Virginia	74.6	66.9
Washington	73.1	65.6
West Virginia	68.1	47.8
Wisconsin	78.1	73.6
Wyoming	63.9	58.9

Source: U.S. Census Bureau. *Voting and Registration in the Election of November 2012.* (Washington, D.C., Department of Commerce, 2014.)

Schedule conflict and lack of interest seem to be the biggest factors cited by eligible people who do not vote, according to the Census Bureau's Current Population Survey for November 2012. The top four cited reasons for not voting were: "Too busy, conflicting schedule" accounting for 19 percent, "Not Interested" accounting for 16 percent, "Illness or disability" accounting for 14 percent, and "Did not like candidates or campaign issues" accounting for 13 percent. Another 9 percent said they were out of town on Election Day, 5 percent said they'd experienced "registration problems," and 4 percent said they'd forgotten to vote. Six percent said they either had "transportation problems" on Election Day or blamed an "inconvenient polling place." Less than 1 percent blamed bad weather, 11 percent cited various other reasons, and 3 percent either refused to answer or said they "don't know" why they didn't vote. (Note: Total is more than 100 percent because of rounding.)

The Census reported that men were much more likely than women to say they were "not interested" or "did not like the candidates." Men were twice as likely as women to report being "out of town" on Election Day. Women, however, were twice as likely as men to cite "illness or disability" for not voting.

All of the information presented so far has been based upon participation rates in presidential elections, which are by far the best-attended voting events. The nature of the electorate changes significantly during so-called "off-year" elections, when control of the White House is not an issue. Generally speaking, the off-year elections show a slight but very significant shift toward men since male voters are at near parity with female voters. The "gender gap" in participation rates closed from a 6-point advantage for women in the 2012 presidential election to just a 2-point advantage in the 2014 congressional election. Since men are much more likely to vote Republican than are women, the consequences of this small-seeming shift can be—and was—enormous.

There were other equally significant shifts in demographics in the 2014 off-year voting. Non-Hispanic white voters enjoyed an increased share of the electorate, as did older voters, who accounted for one-third of the off-year electorate compared to just a quarter of the voters in the presidential campaign. These demographic groups also skew significantly toward the GOP, explaining, in part, why the Democrats did so poorly in the 2014 campaigns. (Note: Exit polling data is used here because U.S. Census estimates for the 2014 off-year campaign were not available at time of publication.)

Finally, an important factor influencing whether Americans choose to vote is how they feel about the two major political parties, which, with very few exceptions, nominate the viable candidates for most national and state political offices. Complicated and conflicting attitudes about the Democratic and Republican parties can increase uncertainty about the issues in an election or lead to doubts about both parties' platforms, especially among independent voters, who have become a growing element within the electorate. Such doubt is unlikely to promote voting. Table 10, based on a survey conducted in October 2000 by Ohio University and the Scripps Howard News Service, suggests that the lack of interest may be partly because of the attitudes the public holds about the two major parties' health, agenda, and position on issues.

Significant percentages of Democrats and Republicans indicated they have doubts about the health of their own parties and the quality of the agendas their parties have undertaken. Republicans and Democrats were especially likely to question whether their own parties have adopted clear issues.

Perhaps even more telling, independent voters rarely believe that the major parties have adopted clear issues. Democrats were much more likely to praise the clarity of Republicans

Table 9 Comparison of Composition of Electorate for the 2012 Presidential and 2014 Congressional Elections

Group	Percentage in 2014 Election	Percentage in 2012 Election
Men	49	47
Women	51	53
White	75	72
Black	12	13
Hispanic	8	10
Asian	3	3
18-29	13	19
30-44	22	26
45-59	32	29
60 or more	34	25
Married	63	60
Not Married	37	40
High School Dropout	2	3
High School Grad	18	21
Some College	29	29
College Grad	31	29
Post Grad	20	18
East	20	21
Midwest	25	24
South	33	33
West	22	22
Family $30,000 or less	16	20
$30,000 to $49,999	20	20
$50,000 to $100,000	34	31
Over $100,000	30	28
Republican	37	32
Independent	28	29
Democrat	36	38
Liberal	23	25
Moderate	40	41
Conservative	37	35

(*Continued*)

Table 9 (*Continued*)

Group	Percentage in 2014 Election	Percentage in 2012 Election
Union Household	17	18
Gay, Lesbian, Bisexual	4	5
Approve of Obama	44	54
Disapprove of Obama	55	45
Voted Democrat	47	51
Voted Republican	53	49

Source: Edison Research for the National Election Pool, a consortium of ABC News, Associated Press, CBS News, CNN, Fox News, and NBC News. National data for 2014 was based on questionnaires completed by 19,441 voters leaving 281 randomly selected precincts across the United States, and includes 2,800 telephone interviews with absentee and early voters.

Table 10 Attitudes toward the Two Major Political Parties among Voters Who Identify with the Democratic Party, the Republican Party, or as Independent (Figures show the percentages of Democrats, Republicans, and Independents who say they agree with each statement.)

Position	Democrat	Republican	Independent
Democratic Party Is Healthy	61.2%	18.8%	20.5%
Republican Party Is Healthy	30.8	49.3	18.9
Democratic Party Has Good Agenda	61.8	15.0	23.2
Republican Party Has Good Agenda	26.3	52.7	21.0
Democratic Party Has Clear Issues	44.7	34.0	20.4
Republican Party Has Clear Issues	36.8	43.0	20.2

Source: Scripps Survey Research Center, Ohio University, October 2000.

and Republicans to believe in the clarity of Democrats than were independents to believe in the clarity of the positions of either party.

One of the driving forces for Republicans' and Democrats' lack of confidence in their own parties is the ideological diversity within the parties. Conventional wisdom holds that Republicans are conservatives and the Democrats are liberals. Yet polling data from the Scripps Survey Research Center have shown consistently that about a fifth of people who describe themselves as conservatives also say they are Democrats or are independent voters who "lean to the Democrats." About a fourth of Republicans say they are not conservatives, most opting for a "middle of the road" ideology. Therefore the major parties, and their candidates, inherently face a nearly impossible task in pleasing all the voters in their party.

How They Vote: An Analysis of Voting Patterns by Demographic Groups

Thomas K. Hargrove and Guido H. Stempel III

How Americans vote is heavily influenced by who they are. The American electorate is a complex quilt of widely varying demographic characteristics that often form bright dividing lines in political preferences. The changing profile of the U.S. population and the subsets of registered voters and participating voters is, again, a matter of enormous political consequence.

Although the electorate has undergone significant change in recent decades, many of the voting preferences of its different groups can be fairly stable. The famous gender gap in America—how women generally are less likely than men to support conservative candidates—has been around for generations. When there are variations from these historical patterns, such as the narrowing of the gender gap in 2004, when women became more likely than usual to support the Republican ticket for president during the nation's war against Middle Eastern-based terrorism, the consequences can become significant in the balance of power between the two major political parties. It was the only election since 1988 when Republicans won the popular vote.

This analysis will examine the general voting preferences of demographic groups in the United States using the very large-sample surveys conducted by consortiums of the nation's major national news organizations among voters as they exited polling places on Election Day for general elections for U.S. president. Methodologies employed in these polls had to change because of changing election practices. The media consortium in 2012, for example, had to conduct telephone interviews in Florida, North Carolina, Ohio, and Wisconsin to account for significant numbers of early voters in those states.

Even before addressing voting groups, it is important to remember that the general political affiliation of voters has seen significant fluctuation with the rising and falling of fortunes for the Democratic and Republican parties. These changes in self-reported allegiance to the parties are usually the result of attitudes for or against the party considered to be in power and therefore responsible for the nation's successes and failures. What might seem to be small percentage-point shifts in party preference usually indicate the outcome and the margin of the presidential contests.

Allegiance to the Democratic Party has shifted only about three percentage points from 1996 to 2012, which helped Democratic candidates win the popular vote in all but

Table 1 Reported Party Preferences by Voters in Presidential Election Exit Polls: 1996 to 2012

Year	Democratic	Republican	Independent
1996	40%	35%	22%
2000	39	35	26
2004	37	37	26
2008	39	32	29
2012	38	32	29

Source: Election Day exit polls conducted in 1996, 2000, 2004, 2008, and 2012 for consortiums of major news organizations by Edison Media Research and Mitofsky International.

one election. Republican Party loyalties have shifted by 5 percentage points, generally to the detriment of the GOP's candidates. But the rise in self-described independents who are loath to commit to either major party has grown by seven percentage points. This would probably indicate an increase in what political professionals call "persuadable voters," who can shift allegiances more easily than voters with clear party preferences.

Table 1 shows how voters who went to the polls in recent president elections identified their party loyalties.

The gender gap was probably around in America when women achieved universal suffrage in 1920, although reliable data for women voters' earliest national elections are difficult to find. The Gallup organization reports the presence of a gender gap at least since 1952, although the gap was in the single digits during some contests in the 1970s. Generally speaking, women can be relied upon to support Democratic presidential candidates significantly more than men, who generally show a preference for Republicans.

In recent elections, the gender gap has been fairly stable, especially for women. The female vote for Democratic presidential candidates has varied only by 5 percentage points from 1996 to 2012. Their 2004 shift toward the Republicans in the aftermath of the terrorist attacks in New York City and Washington, D.C., gave the GOP it's only popular vote win for the national office in recent years.

Male voters have been somewhat more dynamic than women. They showed a greater willingness to defect from the Republican Party in 1996 in favor of independent candidate H. Ross Perot than women were to turn away from the Democrats that year. (Perot got 10 percent of the vote from men, 7 percent from women.) They solidly supported the GOP during the terrorist crisis, but wandered away from the Republican ticket in significant numbers in 2008 following disillusionment with the Iraq war and other perceived failures of GOP leadership. Men varied in their support for the Republican Party by 10 percentage points in recent elections—a rate of variance double that found in the women's vote.

Table 2 shows the gender gap from 1996 to 2012.

The general pattern of voting among the different races and ethnicities in the 21st century has been that non-Hispanic whites support the Republican candidate for president while everyone else—sometimes identified by the phrase "people of color" by minority leaders—generally support Democrats. There has been an increased racial polarization of this trend in recent campaigns, probably exacerbated by the historic position of

Table 2 Support for Democratic or Republican Presidential Campaigns by Gender: 1996 to 2012

Year and Group	Democratic	Republican
Men in 1996	44%	45%
Men in 2000	43	54
Men in 2004	44	55
Men in 2008	49	48
Men in 2012	45	52
Women in 1996	55%	38%
Women in 2000	54	44
Women in 2004	51	48
Women in 2008	56	43
Women in 2012	55	44

Source: Election Day exit polls conducted in 1996, 2000, 2004, 2008, and 2012 for consortiums of major news organizations by Edison Media Research and Mitofsky International.

Barack Obama as America's first black chief executive and by increasing attention on the nation's immigration policies, often condemned by Hispanic and Asian groups as hostile to their interests. Obama's political successes were rooted in the reality that minority voters have become much more numerous and influential. Democratic losses during recent off-year elections, conversely, can partially be attributed to reduced participation by people of color.

While the gender gap has been fairly stable in recent elections, every major racial or ethnic group has experienced a double-digit shift in voting patterns from 1996 to 2012. Non-Hispanic white voter support for the Republican Party ranged from its low-water mark of 46 percent, due to Perot's mostly white-backed independent candidacy, to a high of 59 percent in 2012 when Obama campaigned for re-election on a promise to raise taxes on the wealthy to reduce federal deficits.

Black voters, probably the Democrats' most reliable demographic group, have also shown significant double-digit variations. Their support varied from a low of 84 percent in 1996 when 4 percent of blacks supported Perot, to a high of 95 percent when Obama ran for his first term.

But it was voter groups with significant interest in immigration and the nation's policies about immigration that have shown the greatest swings in loyalty in recent years. Texas-based Republican George W. Bush was able to peel off a major chunk of the Hispanic vote in 2000 and 2004, a testament to his flexibly on immigration issues that angered many in his party.

Asian voters actually flipped their allegiance in national politics in just 16 years, going from a narrow plurality that supported the Republican ticket in 1996 to a nearly three-quarters majority for President Obama in 2012. Polling data should be scrutinized when dealing with such a small subgroup. Yet it is clear that Asians are a rapidly growing constituency that cast about 3 percent of the ballots in 2012, solidly in favor of the Democratic ticket.

Table 3 shows the many shifts in racial voting patterns from 1996 to 2012.

Analyses of voting patterns by different age groups across time are, of course, treacherous since the actual population in each group shifts as voters grow older. But two important trends emerge from such an analysis: the youngest cohort of voters has become increasingly Democratic through the early elections of the 21st century while the eldest voters have become increasingly Republican. Both trends may be short-term, however, because they were heavily influenced by events.

Younger Americans were simultaneously attracted to the charismatic candidacy of Barack Obama while repelled by the military decisions of his predecessor, George W. Bush. The commitment of U.S. troops in Iraq was especially unpopular with young voters. But these same factors helped influence elderly Americans in the opposite political direction. Security concerns prompted by the nation's war on terrorism and Obama's candidacy—unthinkable in their youth—helped push elder voters toward the GOP.

Table 3 Support for Democratic or Republican Presidential Campaigns by Race and Ethnicity: 1996 to 2012

Year and Group	Democratic	Republican
Non-Hispanic Whites 1996	44%	46%
Non-Hispanic Whites 2000	42	55
Non-Hispanic Whites 2004	41	58
Non-Hispanic Whites 2008	43	48
Non-Hispanic Whites 2012	39	59
Blacks 1996	84	12
Blacks 2000	90	9
Blacks 2004	88	11
Blacks 2008	95	5
Blacks 2012	93	6
Hispanics 1996	73	21
Hispanics 2000	62	35
Hispanics 2004	53	44
Hispanics 2008	67	31
Hispanics 2012	71	27
Asians 1996	44	48
Asians 2000	55	41
Asians 2004	56	43
Asians 2008	62	35
Asians 2012	73	26

Source: Election Day exit polls conducted in 1996, 2000, 2004, 2008, and 2012 for consortiums of major news organizations by Edison Media Research and Mitofsky International.

Despite political wrangling over so-called class warfare, economic class has only a modest impact on voting behavior, especially when compared to more powerful factors like gender and race. It is true that economically disadvantaged voters are more likely to vote for Democratic candidates than are more affluent voters, but the political effects of poverty are often offset by other factors, such as geography. For example, the GOP has solid support among white voters in the South even though Southern household incomes lag well behind those in the Northeast, a Democratic stronghold.

The Republican ticket for president in 1996 enjoyed a 16 percentage-point advantage among voters from households in the highest income bracket ($100,000 or more), but that advantage has been shrinking in more recent elections. Barack Obama was able to match the Republican vote among this wealthiest bracket in 2008. The political income gap at the top went back to double digits (although not to the 1996 level) after President Obama campaigned vigorously for re-election on a promise to increase the tax rate on America's

Table 4 Support for Democratic or Republican Presidential Candidates by Age Group: 1996 to 2012

Year and Group	Democratic	Republican
Age 18–29 in 1996	55%	35%
Age 18–29 in 2000	48	47
Age 18–29 in 2004	54	45
Age 18–29 in 2008	66	32
Age 18–29 in 2012	60	37
Age 30–49 in 1996	50	41
Age 30–49 in 2000	48	50
Age 30–49 in 2004	46	53
Age 30–49 in 2008	51	47
Age 30–49 in 2012	51	46
Age 50–64 in 1996	47	45
Age 50–64 in 2000	50	48
Age 50–64 in 2004	47	52
Age 50–64 in 2008	50	49
Age 50–64 in 2012	47	52
Age 65 or more in 1996	50	44
Age 65 or more in 2000	51	47
Age 65 or more in 2004	47	52
Age 65 or more in 2008	45	53
Age 65 or more in 2012	44	56

Source: Election Day exit polls conducted in 1996, 2000, 2004, 2008, and 2012 for consortiums of major news organizations by Edison Media Research and Mitofsky International.

wealthiest citizens. The income gap was greatest among voters from households earning $250,000 or more, who favored Republican challenger Mitt Romney by 55 percent to Obama's 42 percent—a 13 percentage point advantage that nearly matched the GOP advantage among the wealthy in the 1990s.

Organized labor has had a significant impact upon American politics, both through allocation of money to assist politicians friendly to the union cause and through an often potent get-out-the-vote organization. Offsetting these advantages, however, has been organized labor's dwindling share of the labor market as America transitioned to a post-industrialized, more service-based economy, which union leaders have found difficult to organize.

In 1976, when Democratic challenger Jimmy Carter unseated incumbent Republican President Gerald Ford, union households represented 29 percent of the vote. Carter would

Table 5 Support for Democratic or Republican Presidential Campaigns by Income Groups: 1996 to 2012

Year and Group	Democratic	Republican
Less than $30,000 in 1996	56%	34%
Less than $30,000 in 2000	55	41
Less than $30,000 in 2004	59	40
Less than $30,000 in 2008	64	33
Less than $30,000 in 2012	63	35
$30,000 to $49,999 in 1996	49	41
$30,000 to $49,999 in 2000	49	48
$30,000 to $49,999 in 2004	50	49
$30,000 to $49,999 in 2008	55	43
$30,000 to $49,999 in 2012	57	42
$50,000 to $74,999 in 1996	47	46
$50,000 to $74,999 in 2000	46	51
$50,000 to $74,999 in 2004	43	56
$50,000 to $74,999 in 2008	48	49
$50,000 to $74,999 in 2012	46	52
$75,000 to $99,999 in 1996	45	49
$75,000 to $99,999 in 2000	46	52
$75,000 to $99,999 in 2004	45	55
$75,000 to $99,999 in 2008	51	48
$75,000 to $99,999 in 2012	46	52
$100,000 or more in 1996	39	55
$100,000 or more in 2000	43	55

(Continued)

Table 5   (*Continued*)

Year and Group	Democratic	Republican
$100,000 or more in 2004	41	48
$100,000 or more in 2008	49	49
$100,000 or more in 2012	44	54

Source: Election Day exit polls conducted in 1996, 2000, 2004, 2008, and 2012 for consortiums of major news organizations by Edison Media Research and Mitofsky International.

Table 6   Support for Democratic or Republican Presidential Campaigns by Union Households: 1996 to 2012

Year and Group	Democratic	Republican
Union Households in 1996	60	30
Union Households in 2000	59	37
Union Households in 2004	59	40
Union Households in 2008	59	39
Union Households in 2012	58	40
Non-union Households in 1996	47	45
Non-union Households in 2000	45	53
Non-union Households in 2004	44	55
Non-union Households in 2008	51	47
Non-union Households in 2012	49	48

Source: Election Day exit polls conducted in 1996, 2000, 2004, 2008, and 2012 for consortiums of major news organizations by Edison Media Research and Mitofsky International.

have lost without the union vote. But by 2012, union households represented 18 percent of the vote, and Obama probably would have won without the organized labor vote, although his re-election would have been much closer.

As Table 6 demonstrates, union households have provided a steady source of Democratic support over the years, although there have always been significant numbers of people who draw income from union jobs who supported GOP candidates. Much greater swings occur in non-Union households, where the Republican vote has been as high as 55 percent in 2004 to as low as 45 percent in 1996. It was the ability to pull support from non-Union households that gave Democrats victory in 1996, 2008, and 2012.

National polls and Election Day exit polls have generally found that about 4 to 5 percent of adults and nationwide voters answer "yes" to the question: "Are you gay, lesbian, or bisexual?" This group has become a small but reliable source of support for Democratic candidates. It is not impossible that President Obama, who in 2012 became the first sitting president to endorse national recognition for gay marriage, might have lost re-election in 2012 without the support of three-quarters of gay voters.

Table 7 Support for Democratic or Republican Presidential Campaigns by Sexual Orientation: 1996 to 2012

Year and Group	Democratic	Republican
Gay, Lesbian, or Bisexual in 1996	69%	23%
Gay, Lesbian, or Bisexual in 2000	71	25
Gay, Lesbian, or Bisexual in 2004	77	23
Gay, Lesbian, or Bisexual in 2008	70	27
Gay, Lesbian, or Bisexual in 2012	76	22
Not Gay or Bisexual in 1996	48	44
Not Gay or Bisexual in 2000	47	50
Not Gay or Bisexual in 2004	46	53
Not Gay or Bisexual in 2008	53	45
Not Gay or Bisexual in 2012	49	49

Source: Election Day exit polls conducted in 1996, 2000, 2004, 2008, and 2012 for consortiums of major news organizations by Edison Media Research and Mitofsky International.

Table 8 Support for Democratic or Republican Presidential Campaigns According to Voters' Self-Described Political Philosophy: 1996 to 2012

Year and Group	Democratic	Republican
Liberal in 1996	81%	12%
Liberal in 2000	81	13
Liberal in 2004	85	13
Liberal in 2008	89	10
Liberal in 2012	86	11
Moderate in 1996	57	33
Moderate in 2000	53	45
Moderate in 2004	54	45
Moderate in 2008	60	39
Moderate in 2012	56	41
Conservative in 1996	20	72
Conservative in 2000	17	82
Conservative in 2004	16	84
Conservative in 2008	20	78
Conservative in 2012	17	82

Source: Election Day exit polls conducted in 1996, 2000, 2004, 2008, and 2012 for consortiums of major news organizations by Edison Media Research and Mitofsky International.

Pollsters usually instruct their interviewers not to try to define the terms "liberal" or "moderate" or "conservative" when asking survey respondents to self-describe their political ideology. The usual interviewing ploy is to ask voters to assign those terms "in whatever way these words mean to you." It might sound haphazard, but the results voters give when asked to respond to these words are almost always meaningful, even if the terms are not clearly defined.

As proof of the value of these usually undefined terms, political philosophy has shown the smallest variance of any of the commonly used voter groups during the five elections used in this study. There are, of course, people who identify themselves as conservative who also vote Democratic in presidential elections. There are also significant numbers of self-described moderates who regularly vote for the Republicans. But the fluctuation of the vote among these self-described voter groups mostly has been in the single digits from 1996 to 2012.

The most popular of these self-selected terms is "moderate," which was picked by as few as 41 percent of voters in 2012 and by as many as 50 percent in 2000. Not surprisingly, moderate voters have shown the largest variations. Republican candidates must come to near parity with Democrats among moderate voters if they are to be viable.

"Crossover voting" describes the willingness of a voter to cast a ballot for candidates of "the other" party. It is becoming a declining practice because of the nation's increasing

Table 9 Support for Democratic or Republican Presidential Campaigns According to Voters' Self-Described Political Party Preference: 1996 to 2012

Year and Party	Democratic	Republican
Democrat in 1996	85%	10%
Democrat in 2000	87	11
Democrat in 2004	89	11
Democrat in 2008	89	10
Democrat in 2012	92	7
Republican in 1996	13	81
Republican in 2000	8	91
Republican in 2004	6	93
Republican in 2008	9	93
Republican in 2012	6	93
Independent in 1996	44	37
Independent in 2000	46	48
Independent in 2004	50	48
Independent in 2008	52	44
Independent in 2012	45	50

Source: Election Day exit polls conducted in 1996, 2000, 2004, 2008, and 2012 for consortiums of major news organizations by Edison Media Research and Mitofsky International.

tendency to political polarization. The last time significant numbers of Americans crossed party lines was in 1996, a surprise, perhaps, since Ross Perot's independent candidacy could have given a natural vent to voters unhappy with their own party's nominee. Nonetheless, and by double digits, significant numbers of Republicans voted Democratic in 1996 and vice versa.

Crossover voting can be a potent predictor of which candidate will win, but even more important, of course, are the growing numbers of voters who describe themselves as political independents. Generally, Democrats win the White House when they have at least a 5-percentage-point advantage over their rivals. (The 2012 election was an exception. Obama lost the independent vote but attracted so many Democrats to the polls that he was re-elected easily.) Republican nominees, meanwhile, need to at least approach parity with Democrats among independents.

Why People Vote: A Discussion of Motivations for Participating in Elections

Guido H. Stempel III

Research, beginning with the Lazarsfeld and Berelson's study of Erie County Ohio in 1940, has told us a lot about the electoral process. We know, of course, the outcome of an election, and public opinion polls before the election give us a rather accurate impression of who is going to win. We know what turnout is—a little more than 50 percent for presidential elections, about 40 percent for congressional elections, and less than that for most local elections. We know that race, education, income, and age are related to turnout. We know that turnout is usually higher for Republicans than for Democrats. We know that it is the economy and national security that affect elections the most consistently.

However, none of these findings explain why people vote. The differences between demographic groups do not answer this. Why are people more than 55 years old more likely to vote than people less than 25 years old? Why are people with a college education more likely to vote than people with less education? Why are rich people more likely to vote than poor people? What is the real difference between people who vote and people who do not vote? Why do more people vote for president than for congress when in fact it is their congressman who is the closer connection to the federal government?

A perhaps bigger question is why voter turnout in the United States is less than that in almost any democracy you can name. We hope for a 60-percent turnout in presidential elections, but in most other democracies turnout is more than 75 percent. In Austria, Chile, and Italy, it is above 90 percent. In Germany, Greece, and Sweden, it is 86 percent.

Pollsters estimating which candidate or party will win an election find it difficult to predict who will vote. If you ask people a week before the election whether they plan to vote, likely more than 80 percent will say they do. That in part reflects the fact that people know they should vote, that it is a citizen's duty to vote. It seems evident that this is one answer to the why question, but it is obvious that other factors are in play. A sense of duty leads some people to vote simply as a matter of habit. If there is an election, they vote just as they celebrate holidays. No election is too unimportant.

Some people vote because they believe their vote could decide the election. This notion is widely circulated, and we do read about elections, usually local, decided by one vote. In the author's home county, there was a race for nomination for county commissioner that ended up a tie. The votes were recounted, and the tie remained, so they flipped a coin to determine the winner. This was in a primary in which less than a fourth of the eligible voters had cast ballots. In contrast, some people will say they don't vote in presidential elections because the Electoral College is all that matters. Their vote will not count. It perhaps is futile for a Democrat in Nebraska to vote for president because no Democrat has carried Nebraska since Lyndon Johnson did in 1964. It may be almost as futile for a Republican to vote in a presidential election in Massachusetts, where the only Republican to win in the last half century was Ronald Reagan.

Another reason to vote is personal benefit. An issue at stake, either directly or indirectly, may be important to people personally. Perhaps their concern is not for their own welfare but for the welfare of others they care about.

How interesting people find the candidate or the campaign may determine whether they vote. In the 1992 presidential election, turnout was higher than expected. A post-election survey by Ohio University and the Scripps Howard News Service indicated this was because people found Ross Perot and his campaign interesting. He went beyond campaign clichés to discuss matters such as taxes and budgets in some detail. That forced his opponents, Bill Clinton and George H.W. Bush, to discuss matters that candidates usually avoided.

Some people vote as a matter of loyalty and commitment to the political party of their choice. They believe in their party, and they want their party to do well in every election, whether it is a presidential or local election. They believe that it matters to their country, their state, and their community that their party succeeds. A related factor is the confidence and certainty they have in their beliefs. Such confidence makes them more likely to vote, especially if it is the result of considerable thought.

Other affiliations may affect whether or not a person votes. We all belong to various kinds of groups, be they religious, social, or work-related. We strive to be part of these groups and follow the group norms to some extent. There are opinion leaders in these groups, and they influence decisions about whether to vote, for whom to vote, and how important a particular election is.

Two factors that have a negative effect on voter turnout should be mentioned. One is weather. We hear that bad weather will affect, and has affected, turnout, but the evidence is anecdotal. Less than 1 percent of people who didn't vote in 2012 blamed the weather for not voting, according to the U.S. Census Bureau's American Community Survey conducted immediately after the election.

The other factor is that nearly all elections are on Tuesday. Polls typically are open 12 or 13 hours. For people who work eight hours and spend three commuting, finding time to cast a ballot is difficult. Yet people like having elections on Tuesday. An Ohio University-Scripps Howard News Service poll showed that a majority do not want to have elections on Sunday, as a number of countries do.

Further Reading

Lazarsfeld, Paul F., Bernard Berelson, and Hazel Gaudet. 1948. *The People's Choice*. New York: Columbia University Press.

"The Psychology of Voting and Election Campaigns." 2006. Duke University. http://www.election studies.org/conferences/2006Duke/abstracts.html. Accessed February 9, 2015.

Media Effects on Knowledge of Campaign Issues

Thomas K. Hargrove, Jerry Miller, Carl Stempel,
and Guido H. Stempel III

It seems obvious that media use should lead to increased knowledge of issues in a political campaign, but research has produced mixed results. The studies of the Roper Organization, which were so prominent in the 1950s and 1960s, reported that people got most of their news about campaigns for national offices from television, but they studied neither issue knowledge nor media use.

A breakthrough came in the study by Atkin, Galloway, and Nayman of the election of 1972, which found that use of newspapers, television, news magazines, and radio all correlated significantly with a knowledge score that combined issue knowledge and identification of campaign personalities.

The lack of definitive findings in more recent studies is partly because of the changing media environment. Television news used to be nonpartisan, but cable has brought news outlets that are committed to a partisan viewpoint.

When a survey asks about television news, what is it asking about? Does it ask about information gained or merely whether you watched television news in the past 24 hours? The same point applies to the Internet, a new player in the political information scene. Hansen and Benoit examined 33 studies of media use and knowledge gain in eight elections from 1972 to 2000. They found that 48 percent of the studies showed information gain from newspaper use, 33 percent showed information gain from television use, and 7 percent found information gain from radio use. All 33 studies included both newspaper and television use, but only 14 included radio use.

Most studies mentioned here have not dealt with online media or cable media. A study by the Scripps Research Center in 2008 dealt with these expanding options in sources for campaign information. It included the use of 23 possible specific sources of information about the 2008 presidential election. (The 23 media are listed in Table 1.) Interviews were completed with 1,015 randomly selected respondents between September 15 and October 2, 2008. Data were weighted by age, sex, and race to make the sample match census figures for those demographics.

The interviewer asked the respondent whether or not each of the 23 media had been a useful source of information for him or her about the presidential campaign. The interviewer then read six issue position statements to the respondent and asked the respondent whether that position was the one taken by John McCain or by Barack Obama. The issue statements follow:

- Which candidate wants to reduce taxes on American corporations?
- Which candidate says abortion is a woman's right?
- Which candidate wants to increase off-shore drilling for oil as soon as possible?
- Which candidate wants mandatory health care for children?
- Which candidate is willing to have a permanent U.S. peacekeeping force in Iraq?
- Which candidate wants to make changes in the North American Free Trade Agreement, sometimes called NAFTA?

Table 1 shows how many respondents mentioned each of the 23 media as a useful source. The daily newspaper was the most mentioned source, being mentioned by 60.5 percent, but there were five other sources mentioned by at least half of the respondents. Four of the five were television news sources, and the fifth was the Internet source not related to news media. However, 14 of the 23 sources were mentioned by less than a third of the respondents. Eighty-eight percent of respondents mentioned at least one of the mainstream media as a useful source. Although use of each of the online sources is low individually, 70 percent of the respondents indicated they used at least one of them. Respondents 18 to 34 years of age used Internet media substantially more than those 35 and up, and used conservative media a good deal less than those 35 years old and up.

Table 1 also shows the average number of correct answers to the issue questions for those who cited a given medium source as useful. The tests of significance come from conducting analyses of variance comparing users and nonusers of each medium. For 13 of the 23 media, users had significantly higher knowledge scores than nonusers. Hannity and Colmes viewers had the highest knowledge scores, followed closely by blog readers, candidates' website readers, Daily Show/Colbert viewers, and the Lehrer News Hour viewers. Users of four media sources—grocery store tabloids, which had the lowest knowledge scores; network TV morning shows (e.g. *Today Show* or *Good Morning America*), network TV evening news viewers; and CNN viewers—had statistically significantly lower knowledge scores than those who did not use that medium.

In general, users of mainstream media—network TV evening news, network TV morning shows, daily newspapers, local TV, and news magazines—fared worse on the knowledge test than users of web-based sources. None of the five mainstream sources had users who scored statistically significantly higher than nonusers, and the users of two of these scored significantly lower than nonusers. On the other hand, three of the six web-based sources had users who scored significantly higher than nonusers, and none had users who scored significantly lower than nonusers.

We also note that users of partisan media sources fared better on the knowledge test than did mainstream media users. Viewers of *Hannity and Colmes*, *Olbermann*, the *O'Reilly Factor*, the *Daily Show/Colbert Show*, blog readers, and readers of the candidates' websites all had significantly higher scores than nonusers of those media. The three remaining partisan sources—Rush Limbaugh, other talk radio, and Fox news—all had nonsignificant differences on the knowledge test compared to nonusers of those media.

Of course, the issue knowledge averages for those who used a particular medium for presidential campaign information are not the result of that medium alone. The

Table 1 Percent of National Sample of Adult Americans Who Say Each Type of Media Is "Useful" in Understanding the Positions of Presidential Candidates

Media Type	Percent Saying "Useful Source"	Issue Score (average correct answers to six issue questions)
Daily Newspaper	60.5%	4.07
Local TV News	55.6	4.02
Cable News Network	55.3	3.98
ABC/CBS/NBC Evening News	53.9	3.86
Fox News	50.9	4.05
Internet News Webs	50.4	4.17
News Magazines	39.5	4.17
National Public Radio	37.5	4.39
Network Morning Shows	36.7	3.86
TV News Websites	36.5	4.21
CNBC	31.9	4.03
Talk Radio Besides Limbaugh	31.8	4.18
O'Reilly	31.3	4.28
Websites of Major Newspapers	29.6	4.33
Jim Lehrer PBS	27.5	4.43
Daily Show/Colbert	25.1	4.44
Candidate Websites	23.8	4.47
Hannity and Colmes	23.3	4.50
Rush Limbaugh	19.3	4.21
Keith Olbermann	18.9	4.37
Party Websites	18.3	4.24
Online Blogs	15.1	4.48
Grocery Store Tabloids	6.0	3.58

N = 1,015; Overall mean knowledge score = 4.09 out of 6; Standard Deviation = 1.54

other media and social factors associated with a particular media source contributed to the mean knowledge scores. The median number of sources cited as useful was *eight* for Democrats and *seven* for Republicans. The mean issue knowledge scores were 4.28 for Democrats, 4.17 for Republicans, 3.74 for independents (including "Don't Knows"), and 4.09 for the entire sample. Democrats were significantly better informed than Republicans about the three Democratic issues, but the two were virtually equal in knowledge of the three Republican issues. The number of sources the respondent said were useful was not related to his or her issue knowledge score. The highest average was 4.77 for those who said 10 sources were useful; however, the correlation between number of sources and knowledge scores was .08, which means that the number of sources explained less than 1 percent of the variation in knowledge scores. In other words, the total number of sources a respondent finds useful is not a particularly strong predictor of how knowledgeable a respondent is about the candidates' stands on the issues.

A more sophisticated analysis that organizes the types of media into seven groups (called "factors" by a statistical process called "factor analysis with a vari-max rotation") was able to explain 54 percent of the variance. These factors reflect the extent to which a person who uses one medium in a factor tended to use other media in that same cluster. The factor clusters are shown in Table 2. The factors are as follows:

- Factor 1, Conservative Media: These are four media that have declared intent to represent a conservative perspective.
- Factor 2, Mainstream Media: These five media are available to the entire public, seek mass circulation, and have been around longer than most other media.
- Factor 3, News Websites: Included here are websites provided by newspapers and television; websites that offer news only on the Web, such as Yahoo and Google; and blogs, which offer both news and opinion and in some cases are connected to mainstream media.
- Factor 4, Liberal/Cable Media: These are six news outlets available only on cable TV. Three of four prominently feature partisan liberal perspectives.
- Factor 5, Political Websites: These are the candidate and party websites.
- Factor 6, Public Broadcasting: These are the two major daily news
- products of public broadcasting—National Public Radio and the Jim Lehrer News Hour.
- Factor 7, Sensational Media: This includes the sensational grocery store tabloids like the *National Enquirer*.

Table 2, with cross-tabulation of issue scores by party and factor, shows some indication of selectivity by party preference. Remember that respondents were not asked merely whether they used each of these media but whether each medium was a useful source of information about the campaign.

If it really was useful, then the issue score should have been higher than the overall average. It was in most, but not all, cases. As can be seen in Table 2, some sources were positive for one or two political preference categories but not for all three. However, network TV news, early morning TV, and grocery store tabloids showed below-average issue scores for all three political preferences. People who said grocery store tabloids were a useful source had lower issue scores than people who did not say grocery tabloids were useful.

Democrats gained the most issue information from the liberal cable media while Republicans gained the most from the conservative media, yet the best individual source for both Democrats and Republicans was online blogs. Democrats who said blogs were useful had an issue score of 4.83, while Republicans who said blogs were useful had an issue score of 4.69. For both Democrats and Republicans, party and candidate websites proved to be useful sources. Of course, people could have used both blogs and party web sites selectively, seeking out material they agreed with.

Table 2 Issue Knowledge (average correct answer to six issue questions) by Party Preference and Interest Factors

Type of Media	Democrat	Republican	Independent
Conservative Media			
Fox News	3.77	4.38	4.04
Hannity and Colmes	4.58	4. 51	4.59
O'Reilly	4.02	4.47	4.17
Rush Limbaugh	3.63	4.50	3.82
Mainstream Media			
Daily Newspapers	4.00	4.25	3.97
Early Morning TV	4.08	3.90	3.75
Local TV News	4.35	3.87	3.85
Network TV News	4.16	3.70	3.59
News Magazines	4.24	4.33	3.99
News Websites			
Internet News Websites	4.29	4.34	4.08
Online Blogs	4.83	4.65	4.26
TV News Websites	4.31	4.09	3.99
Websites of Major Newspapers	4.40	4.42	4.28
Liberal Cable Media			
CNBC	4.31	3.91	4.00
CNN	4.22	3.92	3.84
Colbert	4.51	4.14	4.32
Olberman	4.44	4.16	4.42
Political Websites			
Candidate Websites	4.60	4.36	4.15
Party Websites	4.14	4.37	3.99
Public Broadcasting			
National Public Radio	4.55	4.12	4.12
PBS TV News	4.49	4.36	4.15
Sensational Media			
Grocery Store Tabloids	3.18	3.94	3.71
Talk Radio except Limbaugh	4.08	4.43	4.41
All	4.28	4.17	3.98

Conclusion

It should be noted that independents were substantially less aware of the issues than other respondents. It also shows that some media seem to be contributing to their awareness. Independents are variously described as very interested and indifferent in election campaigns. Our findings support the latter more than the former.

A major finding is that, with controls, the mainstream media were negatively associated with knowledge of candidates' issue positions. Controlling for party affiliation revealed an interesting pattern that may help explain the mainstream media's negative association with knowledge. Conservative media are more strongly associated with knowledge for Republicans and independents, but negatively associated with knowledge for Democrats. Public broadcasting is associated with knowledge for Democrats and independents, but not Republicans. Part of the explanation for why mainstream media perform poorly in this test of informing consumers may be that their coverage of the campaign focuses more on the horse-race aspects of the campaign. In contrast, both the conservative media and public broadcasting, for different reasons, focus on political ideology and issue positions. The conservative media, from a biased position, make stark contrasts between the candidates' positions, and the Lehrer News Hour strives to create "balance" by giving equal time for opposing viewpoints, thus also bringing ideological and individual positions into view.

Of the three party affiliations, independents were most strongly influenced by both public broadcasting and radio talk shows (minus Limbaugh). This is consistent with the interpretation developed here because those without clear ideological bearings should benefit most from reporting that brings the differences into view. At the same time, there may be a political mismatch effect, whereby exposure to media that oppose one's political orientation may confuse your understanding, as indicated by the negative relationship between conservative media and knowledge for Democrats.

Further Reading

Atkin, Charles, John Galloway, and Oguz B. Nayman. 1976. "News Media Exposure, Political Knowledge and Campaign Interest." *Journalism Quarterly* 53 (Summer): 231–37.

Drew, Dan, and David Weaver. 2006. "Voter Learning in the 2004 Presidential Election: Did the Media Matter." *Journalism & Mass Communication Quarterly* 83 (Spring): 25–42.

Hansen, Glenn, and William Benoit. 2007. "Communication Forms as Predictors of Issue Knowledge in Presidential Campaigns: A Meta-Analytic Assessment." *Mass Communication & Society* 10(2): 189–210.

Electoral Maps of Presidential Elections: 1996–2012

The following are maps showing the state winner of each presidential election from 1996 through 2012. Note that Alaska and Hawaii are not shown, although in all cases Alaska voted Republican and Hawaii voted Democratic.

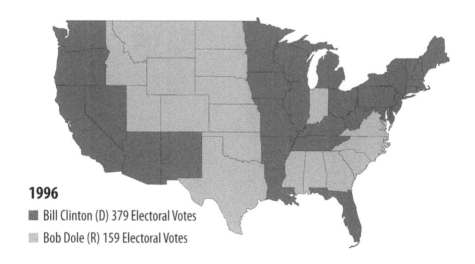

1996

■ Bill Clinton (D) 379 Electoral Votes

▨ Bob Dole (R) 159 Electoral Votes

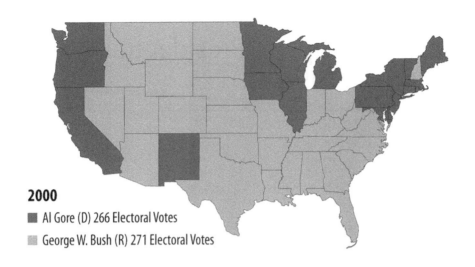

2000

■ Al Gore (D) 266 Electoral Votes

▨ George W. Bush (R) 271 Electoral Votes

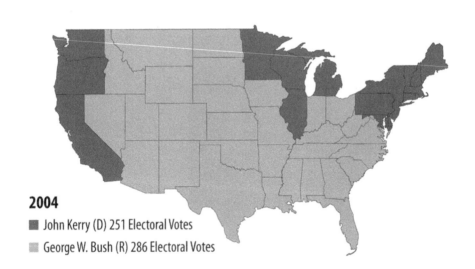

2004

■ John Kerry (D) 251 Electoral Votes

▨ George W. Bush (R) 286 Electoral Votes

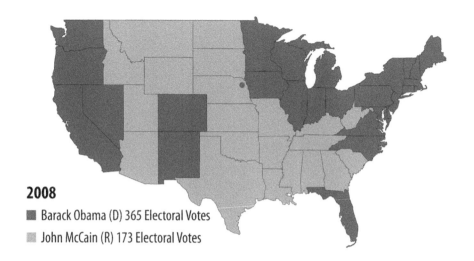

2008
- Barack Obama (D) 365 Electoral Votes
- John McCain (R) 173 Electoral Votes

Note: Although McCain won Nebraska handily, state law allowed the electoral votes to be apportioned by congressional districts, giving Obama one electoral vote from the Second Congressional District which serves Omaha.

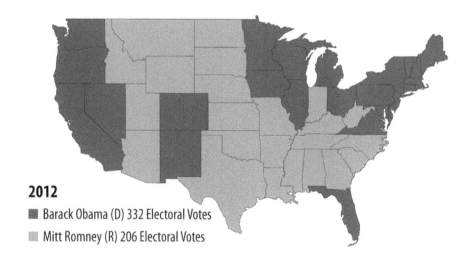

2012
- Barack Obama (D) 332 Electoral Votes
- Mitt Romney (R) 206 Electoral Votes

A

AAPOR (American Association of Public Opinion Research) Standards

Surveys and polls are ubiquitous in today's society. Not only do they allow us to assess and communicate what specific groups of people may know, think, or feel about issues, but they also influence behaviors. These behaviors might include decisions to develop and launch public awareness campaigns or, in anticipated close elections, might spur voters to cast their ballots. A 2012 article in Government Information Quarterly notes the area of policymaking as another major application of opinion research, as it helps "to better anticipate likely impacts of policy measures and better communicate expected benefits and consequences."

The self-proclaimed "leading association of public opinion and survey research professionals," the American Association of Public Opinion Research (AAPOR), was started in Colorado in 1947 by a group of some 75 public opinion researchers. As a result, two organizations were founded: AAPOR and the World Association of Public Opinion Researchers (WAPOR). According to the AAPOR website, these organizations continue to be closely associated and to hold joint meetings in even-numbered years. Both groups seek to advance professional standards in public opinion research; to educate people, so they may assess surveys critically and conduct them responsibly; and to foster related theory and methodology. Each organization also publishes a well-respected academic journal: AAPOR produces *Public Opinion Quarterly*; WAPOR publishes the *International Journal of Public Opinion Research*. In 2013, AAPOR began publishing the *Journal of Survey Statistics and Methodology* as well.

AAPOR members must sign its Code of Professional Ethics and Practice, which includes agreeing to disclose a number of survey specifics to ensure that results may be critically assessed and evaluated by others. These minimal disclosure standards include identifying the following (Survey Disclosure Checklist):

- the population under study;
- the sampling frame;
- how respondents were selected;
- sample size;

- how data were collected;
- when and where data were collected;
- sampling error, if applicable;
- if and how data were weighted and estimated; and
- any reported sample subgroups.

However, AAPOR and other professional organizations, such as the Council of American Survey Research Organizations (CASRO) and the National Council on Public Polls (NCPP), believe that exemplary survey research practice extends beyond minimal disclosure and that researchers should provide sufficient detail to allow survey replication and independent examination of results. According to AAPOR best practices, such additional details might include any or all of the following (Best Practices):

- survey objectives;
- interviewer instructions;
- sample design and selection procedure, including eligibility criteria, screening, and callbacks;
- sample disposition, including the outcome of all sample cases (i.e. number contacted, reached, refused, terminated, completed, not eligible);
- description of response or completion rates and descriptions of nonrespondents, including how they differ from respondents, if at all;
- details about any special data indexing, editing, or other adjustments;
- discussion and description of all percentages on which conclusions are drawn;
- interviewer characteristics and instructions, codebooks, manuals, or other specifications; and
- any additional information relevant for a layperson to adequately assess the findings.

As a professional organization that relies on the public to participate in its research efforts, AAPOR also formally condemns a number of survey practices. These practices include using any form of monetary compensation to influence responses; revealing participahts' identities without their permission; misrepresenting survey or poll methodologies; and participating in "push polls," defined as "a telemarketing technique in which telephone calls are used to canvass potential voters, feeding them false or misleading 'information' about a candidate . . . to see how this 'information' affects voter preferences."

In addition, AAPOR regularly issues new editions of Standard Definitions: Final Dispositions of Case Codes and Outcome Rates for Surveys. It provides formulas and guidelines to describe the final disposition of cases and outcome rates of random digit dialed (RDD) telephone surveys, in-person household surveys, mail surveys of specifically named persons, and Internet surveys of specially named persons. As stated in the report background, "By knowing the disposition of every element drawn in a survey sample, researchers can assess whether their sample might contain nonresponse error and the potential reasons for that error." (Standard Definitions) The organization notes in the document that it is working with others, including academic journals, to further the adoption and use of Standard Definitions to help standardize research codes used to document sampled cases.

The report and its disclosure standards contribute to AAPOR's mission, which includes "advising the science and practice of survey and opinion research to give people a voice in the decisions that affect their daily lives." The organization also publishes detailed best survey practices, which are summarized below (Mission and Goals):

- begin with specific research goals;
- assess whether a survey or poll is the best means to obtain the information desired;
- select samples that accurately reflect the population under study;
- balance survey design errors with the available budget;
- word questions to ensure adequate concept measurement and respondent understanding;
- pretest questionnaires and survey procedures;
- train interviewers on the survey subject and interviewing techniques;
- check quality at each stage of the survey or poll;
- maximize response rates within ethical boundaries;
- use appropriate statistics and reporting procedures;
- have and fulfill confidentiality or anonymity processes;
- disclose all survey methods to ensure replication and evaluation are possible.

As the number of self-selection Internet and social media polls and surveys grows, the public's faith in all survey research could erode. Educating journalists, communicators, and the larger public about legitimate survey research practice and standards is critical to ensure an educated and engaged political populace.

Diana Martinelli

See also: Gallup, George; Roper, Elmo

Further Reading

The American Association for Public Opinion Research. http://www.aapor.org/. Accessed February 2, 2015.

Groves, Robert M., Floyd J. Fowler Jr., Mick P. Couper, James M. Lepkowski, Eleanor Singer, and Roger Tourangean. *Survey Methodology*. Hoboken, NJ: John Wiley and Sons, 2004.

AARP (American Association of Retired Persons)

The American Association of Retired Persons (AARP) consists of three major arms: AARP; AARP Services, Incorporated (ASI); and the AARP Foundation. Based in Washington, D.C., AARP advocates in the nation's Capital, in state houses, and in the courts on behalf of AARP members and their families. AARP is a nonprofit membership organization for persons 50 years of age and older. The organization was founded in 1958 by retired California educator Dr. Ethel Percy Andrus. Today the organization represents more than 35 million members. The organization focuses its efforts and resources on health and wellness, economic security and work, long-term care and independent living, and personal enrichment for the 50-plus population in all 50 states, the District of Columbia, and the U.S. Virgin Islands. The organization reaches out internationally through its Office of International Affairs. It works with governmental and nongovernmental organizations to address worldwide aging concerns.

The organization advocates specifically for long-term solvency of Social Security, pension protection, prescription drug coverage in Medicare, patient protections in managed and long-term care, and other protections for older consumers. The organization fights against age discrimination and predatory home-loan lending. AARP Services, Incorporated, is a wholly owned subsidiary of AARP. ASI manages products and services for members, including health and life insurance, prescription discounts, and travel discounts. Finally, the AARP Foundation, the charity of the organization, engages in litigation, awards grants for research in aging, manages grants, and conducts educational programs on financial security and coping with chronic health conditions.

AARP sets its policy agenda through information gathered from telephone calls, town meetings, letters, surveys, and member polls. Also in keeping with the times, AARP facilitates an Internet blog (discussion board) for its membership population. The organization's National Legislative Council makes policy recommendations based on input from members, experts, and elected officials. The council presents its recommendations to the 21 members of the Board of Directors. The legislative council; board of directors; national officers; field directors; state presidents; and legislative, program, and chapter leaders are all volunteers.

AARP's top three revenue sources in 2001 were membership dues (28%), income from AARP health-care options (17%), and royalties (14%). AARP's top three expense categories for the same year were publications (25%), programs and field services (19%), and facilities and headquarters administration (16%) (AARP 2001).

AARP represents workers and retirees, people living alone or with families, and people of various financial means. Nearly a third of AARP members are under 60, 46 percent are age 60 to 74, and 21 percent are 75 and older.

AARP publishes a monthly magazine, *AARP: The Magazine*, a monthly newspaper, the *AARP Bulletin*, and a quarterly newspaper, *Segunda Juventud*, and maintains a website at www.aarp.org. The organization also produces two national radio network series, *Prime Time* and *Mature Focus*. In addition, AARP compiles organizational expertise, research, and members' concerns and interests in its annual publication of *The Policy Book: AARP Policies*. The organization operates its own research center. The AARP's *Research Center Digest* offers research results and policy insight to members and nonmembers. Researchers may obtain copies of the organization's annual report and archived copies of *AARP: The Magazine* on the AARP website or by contacting the organization.

Kimberly L. Douglass

See also: Baby Boom Generation; Generation X

Further Reading

AARP. Annual Report. Washington, DC: AARP Foundation, 2001.
AARP. Fact Sheet and Background Information. Washington, DC: Author, 2003.
AARP. www.aarp.org. Accessed February 2, 2015, 2015.

Abortion

Few issues have divided and polarized American voters as intensely as legalized abortion. Support or opposition to abortion has become a political bright line dividing Americans in many ways: Democrats from Republicans, women from men, young from old, and residents of the East and West coasts from denizens of the South and Midwest.

States began banning abortion in the 19th century, with Connecticut criminalizing the procedure in 1821 and all other states enacting anti-abortion laws by 1900. Many states, however, permitted abortions in cases of rape, incest, or when the life of the mother was threatened by the pregnancy.

The issue changed dramatically after Norma McCorvey discovered in 1969 she was pregnant with a third unwanted child and tried falsely to claim in Dallas, Texas, that she had been raped. Her attempt at a lawful abortion was unsuccessful since she had no police report documenting a sexual attack, and she was unable to obtain an illegal abortion in Texas. She filed a federal lawsuit in 1970 under the alias of "Jane Roe" and listed the defendant as Henry Wade, Dallas County's District Attorney, who represented Texas' anti-abortion law. Her claim, simply, was that state bans on abortion are unconstitutional.

The U.S. Supreme Court ruled in 1973 in a 7–2 decision that the due process clause of the Fourteenth Amendment extended to a woman's right to have an abortion, although the state was upheld in regulating abortions and banning them in the third trimester of pregnancy. (The court would later amend this trimester standard to a more medically based standard that abortions may be performed until fetal viability, when the unborn child has developed sufficiently to survive outside the mother's womb, usually about seven months into the pregnancy.)

The ruling created a political storm that has never abated. The National Organization for Women and other women's groups upheld the decision as a basic human right, arguing that no government should claim control over a woman's body. But a complex array of national groups coalesced to oppose the "legalized murder" that they said *Roe v. Wade* caused. Among those who've consistently taken stands against abortion in the wake of the Supreme Court case are the Roman Catholic Church, the Republican Party in every party platform written since the ruling, and the many pro-life organizations created to mobilize public opinion against the ruling. Annual "March for Life" events in Washington, D.C., have attracted growing numbers of protesters. The march drew more than half a million people in 2013.

Many attempts to pass an amendment to the Constitution banning abortions have failed in Congress. However, lawmakers did approve the "Hyde Amendment," which barred use of federal Medicaid money to fund abortions, except in cases of rape, incest, or a medical threat to the life of the mother.

The politics of abortion are quite complicated. Generally, men are more likely to describe themselves as "pro-life" while women mostly say they are "pro-choice," according to hundreds of polls conducted over the years. Support for the Roe decision is strongest in Northeastern states and weakest in the Southern states. The polarization, according to political party preference, is enormous, with two-thirds of Democrats approving of legal abortion while a similar margin of Republicans oppose it.

The Gallup Poll, in a series of questions asked from 1975 through 2014, found that Americans are consistently divided on the broad issue of whether and when abortion should be allowed. Generally, about a quarter of American adults have said abortion should be legal "under any circumstances" while slightly more than half have taken a moderate opinion that it should be "legal only under certain circumstances." The position that it should be "illegal in all circumstances" has held fairly steady for one-fifth of the nation over the last 40 years.

"U.S. public opinion on abortion has displayed great stability in recent years, with Americans dividing about evenly into the 'pro-choice' and 'pro-life' camps," poll analyst Lydia Saad concluded in 2014. "Gallup finds roughly half of Americans retain a nuanced view about the legality of abortion, saying it should be legal only in certain cases. However, the percentages on the extremes—those favoring total legality or illegality—have crept up, presumably to the delight of their respective comrades in the Republican and Democratic parties."

The extent to which abortion becomes important in national elections has fluctuated slightly over time, showing indications of polarization. The number of Americans who say a political candidate "must share (my) views on abortion" has risen from 13 percent in 1992 to 19 percent in 2014. Similarly, the percentages who say that abortion "is not a major issue" declined from 36 percent in 1992 to 27 percent in 2014.

Although Democrats and Republicans are likely to continue to take sharply opposing sides, the legality of abortion rights is unlikely to change in the foreseeable future. Even as appointees to the Supreme Court became increasingly conservative during the years of presidents Ronald Reagan, George H.W. Bush, and George W. Bush, the court was content to observe a policy of "stare decisis"—the Latin phrase and legal concept usually translated as "to stand by that which is decided."

Many scholars have concluded the ultimate source of abortion rights is vested in the rising political and leadership powers obtained by women throughout the 20th century. "Abortion was not a central issue in American politics and abortion cases were not so important in 19th and early 20th century American history because women had little to say in lawmaking," concluded historians N.E.H. Hull and Peter Charles Hoffer. The law changed only after "the role and influence of women in society changed," as women became voters; took professional jobs; got elected in increasing numbers to local, state, and federal offices; and started amassing wealth.

Thomas K. Hargrove

See also: Feminism, Gender Gap

Further Reading

Hull, N.E.H., and Peter Charles Hoffer. "*Roe v. Wade*: The Abortion Rights Controversy in American History." Lawrence: University Press of Kansas, 2010.

Saad, Lydia. "U.S. Still Split on Abortion: No Decline in Voters Who Prioritize Abortion Issue, Now at 19 Percent." The Gallup Poll, 2014. http://www.gallup.com/poll/170249/split-abortion-pro-choice-pro-life.aspx. Accessed September 11, 2014.

Absentee Voting

Absentee voting refers to a variety of practices allowing voters to cast ballots before Election Day. While various terms are used to describe these practices, they generally are of three types. Absentee voting: All states allow certain voters to cast a ballot either in person or by mail prior to Election Day. All states allow military personnel stationed overseas, their dependents, and other citizens living abroad to vote absentee. As of late 2012, seven states and the District of Columbia offered a permanent absentee ballot option to all voters; once voters ask, they automatically receive absentee ballots for future elections. In addition, seven states grant permanent absentee voting status to certain persons, usually permanently disabled voters. Alaskans living in remote areas also may be granted such status. As of late 2012, 21 states require an excuse to vote absentee. Excuses generally include military service overseas, illness, or other hardship. Twenty-seven states and D.C. require no excuse.

Early voting: As of late 2012, in 32 states and D.C., voters need no excuse to cast ballots in person during a designated period prior to Election Day. In some states, early voting may take place only at an election official's office while in other states additional satellite voting locations exist. These typically include government offices, schools, libraries, grocery stores, and shopping malls.

Mail voting: Voters in Colorado, Washington, and Oregon receive their ballots only by mail. In these three states, ballots are automatically sent to all eligible voters. Together, these various non-Election Day voting practices are sometimes referred to as "convenience voting."

Absentee voting typically ends a week or less before Election Day. As of late 2012, 11 states allow absentee voting the day before the election; three states end absentee voting five days before the election; and other states are somewhere in-between. Early voting periods range widely by state, from 4 to 45 days before the election. States also vary in how long early voting places remain open daily. Most states give county or local officials the authority to decide the hours for early voting. A smaller number of the 32 early voting states require voting places to be open at least one weekend day during the early voting period. Up-to-date information regarding voting rules in all 50 states and the District of Columbia is available from the National Conference of State Legislatures.

Despite the importance of voting in a modern democracy, remarkably little empirical research has been conducted on when, where, and how Americans vote, and even less research has examined the effects of convenience voting. Surveys consistently have shown strong support from the public for all forms of absentee, early, and mail voting, with the most frequently mentioned reason being, predictably, convenience. Despite public pressure to increase convenience voting, some election experts have identified what they regard as unanticipated, unintended, or unwanted effects of convenience voting (e.g., a ballot cast early for a candidate who withdraws is a vote lost; opportunities for fraud and accidents may increase), and they urge more study and greater caution in adopting non-Election Day, nonprecinct voting practices. (For a recent review, see Stein and Vonnahme, 2011.) Some research suggests that convenience voting generally, and certain practices in particular, such as all-mail voting, lower administrative costs while other research suggests that ballots cast at different times, in different places, and in different forms complicate election administration.

While one might expect convenience voting to increase voter turnout—and perhaps especially among underrepresented groups such as racial and ethnic minorities—research generally finds that increasing convenience voting opportunities alone does not lead to significantly greater participation. A crucial factor has been the extent to which the political parties actively induce their supporters to take advantage of convenience voting opportunities. Oliver found that when states made voting more convenient, the political parties' mobilization efforts were critical to increasing turnout. Today, the question of differential party efforts is perhaps less critical since both major American parties now mount exhaustive efforts to identify potential voters and help them vote absentee. Noting how the early vote gave President Barack Obama his margin of victory in several key states in 2008, the *New York Times* observed that in 2012 the Republicans tried hard to erase the Democrats' earlier advantage by greatly increasing their own efforts. One effect of absentee voting and other forms of convenience voting seems clear: they are affecting the ways political parties conduct their campaigns. Noting that one in three Americans were expected to vote early in the 2012 election, the *Times* maintained that early voting is "reshaping election campaigns" (Cooper and Zeleny, 2012). Given that a majority of voters may soon be casting their ballots before Election Day, the effects of absentee voting on potential fraud and accidents, voter turnout, turnout of particular types of voters, administrative costs, party politics and campaigns, and news media election coverage clearly are topics ripe for research.

Dominic Lasorsa

See also: Advanced voting

Further Reading

Chapin, Douglas. 2011. "Non-Precinct Place Voting and Election Administration." *Election Law Journal* 10(3): 303–305.

Cooper, Michael, and Jeff Zeleny. 2012. "Early Voters, and a Hurricane, Change the Rhythm of the Campaign." *The New York Times*, October 30, 2012, p. A10.

National Conference of State Legislatures. 2012. "Absentee and Early Voting." Updated September 4, 2012. http://www.ncsl.org/legislatures-elections/elections/absentee-and-early-voting.aspx. Accessed February 2, 2015.

Stein, Robert M., and Greg Vonnahme. 2011. "Voting at Non-Precinct Polling Places: A Review and Research Agenda." *Election Law Journal* 10(3): 307–311.

Stewart, Charles, III. 2011. "Adding Up the Costs and Benefits of Voting by Mail." *Election Law Journal* 10(3): 297–301.

Advanced Voting

Advanced voting—also called early voting—allows voters to cast ballots before Election Day at a time that is more convenient for them. It is a reform intended to improve voting participation through absentee balloting by mail or through in-person balloting at early polling stations set up days or weeks prior to Election Day. The practice is rapidly growing in popularity in the United States and now represents a significant percentage of ballots cast in major elections. By the 2008 presidential election, more than 30 percent of all ballots cast resulted from some form of advanced voting procedures, up from 16 percent in 2000 and 7 percent in 1992.

According to the National Conference of State Legislatures, 33 states and the District of Columbia allowed qualified voters to cast a ballot in person prior to Election Day during the 2014 general election. Voters did not need to establish a reason why advanced voting was necessary, making this a "no excuse" voting practice.

Absentee voting does not require that the voter appear in person at a designated polling place, yet is also considered a means of advanced voting. Twenty-seven states and the District of Columbia allow "no excuse" absentee voting, although voters must still make a special effort to request that an absentee ballot be mailed to them. Twenty other states require that voters stipulate reasons that they cannot appear in person to vote on Election Day, the most common of which are that the voter will be out of town or is physically incapable of going to the polling place because of advanced age, illness, physical disability, or other infirmities.

Three states—Colorado, Oregon, and Washington—conduct all of their elections by mail. They automatically mail ballots to eligible voters' homes and request that voters mark and return their ballots by mail within a specified time period. These states forgo the expense of hiring temporary workers to operate temporary polling places. Seventeen states have enacted procedures so that certain elections may be conducted entirely by mail, although the circumstances under which such all-mail elections may be held vary from state to state.

Seven states and the District of Columbia allow permanent absentee voting. Once a voter asks to be added to an official list, he or she will automatically receive an absentee ballot for all future elections. Those states in 2014 were Arizona, California, Hawaii, Minnesota, Montana, New Jersey, and Utah.

A study of election participation rates sponsored by the Pew Charitable Trusts and released in early 2014 found that advanced voting "is actually associated with lower turnout" by "reducing the civic significance of elections for individuals and altering the incentives for political campaigns to invest in mobilization." The team of political science scholars led by Barry C. Burden of the University of Wisconsin-Madison concluded that voters are less motivated to cast ballots because early voting has the effect of "dissipating the energy of Election Day over a longer period of time. . . . Social pressure is less evident, guidance on how or where to vote is less handy, and the prospect of social interactions at the polls is decreased."

The group also noted that another common election reform, same-day registration, has consistently shown increase rates of voter participation. This procedure allows unregistered voters to go to polling places on Election Day, register as a voter, and participate in the day's election. This permits a kind of instant gratification for unregistered citizens who were motivated sufficiently by a political campaign or issue that they wished to become electors.

Thomas K. Hargrove

See also: Absentee voting

Further Reading

Burden, Barry C. and David T. Canon, Kenneth R. Mayer, and Donald P. Moynihan. 2014. "Election Laws, Mobilization and Turnout: The Unanticipated Consequences of Election Reform." *American Journal of Political Science* (January): 95–109.

National Conference of State Legislatures. "Absentee and Early Voting." Updated October 21, 2014. http://www.ncsl.org/research/elections-and-campaigns/absentee-and-early-voting.aspx. Accessed December 6, 2014.

Advertising in Presidential Campaigns

Reflecting a growing trend with little sign of abatement, President Barack Obama and Republican challenger Mitt Romney spent record amounts on campaign ads—more than $1 billion combined—during their 2012 race.

According to the Associated Press, Obama and Romney spent $1.08 billion on more than 1 million ads, most of which were 30- and 60-second TV commercials. The Romney campaign spent about $600 million on ads, and the Obama campaign spent about $400 million. Their combined $1 billion is almost double the combined 2008 total of $515 million. The total number of ads also increased by more than 40 percent from the 2008 race, when Obama defeated GOP nominee John McCain.

Despite a societal shift from television to online/social media, TV ads remained the clear medium of choice for the candidates in 2012. "The decline of television advertising hasn't happened, and it's not going away anytime soon," said Erika Franklin Fowler, director of the Wesleyan University Media Project, which tracks campaign advertising. "TV is where you look for the persuadable voter, and the Internet is what you use to mobilize your base."

Not that online advertising didn't skyrocket from 2008. In fact, online spending increased more than 250 percent, according to the Federal Election Commission. President Obama's campaign spent twice as much on online advertising, $52 million versus $26 million for Romney, reflecting the younger demographic of the incumbent president's supporters.

Although Romney clearly outspent Obama by about $200 million on campaign ads, he actually had fewer ads because of the primary source of his funding. More than half of the GOP nominee's funding came from "outside" sources (political action committees), as opposed to most of Obama's funding coming from contributions within the Democratic Party.

Thus, Obama got more bang for his campaign bucks because television stations, by law, must grant presidential candidates lower ad rates than regular commercial advertisers receive. That cheaper rate is not available to the political parties or the outside groups, which must pay much higher rates in battleground states where ad space is especially high.

For example, more than half of pro-Romney advertising spending came from super PACs, which sometimes pay double and triple what candidates pay for TV time. In Florida during the last month of the campaign, both sides reserved roughly the same amount of time—at $25 million each. But the audience reach of the pro-Obama ads was far greater, sometimes by 20 percent, according to the *New York Times*. Because of that funding advantage, Obama's campaign bought about 503,000 ads since June, while Romney's campaign bought 461,000 ads, according to the *Washington Post*.

Another campaign ad spending trend that carried over from the 2008 race was a further focusing of spending in key battleground states, a source of frustration for those in the remaining states. In the 2012 race, the focus of both parties was on nine states: Colorado, Florida, Iowa, Nevada, New Hampshire, North Carolina, Ohio, Virginia, and Wisconsin. Six other states were considered battleground states in the 2008 race. Thus, record campaign ad dollars were funneled to fewer voters, who were bombarded with more ads than ever from both sides.

Battleground states in 2008 that were not part of the mix in 2012 were New Mexico, Missouri, Indiana, Montana, Georgia, and North Dakota.

Here are some key spending comparisons between 2008 and 2012, according to the *Week* magazine:

- $900 million—Amount spent on ads from June 1 to October 21, including from super PACs, up from $600 million for the same period in 2008.
- 915,000—Total ads aired by the Romney and Obama campaigns, up from 637,000 ads aired by the rival presidential campaigns during the same period in 2008.
- 44.5%—The increase in the number of ads in 2012 compared to the same time period in 2008.
- 438%—The increase in spending on TV ads by Democratic-leaning groups outside the official campaign and party.
- 954%—The increase in ad buys by Republican-leaning groups.

These stunning increases in campaign ad spending from the 2008 race have left pundits both amazed and concerned. "When all is said and done," says Erika Franklin Fowler, codirector of the Wesleyan Media Project, "2012 will go down as a record pulverizing year for political advertising."

However, because Obama enjoyed deeply discounted ad rates and, thus, reached a similar number of voters as Romney, who spent about $200 million more, some advocates of campaign finance reform are concerned. They fear that this unexpected parity will quell campaign finance reform efforts.

"There's a worry that if there's parity in terms of spending on ads, that it will diminish the appetite for reform," said Ellen Miller, the executive director of the Sunlight Foundation, which monitors outside spending. "But this is not about whether the candidates can game the system," she added. "It's about whether Americans can be fairly represented in a democracy that depends on big money, much of it spent in secret."

Robert Nanney

See also: Campaign 2008; Campaign 2012

Further Reading

Associated Press. 2012. "Big Money, Smaller Audience: The 2012 Presidential Ad Blitz Is a Study in Contrasts." As printed in *The Washington Post*, November 4.

Lutz, B.J. 2012. "Obama Nearly Doubles Romney in Online Ad Spending." NBCChicago.com, November 5.

Peters, Jeremy W., Nicholas Confessore, and Sarah Cohen. 2012. "Obama is Even in TV Ad Races Despite PACs." *The New York Times*, October 28.

"Presidential Ad Spending: By the Numbers." 2012. *The Week* magazine, October 25.

Affirmative Action

Affirmative action is the practice of preferential hiring for minorities to ensure that employees in business and government represent population demographics. In politics and the

American business world, there is debate about whether affirmative action is effective, or even necessary.

Affirmative action began largely as a result of the African American civil rights movement of the 1950s and 1960s. The first person to use the term "affirmative action" was President John F. Kennedy. His goal was to use affirmative action to ensure that the demographics of federally funded positions represented the nation's racial demographics more proportionately. With the passage of the 1964 Civil Rights Act, eight months after Kennedy was assassinated, affirmative action began to spread outside of government. Title VI of the act stated that "no person . . . shall, on the ground of race, color, or national origin, be excluded from participation in, be denied the benefits of, or be subjected to discrimination under any program or activity receiving Federal financial assistance." Title VII laid out exemptions to this law, stating that, under special circumstances, gender, religion, or national origin could be used as a basis for employee selection. This was the beginning of the type of preferential hiring that we now refer to as affirmative action.

Since then, affirmative action clearly has helped level the playing field for minority groups. According to one study, although blacks represent approximately 12 percent of the U.S. population, they make up less than 5 percent of the management ranks and considerably less than 1 percent of senior executives. The disparity is prevalent among gender, too. Women who work full-time throughout the year earn approximately 78 percent as much as men, according to a 2009 study.

Kennedy's successor, Lyndon B. Johnson, was the first to use the term affirmative action in legislation. In Executive Order No. 11,246 (1965), Johnson required federal contractors to use affirmative action to ensure that applicants are employed and that employees are treated during employment, without regard to race, creed, color, or national origin. Johnson also wanted to extend Title VII into realms outside government-financed jobs. Johnson's affirmative action was designed to implement institutional change so that American organizations could comply with the Civil Rights Act.

One of the most common misconceptions of affirmative action is that it sanctions quotas based on race or some other essential group category such as gender. It does not. This was affirmed in 1978 when the U.S. Supreme Court, in *Regents of the University of California v. Bakke*, ruled that racial quotas for college admissions violated the Fourteenth Amendment's equal protection clause, unless they were used to remedy discriminatory practices by the institution in the past. In *Bakke*, white applicant Allan P. Bakke argued that his application to the University of California, Davis's Medical School was denied due to the university's use of quotas to admit a specific number of minority students to the medical school each year. The Supreme Court ruled that Bakke's application was rejected because of the quota and ruled quotas unlawful. Muddying the waters, however, was Justice Powell's diversity rationale in the majority decision. The diversity rationale posited that ethnic and racial diversity can be one of many factors for attaining a heterogeneous student body in places of higher education. Thus, while Bakke struck down sharp quotas, the case created a compelling government interest in diversity.

Affirmative action requires companies to perform an analysis of minority employment, establish goals to create a more demographically representative workforce, and develop plans to recruit and employ minority employees. For most companies that have effective programs, affirmative action extends beyond hiring practices to include maintaining a diverse workforce, periodic evaluations of the affirmative action program, educating and sensitizing employees concerning affirmative action policies, and providing a work environment and management practices that support equal opportunity in all terms and conditions of employment. Many of the biggest companies in the United States today have departments and legal staffs dedicated entirely to ensuring diversity in the workplace.

Since its inception, affirmative action has faced harsh critics who would like to see the process changed, altered, or disbanded altogether. The critics of affirmative action claim that the practice actually creates unequal hiring practices; is impractical; is unfair to those who, they claim, lose jobs due to the practice; and is even unfair to those who gain employment because they may not be able to do the work. One of the most common misconceptions about those who are against affirmative action is that they are all white conservative men. Many minorities, even liberal ones, are also opposed to affirmative action, if not as a concept, then to the way it is implemented in the U.S. system.

The most prevalent argument against affirmative action is that the practice creates reverse discrimination. Those who argue this stance point to Title VI of the 1964 Civil Rights Act, which was designed to prevent exclusion of minority groups based on race, religion, sex, or national origin. Those who claim reverse discrimination when arguing against affirmative action claim that white men are now victims of discrimination due to their race and sex.

Legal issues in the application of affirmative action have faced frequent judicial review, even in recent years. In 2003, the Supreme Court upheld the University of Michigan's law school admissions policy, which considered race as a factor. But the court in 2009 ruled in *Ricci v. DeStefano* that nonminority firefighters in New Haven, Connecticut, were justified in claiming reverse discrimination. The city had thrown out the results of advancement exams because it feared the results would prevent a sufficient number of minority candidates from advancing.

William M. Sturkey

See also: African American voters; Asian voters; Hispanic voters

Further Reading

Anderson, Terry H. 2004. *The Pursuit of Fairness: A History of Affirmative Action.* New York: Oxford University Press.

Dobbin, Frank. 2009. *Inventing Equal Opportunity.* Princeton, NJ: Princeton University Press.

Katznelson, Ira. 2005. *When Affirmative Action Was White: An Untold History of Racial Inequality in Twentieth-Century America.* New York: W.W. Norton.

Kellough, J. Edward. 2006. *Understanding Affirmative Action: Politics, Discrimination, and the Search for Justice.* Washington, DC: Georgetown University Press.

AFL-CIO (American Federation of Labor-Congress of Industrial Organizations)

The American Federation of Labor-Congress of Industrial Organizations includes 55 unions with about 14.5 million members. It has been a major force in American politics for many years. When the AFL-CIO was formed in 1955 by the merger of the American Federation of Labor (AFL) and the Congress of Industrial Organizations (CIO), there were 15 million members. Although many observers point out that union membership has declined, the fact is that this decline is less than some analysts suggest. At the turn of this century there were 16.2 million union members. By 2010 the number had declined to 14.7 million and stayed at that level for the next five years.

To assess the impact of AFL-CIO, it is important to consider also the spouses, brothers, sisters, sons, and daughters of union members and former union members. This adds up to considerably more than 14.5 million voters, and many politicians are aware of this.

The AFL-CIO spends a great deal of money on politics. It is estimated, on the basis of reports to the Federal Elections Commission and the Department of Labor, that the AFL-CIO spent $4.4 billion between 2005 and 2011. One-fourth of these expenditures were contributions to Democratic candidates. The rest was for lobbying, educating, and recruiting voters. These are national figures and do not include contributions of money and time contributed by local unions.

While virtually all the AFL-CIO contributions go to Democratic candidates, not all AFL-CIO members vote for Democratic candidates. Several polls in 2012 indicated that about a third of union members voted for the Republican nominee for president, Mitt Romney.

That the AFL-CIO's influence remains was demonstrated in at least two ways in 2013. The AFL-CIO led a repeal drive in Ohio against legislation sought by Gov. John Kasich and passed by the state legislature that severely limited contract-negotiating rights of public employees. The repeal succeeded by a 2-to-1 margin, prompting Kasich to back away from the issue. Similar legislation in Wisconsin led to an AFL-CIO-led effort to recall Gov. Scott Walker. The recall failed, but post-election surveys indicated the reason was not that Wisconsin people favored the law but that they were reluctant to recall a governor, something that never had happened in that state.

AFL and CIO had different histories and philosophies and once were in competition with each other. Merger was not anticipated until Congress passed the Taft-Hartley Act of 1947. That law reversed many of the gains labor received in the Wagner Act of 1935, a major part of the New Deal, which created the National Labor Relations Board and guarantees basic rights of employees to organize into unions, engage in collective bargaining, and take collective action, including strikes, if necessary. The Taft-Hartley Act went so far in the opposite direction that the AFL and CIO decided to put their differences aside and join forces to protect labor. The Taft-Hartley Act drove unions to the Democratic side, and subsequent antilabor actions by Republicans have solidified that.

The AFL was created by Samuel Gompers in 1886. It was an organization of craft and trade unions and focused on economic reform. It believed that higher pay for workers would benefit management as well. It was politically neutral at the outset but became involved in Democratic Party politics. The AFL supported William Jennings Bryan in his bids for the presidency and opposed the nomination of Woodrow Wilson in 2012. Wilson appointed Gompers to the Council of National Defense, and the Wilson years were the best years AFL had had. The AFL had 50,000 members when it was founded and grew to three million members by the time of Gompers' death in 1924.

In contrast to the AFL concept of organizing by trades and skills, the CIO organized by industries, such as steel, coal mining, and automobiles. Some labor leaders tried to get the AFL to accept this type of union along with those involving skills and trades. When the AFL continually refused, 10 AFL unions broke away to form the CIO in 1935. The two groups were rivals until Taft-Hartley brought them together.

The CIO supported the Democratic Party from the start. In the wake of Taft-Hartley, AFL-CIO became more strongly Democratic, causing Republican Party positions on labor to intensify. While not all AFL-CIO members vote Democratic, the AFL-CIO, despite its decline in membership, remains a major force in American politics.

Guido H. Stempel III

See also: Political Action Committees

Further Reading

Skurzynski, Gloria. 2008. *Sweat and Blood: A History of U.S. Labor Unions*. Minneapolis: Twenty-First Century Books.
Yates, Michael D. 2009. *Why Unions Matter*. New York: Monthly Review Press.

African American Voters

African American voters, over a 50-year period, have risen from widespread political disenfranchisement throughout much of the American South during the Jim Crow era to become a key voting bloc that turned out in greater numbers than any other racial or major ethnic voter group during the 2012 presidential election. Black voters were widely credited by conservative and liberal news media alike as an important factor in President Barack Obama's reelection.

The Census Bureau estimates there were 28.7 million black Americans of voting age in 2012, of whom 19.7 million were registered to vote and 17.8 million reported casting a ballot in the general election. That means blacks accounted for 12.2 percent of the voting age population, 12.8 percent of the nation's registered voters, and 13.4 percent of the ballots cast for president in 2012. Blacks of eligible voting age actually cast a ballot 66.2 percent of the time, surpassing, for the first time in history, the non-Hispanic white voting rate which was 64.1 percent that year. Turnouts for Hispanic and Asian voters were less than 50 percent that year.

"This is a historic event, given the history of black disenfranchisement," Brookings Institution demographer William Frey concluded when the Census Bureau voting estimates were released in 2013. "It has a lot to do with the first black president."

Black voters have become key to Democratic Party hopes in national elections and in many city, county, and statewide contests. They have proven for decades to be among the Democrat's most loyal voters, usually voting for Democratic presidential candidates 88 percent of the time or more. Their loyalty peaked in 2008 and 2012 when they supported Obama 95 percent and 93 percent of the time, respectively.

Historically, when Southern blacks first gained voting rights in the turbulent period of Reconstruction following the Civil War, they often sided with "the party of Lincoln." Republicans in Congress, at Lincoln's behest, fought Democrats to win passage of the Thirteenth Amendment to the Constitution outlawing slavery in 1865. Blacks often voted Republican in the decades that followed, although Jim Crow laws increasingly reduced their access to the polls.

But black allegiance swung toward the Democratic Party during the 20th century, with many African Americans opting to become part of Franklin Delano Roosevelt's New Deal coalition. Since blacks were moving out of the rural South and into Northern cities in search of better jobs and broader opportunities, they naturally gravitated to the increasingly urban-based Democratic Party. Their migration to the Democrats solidified even as white Southerners began a reverse migration.

At first, white Southerners were obliged to reject the Republican Party precisely because it was "the party of Lincoln" and because of the raw emotions that the Civil War still evoked. White Southern Democrats were the architect of Jim Crow legislation even as national Democratic leaders were becoming increasingly sensitive to the human rights plight of blacks.

The tensions between white Southern Democrats and national Democrats came to a boil with the 1948 "Dixiecrat revolt," in which white Democrats broke ranks with their national party after President Harry Truman ordered an end to racial discrimination in the armed forces and created the President's Committee on Civil Rights. Southern whites increasingly voted for the GOP in national elections and, eventually, for Republicans in local and state contests as well.

Black Southern Americans, meanwhile, were excluded from voting because of discriminatory Jim Crow laws passed by Southern state legislatures from the 1880s into the early 20th century. These acts imposed barriers to blacks' registering to vote through poll taxes, literacy tests, requirements that voters own property, so-called "moral character" tests, and "grandfather" clauses that allowed otherwise-ineligible persons to vote if their grandfathers voted—legislation that effectively barred African Americans whose grandfathers were slaves.

Southern blacks increasingly resisted these barriers, resulting in a broad civil rights movement under the leadership of Martin Luther King Jr., Ralph Abernathy, Malcolm X, and many others. Sympathy over the unfair conditions and outrage at the often-fatal attacks on black leaders during the civil rights struggle prompted Congress to enact the Civil Rights Act of 1964—which broadly outlawed discrimination based on race, color, religion, sex, or national origin—and the Voting Rights Act of 1965 which specifically prohibited racial discrimination in voting.

Southern black voting registration grew steadily as a result. In 1950, only about 17 percent were registered to cast ballots. Black registration rose rapidly to 29 percent in the South by 1960 and 43 percent four years later. In 2012, the Census Bureau estimated that 73 percent of black residents were registered to vote, only slightly behind the 73.7 percent registration rate of non-Hispanic whites.

According to a study by the Congressional Research Service, the rate of black voting participation had an enormous impact on the racial makeup of Congress. The first three African American federal lawmakers took office in 1869: two black representatives and a black senator. Black representation rose in subsequent elections and reached its 19th-century zenith in 1875, when seven black representatives and one senator took office. But the ranks of black members of Congress fell off rapidly as Jim Crow laws were enacted until there were none during the period from 1901 through 1929, and then only one or two until the late 1950s.

The size of the black congressional delegation grew slowly, despite rapid increases in black voter registration. Many Southern black voters continued to support white Democratic incumbents, gaining black representation only after a white incumbent retired. By 1967, there were only six black members, but the black caucus started rising steadily from 1969, when it reached 11 members. Blacks accounted for 21 House seats in 1983, 27 in

1991, 39 representatives and one senator in 1993, and they achieved an all-time high of 44 House members in 2011.

The rapid increase in black representation was also influenced by federal court orders that permitted racially conscious design of congressional districts, a judicial policy that Democrats could hardly refuse and Republicans actually embraced. Drawing congressional lines to create majority black districts concentrated loyal Democratic voters into one or two districts in each state, allowing Republican candidates greater strength in the heavy majority white districts.

Thomas K. Hargrove

See also: Jackson, Jesse; Obama, Barack

Further Reading

Beyerlein, Kraig, and Kenneth T. Andrews. 2008. "Black Voting During the Civil Rights Movement, a Micro-Level Analysis." *Journal of Social Forces.* Chapel Hill: University of North Carolina Press.

Manning, Jennifer E., and Colleen J. Shogan. 2012. "African American Members of the United States Congress: 1870–2012." Congressional Research Service. http://www.senate.gov/CRSReports /crs-publish.cfm?pid=%270E%2C*PLW%3C%20P%20%20%0A. Accessed September 10, 2014.

May, Gary. 2014. *Bending Toward Justice: The Voting Rights Act and the Transformation of American Democracy.* New York: Basic Books.

McCormick, John. 2013. "Blacks Made History Surpassing White Voter Turnout Rates" Bloomberg News. http://www.bloomberg.com/news/2013-05-08/blacks-made-history-surpassing-white-voter -turnout-rates.html. Accessed September 7, 2014.

Agenda Setting

In its simplest form, the agenda-setting theory suggests that "The press may not be successful much of the time in telling people what to think, but it is stunningly successful in telling them what to think about," according to mass media scholar Bernard C. Cohen. The genesis of the theory, however, can perhaps be traced back to the 1922 publication of Walter Lippmann's classic work *Public Opinion*, in which he noted there are significant differences between the "the world outside and the pictures in our heads." Agenda-setting theory says it is the media that create an impression of the importance of these pictures in our head, which may differ significantly from what is important in the world outside.

It is important to note that, unlike other cause-and-effect theories (observational learning, aggressive cues, etc.), agenda-setting theory does not say the media make us do anything. Rather, agenda setting says the media suggest what is important and what is not.

In this form, agenda setting is similar to George Gerbner's cultivation theory; both suggest that the world we perceive in our heads may not be the objective world that actually exists. But whereas cultivation theory proposes that we actually "inhabit" a media-created world (that is, we behave as if the mediated world objectively exists), agenda-setting is more concerned with what we think than how we act.

In 1951, philosopher of science James Conant, in his book *Science and Common Sense*, outlined the characteristics of a good scientific theory: (1) other publications based on the theory, (2) integration with other theories, and (3) Generation of new research across a variety of disciplines. Agenda-setting theory, first introduced as a formal theory in the seminal 1972 work, "The Agenda Setting Function of Mass Media," certainly meets Conant's three criteria. Since that publication, based on the 1968 presidential election, hundreds of other studies have examined agenda setting in relation to political and nonpolitical communication, in media and nonmedia settings, around the world. The agenda-setting theory stands in contrast to the older "hypodermic" or "magic bullet" theory, which suggests the media have direct and powerful influences on behavior.

Although development of a formal theory of agenda setting can be traced to the mid-twentieth century, its application can be seen in the earliest writings. Caesar's *Commentaries* through Machiavelli's *The Prince* on through Thomas Paine's *Common Sense* can all be viewed as treatises on influencing public opinion. Indeed, in his book *Mightier Than the Sword*, Roger Streitmatter traces the influences of media on public policy from the Civil War through the 2008 election, all without explicit reference to "agenda setting."

In terms of elections and voting behavior, agenda-setting theory and the two-step flow theory of communication are linked. In their original research, McCombs and Shaw (and many researchers since) showed a strong correlation between what the news media considered to be important issues and what voters considered to be important issues. However, it is also apparent that politicians set the agenda for reporters (thus two-step flow). Out of the universe of issues they can discuss, politicians choose which ones to emphasize, and these are the issues that are then relayed to the public.

In addition, it must be noted that if media are setting an agenda for what is important, they are by default also deciding what is not important. Agenda setting seems to be most effective in moving "undecided" voters into a "decided" column whereas political partisans (who are less likely to be swayed by media messages with which they disagree) will tend to see messages favorable to the other side as biased, and messages from their side as fair and impartial. What is important for one side is generally unimportant for the other, and what is unimportant for one side is important for the other.

Of course this information flow is not a one-way street, and many times the news media report information politicians would rather be kept out of the public eye. The Thomas Eagleton affair in the 1972 election and the Barak Obama/Jeremiah Wright disclosures in the 2008 election are two examples of how what were perhaps nonissues became important because of media coverage. Of course, depending on one's political persuasion, the Eagleton and Wright issues were important, which perhaps validates the agenda-setting theory: for true believers, the issues were clear-cut; for those who did not have strong opinions, the media made these issues important but did little to actually change beliefs and perceptions.

Another aspect of agenda-setting is carried out by the candidates themselves. "Pseudo-agenda setting," similar to Daniel Boorstein's pseudo-event, is when a candidate diverts questions from what reporters and/or the public wants to know to subjects the candidate wants to address. Such spin is common in candidate debates, where the question and answer may be similar to the following:

Question: Candidate, can you describe your plan for medical care for the elderly?
Answer: Yes, medical care is a critical part of the economy, much like education funding. As you know, my administration, has taken the lead in trying to help low-performing schools. . . .

Here the candidate may be saying he believes education is more important than medical care, or he may simply be trying to avoid discussing medical care. Thus the question arises: What is the real agenda—discussing education or avoiding discussing health care?

The media have three choices in reporting this dialogue, thus setting an agenda: the candidate's emphasis on education, the candidate's lack of emphasis on health care, or the candidate's attempt to spin the question to provide a less salient response.

Larry Burriss

See also: Gatekeeping

Further Reading

Cohen, Bernard. 1963. *The Press and Foreign Policy*. Princeton, NJ: Princeton University Press.

Erbring, Lutz, Edie Goldenberg, and Arthur Miller. 1980. "Font-Page News and Real-World Cues: A New Look at Agenda Setting by the Media." *American Journal of Political Science* 24:16–49.

Lippmann, Walter. 1997. *Public Opinion*. New York: Simon and Schuster.

McCombs, Maxwell E., and Donald L. Shaw. 1972. "The Agenda Setting Function of Mass Media." *Public Opinion Quarterly* 36:176–187.

McCombs, Maxwell E., and Donald L. Shaw. 1993. "The Evolution of Agenda Setting Research: Twenty-Five Years in the Marketplace of Ideas." *Journal of Communication* 43: 58–67.

Streitmatter, Roger. 2012. *Mightier Than the Sword: How the News Media Have Shaped American History*. 3rd ed. Boulder, CO: Westview Press.

Ailes, Roger (1940–)

Roger Ailes is president of Fox News, which he founded in 1996. It has the highest Nielsen Ratings of any cable news program and has had the highest ratings continuously since 2002. Its ratings typically are about twice as high as those of major competitors—cable networks CNN, CNBC, and MSNBC.

Polls show that 20 to 25 percent of Americans are conservative, and Fox News has that audience to itself, while the rest of the audience is divided between the other cable networks and the over-the-air networks, ABC, CBS, and NBC. Fox News has offered a conservative perspective heavy on commentary with such people as Geraldo, Glenn Beck, Bill O'Reilly, and Sean Hannity. This obviously appeals to conservatives, but research shows that, while the audience is predominantly conservative, it is not entirely so. The study about "media effects" in the fourth introductory essay at the beginning of this encyclopedia shows that some Democrats and independents find Fox News a useful source of campaign information.

The tagline of Fox News is "fair and balanced," but many observers question that. However, Ailes says the difference between Fox and other cable news is that the others ignore news about conservatives. From time to time Fox News goes to an extreme and draws widespread criticism, but Ailes is supportive of his staff in such situations, and Fox News is affected slightly, if at all.

A 1962 graduate in radio-TV from Ohio University, Ailes began his career on the *Mike Douglas Show* as a property assistant. He became producer of that program in 1965 and executive producer in 1967. While Ailes was with the Douglas program, Richard Nixon was a guest. Ailes and Nixon had a discussion about the role television plays in politics. Nixon, who had lost the 1960 presidential election largely because he fared badly in televised debates and who had become mistrustful of television, was impressed. He appointed Ailes media adviser for his 1968 campaign, and Ailes helped Nixon use television more effectively and go on to win the election.

Ailes assisted other political candidates for almost a quarter of a century. He helped Ronald Reagan in both 1980 and 1984 and was a major factor in George H.W. Bush's victory in 1988. With this background, he went to work for Richard Thornburg, former governor of Pennsylvania, who was running for U.S. senator in 1992. Thornburg was expected to win easily but lost, and Ailes did not work for a political candidate again.

Ailes's most noteworthy effort was as communication manager for George H.W. Bush in the 1988 presidential campaign. The Democratic candidate, Michael Dukakis, had a substantial lead in early polling, but the Bush campaign successfully attacked Dukakis for his policy of furloughs for prison inmates. A main feature of this was a cable television ad about Willie Horton, a convict who had committed assault and rape while out on furlough. Ailes was criticized for this but maintained he had nothing to do with the ad.

Ailes also worked with Reagan in 1984 after he had lost the first debate to Walter Mondale. He advised Reagan not to emphasize statistics because the public would not be interested. Ailes also was credited with giving Reagan, who was the oldest president in U.S. history, a way to deal with the issue of age. When the issue came up in the second debate, Reagan responded by saying he was not going to make his opponent's youthfulness and lack of experience an issue. That was the most memorable line of the campaign and essentially ended discussion of Reagan's age.

In 1992, Ailes created the Rush Limbaugh television program. It lasted four years before it was dropped, apparently by mutual agreement. It did not draw the large audience that Limbaugh has drawn on radio.

Ailes became president of CNBC in 1993, and also planned and implemented another CNBC channel called "America Today," which lasted only three years. When NBC started MSNBC in 1996, Ailes left CNBC. That made him available when Rupert Murdoch asked him to start Fox News. Ailes became chairman of the Fox Television Station Group in 2005.

Ailes says that his education at Ohio University has been a major factor in his success. He has contributed scholarships to broadcasting students for two decades. He also contributed funding for the renovation and expansion of the newsroom of WOUB, the public radio and television station at Ohio University.

Guido H. Stempel III

See also: Fox News, CNN, MSNBC

Further Reading

Collins, Scott. 2004. *"Crazy Like a Fox": The Inside Story of How Fox News Beat CNN.* New York: Penguin Group.

Sherman, Gabriel. 2014. *The Loudest Voice in the News: How the Brilliant Bombastic Roger Ailes Built Fox News and Divided a Country.* New York: Random House.

American Association of Public Opinion Research (AAPOR)

See AAPOR (American Association of Public Opinion Research) Standards

American Association of Retired Persons (AARP)

See AARP (American Association of Retired Persons)

American Federation of Labor-Congress of Industrial Organizations (AFL-CIO)

See AFL-CIO (American Federation of Labor-Congress of Industrial Organizations)

American Society of Newspaper Editors (ASNE)

See ASNE (American Society of Newspaper Editors)

Antiestablishment Political Rhetoric

In recent decades, American politicians increasingly have used anti-establishment political rhetoric, urging voters to select them so that they will correct the excesses and abuses of government. The message that government is essentially wrong and contrary to the common good is at odds with much of the rhetoric of the past, starting with George Washington's famous use of a biblical metaphor that the national government of the United States is a "city on a hill."

Deeply ingrained in the American political psyche is a belief that individualism is a heroic force that must struggle with—and eventually transcend—a broader social and governmental establishment. This theme was eloquently voiced throughout the first 200 years of the American republic, whether in Thomas Jefferson's "Declaration of Independence" or Martin Luther King Jr.'s "Letter from a Birmingham Jail." The righteous individual must triumph over institutions, no matter how powerful or ingrained they may be.

The willingness to "speak truth to power," to "fight the man" or to "rage against the machine" have become major themes in our social and political mythos, perhaps one of the few political values over which both conservatives and liberals usually agree. So powerful has antiestablishment rhetoric become that it is even a mainstay of modern presidential politics—an irony since whoever seeks this office, by definition, wants to become "the man."

Antiestablishment rhetoric widely flourished during the 1960s in the civil rights struggle of African Americans and in the youth-centric counter-culture.

Martin Luther King Jr. wrote famously in 1963 that the greatest threat to the civil rights movement was not the Ku Klux Klan nor the white citizen's councils, but "the white moderate who is more devoted to 'order' than to justice; who prefers a negative peace which is the absence of tension to a positive peace which is the presence of justice; who constantly says: "I agree with you in the goal you seek, but I cannot agree with your methods of direct action"; who paternalistically believes he can set the timetable for another man's freedom; who lives by a mythical concept of time and who constantly advises the Negro to wait for a 'more convenient season'." King's challenge from his Birmingham jail cell was aimed at America's too complacent white establishment, which allowed repressive Jim Crow laws to subjugate blacks.

Perhaps one of the great American expressions of anti-establishmentism can be found in the Students for a Democratic Society's 1962 "Port Huron Statement," which announced that "there is an alternative to the present, that something can be done to change circumstances in the school, the workplaces, the bureaucracies, the government. It is to this latter yearning, at once the spark and engine of change, that we direct our present appeal. The search for truly democratic alternatives to the present, and a commitment to social experimentation with them, is a worthy and fulfilling human enterprise, one which moves us and, we hope, others today."

American conservatives hold very similar notions. Arizona Senator Barry Goldwater expressed a call for individualism when he accepted the Republican nomination for president in 1964, to which most of the counter-culture authors of the Port Huron Statement would probably agree: "Equality, rightly understood as our founding fathers understood it, leads to liberty and to the emancipation of creative differences; wrongly understood, as it has been so tragically in our time, it leads first to conformity and then to despotism."

Antiestablishment rhetoric was masterfully employed by President Ronald Reagan in his farewell speech of 1988. He clarified for conservatives that government, by its nature, represents a threat to individualism: "I hope we have once again reminded people that man is not free unless government is limited. There's a clear cause and effect here that is as neat and predictable as a law of physics: as government expands, liberty contracts."

Antiestablishment politics requires that politicians promise to change the nation's culture within the halls of power. President Barak Obama crystallized the theme of his successful campaign when describing the intention of his administration in 2009 during one of his first radio addresses as president: "It's time to fundamentally change the way that we do business in Washington. To help build a new foundation for the 21st century, we need to reform our government so that it is more efficient, more transparent, and more creative. That will demand new thinking and a new sense of responsibility for every dollar that is spent."

It has become nearly impossible for successful American politicians to voice support of the nation's establishment, government, or current social order. These are all negative ideas in the modern political lexicon.

Antiestablishment rhetoric may be producing a long-term impact on how Americans view their nation. The Gallup Poll since 1979 has asked Americans whether they generally are "satisfied" or "dissatisfied" with "the way things are going in the United States at this time?" It became a stock question used by pollsters to gauge the general public mood, which has often varied with economic conditions and according to the party that occupies the White House. Democratic voters are dissatisfied when Republicans rule, and vice versa, but the broad trend on this question has definitely been downward, regardless of economic conditions or which party carried the last election. It was not uncommon in the 1980s and 1990s for 70 percent or more of Americans to say they were generally "satisfied" with conditions in the nation. The last time this statistic reached 70 percent was in the immediate aftermath of the September 11, 2001, terrorist attacks, when to express "dissatisfaction" was viewed as unpatriotic. Satisfaction hit an historic low of 7 percent in the final days of President George W. Bush's administration in late 2008. It generally has hovered around 25 percent during Obama's presidency.

The antiestablishment politics of the 20th century helped produce a widespread and, so far, lasting cynicism into the 21st century.

Thomas K. Hargrove

See also: Reagan, Ronald; Conspiracy Theories

Further Reading

Heath, Joseph, and Andrew Potter. 2004. "Nation of Rebels: Why Counterculture Became Consumer Culture." New York: HarperCollins.

Horwitz, Robert B. 2013. *America's Right: Anti-establishment Conservatism from Goldwater to the Tea Party.* Cambridge: Polity Press.

Arnett, Peter (1934–)

American journalists in recent decades have proven that the press, for better or worse, truly should be considered a "fourth estate," sharing power with government and other organs of power. Perhaps no one exemplifies the breadth and controversial nature of journalism's political power than the career of Pulitzer-prize-winning war correspondent Peter Arnett.

The title of Arnett's memoir published in 1994, *Live from the Battlefield from Vietnam to Baghdad: 35 Years in the World's War Zones,* just about sums up his career. But what the title does not divulge is Arnett's impact on relations between the media and the military and the fact that he continued to report from the battlefield, covering a total of 19 wars over a 40-year career.

Born in Bluff, "a gale-lashed town at the bottom end of New Zealand," in 1934 to parents of Maori and English descent, Arnett began his journalistic career at the *Southland Times*, Invercargill, and then at the Standard, Wellington. He did a brief stint at the *Sydney Sun*, Sydney, Australia, before moving to Bangkok, where he worked on the *Bangkok World*. He left for Laos, where he founded a newspaper and served at once as a correspondent for the Associated Press, United Press International, and Agence France Presse. After a stint with the Associated Press in Jakarta, he moved to the AP's Saigon bureau in 1962. He stayed in Vietnam for 13 years, tenaciously covering the war by jumping in helicopters and getting a bird's eye view of the action on the ground. "I got closer to the action there than anywhere else," Arnett has said. "We were allowed to go where we wanted to go. I haven't been able to do that since." He won a Pulitzer Prize in 1966.

Producing reports from the front that were sharply at odds with Pentagon accounts, Arnett helped change the cozy relationship between foreign correspondents and American officials. Arnett's reports infuriated presidents Kennedy, Johnson, and Nixon and generals Harkins, Westmoreland, and Wheeler. Johnson's presidential assistant Jack Valenti wrote a memo to the president before a meeting with AP executives that noted, "You may want to bring up the problem of Peter Arnett who has been more damaging to the U.S. cause than a whole battalion of Viet Cong."

Arnett said, "I believed the truth was to be found in the battlefield and not in the briefing rooms." During the Tet offensive, he got from a senior U.S. officer the famous quote: "It became necessary to destroy the town to save it," a line that came to symbolize what the war had become for much of America.

Having joined the fledgling CNN in 1981, Arnett reported in war zones from Central America to Asia. In 1991, having been asked to go to Baghdad to cover the first Gulf War, he became a household name for reporting from the El Rashid Hotel via a smuggled-in satellite phone. On the scene, he described how the newest, sophisticated, target-specific weapons often went awry, killing civilians and "friendly" troops (U.S. soldiers).

When a U.S. bomb hit what the White House called a biological weapons center and what the Iraqis said was their country's only baby-milk plant, Arnett toured the plant and stood before the cameras with measuring cups and milk-powder containers, saying the plant looked like a milk plant to him. He interviewed Saddam Hussein, outraging U.S. officials who said the Iraqi president was scoring propaganda points.

Sen. Lawrence Coughlin denounced Arnett in Congress, saying, "Arnett is the Joseph Goebbels of Saddam Hussein's Hitler-like regime." Thirty-four House members signed a letter accusing Arnett of giving "the demented dictator (Hussein) a propaganda mouthpiece to over 100 nations."

Arnett's most high-profile clash with the U.S. government during the Gulf War was over collateral damage (casualties) in what the Iraqis insisted was a civilian center and the Pentagon insisted was a command-and-control military bunker. About two hundred people were killed. The televised report started Americans questioning the Pentagon's—and not Arnett's—truthfulness.

Just seven years later, Arnett would be in trouble again, this time with CNN itself and Time Warner, owner of *TIME* magazine, in which he had a bylined article about the use of sarin gas on American defectors in Laos during the Vietnam War. Arnett maintained he was merely the anchor for the "Tailwind" CNN investigation and that his byline in *TIME* was simply a marketing ploy. He had contributed "not one comma" to the report, he said. However, there was widespread criticism. Christiane Amanpour, CNN's chief international correspondent, criticized Arnett, saying, "I object to the new image of correspondent as nincompoop."

In April 1999, CNN and Arnett brought Arnett's 18-year service to an amicable conclusion with two years left on a five-year contract.

The fallout from "Tailwind" helped drive the press's credibility to a record low. A *Newsweek* poll published shortly after the program showed that more than half of Americans characterized news reporting as "often inaccurate" and 76 percent said the race for ratings and profits had made the media too entertainment oriented.

Within months of leaving CNN, Arnett conducted interviews of world leaders for a website, ForeignTV.com. He became editor and chief of Global Vision, a quarterly business magazine; covered the end of the 2000 presidential campaign for ATV, the Turkish television network; and in late 2001 joined BNN, an independent video company that made documentaries for the Discovery Channel and MSNBC. As a member of the Committee to Protect Journalists, he visited Algeria and Uzbekistan. With the start of the second Gulf War—Operation Iraqi Freedom—in March 2003, Arnett was back in Baghdad, this time reporting for National Geographic Explorer, exclusively on MSNBC.

Just a week into the war, Arnett told state-controlled Iraqi TV that the U.S. effort so far was a failure. "It is clear within the United States there is growing challenge to President Bush about the conduct of the war and also opposition to the war," he said. "So our reports about civilian casualties here, about the resistance of the Iraqi forces . . . help those who oppose the war."

Sen. Alan Simpson, Republican-Wyoming, criticized Arnett as an Iraqi sympathizer. More protests followed. Although they defended him initially, MSNBC, National Geographic, and NBC fired him. Marvin Kalb—senior fellow at the Shorenstein Center on the Press, Politics, and Public Policy at Harvard University—said Arnett's mistake was not necessarily his criticism of U.S. war policy but where he said it.

"He was fired because he was critical of the U.S. on Iraqi television," Mr. Kalb said. "That is similar to Tokyo Rose in World War ll. It has the appearance of participating in enemy propaganda."

Britain's *Daily Mirror* immediately hired Arnett and announced his appointment with the headline, "Fired by America for telling the truth . . . Hired by the *Daily Mirror* to carry on telling it."

In the decade since, Arnett has taught journalism at Shantou University, China. He has received multiple honors and awards, among them the Premio Ischia award (Italy), the Freedom of Speech Award (National Association of Radio Talk Show Hosts, United States), and the National Press Club's Lifetime Achievement Award in Journalism (United States). He has been made an officer of the New Zealand Order of Merit, and the Southern Institute of Technology, Invercargill, New Zealand, has named a school after him—the Peter Arnett School of Journalism.

Maria Marron

See also: Koppel, Ted; Moyers, Bill; Presidents and the Press

Further Reading

Alabiso, Vincent, Kelly Smith Tunney, and Chuck Zeller, eds. 1998. *Flash! The Associated Press Covers the World.* New York: The Associated Press in association with Harry N. Abrams.

Arnett, Peter. 1994. *Live from the Battlefield from Vietnam to Baghdad: 35 Years in the World's War Zones.* New York: Simon & Shuster.

Asian Voters

According to the 2010 Census, the Asian American population was 6 percent of the U.S. population and was the fastest growing racial group between 2000 and 2010, increasing by 46 percent compared to a growth rate of 43 percent for Hispanics, 40 percent for Native Hawaiian/Pacific Islander, 27 percent for American Indian/Alaska Native, 15 percent for African American and 1 percent for non-Hispanic whites. The Asian American population continues to be concentrated in several states, including, in descending order, California, New York, Texas, New Jersey, Hawaii, Illinois, and Washington. In terms of growth, Asian American populations increased the most over the past decade in Nevada (by 116 percent), Arizona (95 percent), North Carolina (85 percent), North Dakota (85 percent), Georgia (83 percent), and New Hampshire (80 percent).

The Asian American population is diverse, including people from 19 ethnic groups. Ranked in order of population, these groups are Chinese (except Taiwanese), Filipino, Indian, Vietnamese, Korean, Japanese, Pakistani, Cambodian, Hmong, Thai, Laotian, Taiwanese, Bangladeshi, Burmese, Indonesian, Nepalese, Sri Lankan, Malaysian, and Bhutanese. The fastest growing groups 2000 to 2010 were Bangladeshi (157 percent), Pakistani (100 percent), Sri Lankan (85 percent), and Indian (68 percent).

Asian Americans are more likely than any other ethnic group to be foreign-born. According to the U.S. Census Bureau's American Community Survey, about 60 percent of Asian Americans were born outside the United States, and about one in three has limited English proficiency.

Among the voting-age population, 68 percent of Asian Americans were citizens in 2008 compared to 91 percent of the total U.S. population. Voter registration among

Asian Americans was 55 percent compared to 71 percent for the U.S. population. Of those registered to vote, 86 percent voted, compared to 90 percent for the entire U.S. population.

Over the past two decades, Asian Americans have shown a significant shift towards the Democratic Party. In 1992, only 31 percent of the Asian American electorate voted for Bill Clinton. But by 2012, 73 percent voted for Barack Obama, according to exit polling conducted by a consortium of news organizations.

In 2008, 48 percent of Asian Americans identified as Democrat, 31 percent as independent, and 22 percent as Republican. Among the Asian American groups, the most likely to identify as Democrats were Japanese (59 percent), Korean (59 percent), Asian Indian (54 percent), and Filipino (50 percent), according to Ramakrishnan.

The 2012 elections showed a range in Asian American voting across ethnic lines. Support for Barack Obama, in each ethnic group, from highest to lowest, was Bangladesh American (96 percent), Pakistani American (91 percent), Indian American (84 percent), Chinese American (81 percent), Korean American (78 percent), Filipino American (65 percent), and Vietnamese American (44 percent). The exit polling found that Obama's support was overwhelming among all age cohorts of Asians.

The shift of Asian Americans toward the Democratic Party in the 2012 elections has been attributed to the Obama administration's policies on health care, education, the environment, and national security, according to a 2012 survey by the Asian American Justice Center. The post-election survey showed that the issues most important to Asian Americans were the economy and jobs (86 percent), education (81 percent), health care (80 percent), national security (72 percent), social security (71 percent), the environment (59 percent), racial discrimination (54 percent), and immigration. The percentages of Asian Americans voting for Obama and Romney, and rating each issue as important were as follows: economy and jobs (67 percent Obama, 33 percent Romney); education (71 percent Obama, 29 percent Romney); health care (71 percent Obama, 29 percent Romney); national security (66 percent Obama, 34 percent Romney); social security (70 percent Obama, 30 percent Romney); environment (72 percent Obama, 28 percent Romney); racial discrimination (74 percent Obama, 26 percent Romney); immigration (70 percent, 30 percent Romney).

Voting patterns in congressional elections among Asian Americans were similar to presidential voting in 2012. For the U.S. Senate, 74 percent voted for the Democratic candidate and 18 percent voted for the Republican candidate. For the U.S. House of Representatives, 73 percent voted for the Democratic candidate and 17 percent voted for the Republican candidate. Among Asian Indians, Chinese, Filipinos, Japanese, Koreans, and Vietnamese, the main media source of political information in 2008 was television (85 percent), followed by newspapers (65 percent), the Internet (52 percent), and radio (45 percent). Foreign-born Asian Americans in these groups used ethnic media sources (particularly ethnic newspapers) more than English news sources.

Alexis Tan

See also: African American Voters; Hispanic Voters

Further Reading

Asian American Center for Advancing Justice. 2011. *A Community of Contrasts: Asian Americans in the United States: 2011*. Los Angeles: Asian American Center for Advancing Justice.

Asian American Justice Center. 2012. *Behind the Numbers: Post-Election Survey of Asian American and Pacific Islander Voters in 2012*. Los Angeles: Asian American Center for Advancing Justice.

Wong, Janelle, with Karthiok Ramakrishnan, Tapku Lee, and Jane Junn. 2011. "Asian American Political Participation: Emerging Constituents and Their Political Identities." New York: Russell Sage Foundation.

ASNE (American Society of Newspaper Editors)

The American Society of Newspaper Editors (ASNE) was organized in 1922, a time when there was major criticism of journalistic behavior and ethics. Some consider the founding a response to articles critical of newspaper standards appearing in the *Atlantic Monthly*. Moorfield Storey, a well-known political independent and the first president of the NAACP, and Frederick Lewis Allen, a secretary to Harvard Corp., penned the lengthy critiques.

Storey's article, "The Daily Press" asked why the press "claims for itself great rights and great privileges—practically unrestrained free speech and reduced postage, among others" yet did not exercise those rights responsibly. Storey wrote, "The press must either lead or follow; and, if it follows by catering to a depraved public taste or a popular prejudice, it is largely responsible for the taste or the prejudice, for both grow by what feeds them. To every editor is presented the question, 'Shall I seek money through increased circulation and advertisements, or shall I try to create a sound public opinion and make my journal a power for good?'"

Allen attacked the press and suggested, "A deliberate attempt ought also to be made by the more conscientious newspaper publishers and editors, acting presumably though their various professional associations, to formulate in more definite terms a code of newspaper ethics. . . . Associations of publishers or editors might also advantageously offer prizes for accuracy in the treatment of critical events, the awards to be made after thorough investigation by an impartial jury. . . . The important thing is to stimulate newspapers to present the unbiased truth."

These articles prompted editors to act on an idea tossed around a decade earlier. One of the group's founding members attributed its beginning to a gathering around a campfire at Glacier National Park in 1912, where editors were guests on a press junket designed to promote the park. They talked of creating an ethical organization of editors, banded together on the common ground of high purpose. Whatever the catalysts were, the Society produced one of America's first major journalism codes of ethics in 1923 and helped change global journalistic standards.

The first ASNE Constitution, created by a group of men lead by Casper S. Yost of the St. Louis Globe-Democrat, described the purposes of the new organization: "To promote acquaintance among members, to develop stronger and professional esprit de corps, to maintain the dignity and rights of the profession, to consider and perhaps establish ethical standards of professional conduct, to interchange ideas for the advancement of professional ideals and for the more effective application of professional labors, and to work collectively for the solution of common problems."

By 1975, the ASNE original "Canons of Journalism" code was renamed as "Statement of Principles" and became more tightly focused on press freedom and social responsibility. The preamble reads: "The First Amendment, protecting freedom of expression from abridgment by any law, guarantees to the people through their press a constitutional right, and thereby places on newspaper people a particular responsibility. Thus journalism demands of its practitioners not only industry and knowledge but also the pursuit of a standard of integrity proportionate to the journalist's singular obligation."

Along with its focus on ethics and press freedoms, ASNE's key initiatives in the 21st century are promoting diversity in newsrooms, recognizing journalism excellence through awards, developing leadership, and fostering youth journalism. The group also provides support for news literacy and technology advances. While its stated mission did not include wielding political clout, the ASNE, over its history, has become an important influence on American politics and policy.

The Society, which has shed it elitism over time, had been an exclusive organization of the most influential editors in the United States. At one point, membership was limited to editors of newspapers with more than 100,000 subscribers. During its history, ASNE has expected and received access to the nation's most powerful leaders and has been invited to consultations at the White House and in Congress. During World War II, ASNE members played key roles in helping to lead war efforts and were drawn into service on government committees. Newspapers also observed self-restraint in concert with a federal government censorship code.

During election seasons, presidential candidates have also been frequent visitors at ASNE events. Politicians flocked to ASNE looking for editorial support for policy ideas. That was particularly the case at the ASNE's annual conventions, usually held at a Washington hotel. It has been a coveted opportunity to speak to a room full of editors who controlled some of the nation's most influential newspapers and editorial pages. For example, every sitting president since its organization has addressed ASNE members. The association's conventions have been forums for major presidential speeches and initiatives. Franklin D. Roosevelt asked ASNE members during a private session to help him sell his New Deal. In President Coolidge's "Press under a Free Government" speech, he said he was unconcerned that the wealth of newspaper owners would taint news coverage, Coolidge said, "It seems to me, however, that the real test is not whether the newspapers are controlled by men of wealth, but whether they are sincerely trying to serve the public interests."

In April 1953, President Dwight Eisenhower used the ASNE stage to deliver his famous Cold War "The Chance for Peace" speech. He attempted to contrast the philosophies of the United States and Soviet Union by showing how military spending was robbing humanity. After only three months in office he delivered this memorable line: "This is not a way of life at all, in any true sense. Under the cloud of threatening war, it is humanity hanging from a cross of iron."

ASNE has led the fight for access to government meetings and records as the American press has become more adversarial with local, state, and national leaders since the 1960s. ASNE took on the John F. Kennedy White House and its attempts to manage news, particularly over the failed Bay of Pigs invasion in Cuba. After Kennedy's assassination, ASNE's Freedom of Information committee kept the pressure on Lyndon B. Johnson and the secrecy surrounding the Vietnam War. ASNE helped lobby for the federal Freedom of Information Act that Johnson begrudgingly signed into law in 1966. Some members also became critical of the war itself. Early in the Nixon administration, White House spokesman Herb Klein followed ASNE recommendations for open media relations, but that quickly faded as the White House became nearly impenetrable to the press.

ASNE was also an early leader in strengthening press freedom and access to government information around the globe. ASNE has also been an active litigant in First Amendment and information access cases at the U.S. Supreme Court. Specifically, ASNE has battled attempts to restrict press access and coverage of trials and has been an advocate for a federal reporter's shield law. In 2013, ASNE joined with other media groups to oppose new White House restrictions limiting photographer access to President Barack Obama.

ASNE has also transformed itself over the years from a white male dominated group to embrace goals of diversity inside the organization and in the nation's newsrooms. As historian Alfred Pratte wrote, ASNE, over the years, has lost some of its more outspoken and visible advocacy as leaders have become editor-business people and taken more conservative stands reflected by a media shift to corporate culture. The expansion of membership and less elitist makeup has also meant participation from leaders from smaller news organizations and from journalism education. By 2014, the board of directors included leaders of university journalism schools, large media companies, small nonprofit journalism newsrooms, the Associated Press wire service, and even a public radio system.

Faced with the challenges of declining revenue for newspapers, the closure of newspapers, and the growth of competitive new media channels, ASNE has retrenched. Perhaps symbolic of the times, ASNE has moved its offices to the University of Missouri School of Journalism in Columbia to save money. For the first time, ASNE and the Associated Press managing editors planned a joint convention for 2014 away from Washington in Chicago. As the news industry faces a critical juncture, it remains to be seen if the political clout of ASNE will diminish over time.

Joel J. Campbell

See also: Presidents and the Press; Presidential Press Conferences

Further Reading

De Wolfe, M.A. 1932. *Portrait of an Independent, Moorfield Storey, 1845–1929*. New York: Houghton Mifflin.

Meyer, Philip. 2006. *Newspaper Ethics in the New Century: A Report to the American Society of Newspaper Editors*. Chapel Hill, NC: Carolina Academic Press.

Pratte, Paul A. 1995. *Gods within the Machine: A History of the American Society of Newspaper Editors, 1923–1993*. Westport, CT: Praeger.

B

Baby Boom

The baby boom describes a remarkable period of increased birth rates in the United States that occurred immediately after World War II. About 78 million Americans were born between 1946 and 1964 and became the generation informally called "boomers." This generation was the most affluent, best educated, and most diverse generation in U.S. history up to that time.

Scholars and writers often speak of boomers as an intensely generationally self-aware group since they were told of their unique attributes even while they were growing up. Because of their large numbers, the boom generation became a social, economic, cultural, and political force in America. Entire musical genres like rock-and-roll and modern country music came into being in response to the consumer purchasing power of this very large generation that wanted their own unique sounds.

The baby boom was ethnically and racially diverse compared to previous generations. About 73 percent were non-Hispanic white, down from 83 percent among the Greatest Generation that waged and won World War II. The boom was increasingly black and Hispanic compared to previous generations.

The baby boom grew up during a period of almost chaotic social change. Young African Americans in the South rejected the legal and social limitations placed upon them and began protesting for voting and civil rights with guidance from the Rev. Martin Luther King Jr. and a new generation of black leadership. Boomers nationwide sought to reevaluate America's Cold War military policy, which the Vietnam War had forced upon them. Many rejected the war, protesting against the military draft, sometimes violently. Women also reevaluated their place in society, giving rise to the feminist movement and to sexual freedoms and experimentations made possible by oral contraception and other advances in medical birth control. Many boomers experimented with recreational drugs like marijuana and LSD. Others experimented with social communes, forming small groups with nontraditional lifestyles.

The boom generation became more traditional in many ways as it aged. Although never as prolific as their parents, boomers married and produced a "boomlet" generation, commonly referred to as the millennial generation. Their politics also seem to change over time. Although often identified as iconoclastic and antiestablishment, boomers became the bulk of the so-called "Reagan Democrat" movement in which white, blue-collar voters who had generally supported Democrats in their youth joined Ronald Reagan's conservative revolution in the 1980s.

In fact, many commentators have speculated that the boom generation should be divided into two groups since the older element of the boom has behaved differently over time from the younger boom. Author Jonathan Pontell suggested that the later boom should be called "Generation Jones" because these are people born under different economic conditions during the period from 1954 to 1965. The phrase evolved from the term "keeping up with the Joneses" and describes a cohort born in a time of great expectations that was later challenged by the difficult economic realities of unemployment and declining industrialization.

Pew Research has found that early boom voters were, indeed, more likely to support Barack Obama in 2008 and more likely to identify as Democrats than were Generation Jones voters. Voters born in the last half of the baby boom were much more likely to support the Republicans in 2008. Pew also found that most generations tend to vote more conservatively as they age.

Thomas K. Hargrove

See also: Generation X, Millennials

Further Reading

Strauss, William, and Neil Howe. 1991. *Generations: The History of America's Future, 1584 to 2069.* New York: William Morrow and Co.

Taylor, Paul, and Scott Keeter. 2010. "Millennials: A Portrait of Generation Next, Confident. Connected. Open to Change." Published online by Pew Research. www.pewresearch.org/millennials. Accessed January 13, 2015.

Balanced Budgets

In balanced budgets, the generated revenue (input) is the equivalent of, or exceeds, the necessary expenditures (output). Though surplus receipts can be associated with a balanced budget, often in public budgeting, simply matching income with debts is sufficient. The desirability (and feasibility) of balanced budgets is debated by advocates of varying economic principles. The applicability of balanced budgets differ in state government and federal government, in part because the size of their budgets, the services they provide, and the ways in which they generate revenue.

Economic rationale traditionally holds that government expenditures should refrain from exceeding the predicted revenue coming in through taxation, fees, etc. This prevents the creation or extension of debt, which is more impersonal on the larger level (compared to a personal budget) because of the leadership turnover and diffused accountability in the budgeting appropriation process. One of the most influential economists, John Maynard Keynes (1883–1946) endorsed a new economic theory supporting government intervention within the economy and forgoing a balanced budget for a deficit budget. Politically, this choice can be popular, as it prevents the unpleasant task of eliminating programs that enjoy a loyal constituency base.

Adherence and feasibility in keeping a balanced budget varies depending on the level of government. Federal governments can utilize loans from other nations or savings bonds as a way to supplement the revenue to pay expenditures. The United States follow this concept and relies on loans and debt to other countries, such as China, to provide all the goods and services outlined in the budget. Because of the opportunity to borrow money from both external and internal sources, maintaining a balanced budget can be more challenging for federal governments. Local governments often do not have sources from which they can borrow and, though they can supplement their revenue with grants from the state and federal governments, typically must maintain balanced budgets to remain effective. State governments vary: some states, such as California, are known for their large levels of state debt, while other states adhere more strictly to balanced or near-balanced budgets.

The reason a government might fail to stick to a balanced budget lies in the inherently complex political process of public budgeting. Governments provide a number of services that develop their own "constituencies," or individuals who enjoy and benefit from that service and would be upset if it were removed. Often we think of entitlement programs (such as Social Security, Medicare, and Medicaid) as examples, but even nice parks, good schools, college student loans, and homeowner tax credits can all build political popularity. Curbing the spending on these programs (which leads to fewer goods or services enjoyed by the same recipients or fewer recipients enjoying the same goods or services) can be politically unfeasible, as citizens will voice their dissatisfaction through elections, among other ways. Public officials may find prioritizing the needs of one group over another, while remaining in office, immensely challenging.

Unforeseen changes that prompt program cuts can also serve as a barrier to balanced budgets. Some changes that influence the budget can be foreseen (though that does not mean they are always taken into account successfully). An increase in the birth rate, as occurred in the 1950s during the beginning of the baby boom, will lead to an increasing need for services (such as hospitals and schools) and later an increase in the tax base. Negative changes, such as war or economic recession, can increase the need for expenditures drastically while the revenue remains the same or even falls. For state governments, federal mandates that require an expansion or creation of a program but do not provide the full funds can be an unforeseen expense. Because these events cannot always be determined in advance, even governing bodies that prefer to follow balanced budgets must allow for some elasticity.

Historically, balanced budgets were common when the budgeting process was highly centralized in Congress so that the appropriations committee maintained nearly exclusive control. Members of this committee were often long-time incumbents from "safe" districts who were considered competent because their budgeting decisions were not generally guided by providing pork to constituents as a way to ensure reelection. By the 20th century, however, the budgeting process had expanded to include a number of political players, including the growing position of the president and multiple committees within Congress. Dispersed power meant less accountability and more incentive to serve personal interests. Coupled with mounting national defense expenditures and Keynesian economics, balanced budgets fell by the wayside and were replaced by deficit budgets. In an attempt to return to a balanced budget, the Gramm-Rudman-Hollings Balanced Budget Act was passed in 1986, which prescribed fixed deficit targets and mandated automatic spending cuts if those targets were not met. Though it made some improvements, on the whole it could not prevent large budget deficits and failed to provide balanced budgets. Later, the Budget Enforcement Act of 1990 and its successor, the Statutory Pay-As-You-Go Act of

2010 or PAYGO, have all had similar goals of minimizing the deficit and steering Congress back to balanced budgets, but with little avail.

Laura Merrifield Sojka

See also: Keynesianism

Further Reading

Hager, George. 1998. *Balancing Act: Washington's Troubled Path to a Balanced Budget.* New York: Vintage.
Savage, James D. 1990. *Balanced Budgets and American Politics.* Ithaca, NY: Cornell University Press.

Blue States

See Red States and Blue States

Bork, Robert H. (1927–2012)

The grueling political fight over President Ronald Reagan's 1987 nomination of Yale Law School professor Robert H. Bork to the U.S. Supreme Court resonates into the 21st century for at least two reasons. His name is still a political verb. To be "borked" is to suffer withering public scrutiny, especially because of personal ideology. The rejection of his nomination by the Democratic-controlled Senate also is widely seen as an important moment in the increasing political polarization among America's leaders.

Robert H. Bork was a law professor at Yale Law School from 1962 to 1975 and from 1977 to 1981. He served in the Department of Justice from 1972 to 1977 in both the Richard Nixon and Gerald Ford administrations, and it was during this time that he rose to national prominence. However, he is best known as President Ronald Reagan's failed nominee to the U.S. Supreme Court. Bork's views on civil liberties and civil rights, based on his theory of constitutional interpretation, were central in the Senate's rejection of his nomination.

President Richard Nixon named Robert Bork as U.S. solicitor general in 1972. Shortly thereafter Archibald Cox was appointed as special prosecutor to investigate the Watergate scandal, which involved the burglary of the Democratic National Committee Headquarters by men with ties to President Richard Nixon. In the course of the investigation, Cox obtained a subpoena requiring Nixon to turn over audiotapes of conversations recorded in the Oval Office. On October 20, 1973, Nixon ordered Attorney General Elliot Richardson to fire Cox; Richardson resigned instead. Richardson's deputy, William Ruckelshaus, also resigned rather than fire Cox.

Nixon then turned to Bork as the third-ranking Justice Department officer to carry out his order. Describing what was referred to in the press as the "Saturday Night Massacre," the president indicated in his memoirs that although Bork may have personally opposed the order, "he was a constitutional scholar and he felt that I had the constitutional right to do so and that he therefore had the duty to carry out my orders. He said he would fire Archibald Cox." His views as a constitutional scholar ultimately led to his appointment to the United States Court of Appeals for the District of Columbia by President Ronald Reagan in 1982.

When Justice Lewis Powell announced his retirement from the U.S. Supreme Court in June 1987, President Reagan had an opportunity to significantly alter the ideological balance to be more favorable to conservative views. Powell, according to constitutional law scholar Henry Abraham, had "played a pivotal role as the tie-breaking vote in cases determining the Court's interpretation of constitutional law on such controversial issues as abortion, criminal justice, affirmative action, and separation of church and state." As a moderate, Powell provided the crucial swing vote that favored conservative positions on some issues and liberal positions on others. Bork, who had often been mentioned as a potential Supreme Court nominee, had amassed a judicial and scholarly record that exhibited his conservative views.

Bork believes that judges should interpret the Constitution by following the framers' intent or their "original understanding" of the Constitution's provisions. Bork's position is that, to promote consistency and leave policy-making to the other branches of government, judges should be faithful to the historical foundations upon which the Constitution is based. He was opposed to Supreme Court rulings concerning the right to privacy, such as *Griswold v. Connecticut* (1965) and *Roe v. Wade* (1973), because there is no explicit right to privacy in the Constitution. Therefore, these matters are better left to the legislative branch. Bork, according to his autobiography, believed that law should reflect the views of the populace and not the views of unelected judges.

Despite a significant paper trail in judicial opinions and scholarly writings that explicated these beliefs, President Reagan, upon announcing his nomination of Bork to fill Powell's seat on July 1, 1987, characterized his nominee as "neither a conservative nor a liberal." A mere 45 minutes after Reagan's announcement, Senator Edward Kennedy—in what Abraham called "a patent fit of gross hyperbole"—stated, "Robert Bork's America is a land in which women would be forced into back alley abortions, blacks would sit at segregated lunch counters, rogue police could break down citizens' doors in midnight raids, school children could not be taught about evolution, writers and artists could be censored at the whim of government, and the doors of the federal courts would be shut on the fingers of millions of citizens for whom the judiciary is—and is often the only—protector of the individual rights that are the heart of our democracy."

The intense opposition manifested in Senator Kennedy's statement led to an unprecedented public relations campaign against Bork's nomination during the course of the confirmation hearings. Although Bork received an exceptionally well-qualified rating from the American Bar Association, he garnered sharp criticism from a wide range of political opponents of the Reagan administration. The focus was on Bork's own judicial philosophy rather than on his overall legal qualifications for the bench. In hearings before the Senate Judiciary Committee, he was asked how he might rule in hypothetical cases on obscenity, school desegregation, and abortion rights, to which he responded with his view on the role of a judge, not possible decisions he might make as a Supreme Court justice.

During the hearings, Bork did much to undermine his chance for confirmation. For instance, he responded to questions from committee members in a "scholarly, lecture-like" manner. "Moreover, Bork's personal appearance and demeanor seemed as suspect as his ideology. His devilish beard and sometimes turgid academic discourse did not endear him to wavering Senators or the public," Abraham concluded. Bork's nomination was also hindered by several political factors: the Democrats won control of the Senate in the 1986 midterm elections, Southern Democrats in the Senate feared losing African American votes if they supported Bork, and President Reagan's political standing had been damaged by the Iran-Contra scandal and concerns about the economy.

On October 23, the Senate rejected the nomination by a vote of 58 to 42. Out of this came a new verb—to be borked—meaning to have one's professional career held up to extensive public and highly partisan scrutiny leading to political defeat. In his 1990 book, Bork suggested the episode had the potential to shape future court nominations along more ideological than purely legal lines. Since his confirmation battle, Bork authored several books and was a senior fellow at the American Enterprise Institute, a conservative think tank. More recently, he was a lecturer at the University of Richmond law school.

James Gilchrist

See also: Polarization

Further Reading

Abraham, Henry. 1999. *Justices, Presidents, and Senators.* Lanham, MD: Rowman & Littlefield.
Bork, Robert H. 1990. *The Tempting of America: The Political Seduction of the Law.* New York: Simon & Schuster.

Brennan, William (1906–1997)

William J. Brennan Jr. was an American jurist and associate justice of the United States Supreme Court who served on the high court from 1956 to 1990. He was commonly seen as a key liberal leader on the court because of his positions on issues like abortion and the death penalty. He authored the landmark decision in *Baker v. Carr,* in which the high court claimed jurisdiction over legislative reapportionment matters, a judicial policy that will resonate throughout the 21st century as future jurists must weigh the increasingly difficult issue of how political power should be fairly apportioned.

When William Rehnquist first assumed the mantle of chief justice, the Court held a formidable lineup of liberal justices anchored by Warren Court appointee William Brennan, who was appointed by President Dwight D. Eisenhower in 1956. Eisenhower selected Brennan, a little-known jurist from New Jersey, in part because he was Catholic and a politically inactive Democrat. He had thought Brennan would be a moderate justice. Instead, he appointed the future liberal craftsman of the Warren Court. Later, Eisenhower would regret the nomination. When asked what mistakes he had made, the president allegedly replied that two of them sit on the U.S. Supreme Court, referring to Chief Justice Warren and Justice Brennan.

Brennan obtained his law degree from Harvard University, studying under Supreme Court justice Felix Frankfurter, who was known on the Court as a practitioner of judicial restraint. Once, when asked about his former pupil, Frankfurter said he had encouraged his students to think for themselves but that Brennan had taken it too far. Brennan was appointed to the New Jersey Superior Court in 1949, the Appellate Division of the Superior Court in 1950, and the New Jersey Supreme Court in 1952. When Justice Sherman Minton retired, President Eisenhower apparently wanted to appoint a state court jurist who was a Democrat, a moderate, and a Catholic. William Brennan seemed to fit the bill, and he received the nomination of a lifetime.

Eisenhower appointed Brennan to the bench in October 1956 when the Senate was in recess (not in session), allowing Brennan to take his seat on the high court before confirmation.

The Senate confirmed him in March 1957 with one dissenter—Senator Joseph McCarthy, who was famous, or infamous, for his extreme efforts to ferret out communists in America.

Brennan served nearly 34 years on the Court; many scholars considered him to be the leading intellectual force of the Warren Court. He believed strongly in a living Constitution and used his position on the Court to sway many of his colleagues to his positions. Even when he was a member of the more conservative Burger and Rehnquist Courts, Brennan was a formidable ideological foe. Brennan effectively led the Court, in part because of his intelligence, but perhaps more so because of his magnetic personality and persuasive powers. He got along well with his colleagues—even those with whom he disagreed. Rehnquist wrote in his book on the Supreme Court, "Bill Brennan and I disagreed with each other about a lot of constitutional issues, but his buoyant outlook on life and friendly warmth toward his colleagues ensured that disagreements about the Constitution would not mar personal relationships" (Rehnquist, 227).

Brennan authored some of the Court's landmark decisions, from the ruling in *Baker v. Carr*, in which the Court entered the "political thicket" and claimed jurisdiction over legislative reapportionment claims, to the libel case *New York Times Co. v. Sullivan*, to the leading free exercise of religion opinion in *Sherbert v. Verner*. Brennan's magnetic personality endeared him to his colleagues, and he became a master at obtaining five votes. A lasting testament to his persuasive powers was that in 1990, he managed to obtain five votes to uphold an affirmative action policy at the Federal Communications Commission, even though the Court had invalidated a similar affirmative action policy in Richmond, Virginia the year before. Brennan retired from the Court shortly after the 1989–1990 term because of a stroke.

Brennan and Rehnquist—though they often disagreed on legal matters—were both legal giants. "Brennan and Rehnquist were the two modern masters of manipulating precedents in U.S. Reports," says constitutional law scholar Thomas Baker. "They both possessed an encyclopedic knowledge of the law and facile, plastic minds."

David L. Hudson, Jr.

See also: Judicial Activism

Further Reading

Hopkins, W. Wat. 1991. *Mr. Justice Brennan and Freedom of Expression*. New York: Praeger.

Hudson, David L. Jr. 2006. *The Rehnquist Court: Understanding Its Impact and Legacy*. New York: Praeger.

Rehnquist, William H. 2001. *The Supreme Court*. New York: Knopf.

Tribe, Laurence. 1990. "Common Sense and Uncommon Wisdom: A Tribute to Justice Brennan." *Harvard Law Review* 1–1990.

Wermiel, Stephen J. 1994. "William Joseph Brennan Jr." In Melvin I. Urofsky, ed. *The Supreme Court Justices: A Biographical Dictionary*. New York: Garland Publishing.

Brinkley, David (1920–2003)

David McClure Brinkley epitomized both the rising power of network broadcast journalism and the entrenched power of the news media based in Washington, D.C. He was a master of both.

Brinkley's autobiography—*11 Presidents, 4 Wars, 22 Political Conventions, 1 Moon Landing, 3 Assassinations, 2,000 Weeks of News and Other Stuff on Television and 18 Years of Growing Up in North Carolina*—published in 1995 before he retired from ABC sums up his influential career.

An electronic journalist for more than 50 years, Brinkley covered the civil rights movement, protests, riots, politics, presidents, assassinations, and other news. When he retired on November 10, 1996, as host of ABC-TV's *This Week With David Brinkley*, he had either anchored or hosted a daily or weekly television show for more than 40 years—longer than anyone else in the business.

Brinkley had started out in print journalism, at the age of 16, writing about his high school activities for the *Wilmington Morning Star* at the invitation of a relative in Wilmington, North Carolina.

He wrote for the United Press wire service in Atlanta, Charlotte, and Nashville before going to Washington, D.C., in 1943 to interview for a job with CBS Radio. When he got to D.C., however, the CBS management pretended not to know him, so he went over to NBC and got hired.

When Brinkley started work for NBC, he covered the White House during the presidency of Franklin D. Roosevelt. "Covering in quotes," was the way Brinkley put it. He was one of the few radio journalists to make a smooth transition to the new medium of television. From 1951 until 1956, Brinkley was Washington correspondent for NBC's nightly news show, *Camel News Caravan*.

When he was teamed up with Chet Huntley to cover the Democratic and Republican national conventions in 1956, the combination was so successful that the 15-minute evening *NBC News Report* became the "Huntley-Brinkley Report" from New York and Washington. They reached an audience of 20 million viewers every night. The show, which ended with the signature sign-off—"Good night, Chet," from Brinkley in Washington, and "Good night, David," from Huntley in New York, won Emmy awards in 1959 and 1960.

Brinkley's skeptical approach to his subjects often aroused the wrath of people on both sides of the political fence. He was called everything from a left-wing radical to a right-wing reactionary.

During the Kennedy and Johnson presidencies, Brinkley was on good terms with the administrations' highest officials. He spent a weekend at Camp David with President Lyndon B. Johnson. However, the Johnson administration placed a tap on his home telephone during the Vietnam protests. He was on President Richard M. Nixon's enemies list, and Vice President Spiro T. Agnew attacked him as "anti-American."

President Bill Clinton attributed his early interest in politics to the Huntley-Brinkley coverage of the conventions. ABC News political analyst Jeff Greenfield has said that Brinkley created a whole generation of political junkies because he appreciated the human side of politics.

After the "Huntley-Brinkley Report" ended August 1, 1970, when Huntley retired, Brinkley drifted in professional limbo. A news anchoring partnership with John Chancellor lacked chemistry; a magazine show failed to get high ratings. Brinkley, age 61, quit NBC in September 1981 after 38 years.

Almost immediately, Roone Arledge, then president of ABC News, offered him the opportunity to host a Sunday morning talk show, *This Week with David Brinkley*. Journalists such as Sam Donaldson, George Will, and Cokie Roberts appeared, and the format included interviews with a guest newsmaker, followed by analysis and opinion in a roundtable discussion format. In November 1981, *TIME* magazine described the show as "a true innovation in television journalism." The show became a ratings leader and remained in continuous production for the next 15 years. Brinkley stepped down as host of his show in November 1996 but continued to do commentaries.

Controversy struck again when Brinkley became a spokesman for the Archer Daniels Midland Co. after his "retirement" from *This Week with David Brinkley*. Some in the media criticized his appearing in ads on a program he had anchored for fifteen years, saying he was leading viewers to believe the network was endorsing ADM products.

Former President George H.W. Bush called Brinkley the elder statesman of broadcast journalism, but Brinkley thought of himself in more modest ways. "Most of my life," he said in a 1992 interview, "I've simply been a reporter covering things, and writing and talking about it."

Although he often was dissatisfied with what he saw in Washington, Brinkley always remained polite. When he chided politicians and government bureaucrats, he did so gently and wryly. Politics was his passion. One writer described him as "a constant, pungent election night presence—first on NBC, then on ABC."

Brinkley attributed the emergence of the trend of reporters interviewing reporters to himself. The trend began, Brinkley said, the day in November 1969 when President Nixon delivered his most historic address on Vietnam. Nixon spoke longer than expected, and, because his speech had spilled over to the networks' next half-hour time block, the networks had to fill in whatever part of the block was left. Brinkley and his colleagues had to discuss Nixon's speech until the beginning of the next hour of programming.

Brinkley was hugely successful. After 50 years in the business, he continued to be a shrewd and witty observer, but he came to be seen as too much of a Washington insider. He did, for example, own a condo in a posh Florida complex—the Sea View Hotel in Bal Harbour, Florida—where Senator Bob Dole and Elizabeth Dole, Howard Baker, Bob Strauss, Tip O'Neill, and Dwayne Andreas, owner of Archer Daniels Midland, also had units.

Brinkley was aware of the enormous fame that accrued to television anchors. In *Brinkley's Beat*, he wrote, "Most of my adult life has been shaped by that reality. But I do not believe that I, or my fellow anchors, have become famous for our power to influence uncritical masses of people, or for our ability to change the social or political order, or to elect a candidate or defeat one. So what are we famous for? Mainly, we are famous for being famous."

In 1958, Brinkley was given the DuPont Award for his "inquiring mind sensitive to both the elusive fact and the background that illuminates its meaning." Over the years that followed, he collected ten Emmy awards, three Peabody awards, and, in 1990, the Peabody for Lifetime Achievement. In 1989, he was inducted into the Academy of Television Arts and Sciences' Hall of Fame, and in 1992, he received the Presidential Medal of Freedom, the nation's highest civilian honor.

He wrote three books—*Washington Goes to War*, in 1988; his autobiography in 1995; and *Everyone Is Entitled to My Opinion* in 1996. He wrote his memoir, *Brinkley's Beat: People, Places and Events That Shaped My Time*, in 2003 shortly before his death.

Interviewed by his son Joel in 1997, then an editor with the *New York Times*, Brinkley said, "If I were 20 years old, I would try to do the same thing again, all of it. I have no regrets. None at all."

David Brinkley died June 11, 2003.

Maria Marron

Further Reading

Brinkley, David. 1995. *11 Presidents, 4 Wars, 22 Political Conventions, 1 Moon Landing, 3 Assassinations, 2,000 Weeks of News and Other Stuff on Television and 18 Years of Growing Up in North Carolina.* New York: A.A. Knopf.
Brinkley, Joel. 1997. "A Talk with David Brinkley: Son Knows Best: There Sure Is a Story Here." *The New York Times*, February 5.

Bush, George Walker (1946–)

Republican Party politician, governor of Texas (1995–2001), and president of the United States (2001–2009), George Walker Bush was born in New Haven, Connecticut, on July 6, 1946, and grew up in Midland and Houston, Texas. He is the son of George H.W. Bush, president of the United States during 1989–1993.

The younger Bush graduated from the exclusive Phillips Academy in Andover, Massachusetts, and from Yale University in 1968. He volunteered for the Texas Air National Guard after graduation and became a pilot, although questions later surfaced about his actual service. He earned an MBA from Harvard University in 1975 and returned to Texas, founding Arbusto Energy Company in 1977. He served as a key staffer during his father's 1988 presidential campaign and later became one of the owners of the Texas Rangers baseball team.

In 1994, Bush was elected governor of Texas. As governor, he worked with the Democratic-dominated legislature to reduce state control and taxes. In 1996 he won reelection, by which time he had earned a reputation as an honest broker who could govern in a bipartisan manner.

In 2000, having set records for fund-raising and having campaigned as a "compassionate conservative," Bush easily won the 2000 Republican nomination for the presidency of the United States. His platform included tax cuts, improved schools, Social Security reform, and increased military spending. On foreign policy issues, he downplayed his obvious lack of experience but eschewed foreign intervention and nation-building.

The U.S. presidential election of November 2000 was one of the most contentious in American history. The Democratic candidate, Vice President Al Gore, won a slim majority of the popular vote, but the electoral vote was in doubt. Confusion centered on Florida. Eventually, after weeks of recounts and court injunctions, the issue reached the U.S. Supreme Court. On December 12, 2000, a deeply divided Court halted the recount in Florida, virtually declaring Bush the winner. For many Americans, Bush was an illegitimate and unelected president.

As president, Bush secured a large tax cut in hopes that this would spur the economy, and he pushed forward Social Security reform. He and the Republican-controlled Congress also enacted a tax rebate for millions of Americans in the late summer and early autumn of 2001. That same year, with prodding from the White House, Congress passed the No Child Left Behind Act, a standards-based reform measure designed to build more accountability into public education. Although the measure won broad bipartisan support, it later was criticized for being too narrowly conceived and incapable of accounting for differences in the way children learn. Many also came to believe that the mandate was not properly funded, especially in poorer school districts. In 2003, Bush was successful in passing a prescription drug act for U.S. citizens over the age of 65, but the measure ended up being far more expensive than originally forecast. Many also criticized the plan for being too complicated and offering too many options.

The course of Bush's presidency was forever changed on September 11, 2001, when 19 hijackers associated with the Al Qaeda terrorist organization seized commercial airliners and crashed them into the World Trade Center and the Pentagon. The attacks killed nearly 2,700 Americans and 316 foreign nationals. Over the next few days, Bush visited the scenes of the attacks, reassuring the public and promising to bring those responsible to justice. The catastrophe of September 11 seemed to bring legitimacy and purpose to Bush's presidency, although it tilted the economy further into recession.

On September 20, 2001, Bush appeared before Congress and accused Al Qaeda of carrying out the attacks. He warned the American people that they faced a lengthy war against terrorism. He also demanded that the Taliban government of Afghanistan surrender members of Al Qaeda in their country or face retribution. When the Taliban failed to comply, U.S. and British forces began a bombing campaign on October 7. Initially, the United States enjoyed broad international support for the War on Terror and its campaign to oust the Taliban from Afghanistan. Indigenous Northern Alliance forces, with heavy American support—chiefly in the form of air strikes—handily defeated the Taliban and by November 2001 had captured the capital of Kabul. Taliban resistance continued thereafter, but the multinational coalition was nevertheless able to establish a new government in Afghanistan.

The Bush administration also sought to improve national security in the wake of September 11. A new Department of Homeland Security was created to coordinate all agencies that could track and defeat terrorists. In October 2001, at the behest of the Bush administration, Congress passed the Patriot Act, giving the federal government sweeping powers to fight the War on Terror. Many Americans were uncomfortable with this legislation and feared that it might undermine American freedom and civil liberties.

In 2002, the Bush administration turned its attentions toward Iraq. Intelligence reports suggested that Iraqi dictator Saddam Hussein was continuing to pursue weapons of mass destruction (WMDs). When Bush demanded that he comply with United Nations resolutions seeking inspection of certain facilities, Hussein refused. By the end of the year, the Bush administration had formulated a new policy of preemptive warfare (the Bush Doctrine) to destroy regimes that intended to harm the United States before they were able to do so. In October 2002, Bush secured from Congress a bipartisan authorization to use military force against Iraq if necessary.

By the beginning of 2003, a military buildup against Iraq was already taking place. However, Bush's efforts to create a broad, multinational coalition failed to achieve the success his father enjoyed with the Persian Gulf War coalition against Iraq in 1991. Nearly all of the forces were American or British, and the United Nations failed to sanction military action against Iraq, as it had done in 1990. The virtually unilateral U.S. approach angered much of the international community and even some U.S. allies.

Military operations commenced on March 19, 2001, and Baghdad fell on April 9. At that point, organized resistance was minimal, but manpower resources, while sufficient to topple Hussein, were clearly insufficient to maintain the peace. Rioting and looting soon broke out, and weapons stockpiles were pillaged by insurgents. Religious and ethnic tensions came to the fore between Sunnis, Shias, and Kurds. Far more American troops were killed trying to keep order in Iraq than had died in the overthrow of the regime.

Although Bush won reelection in November 2004 in large part because of his tough stance on the so-called War on Terror, support for the war in Iraq gradually waned because of mounting American military and Iraqi civilian dead, reports of American atrocities committed in Iraq, the war's vast expense, revelations that the White House trumped up or knowingly used questionable intelligence about Iraqi WMDs, and general mismanagement of the war effort. Meanwhile, large budget deficits and trade imbalances piled up.

The Bush administration suffered stunning setbacks at home. The White House was roundly denounced for its poor handling of relief efforts following Hurricane Katrina in the autumn of 2005, in which hundreds died in Louisiana and along the Gulf Coast. In the November 2006 midterm elections, the Republicans lost both houses of Congress, and Bush was forced to fire Secretary of Defense Donald Rumsfeld.

In January 2007, amid increasing calls for the United States to pull out of Iraq, Bush decided on just the opposite tack. His administration implemented a troop surge strategy that placed as many as 40,000 more U.S. soldiers on the ground in Iraq. Within six months, the surge strategy seemed to be paying dividends, and violence in Iraq was down. At the same time, however, a growing Taliban insurgency in Afghanistan was threatening to undo many of the gains made there since 2001. Many critics argued Bush's Iraq policies had needlessly diluted the U.S. effort in Afghanistan, but Bush was hard-pressed to send significantly more troops to Afghanistan because the military was already badly overstretched.

In the meantime, the White House's controversial policy of indefinitely detaining non-U.S. terror suspects, most of whom were being held at the Guantánamo Bay Detainment Camp in Cuba, drew the ire of many in the United States and international community. Even more controversial has been the use of "coercive interrogation techniques" on terror suspects and other enemy combatants. A euphemism for torture, this has included water-boarding, which forced detainees to endure near drowning. The White House, and especially Vice President Dick Cheney, however, asserted the technique did not constitute torture.

By 2008, Bush's approval ratings were among the lowest for any U.S. president in history, dropping to 25 percent in a Gallup poll. (Only Richard Nixon scored lower with a 24 percent rating immediately before he resigned.) In the fall, the U.S. economy went into near free fall following a spectacular series of bank, insurance, and investment house failures, necessitating a massive government bailout worth more than $800 billion. Other corporate bailouts followed as many major businesses teetered on the brink of insolvency. Unemployment rose dramatically in the fourth quarter of 2008, and consumer spending all but collapsed. By the time Bush left office in January 2009 the nation was facing the worst economic downturn in at least 35 years.

Tim J. Watts and Paul G. Pierpaoli, Jr.

See also: 9/11 Terrorist Attacks, Campaign 2000, Campaign 2004, Vote Counting Problems

Further Reading

Bruni, Frank. 2002. *Ambling into History: The Unlikely Odyssey of George W. Bush*. New York: HarperCollins.

Daalder, Ivo H., and James M. Lindsay. 2003. *America Unbound: The Bush Revolution in Foreign Policy*. Washington, DC: Brookings Institution.

Schweizer, Peter. 2004. *The Bushes: Portrait of a Dynasty*. New York: Doubleday.
Singer, Peter. 2004. *The President of Good & Evil: The Ethics of George W. Bush*. New York: Dutton.
Woodward, Bob. 2002. *Bush at War*. New York: Simon and Schuster.
Woodward, Bob. 2004. *Plan of Attack*. New York: Simon and Schuster.
Woodward, Bob. 2006. *State of Denial: Bush at War, Part III*. New York: Simon and Schuster.
Woodward, Bob. 2008. *The War Within: A Secret White House History, 2006–2008*. New York: Simon and Schuster.

Bush Doctrine

The Bush Doctrine is a foreign and national security policy articulated by President George W. Bush in a series of speeches following the September 11, 2001, terrorist attacks on the United States. Future presidents will struggle with the questions raised by this policy and whether America is ever justified in waging a preemptive war.

The Bush Doctrine identified three threats against U.S. interests: terrorist organizations; weak states that harbor and assist such terrorist organizations; and so-called rogue states. The centerpiece of the Bush Doctrine was that the United States had the right to use preemptory military force against any state that is seen as hostile or that makes moves to acquire weapons of mass destruction, be they nuclear, biological, or chemical. In addition, the United States would "make no distinction between the terrorists who commit these acts and those who harbor them."

The Bush Doctrine represented a major shift in American foreign policy from the policies of deterrence and containment that characterized the Cold War and the brief period between the collapse of the Soviet Union in 1991 and 2001. This new foreign policy and security strategy emphasized the strategic doctrine of preemption. The right of self-defense would be extended to use of preemptive attacks against potential enemies, attacking them before they were deemed capable of launching strikes against the United States. Under the doctrine, furthermore, the United States reserved the right to pursue unilateral military action if multilateral solutions cannot be found. The Bush Doctrine also represented the realities of international politics in the post–Cold War period; that is, the United States was the sole superpower and it aimed to ensure American hegemony.

A secondary goal of the Bush Doctrine was the promotion of freedom and democracy around the world, a precept that dates to at least the days of President Woodrow Wilson. In his speech to the graduating class at West Point on June 1, 2002, Bush declared that "America has no empire to extend or utopia to establish. We wish for others only what we wish for ourselves—safety from violence, the rewards of liberty, and the hope for a better life."

The immediate application of the Bush Doctrine was the invasion of Afghanistan in early October 2001 (Operation Enduring Freedom). Although the Taliban-controlled government of Afghanistan offered to hand over Al Qaeda leader Osama bin Laden if it was shown tangible proof that he was responsible for the September 11 attacks and also offered to extradite bin Laden to Pakistan where he would be tried under Islamic law, its refusal to extradite him to the United States with no preconditions was considered justification for the invasion.

The administration also applied the Bush Doctrine as justification for the Iraq War, beginning in March 2003 (Operation Iraqi Freedom). The Bush administration did not wish to wait for conclusive proof of Saddam Hussein's weapons of mass destruction (WMDs), so in a series of speeches, administration officials laid out the argument for invading Iraq. To wait any longer was to run the risk of having Hussein employ or transfer the alleged WMDs. Thus, despite the lack of evidence of an operational relationship between Iraq and Al Qaeda, the United States, supported by Britain and a few other nations, launched an invasion of Iraq.

The use of the Bush Doctrine as justification for the invasion of Iraq led to increasing friction between the United States and its allies, as the Bush Doctrine repudiated the core idea of the United Nations (UN) Charter. The charter prohibits any use of international force that is not undertaken in self-defense after the occurrence of an armed attack across an international boundary or pursuant to a decision by the UN Security Council. Even more vexing, the distinct limitations and pitfalls of the Bush Doctrine were abundantly evident in the inability of the United States to quell sectarian violence and political turmoil in Iraq. The doctrine did not place parameters on the extent of American commitments, and it viewed the consequences of preemptory military strikes as a mere afterthought.

Keith A. Leitich

See also: 9/11 Terrorist Attacks; Campaign 2004

Further Reading

Buckley, Mary E., and Robert Singh. 2006. *The Bush Doctrine and the War on Terrorism: Global Responses, Global Consequences*. London: Routledge.

Dolan, Chris J. 2005. *In War We Trust: The Bush Doctrine and the Pursuit of Just War*. Burlington, VT: Ashgate.

Gurtov, Melvin. 2006. *Superpower on Crusade: The Bush Doctrine in U.S. Foreign Policy*. Boulder, CO: Lynne Rienner.

Heisbourg, François. 2003. "Work in Progress: The Bush Doctrine and Its Consequences." *Washington Quarterly* 6(22) (Spring): 75–88.

Jervis, Robert. 2005. *American Foreign Policy in a New Era*. New York: Routledge.

Schlesinger, Arthur M. 2004. *War and the American Presidency*. New York: Norton.

C

Cable News Network (CNN)

See CNN (Cable News Network)

Campaign 2000

The 2000 presidential election between Democratic Vice President Al Gore and Republican Texas Governor George W. Bush was one of the closest elections in American history. The contest underscored the inexact nature of the nation's system of ballot counting due to outdated voting machines and imprecise ballot auditing procedures. Bush was declared the winner after the U.S. Supreme Court ordered local election officials in Florida to cease a recount and accept the certified result that the Republican had carried the Sunshine State by 537 votes. The Republicans narrowly won the Electoral College vote after losing the popular vote by more than 500,000 ballots.

Bush, thus, became the fourth U.S. president to assume office after losing the popular vote, following in the footsteps of John Quincy Adams in 1824, Rutherford B. Hayes in 1876, and Benjamin Harrison in 1888.

Although they lost control of the White House, Democrats made gains in the Republican-controlled Congress. They unseated five GOP incumbents to force a 50-50 tie in the Senate and picked up one seat to narrow the GOP's control of the House of Representatives to a 221-211 majority. Democrats technically controlled the Senate for 17 days when senators' new terms began on January 3, 2001 since Vice President Al Gore could vote to break any ties. But Republicans took back control January 20 when Bush and Vice President Dick Cheney were sworn into office.

As might be expected, one of America's most contentious elections began contentiously. The 2000 race would decide who'd replace retiring Democratic President Bill Clinton, who himself was impeached by the Republican-controlled House of Representatives in 1998 for lying under oath about a sexual affair with a White House intern. Clinton was allowed to complete his term after Senate Republicans failed to muster the two-thirds majority necessary to remove him.

Although both Bush and Gore were widely perceived by their party's hierarchy as the clear front runners, they each faced significant challenges from within their parties. Gore drew Democratic challenges from former U.S. Senator Bill Bradley of New Jersey and, to a lesser extent, from political activist Lyndon LaRouche. Bush, meanwhile, drew significant challenges from half a dozen Republicans including Sen. John McCain of Arizona, a combat pilot during the Vietnam War who'd become a prisoner of war when he was shot down in 1967.

Gore was able to dispatch his challenger first, forcing Bradley to suspend his campaign on March 9 after the vice president won all 15 "Super Tuesday" primaries two days earlier. But Bush unexpectedly lost the New Hampshire primary to McCain, who went on to carry six other states before also bowing out in early March. Another Republican, former U.S. Ambassador Alan Keyes of Maryland, stayed in the race through July, although he failed to win in any primary or state caucus.

Bush, in his acceptance speech at the Republican Party National Convention in Philadelphia, thanked McCain and his other challengers since "their convictions strengthen our party." The Texan also told delegates, prophetically, that the coming general election campaign against Gore "will be a tough race, down to the wire."

Gore, three weeks later at the Democratic convention in Los Angeles, made a point of greeting his wife, Tipper, with a protracted on-stage kiss and reminding delegates that "we just celebrated our 30th wedding anniversary." After thus assuring the nation that Gore had a stable marriage, he concluded that "There are big choices ahead, and our whole future is at stake."

Bush campaigned by repeatedly promising to restore "honor and dignity" to the White House, a regular reminder to voters about the sexual scandals involving the incumbent. Gore rarely appeared with the president during the summer and fall months. He reminded voters that "We're entering a new time. We're electing a new president."

Issues in the race were plentiful. Gore promised to use the projected federal budget surplus to reform and strengthen Social Security and Medicare, which he vowed to place in a "lockbox" safe from special interests. Bush, meanwhile, criticized Clinton's military policies in Somalia and the Balkans. "I don't think our troops ought to be used for what's called nation-building," the Republican said. (That remark in one of the debates would become high irony since more than 4,000 U.S. troops would perish under President Bush in the attempts to stabilize a new regime in Iraq.) Public opinion polls showed the race was close, although no one knew how close.

Both candidates knew that Florida would be key. Bush campaigned across the state November 5, two days before the election, by telling voters it was his 23rd wedding anniversary with his wife, Laura. "We need to get rid of the politics of anger and name-calling and ugliness," the Republican said. Gore made Florida his last campaign stop, doing late-night interviews on Election Eve.

What followed on Election night was a statistical, journalistic, and political nightmare. The Associated Press and all major TV networks projected around 8:00 p.m. that Gore had won Florida, prompting Bush in Texas to tell reporters that they'd "called this thing awfully early." As the actual vote counts started to be tallied, however, the race in Florida proved to be much closer. The networks began retracting their projections at 10:00 p.m.

Shortly after 2:00 a.m. the next day, Bush appeared to have a 50,000-vote lead. Network statisticians began declaring the Republican the victor in Florida. Within half an hour, Gore telephoned his opponent to concede and congratulate Bush. The vice president then traveled by motorcade toward a rally of supporters at War Memorial Plaza in Nashville, Tennessee, where he planned to concede publicly. But while en route, aides contacted the vice president to warn that the count had tightened dramatically to less than a 1,000-vote advantage for Bush. Gore called the Texan again to retract his concession at about 3:30 a.m. Realizing the new vote trend, the networks again began retracting their projections at about 4:00 a.m. and declared Florida was simply too close to call.

With Florida undecided, the unofficial tally by the news media on November 10 showed that Gore had won 19 states and the District of Columbia for a total of 261 electoral votes, while Bush had won 29 states for a total of 246 electoral votes. Since 270 were needed to win, neither candidate could declare victory. Although New Mexico was also deemed too close to call, its 5 electoral votes didn't matter. Whoever got Florida's electoral votes would be president.

The scrutiny that Florida's election process received was harsh. Nearly 3 percent of the state's ballots cast did not register a vote for president. Most of those 178,145 nonregistering ballots were old-fashioned punch cards, which could easily generate errors if voters failed to completely remove the cardboard "chads" so that machines could tally them correctly. Local election officials began hand recounts, holding punch cards aloft so they could squint to determine a voter's intent through indentations on the cardboard. There were also questionable ballot designs, especially a so-called "butterfly ballot" in Palm Beach County in which voters were expected to follow printed indicator arrows connecting candidates' names to the appropriate punch card location. Independent candidate Pat Buchanan agreed with the Gore campaign that many of the 5,566 votes he'd received in Palm Beach actually belonged to the Democrat.

As confusion over the many recounts mounted, the Bush campaign appealed to the U.S. Supreme Court, which ordered a halt to the process while it deliberated the historic case *Bush v. Gore*. Thirty-six days after the election, on December 12, the high court issued a 5-4 decision that no constitutionally valid recount could be completed by the legally mandated deadline for declaring the outcome. The minority justices' dissent, written by Justice John P. Stevens, was unequivocal: "One thing . . . is certain. Although we may never know with complete certainty the identity of the winner of this year's presidential election, the identity of the loser is perfectly clear. It is the Nation's confidence in the judge as an impartial guardian of the rule of law."

"I believe things happen for a reason, and I hope the long wait of the last five weeks will heighten a desire to move beyond the bitterness and partisanship of the recent past," Bush said in a much-delayed victor statement after the ruling. "Our nation must rise above a house divided. Americans share hopes and goals and values far more important than any political disagreements."

Thomas K. Hargrove

See also: Bush, George Walker; Candidates, presidential 2000; Vote Counting Problems

Further Reading

Ceaser, James W., and Andrew E. Busch. 2001. *The Perfect Tie: The True Story of the 2000 Presidential Election.* New York: Rowman & Littlefield.

Gillman, Howard. 2001. *The Votes That Counted: How the Court Decided the 2000 Presidential Election.* Chicago: University of Chicago Press.

Posner, Richard A. 2001. *Breaking the Deadlock: The 2000 Election, the Constitution, and the Courts.* Princeton, NJ: Princeton University Press.

Sabato, Larry J. 2001. *Overtime! The Election 2000 Thriller.* New York: Longman.

Toobin, Jeffery. 2002. *Too Close to Call: The Thirty-Six-Day Battle to Decide the 2000 Election.* New York: Random House.

Campaign 2002

America was still numb from the September 11, 2001, terrorist attacks upon the World Trade Center in New York City and the Pentagon in Washington, D.C., as it headed into the 2002 off-year general elections. President George W. Bush, despite his close and disputed election two years earlier, rallied the nation to what he correctly predicted would be a protracted struggle against Middle Eastern extremists. "This crusade, this war on terrorism is going to take a while. And the American people must be patient," Bush said days after the attacks. What followed were U.S. military commitments in Afghanistan, the base from which Al Qaeda plotted the attacks, and a buildup for the 2003 invasion of Iraq with the stated purpose of removing President Saddam Hussein and the nation's alleged stockpile of chemical weapons.

Political historians widely attribute this political environment of war and impending war to the modest gains Republicans achieved in Congress, despite the disputed presidential election of 2000. Those few additional seats gave the GOP control of the Senate and solidified its hold on the House. The last time the in-power party made gains in its first off-year election was 1934, when Franklin D. Roosevelt was rallying voters for political majorities in both houses of Congress that would permit him to launch the New Deal. It should be noted, however, that older, richer, and better educated conservative voters usually have greater sway in the off years when turnouts are lower.

For these reasons, Republicans gained 2 seats in the Senate and 8 seats in the House. Exit polling (delayed for 10 months because of technical problems that led to the disbanding of the Voter News Service) showed that 40 percent of the 2002 voters identified themselves as Republicans, a significant increase from 35 percent in the 2000 election. Democratic identification dropped slightly to 38 percent. Yet it was the first time in many years that the GOP had more voters in polling booths than did the Democrats. Independent voters, who usually decide the outcome of elections, also broke for the conservatives that year.

Congressional Democrats were deeply divided on the coming Iraqi war. Their troubles with Bush's war on terrorism could be summarized, perhaps, by the campaign of House Minority Leader Richard Gephardt of Missouri. He tried to focus voters on widespread concerns about Social Security and the lackluster economy. Democrats frequently noted that pocketbook issues, not terrorism, led most public opinion polls as the nation's top issue. Gephardt bitterly criticized Bush for not winning wider global support for the U.S. invasion into Iraq, but in the end voted to allocate $87 billion to pay for the military action. "I can't find it within myself to not vote for the money to support our men and women who are over there protecting us," Gephardt told reporters. After the modest, but historic, losses in 2002, Gephardt stepped down as House minority leader in January of 2003.

The GOP takeover of the Senate was aided by the October 25, 2002, private aircraft crash that killed Democratic Sen. Paul Wellstone of Minnesota and seven members of his family and campaign staff. Wellstone had voted against the Iraq war just two weeks earlier, one of 23 senators to do so. He has also voted against the 1991 Senate bill authorizing the use of force for the first Persian Gulf War. Democrats selected former Vice President Walter Mondale to take Wellstone's place to face Republican Norm Coleman. Mondale, who said he also would have voted against the Iraqi war resolution, was narrowly defeated by Coleman.

The small pro-GOP wave continued down the ballot to state legislative races. Republicans gained majorities in eight state legislative bodies, giving them a majority of state legislative seats for the first time since the Eisenhower sweep of 1952. It was a narrow win, perhaps, but Republicans gained 105 seats in state house races and 36 seats in state Senates among the 46 states that held legislative elections that year.

The only bright spot for Democrats was a small pickup in governorships. The Democrats won 10 governorships previously held by Republicans as well as the seat previously held by Maine independent Gov. Angus King. Republicans won eight governorships formerly held Democrats and the seat of Minnesota Gov. Jesse Ventura, elected on the Reform Party. Despite the losses, Republicans still maintained a slight majority of governorships.

Yet 2002 can only be described as a Republican victory, ending several years of razor-thin majorities that allowed Democrats to rule most legislative issues. "September 11 changed everything," concluded political author Michael Barone.

Thomas K. Hargrove

See also: 9/11 Terrorist Attacks; Bush, George W.; Bush Doctrine; Campaign 2000

Further Reading

Barone, Michael, Richard E. Cohen, and Grant Ujifusa. 2003. *The Almanac of American Politics 2004*. Washington, DC: National Journal Group

Nutting, Brian, and H. Amy Stern. 2001. *CQ's Politics in America 2002: The 107th Congress*. Washington, DC: Congressional Quarterly.

Campaign 2004

The 2004 presidential election season saw a crowded field of Democrats vie for the chance to challenge incumbent Republican President George W. Bush, who was reelected by a small but unequivocal majority of the popular vote. Republicans also picked up four seats in the United States Senate and three seats in the House of Representatives, making it the first time a political party both reelected a president and made gains in both houses of Congress since 1964, when Democrats made sweeping gains in the landslide election of incumbent President Lyndon B. Johnson, who took office after the assassination of President John F. Kennedy.

The election was dominated by national security concerns following the September 11, 2001, terrorist attacks by the al-Qaeda Islamic terrorist group upon the twin towers of the World Trade Center in New York City and on the Pentagon outside Washington, D.C. Nearly 3,000 Americans perished in those attacks, making it the bloodiest act of terrorism ever committed on U.S. soil. A profound "rally effect" following the attacks gave President Bush the highest approval ratings ever recorded by pollsters.

Against this backdrop, it might seem hard to understand why so many Democrats queued up for a chance to unseat President Bush. After all, no sitting American president has been ousted from power during a time of war. But the Democrats were still stinging from the deeply divided election of 2000, when incumbent Democratic Vice President Al Gore won the popular vote by half a million ballots but lost the Presidential Electoral College vote because of a bitterly disputed 537-vote majority for Bush in the state of Florida. No president who gained the White House after losing the popular vote was reelected. No matter who won, the stage was set in 2004 to break a major political precedent.

Ten prominent Democrats indicated in 2003 that they intended to seek the presidency, although Sen. Bob Graham of Florida withdrew his name more than three months before the start of party caucuses and primaries. Still left in the race at the start of the Iowa caucuses were Sen. John Kerry of Massachusetts, Sen. John Edwards of North Carolina, former Vermont Gov. Howard Dean, retired U.S. Army Gen. Wesley Clark, Rep. Dennis Kucinich of Ohio, Rev. Al Sharpton of New York, Sen. Joe Lieberman of Connecticut, Rep. Dick Gephardt of Missouri, and former Sen. Carol Moseley Braun of Illinois.

There was no early favorite among the crowded pack of Democrats, although considerable press attention was paid to Dean, a medical doctor who ran a populist campaign, and Clark, whose military credentials seemed attractive during a time of war. But the Iowa caucuses unexpectedly had Kerry, who repeatedly reminded voters he'd earned three Purple Heart citations while a junior Navy officer during the Vietnam War, taking first place with 38 percent of the ballots, followed by Southerner Edwards with 32 percent. Dean came in third, followed by Gephardt.

Kerry won the New Hampshire primary, which was not a surprise since New England voters often favor politicians from Massachusetts. Edwards won the South Carolina primary the following week, and Clark won in Oklahoma, but these defeats for Kerry were only minor setbacks. Kerry went on in February to win contests in Hawaii, Idaho, Michigan, Nevada, Tennessee, Maine, Utah, Washington, Wisconsin, and Washington, D.C. Both Clark and Dean dropped out during these campaigns. The stage was set for Super Tuesday in March when Kerry guaranteed his nomination with victories in California, Connecticut, Georgia, Maryland, Massachusetts, Minnesota, New York, Ohio, and Rhode Island.

Kerry accepted the Democrat's nomination for president at the party's national convention in 2004 by reminding Americans that he was a politician with military experience. "I'm John Kerry and I'm reporting for duty," he said at the beginning of his acceptance speech. "The stakes are high. We are a nation at war—a global war on terror against an enemy unlike any we've ever known before. And here at home, wages are falling, health care costs are rising, and our great middle class is shrinking."

Bush, in his acceptance speech for the Republican nomination delivered in New York a month later, reminded voters that the issues in 2004 were unusually significant. "I believe the most solemn duty of the American president is to protect the American people. If America shows uncertainty and weakness in this decade, the world will drift toward tragedy. This will not happen on my watch," Bush said.

The political campaign between Bush and Kerry became unusually personal. Bush accused his Democratic challenger of being a "flip flopper" on important issues that demonstrated Kerry would show uncertainty "in the face of danger."

Critics accused Bush of failing to fulfill his required service to the Texas Air National Guard when he was a young airman in the early 1970s. CBS News broadcast a segment on the popular *60 Minutes* news show citing documents that Bush had been grounded for "failure to perform" to air guard standards by not appearing for a physical examination and that Bush was given preferential treatment as the son of his prominent political father, future President George H.W. Bush. But CBS had not properly authenticated the documents, which appeared to have been produced using word processing equipment that did not exist in 1973, eventually leading to the firing of the segment's producer.

Kerry, meanwhile, was savaged by a group called "Swift Boat Veterans for the Truth," which began airing attack ads in May that disputed his record as a much-decorated Navy officer during the Vietnam War. "John Kerry has not been honest about what happened in Vietnam," one veteran said. "He is lying about his record," said another. Republican Sen. John McCain condemned the ad as "dishonest and dishonorable," but the allegations dogged Kerry throughout the campaign. The incident created a new political term—"swiftboating"—which describes untrue political attacks that successfully undermine a political campaign.

The bare-knuckle campaign ended November 2, 2004, when Bush won with 62 million votes against Kerry's 59 million. Bush had improved his showing from 2000 thanks to a significant shift by female voters who changed from so-called "soccer moms" to "security moms" over concerns of national safety during the war on terror. It was, however, an unusually close election for an incumbent president during a time of war. The election set modern-day records in the percentage of eligible Americans who registered to vote (72 percent) and tied the 1960 record when 64 percent of American citizens cast a vote in the hard-fought 1960 race between Democrat John F. Kennedy and Republican Richard Nixon.

Bush proved to have some coattails in the 2004 election, improving his party's position in both the House and Senate. This was not to last long, however, since the GOP lost control of both houses of Congress in the Democratic wave that broke in the 2006 off-year elections.

Thomas K. Hargrove

See also: Campaign 2000, Campaign 2006, Swift Boat Veterans for Truth

Further Reading

Hillygus, D. Sunshine, and Todd G. Shields. 2008. *The Persuadable Voter: Wedge Issues in Presidential Campaigns.* Princeton, NJ: Princeton University Press.
Sabato, Larry J. 2005. *Divided States of America: The Slash and Burn Politics of the 2004 Presidential Election.* New York: Longman Publishing Group.

Campaign 2006

The 2006 off-year election was dominated by an anti-Republican wave strong enough to bring a flood of Democrats into control of the United States Senate and House of Representatives as well as 36 governorships and a plurality of state legislatures. This wave had many sources, including a widespread and general political dissatisfaction following the Republicans' six-year control of the White House and four-year domination of Congress, and declining support for the policies of President George W. Bush, especially his administration of the U.S. invasion and military occupation of Iraq.

The American electorate had also become gradually but steadily more diversified as the participation rates among women and racial and ethnic minorities grew. Only about one-third of the U.S. electorate was non-Hispanic white male—the only major voter bloc that was reliably, even overwhelmingly, Republican. White men had once accounted for the overwhelming majority of voters in the U.S., but their political strength had dipped to its lowest level in U.S. history.

American politics usually follows a cyclic pattern often compared to a swinging pendulum. Historically, the party that controls the White House almost always suffers defeats in the next off-year election. The effects of these anti-incumbent defeats are a natural safety valve to reduce dissatisfaction among sympathizers to the out-of-power party. But Democratic anger, which raged with President Bush's contentious ascension in 2000 after losing the popular vote, was not assuaged in either the 2002 or 2004 elections. Republican control continued unabated, thanks to the September 11, 2001, terrorist attacks in New York City and Washington, D.C., which prompted considerable U.S. military commitments in the Middle East. The political dam burst in a torrent of anti-Republican rage in 2006.

Much of the wave can be attributed to Bush, who was reelected in 2004 over Democratic Sen. John Kerry of Massachusetts with less than 51 percent of the popular vote and only 286 electoral votes (270 were needed to win). Bush said he had gained "political capital" because of the vote, but it was hardly a mandate from voters for his policies. The second term quickly became tarnished. Bush was widely criticized for his handling of the federal response to Hurricane Katrina in 2005, which left more than 1,800 dead in New Orleans and along the coast of the Gulf of Mexico.

Nevertheless, growing dissatisfaction with Bush's handling of Iraq was the central target of anti-incumbent anger. Iraqi President Saddam Hussein had first incurred U.S. wrath when he occupied Kuwait, prompting the first Persian Gulf War, which ended on February 28, 1991, with an overwhelming show of force by the United States and its allies. Bush's father, President George H.W. Bush, decided not to make removal of Saddam a goal of that war, opting instead for a policy of military and economic containment of the Iraqi strongman.

The younger Bush made Iraqi regime change a priority after the 9/11 terrorist attacks. He said Saddam had supported terrorism and maintained a stockpile of weapons of mass destruction. The U.S. invasion of Iraq lasted from March 19 until May 1, 2003, at the relatively modest cost of fewer than 400 U.S. fatalities. But U.S. casualties mounted alarmingly during the occupation, which saw a dramatic rise in violence between Iraqi Sunni and Shia groups. More than 4,400 American military personnel died in Iraq, the overwhelming majority during the U.S. occupation rather than the actual invasion. The White House also conceded that U.S. intelligence estimates of Iraqi chemical weapons stockpiles were wrong, undermining one of the major goals of the U.S. invasion. "The main reason we went into Iraq at the time was (that) we thought he (Saddam) had weapons of mass destruction. It turns out he didn't," Bush admitted during a press conference two months before the 2006 elections.

Completing the so-called "perfect storm" against Republicans were a series of scandals highlighted by the 2006 conviction of Republican lobbyist Jack Abramoff, who was sentenced to six years in federal prison for illegal deals on behalf of Indian casinos that included nearly a dozen White House and GOP congressional aides.

The Democrats also appointed talented political leaders to supervise the 2006 elections, especially Rep. Rahm Emanuel of Illinois who, as chairman of the Democratic Congressional Campaign Committee, scoured the nation for able Democrats to challenge Republican incumbents. As a result of the 2006 general election, Democrats picked up 31 House and six Senate seats, effectively giving them majorities in both chambers. They also won stunning victories further down the ballot, ending Republican control of six governorships. Twenty-eight governors were Democrats after the election while Republicans accounted for 22, reversing GOP dominance. Democrats gained more than 300 state legislative seats nationwide, increasing their control of both state houses from 19 states to 23 states.

The election also brought an historic milestone for U.S. women since California Rep. Nancy Pelosi was elected Speaker of the House by the new Democratic majority in 2007. Pelosi became the highest-ranking woman in U.S. history, second only to the vice president in line of succession to the presidency.

The election set the stage for the coming Democratic victory in the 2008 presidential race since women and minority groups were establishing unprecedented control of the electorate. Republicans were stung by their failures under the Bush administration and would have to develop wholly new strategies if they ever were to win national elections again.

"The Democrats haven't been this happy since 2000 when CNN declared for Al Gore," Emanuel told the *Washington Post* the day after the election. "And that lasted all of about an hour." Emanuel's words were prophetic. The Democratic glow would last another two years, but the pendulum of U.S. politics was not finished, as the next off-year contest in 2010 would prove.

Thomas K. Hargrove

See also: Bush Doctrine; Campaign 2002, Campaign 2004; 9/11 Terrorist Attacks

Further Reading

Barone, Michael, Richard E. Cohen, and Grant Ujifusa. 2007. *The Almanac of American Politics 2008.* Washington, DC: National Journal Group.

Bendavid, Naftali. 2007. *The Thumpin': How Rahm Emanuel and the Democrats Learned to Be Ruthless and Ended the Republican Revolution.* New York: Doubleday.

Campaign 2008

When prognosticators and pundits looked toward the 2008 presidential election, as early as just after George W. Bush's victory over John Kerry in 2004, they saw a fait accompli on the Democratic side. Only one candidate could possibly rally a defeated and dispirited Democratic Party: Hillary Clinton, the wife of the former president. The Clinton steamroller gathered momentum all through 2006 and 2007 as she accumulated a huge war chest; endorsements from many, if not most, party leaders, congress members, governors, and senators; and built a nationwide, lavishly funded campaign organization. More important, she had near universal name recognition and very high polling numbers in key Democratic constituencies, from middle-aged women to union household members to African Americans. The race for the nomination was famously dubbed "Hillary and the Seven Dwarves." But early on there were signs of trouble, particularly on the left wing of the Democratic Party. There was resentment against anyone being "inevitable," perceptions that Clinton was yet another middle-of-the-road Democratic, and lingering resentment over the scandals and stumbles of the first Clinton presidency. There was widespread speculation that a fresh face with new ideas might be an attractive "not-Hillary."

On the Republican side, there was much greater uncertainty. Vice President Richard Cheney was not running for the nomination, and there was no true bankable star among the Republican governors or senators who could carry the party past many of the unpopular decisions and policies of the Bush administration. The two highest in name recognition, both nationally and among the press and punditry, were John McCain (longtime Arizona senator) and Rudy Giuliani (the world's most famous mayor, who had stewarded the city through the 9/11 terrorist attacks). Neither was seen as either mainstream or hard conservative Republicans, however, and both had made many political enemies within their own party. Neither held any great attraction for the evangelical wing of the GOP.

As the Bush administration's second term in office continued into 2005, speculation for the 2008 election candidates began promptly. By the 2006 midterm elections, early polls anticipated New York Senator Hillary Clinton and Illinois Senator Barack Obama as potential Democratic candidates as well as Giuliani and McCain as potential Republican candidates. Clinton formerly announced her candidacy on January 20, 2007, Giuliani did so on January 28, Obama on February 10, and McCain on March 1. Former North Carolina Senator John Edwards also campaigned as a Democratic contender throughout 2007 with polls indicating he stood in third place behind Clinton and Obama. At the time, McCain stood in second behind Giuliani. The Iowa caucuses and the New Hampshire primary, as expected, served as tipping points for the nomination process. On January 3, 2008, Obama won the Iowa caucus with 38 percent of the votes, placing Edwards in second with 30 percent, and Clinton in third with 29 percent. Obama's win in Iowa made him the new front-runner for New Hampshire. However, following Clinton's successful performances leading up to New Hampshire's primary, the New York senator won New Hampshire on January 8, 2008, with 39 percent. Obama was second with 37 percent, and Edwards third with 17 percent. Edwards withdraw his candidacy on January 30. The New Hampshire primary also established McCain as the Republican nominee with 39 percent of votes beating out Giuliani and bouncing back from a loss in Iowa to Arkansas Governor Mike Huckabee. On February 5, 2008, the results of Super Tuesday's elections established a near tie between Clinton and Obama with 834 and 847 delegates respectively. McCain took 574 delegates, beating out Huckabee's 218 delegates and former Massachusetts Governor Mitt Romney's 231. Two days later, Romney withdrew to endorse McCain, and Huckabee did the same on March 4. Following the last of the primaries in June 2008, Obama claimed the Democratic presidential nomination. Clinton then officially withdrew from the race on June 7 to endorse Obama, leaving McCain and Obama as the final nominees.

The race became the first major election since 1952 in which neither nominee was an incumbent president or vice president and the first time in U.S. history that both candidates were sitting U.S. Senators. The three presidential debates took place on September 26, October 7, and October 15. All resulted in more favorable views of Obama over McCain according to opinion polls. All debates drew huge audiences. The vice presidential debate between Democratic nominee Senator Joseph Biden of Delaware and Republican nominee Governor Sarah Palin of Alaska drew 73 million viewers, the second largest audience for a presidential or vice-presidential debate ever.

On general election day November 4, 2008, exit polls indicated an Obama victory with the McCain-Palin ticket winning the white vote, voters 65 and older, conservatives, and Republicans, while the Obama-Biden ticket was winning over non-white voters, young voters, voters with the lowest and highest incomes, as well as 29 percent of independent voters. Following the final announcements of wins in California, Oregon, Washington, and Hawaii, Obama was declared the country's winner. Shortly afterward, McCain conceded with a speech in Phoenix, and Obama followed with a victory speech in Chicago. After all states' votes were finally accounted for, the McCain-Palin ticket won

173 electoral votes and received 46 percent of popular votes. The Obama-Biden ticket won both the electoral (365 votes) and popular (53 percent) votes, making Barack Obama the first African American U.S. president as well as the presidential candidate with the most votes in U.S. history.

Throughout the campaign, wars in Iraq and Afghanistan became increasingly unpopular during the Republican Bush administration's outgoing term. Polls indicated that, of the likely voters for the upcoming election, 80 percent felt the country was not moving in the right direction. The next president would determine the fate of the United States' involvement with the war and shape the future of American domestic and foreign policy as well as an economy in the onset of recession. Voters needed to decide which of the candidates' Iraq exit strategy was preferable. Additionally, with approximately 12 million illegal immigrants in the country at the time, voters felt an increased sense of urgency regarding the controversy of the costs and benefits of illegal immigration. Abortion also polarized the public since several conservative jurists had been appointed to the Supreme Court. And with nearly 50 million Americans living without health insurance at the time, health care and the future of Medicare were important voting issues as well. Each candidate was touting his own solution to the American people with McCain's campaign slogan stating "Country First." and Obama's rallying for "Change We Can Believe In." Typically in a primary election, only the party out of power calls for change, yet the 2008 election saw both parties offering a new plan for change, as opposed to "more of the same."

Each candidate stated his claims in a war of advertisements that, until that point in American history, had never been seen. The Obama campaign outspent McCain's 3:1, raising $750 million from more than three million contributors, which changed the country's previous boundaries of money and politics. In true reflection of the boom in social media at the time, advertisements were created quickly and for the specific purpose of mass sharing, with many observers noting that the 2008 advertisements were "noticeably sharper and more aggressive than that of previous elections."

The year 2008 was definitely the year that social media arrived in presidential campaigning. No one could doubt that the Obama campaign's skillful use of Facebook, YouTube, Twitter, blogs, texting, and other interactive online media not only helped propel awareness of their candidate and raise money but created a new venue for self-organization of would-be supporters and voters. The difference from the prototype 2004 Howard Dean effort was striking. The Dean campaign initiated social media as a way to excite voters and spread the message of the candidate, but the campaign often stumbled on traditional organizational efforts and all-important Get Out the Vote (GOTV) primary and caucus day turnout. Obama '08, in contrast, did both the old and the new well and in sync.

Second, in 2004, social media for Howard Dean was compared to "dating the candidate," an impossibility for one person building a relationship with a million. But the Obama campaign created venues, encouragement, and motivation for voters to self-organize and fundraise via social media to win influence for the candidate among their own friends. Not without cause, then, that as Franklin Roosevelt was often called the radio president and John F. Kennedy the master of television, Barack Obama could be called our first Facebook president.

Andrea M. Weare and David D. Perlmutter

See also: Campaign 2010; Campaign 2012; Candidates, presidential, 2008; Clinton, Hillary Rodham; Obama, Barack

Further Reading

Day, Jonathan. 2008. "Presidential Election of 2008." In Kenneth F. Warren, ed. *Encyclopedia of U.S. Campaigns, Elections and Electoral Behavior.* Twin Oaks, CA: Sage Publications.

Johnson, Dennis. 2008. *Campaigning for President, 2008.* New York: Routledge.

Perlmutter, David D. 2008. *Blogwars: The News Political Battleground.* New York: Oxford University Press.

Campaign 2010

The 2010 off-year political season saw one of the largest so-called "wave elections" in history, which political analyst Stuart Rothenberg defines as an election that results in at least a 20-seat party shift in the U.S. House of Representatives. The Republicans gained 63 seats, giving them control of the House. The GOP also picked up six seats in the Senate, although the Democrats clung to a 51-seat majority after the election. Republicans made vast gains in state house races, picking up 680 seats to give them control of 26 state legislatures, a pickup of five states. The GOP also won control of 29 of the nation's 50 governorships.

It was the largest anti-incumbent wave since 1948, when Democrats took 75 seats on the broad coattails of Harry Truman's reelection campaign, in which the president railed against the "do-nothing" Republican Congress. The 2010 campaign was the largest off-year wave since 1938, when Republicans picked up 81 House seats as voters became disenchanted with New Deal policies that they blamed for another decline in economic conditions.

Political waves are usually fueled by anger, and 2010 was no exception. Voters were deeply dissatisfied by a record increase in federal deficit spending mandated by President Barack Obama's American Recovery and Reinvestment Act of 2009, which allocated more than $800 billion for new infrastructure and education initiatives in hopes of stimulating the economy out of the Great Recession. Voters were also widely unhappy with the federal bailout of major financial institutions, an initiative begun under President George W. Bush with the $700 billion Emergency Economic Stabilization Act of 2008.

Further fueling the wave was the creation of a new political force—the "Tea Party" movement—which protested Obama's federal deficit largesse. The fiscally conservative movement drew its name from the Boston Tea Party anti-British tax protest of 1773. "America is ready for another revolution," former Republican vice presidential nominee Sarah Palin told thousands of participants at the National Tea Party Convention meeting in Nashville, Tennessee, in February 2010. Although mostly Republican in orientation, members of the Tea Party movement were also deeply critical of bailout spending under the Bush administration.

The election also focused on criticism of the passage of the Democrat's Affordable Care Act—which conservatives characterized as a massive federal health care reform initiative that would unfairly burden small businesses—and a general dissatisfaction that the unemployment rate remained stubbornly high despite the massive infusion of federal stimulus dollars.

Senate Republican leader Mitch McConnell neatly summed up the GOP's campaign theme: "In the first year of the trillion-dollar stimulus, Americans have lost millions of jobs, the unemployment rate continues to hover near 10 percent, the deficit continues to soar and we're inundated with stories of waste, fraud and abuse," McConnell said. "This was not the plan Americans asked for or the results they were promised."

Obama chided congressional Republicans as hypocrites who hotly criticize stimulus spending and yet "still show up at ribbon-cutting ceremonies for projects in their districts." But the president had a tough message to sell since he was urging voters to be patient. "Millions are struggling to make ends meet. So it doesn't yet feel like much of a recovery. And I understand that. It's why we're going to continue to do everything in our power to turn this economy around," Obama said in February.

But the economy did not improve during the campaign season. The U.S. Labor Department estimated that unemployment was 9.7 percent in January 2010 and had ticked up to 9.8 percent in November as voters went to the polls. What followed can only be described as Democratic slaughter.

Fifty-four House Democrats were defeated, including two who lost in primary fights with challengers who, in turn, were defeated by Republicans. There were nine House Democrats who survived reelection despite the so-called "Republican Revolution" in 1994 but were defeated in the 2010 wave.

Virginia Gov. Tim Kaine, who was chairman of the Democratic National Committee for the 2010 season, concluded that Democratic incumbents faced "stiff historical and economic headwinds" that doomed many of them. "The American people are rightly frustrated by the economy," he said.

Republican House Speaker John Boehner was subdued in his reaction to news reporters when asked about one of the biggest GOP wave victories in history. "Frankly, this is not a time for celebration, not when one out of 10 of our fellow citizens are out of work and not when our Congress is held with such low esteem," Boehner said.

The wave elections themselves often come in spurts. The 2010 wave was the biggest of a three-cycle cluster that saw significant gains for Democrats with a 31-seat pickup in the House in 2006 and a 21-seat pickup in 2008. Those significant gains were crushingly reversed in 2010. The wave elections ended in 2012 with the reelection of President Obama when very few incumbents were defeated. The last big wave occurred in the "Republican Revolution" of 1994, which was the first off-year election for Democratic President Bill Clinton. The GOP picked up 53 seats then. But the next five election cycles were quiet with virtually no change in the balance of power between the two parties.

Rothenberg notes the last time that partisan swings of at least 20 House seats occurred for four consecutive elections was during the 1946-48-50-52 cycles, when Democrats won huge gains in 1948 only to be steadily reversed by large Republicans wins in the next three elections.

There was an even longer string of political waves from 1910 to 1924, when 20 or more House seats changed hands for each of eight consecutive elections. "This was, of course, a period of considerable churning in American politics, with the progressive movement and the socialists challenging the major parties," Rothenberg said.

More recent waves have focused exclusively on the struggle between Democrats and Republicans.

Thomas K. Hargrove

See also: Health Reform Attempts; Obama, Barack

Further Reading

Barone, Michael, and Chuch McCutcheon. 2011. *The Almanac of American Politics 2012*. Chicago: University of Chicago Press.

Haas, Karen L. 2011. *Statistics of the Congressional Election of November 2, 2010*. Washington, DC: United States House of Representatives.

Rothenberg, Stuart. 2011. "Are We Headed for Four Wave Elections in a Row?" Column published February 3. Washington, DC: The Rothenberg Political Report.

Campaign 2012

The 2012 election cycle saw Democrats' hopes renewed following the drubbing they received in the 2010 conservative "wave election" that swept Republicans into control of the House of Representatives and gave the GOP a considerably stronger hand at the state level with solid majorities of both state legislatures and governorships. President Barack Obama countered in 2012 with an extremely disciplined "ground-game" campaign in which he established hundreds of local campaign offices, made effective use of social media and information technology to track millions of individual households for specially crafted appeals by volunteers, and targeted mail and mass-media appeals.

Obama and Vice President Joe Biden were easily reelected by a four-percentage-point majority of the popular vote. Democrats picked up 8 seats in the House of Representatives, although still 16 seats shy of the wins necessary for them to regain a majority. They picked up two U.S. Senate seats to increase their slim majority from 51 to 53 seats in the 100-seat body. Republicans did manage to gain one additional governorship in 2012, when North Carolina elected Republican Pat McCrory to replace retiring Democratic Governor Bev Perdue. (Wisconsin Republican Scott Walker also survived a recall election attempt in June by labor leaders angered at his attempts to undermine government unions.)

That outcome was anything but foreordained given the economic crisis America had weathered during the so-called Great Recession of 2008 and 2009. The deflation of housing prices forced millions of Americans into "underwater" mortgages, in which their debts were greater than the value of their homes. Unemployment crept to 10 percent of the labor force in October of 2009 before starting a decline that, for most Americans, seemed agonizingly slow. At the first of January in 2012, the official jobless rate stood at a politically unacceptable 8.3 percent while the millions of "discouraged workers" also counted by the Labor Department (adults who don't look for work because they don't think they can get a job) meant that the "real" unemployment rate was significantly higher.

Democrats were also on the defensive for their "big government" solutions to the nation's crises. The American Recovery and Reinvestment Act of 2009 pumped more than $800 billion by raising the national debt to unprecedented levels to stimulate the economy through infrastructure investment, tax incentives, and increased unemployment benefits. Democrats also pushed through Congress the Patient Protection and Affordable Care Act, which was signed into law on March 23, 2010, to expand health care insurance through private insurance contracts with mandated coverage standards that eliminated unpopular "pre-existing conditions" exemptions. But the bill also created tax penalties for Americans who refuse to obtain insurance, pushing Americans to obtain insurance coverage whether they wanted it or not. It was the most sweeping reform of the U.S. health care system since 1965 when Congress enacted the Medicare and Medicaid programs.

As a result of the tough economic and political realities the Democrats faced, a crowd of nationally prominent Republicans announced their intentions to seek the White House that year. Among them were Former House Speaker Newt Gingrich of Georgia, Texas Gov. Rick Perry, former Massachusetts Gov. Mitt Romney, former U.S. Sen. Rick Santorum of Pennsylvania—whose strong anti-abortion stance made him the darling of social conservatives—and at least five others who might have had a chance of taking the White House.

When Governor Perry's campaign unexpectedly imploded after some disappointing appearances on televised candidate debates—including a disastrous moment when Perry said he couldn't remember the names of all three federal departments he wanted to abolish—the Republican primary season turned into a long, tough slog comparable to the 2008 marathon campaign between Democrats Hillary Rodham Clinton and Obama. But the Democrats campaigned for months with a soft-glove campaign in which both said they were thrilled to be, respectively, their party's first viable female and black candidates.

The Republicans in 2012, in contrast, had to go after each other in a three-way, bare-chested knife fight between Romney, Santorum, and Gingrich. Each challenged the conservative vision of the other. Santorum and Gingrich had to be especially brutal in their attacks on front-runner Romney, reminding voters that the Affordable Health Care Act was modeled on a Massachusetts bill that Romney signed into law. "The whole reason this issue is alive is because of the bill that you drafted in Massachusetts—'Romneycare'—which was the model for 'Obamacare' and the government takeover of heath care." Santorum told Romney during a heated TV debate in Arizona in February.

When Romney finally mathematically cinched the GOP nomination when he won the May 29 Texas primary, he issued a victory statement that was almost wistful: "Our party has come together with the goal of putting the failures of the last three and a half years behind us."

Romney campaigned hard and prepared for the presidential debates that would start October 3 in Denver. Although Obama was already an experienced debater, Romney came out aggressively and was widely perceived by the press and public opinion polls to have won the debate. "Under the president's policies, middle-income Americans have been buried. They're just being crushed. Middle-income Americans have seen their income come down by $4,300. This is a tax in and of itself. I'll call it the economy tax. It's been crushing," Romney said. The president's responses were measured, respectful, but came off almost subdued. The Gallup Poll found that 72 percent of people it interviewed believed Romney had won the debate.

"I've got this," Obama promised his supporters afterwards. The president's appearances in the next two debates were much more aggressive, even combative. Obama came out swinging two weeks later at Romney's promise in the first debate to end federal subsidies for National Public Broadcasting. "We haven't heard from the governor any specifics, beyond Big Bird and eliminating funding for Planned Parenthood," the president said. Polls showed Obama winning in a close vote.

By the third debate, Obama was almost cocky. "Governor, when it comes to our foreign policy, you seem to want to import the foreign policies of the 1980s, just like the social policies of the 1950s and the economic policies of the 1920s," he told Romney. All polls showed the president won the last two debates.

However, if there was a major recorded gaff made by Romney during the campaign, it wasn't something he said during a television debate. Someone secretly video-recorded Romney's comments to a small gathering of Republican supporters in Florida about why Obama was guaranteed to receive at least 47 percent of the vote that year. "There are 47 percent who are with him, who are dependent upon government, who believe that they are victims, who believe that government has a responsibility to care for them, who believe that they are entitled to health care, to food, to housing, to you-name-it," Romney said on hidden camera. The video went viral.

"That hurt. There's no question that hurt and did real damage to my campaign," Romney admitted five months after the election. The quote was deeply divisive, accusing every American who receives federal benefits of being a victim. It underscored criticisms that Romney was an out-of-touch millionaire. It also technically insulted elderly Social Security beneficiaries and recipients of Veterans Administration assistance—both important parts of the Republican coalition—who are also major parts of the 47 percent of America that gets some kind of government assistance.

On election night, Obama racked up 65.9 million votes to Romney's 60.9 million, or 51 percent to 47 percent and 2 percent going to third-party candidates. Obama's margin in the all-important Electoral College vote was even larger, winning 332 to Romney's 206. Although his win in Florida was by a very narrow margin, Obama carried every so-called battleground state except North Carolina.

"Tonight, in this election, you, the American people, reminded us that while our road has been hard, while our journey has been long, we have picked ourselves up, we have fought our way back, and we know in our hearts that for the United States of America the best is yet to come," Obama told a cheering crowd in Chicago immediately after all news networks had declared him the winner.

Thomas K. Hargrove

See also: Campaign 2008; Campaign 2012; Get-Out-The-Vote Efforts

Further Reading

Balz, Dan. 2013. *Collision 2012: The Future of Election Politics in a Divided America.* New York: Viking.
Halperin, Mark, and John Heilemann. 2013. *Double Down: Game Change in 2012.* New York: The Penguin Press.

Campaign 2014

The 2014 off-year political season saw the Republican Party rise to its greatest dominance of state and national offices in nearly a century, as voters who were unhappy—even outright angry—with President Barack Obama marched to the polls while much of the president's political base made a lackluster showing. The GOP picked up nine Senate seats, giving Republicans control of both houses of Congress. The GOP even picked up 13 House seats, further cementing the majority it claimed in the 2010 "wave election." Perhaps more importantly, conservatives gained control of both legislative houses in 29 states and held

31 governorships, giving the Republican Party its widest control of state policy in many generations.

Republican candidates at every level focused their campaigns on an anti-Obama theme, criticizing the president for national health care reforms that financially penalized people who did not sign up for health insurance, for his promised immigration reforms through executive orders without congressional approval, and for failures to prevent scandals at the Veterans Administration that falsified reporting about a serious backlog in medical services for veterans.

"You will be heard in Washington. That's what this campaign was all about," said future Senate Majority Leader Mitch McConnell in his Election Night victory speech. "It was about a government people no longer trust to carry out its most basic duties: to keep them safe, to protect the boarder, to provide dignified and quality care for our veterans. A government that can't be trusted to do the basic things because it's too busy focusing on things it shouldn't be focused on at all."

Although the election was a testament to voter anger at Obama, it was also a powerful demonstration of how different the electorates are in the off-year elections and years when voters decide control of the White House. Turnout was estimated to be just 36.4 percent of eligible voters in 2014, the worst showing for a midterm election since 1942 and a far cry from the 61.8 percent showing in the 2012 presidential election. Exit polls found that Republicans actually outpolled Democrats in 2014—a very rare occurrence. Republicans accounted for 37 percent of the voters, while Democrats were in the minority at 36 percent and independent voters accounted for 28 percent. By contrast, Democratic voters enjoyed a 6-percentage point lead over Republicans in the 2012 election that gave Obama a second term.

The exit polls also provided some troubling news for Democrats in the future. The party's congressional candidates solidly lost the working-class white vote—which was a key component in Ronald Reagan's conservative revolution in the 1980s. Working-class whites voted for Democrats only 34 percent of the time in 2014 and for Republicans 64 percent of the time. That trend indicated liberals must regain what had been one of their historic advantages—a populism that promises bread-and-butter economics to support the middle and lower economic classes.

The *New York Times* editorial board concluded the abysmal voter turnout in 2014 was bad for the Democrats but even worse for democracy. "Republicans ran a single-theme campaign of pure opposition to President Obama, and Democrats were too afraid of the backlash to put forward plans to revive the economy or to point out significant achievements of the last six years. Neither party gave voters an affirmative reason to show up at the polls," the editors concluded.

As a result, many Democratic incumbents were forced from office, including senators Mark Begich of Alaska, Mark Udall of Colorado, and Mary Landrieu of Louisiana. "You all know I am a mountain climber," Udall said in his concession speech. "And I said over and over again as I approached this campaign that I thought of it as the biggest, baddest mountain that I'd ever faced."

Conservative Republican Sen. Ted Cruz of Texas concluded that in the 2014 election "there was no ambiguity" in that the number one issue was President Obama's health care reform. "The American people overwhelmingly said: 'We don't want Obamacare. It's a disaster.'" But the exit polls found the issue was not so clear. Among voters who participated in the off-year election, 49 percent said the Patient Protection and Affordable Care Act "went too far" while 46 percent said the law was "about right" or "did not go far enough" to provide broader health coverage. Republicans vowed they'd resume their efforts to repeal the law signed by Obama in March of 2010. The president vowed he'd veto any such attempts, positioning Democrats and Republicans in a confrontation that would continue into the 2016 presidential election.

The 2014 campaign also saw a stunning rise in the use of "dark money"—funds from undisclosed donors given to politically active nonprofit organizations. According to the Center for Responsive Politics, there were 29 House and Senate races in 2014 in which outside groups actually outspent the candidates themselves. Conservative groups accounted for nearly three-quarters of these undisclosed donations, according to the center.

The conservative victories in 2014 represented a small "wave" election that solidified the remarkable gains made in the 2010 off-year election when the GOP picked up 63 seats to gain control of the House of Representatives. If the 2014 and 2010 waves were added together (not unreasonable since both waves were based on anti-Obama voter anger), the Republicans surpassed by one seat the remarkable wave of 1948 when Democrats gained 75 House seats in President Harry Truman's reelection that focused on a do-nothing Congress.

Thomas K. Hargrove

See also: Campaign 2010; Dark Money

Further Reading

Editorial Board of the *New York Times*. 2014. "The Worst Voter Turnout in 72 Years." November 11, Editorial Page.

Hirschfeld Davis, Julie, and Peter Baker. 2014. "After Election, Obama Vows to Work With, and Without, Congress." *The New York Times*, November 5. http://www.nytimes.com/2014/11/06/us /politics/midterm-democratic-losses-grow.html. Accessed January 1, 2015.

Topaz, Jonathan. 2014. "What We Learned About the American Voter in 2014: Have Republicans Disrupted Democrats' Demographic Advantage?" *Politico*, December 31. http://www.politico. com/story/2014/12/2014-american-voter-elections-113883.html Accessed December 31, 2014.

Candidates, Presidential Election 2000

The 2000 U.S. presidential election will be remembered as a political turning point as America entered the 21st century. Vice President Albert Arnold "Al" Gore Jr., Democrat of Tennessee, faced challenger George Walker Bush, Republican of Texas, in a tightly contested race that, more than a month after Election Day, wound up being decided by the U.S. Supreme Court.

George W. Bush was born in 1946, the son of politically active parents. His father, George H.W. Bush, was a Congressman, ambassador, CIA director, vice president in the Reagan Administration, and president for one term during 1989–93. The younger Bush graduated from Yale University in 1968 and Harvard Business School in 1975. Living in Texas, he worked in the oil business and ran for the 19th district seat in the U.S. House of Representatives in 1978 but was defeated. He continued working with his oil business and purchased co-ownership of the Texas Rangers professional baseball team in 1989.

After five years, he gave politics another try. He announced candidacy for governor of Texas and won the office in 1994. Not long after easily winning his second term as governor, Bush announced his candidacy for president in 1999 and campaigned against a large field of other Republicans for the party nomination. He secured the nomination by the end of the March 2000 primaries. When he was declared winner of the 2000 general election, he became only the second son of a former president to be elected president—the other being John Quincy Adams, son of John Adams, two centuries earlier. Bush campaigned with vice presidential nominee Richard Bruce "Dick" Cheney of Wyoming and focused on Republican themes of what he called "compassionate conservatism"—less international intervention, tax breaks for all taxpayers, tax cuts, a "No Child Left Behind" education program, energy reform, and redesign and technology modernization of the military. He was reelected in 2004.

Al Gore was born in 1948, also the son of a politically active father and mother. His father, Albert Gore Sr., was U.S. Senator from Tennessee and his mother, Pauline, was an attorney. The younger Gore graduated from Harvard University, and he entered military service and spent part of his enlistment in Vietnam during the Vietnam War. Returning home, he worked as a reporter for the *Tennessean* daily newspaper in Nashville but soon entered Vanderbilt Law School. However, he left school after two years to run for U.S. House of Representatives and won four consecutive terms, 1977–85. He next ran for U.S. Senate in 1984, winning the seat he held until he was selected as vice presidential running mate with Governor Bill Clinton of Arkansas in 1992. Clinton's victory and reelection in 1996 put Gore in the vice presidency for eight years, culminating in his candidacy for president in 2000.

Gore announced his candidacy for the nomination in June 1999 and was given the nomination at the party convention in Los Angeles in August 2000. Gore's campaign, with Connecticut Senator Joe Lieberman as his running mate, reflected Democratic Party social values, emphasizing investment in technology and communities; tax cuts; creating trust funds for health care, the environment, and education; opening international markets; and keeping defense strong.

The long 2000 presidential campaign began in 1999 as both Democrats and Republicans organized their campaigns and announced their candidacies for the nominations of their parties. Gore was challenged by fellow Democrat and New Jersey Senator Bill Bradley (born 1943) for the party nomination. Following a series of town-hall-meeting format debates, Gore pulled ahead and won the party primaries and the nomination. At least eleven other well-known and popular Republicans challenged Bush for the nomination of their party. Bush's competitors included U.S. senators, governors, and a former vice president before Bush was given the nomination at the party convention in Philadelphia in August 2000. The list included the following:

- Tennessee Senator Andrew Lamar Alexander (born 1940)
- Conservative Gary Lee Bauer (born 1946)
- Conservative commentator Patrick Joseph "Pat" Buchanan (born 1938)
- Business executive Herman Cain (born 1945)
- Publishing executive Malcolm Stevenson "Steve" Forbes Jr., (born 1947)

- Utah Senator Orrin Grant Hatch (born 1934)
- Ohio Governor John Richard Kasich (born 1952)
- Conservative Alan Lee Keyes (born 1950)
- Arizona Senator John Sidney McCain (born 1936)
- Former Vice President James Danforth "Dan" Quayle (born 1947)
- New Hampshire Senator Robert Clinton Smith (born 1941)

Since the Republicans had no incumbent and no clear leader, the nomination process was open at the outset. While George W. Bush had sought and been given considerable party leader support as the son of the most recent Republican president and the sitting governor of a large conservative state, he had a long and potentially divisive campaign in fall 1999 and spring 2000 before securing the nomination through a series of primary victories. Senator John McCain, who would win his party's nomination for president in 2008, was Bush's leading challenger in a large field of hopefuls. In the end, Bush won 43 state primaries, and McCain carried only seven states.

Following their party nominations in summer 2000, Bush and Gore waged a spirited campaign with neither candidate far ahead in polls. Ultimately, Bush won the closest election in the modern era after weeks of recounts and court arguments over the results in the State of Florida. Bush took office on January 20, 2001. He was reelected in November 2004. Since leaving office in January 2009, he has led a limited public life, occasionally speaking and making other public appearances, but devoting much of his time to developing his presidential library, which opened at Southern Methodist University in Dallas in 2013.

Gore, after conceding defeat in December 2000, turned his attention to the environment at a global level. An author of numerous books, Gore authored several works about climate change. Gore pushed for both public and private sector actions designed to slow global warming, and he spoke extensively to advocate social change with regard to the environment. His work on global warming was recognized with the award of a Nobel Prize on December 10, 2007.

Bruce Garrison and Zongchao Li

See also: Bush, George W.; Campaign 2000; Vote Counting Problems

Further Reading

Brinkley, David. 2001. *36 Days: The Complete Chronicle of the 2000 Presidential Election Crisis.* New York: Times Books.

Bush, George W. 2010. *Decision Points.* New York: Random House.

Ceaser, J.W., and A. Busch. 2001. *The Perfect Tie: The True Story of the 2000 Presidential Election.* Lanham, MD: Rowman & Littlefield Publishers.

Dover, E.D. 2003. *The Disputed Presidential Election of 2000: A History and Reference Guide.* Westport, CT: Greenwood Press.

Gillman, H. 2001. *The Votes That Counted: How the Court Decided the 2000 Presidential Election.* Chicago: University of Chicago Press.

Johnston, R., M.G. Hagen, and K.H. Jamieson. 2004. *The 2000 Presidential Election and the Foundations of Party Politics.* Cambridge: Cambridge University Press.

Pomper, G. 2001. "The 2000 Presidential Election: Why Gore Lost." *Political Science Quarterly* 116(2): 201–223.

Posner, R.A. 2001. *Breaking the Deadlock: The 2000 Election, the Constitution, and the Courts.* Princeton, NJ: Princeton University Press.

Schlesinger, A. M., F.L. Israel, and J.H. Mann. 2003. *The Election of 2000 and the Administration of George W. Bush.* Philadelphia: Mason Crest Publishers.

Toobin, J. 2001. *Too Close to Call: The Thirty-Six-Day Battle to Decide the 2000 Election.* New York: Random House.

Watson, R.P. 2004. *Counting Votes: Lessons from the 2000 Presidential Election in Florida.* Gainesville: University Press of Florida.

Wayne, S.J. 2000. *The Road to the White House, 2000: The Politics of Presidential Elections.* Boston: Bedford/St. Martin's.

Weisberg, H.F., and C. Wilcox. 2004. *Models of Voting in Presidential Elections: The 2000 U.S. Election.* Stanford, CA: Stanford Law and Politics.

Candidates, Presidential Election 2004

The 2004 presidential election may be viewed as a referendum on the war on terrorism and the national economy. The September 11, 2001, attacks, the invasion of Iraq, and American employment were the leading issues that dominated debates and stump speeches of the major candidates.

Republican Party incumbent President George W. Bush sought reelection in 2004. As sitting president, the former Texas governor faced little or no opposition within his own party and easily gained the party nomination at the summer convention in New York City. Bush retained Vice President Richard Bruce "Dick" Cheney, a conservative from Wyoming, on the ticket.

Bush was born in 1946, the son of former President George H.W. and Barbara Bush. He graduated from Yale University in 1968 and Harvard Business School in 1975. A Texan, he worked in the oil business and ran for the 19th district seat in the U.S. House of Representatives in 1978 but lost. While continuing to develop his oil interests, he purchased co-ownership of the Texas Rangers professional baseball team in 1989. After five years, he returned to politics by announcing his candidacy for Texas governor. He won the office in 1994 and again in 1998. Bush announced his candidacy for president in 1999, winning the position in November 2000.

He became the second son of a former president to be elected president—the other being John Quincy Adams, son of John Adams, two centuries earlier. Bush's first term in office was marked early by the historic September 11, 2001, attacks on the World Trade Center in New York and the Pentagon in Washington, D.C., as well as a fourth hijacked commercial jet airliner that crashed in Pennsylvania—not quite eight months after Bush took office. The remaining three-plus years of his first term centered on the global war on terrorism with much of that focus on Iraq.

John Forbes Kerry, the Democratic Party nominee for president in 2004, was born in 1943 to Richard Kerry, a career foreign service officer, and Rosemary F. Kerry. He graduated from Yale University in 1966 and entered the U.S. Navy Reserve later that year. After serving a four-month assignment in Vietnam during the conflict there, he returned to the United States, settling in Massachusetts, and soon announced his candidacy for Congress in early 1972. He won the party nomination but lost the election. Kerry entered Boston

College Law School and graduated three years later, in 1976. After working two years as a district attorney, he opened his own law firm in 1979. In 1982, however, he again sought elected public office, winning the Democratic Primary for lieutenant governor. Campaigning with Michael Dukakis, the pair won the fall election without difficulty.

Two years later, in 1984, Kerry announced he would run for U.S. Senate when Paul Tsongas announced his retirement. Kerry won a close primary race in the heavily Democratic state and was elected that fall. He served Massachusetts from 1985 through his campaign for president in 2004. He earned the party nomination following a series of primary election victories in the spring. Kerry campaigned with former Democratic nomination rival and U.S. Senate colleague Johnny Reid "John" Edwards, from North Carolina.

The Democratic Party faced an internal battle for its nominee before selecting Kerry in the January to March state primary elections. There were at least nine other Democratic Party primary candidates. The list included the following:

- Former Illinois Senator Carol Mosley Braun (born 1947)
- Retired Army General Wesley Kanne Clark, Sr. of Arkansas (born 1944)
- Former Vermont Governor Howard Brush Dean III (born 1948)
- North Carolina Senator Johnny Reid "John" Edwards (born 1953)
- Missouri Congressman Richard Andrew "Dick" Gephardt (born 1941)
- Florida Senator Daniel Robert "Bob" Graham (born 1936)
- Ohio Congressman Dennis Kucinich (born 1946)
- Connecticut Senator Joseph Isadore "Joe" Lieberman (born 1942)
- Baptist minister Alfred Charles "Al" Sharpton Jr. of New York (born 1954)

The summer and fall campaign between Bush and Kerry centered on the war on terrorism since the September 11, 2001, attacks; U.S. involvement in Iraq; overall national security; and the national economy. Republicans, according to national opinion polls in 2004, were most interested in terrorism and national safety while Democrats emphasized domestic issues such as employment, education, and health care in addition to foreign policy. Gallup polls, for example, indicated strong public interest in the economy and terrorism as the campaign began. Bush defended his administration's actions and his leadership. He argued he would continue to be tough on terrorism and national security, strengthening safety and security at home, positions popular with his conservative base. Kerry, more liberal on both foreign and domestic matters, frequently criticized the administration's policies of the past four years and campaigned to be, as one slogan suggested, stronger at home and respected abroad. While much of the campaign was devoted to foreign policy, domestic issues were not overlooked. Kerry often campaigned on economic and employment proposals as well as his plans to improve national health care.

When the campaign concluded on Election Day, November 2, 2004, Bush won a fiercely contested vote with 50.7 percent of the approximately 121 million ballots cast.

After completing his second term in January 2009, Bush moved back to Texas and worked to develop his presidential library at Southern Methodist University in Dallas. He has occasionally made public appearances, traveled internationally on behalf of his global health initiative, and worked on other special projects of personal interest to him and his wife, Laura.

After the 2004 election, Kerry continued to serve in the U.S. Senate for nine more years, with a strong foreign policy role as Senate Foreign Relations Committee chair from

2009–13. Kerry was considered a possible presidential candidate again for 2008, but he endorsed Illinois Senator Barack Obama as party nominee in early 2008. After 28 years in the Senate, he accepted the nomination of President Obama to become the 68th U.S. Secretary of State in early 2013, replacing Hillary Clinton.

Bruce Garrison and Zongchao Li

See also: Bush, George H.; Campaign 2004; 9/11 Terrorist Attacks

Further Reading

Denton Jr., Robert E., ed. 2005. *The 2004 Presidential Campaign: A Communication Perspective.* Lanham, MD: Rowman & Littlefield.

Mayer, William G., ed. 2004. *The Making of the Presidential Candidates 2004.* Lanham, MD: Rowman & Littlefield.

North, David. 2004. *The Crisis of American Democracy: The Presidential Elections of 2000 and 2004.* Oak Park, MI: Mehring Books.

Sabato, Larry J. 2006. *Divided States of America: The Slash and Burn Politics of the 2004 Presidential Election.* New York: Pearson/Longman.

Thomas, Evan, and the Staff of *Newsweek.* 2004. *Election 2004: How Bush Won and What You Can Expect in the Future.* New York: Public Affairs.

Candidates, Presidential Election 2008

The 2008 presidential campaign was the first in U.S. history in which both presidential nominees were sitting U.S. senators, as well as the first time since 1952 that neither nominee was an incumbent president or vice president.

Nevertheless, not all candidates started the primaries and caucuses on an equal footing. On the Democratic side, Hillary Clinton was the presumptive nominee. As innumerable pundits and pollsters throughout 2006 and 2007 proclaimed, she had accumulated a huge war chest, garnered endorsements from many major party leaders and donors, fielded a wide and professional organization, attained near 100 percent name recognition, and enjoyed high polling support among key Democrat constituencies like union members and African Americans.

Yet, via the new campaign and political venue of online social media there was great resistance, especially in the left of the party, to another Clinton and a perceived moderate. A new face with charisma and a game plan could possibly win—and the backers of freshman Illinois Senator Barack Obama saw him as the outsider who could topple the Clinton giant. On the Republican side, George F. Will's famous comment that the GOP was a "primogeniture party" that tended to give the job of candidate to the next man in line seemed to predict longtime aspirant and maverick Senator John McCain.

Among the Republican Party candidates running were those who withdrew before and during the primaries, as well as the primary delegates. Before the primaries, four candidates withdrew, officially endorsing McCain of Arizona. These included senior Kansas Senator Sam Brownback, former Virginia Governor Jim Gilmore, Colorado U.S. Representative Tom Tancredo, and former Wisconsin Governor Tommy Thompson.

During the primaries, four more candidates withdrew, endorsing another party, Senator McCain, or former Arkansas Governor Mike Huckabee. These candidates included former New York City Mayor Rudy Giuliani, California U.S. Representative Duncan Hunter, U.S. Ambassador Alan Keyes, and former Tennessee Senator Fred Thompson. Of the four candidates remaining as Republican Party primary delegates, Huckabee and former governor of Massachusetts Mitt Romney withdrew to endorse Senator McCain, while Texas U.S. Representative Ron Paul endorsed the Constitution Party's Chuck Baldwin.

Three other outside party candidates were accepted on enough state ballots that they could, in theory, win a majority in the U.S. Electoral College: the Independent Party's Ralph Nader, the Libertarian Party's Georgia U.S. Representative Bob Barr, and the Green Party's former Georgia U.S. Representative Cynthia McKinney. The primaries' results marked Senator McCain as the Republican Party nominee.

Bouncing back from a loss in Iowa to former Governor Huckabee, McCain beat former Mayor Giuliani in the New Hampshire primary with 37 percent of the votes, positioning him as the Republican nominee for presidency.

With Alaska Governor Sarah Palin as McCain's running mate, the McCain-Palin ticket saw near wins in five states, ultimately losing within just one to six percentage points to Senators Barack Obama and Joe Biden. After conceding, McCain continued serving as senior U.S. Senator for Arizona.

Democratic Party candidates included two withdrawals before the primaries: Indiana Senator Evan Bayh and former Iowa Governor Tom Vilsack, who endorsed senators Obama and Hillary Clinton respectively. Former Governor Vilsack subsequently assumed the office of Secretary of Agriculture in the Obama administration. During the primaries, seven more candidates withdrew, of whom six endorsed Senator Obama and one endorsed Green Party candidate Jesse Johnson. These included Pennsylvania Senator Joe Biden, Connecticut Senator Christopher Dodd, former North Carolina Senator John Edwards, former Massachusetts Senator Mike Gravel, former Cleveland Mayor Dennis Kucinich, and New Mexico Governor Bill Richardson.

Following his withdrawal, Biden was selected as Obama's running mate and assumed the vice presidency in the Obama administration. Remaining Democratic hopefuls included most notably senators Hillary Clinton of New York and Obama of Illinois. If elected, both senators stood to mark milestones in U.S. presidential politics, with Clinton the potential first woman president and Obama the potential first African American president in history. Although Clinton possessed notable momentum, winning New Hampshire and creating a near tie with Obama on Super Tuesday, her campaign resulted in a withdrawal and endorsement for Obama. Clinton subsequently assumed the office of Secretary of State in the Obama administration.

Before winning the 2008 presidency, Barack Obama was an Illinois state senator for eight years before being elected into the U.S. Senate in 2004. With an early win in Iowa, Obama maintained a competitive presence in the Democratic race, ultimately winning the presidency with Biden as vice president. The Obama-Biden ticket won both the electoral (365 votes) and popular (53 percent) vote, making Obama the presidential candidate with the most votes in U.S. history.

In retrospect, the Republican campaign was heavily criticized as being singularly weak and led by a candidate whose historical moment, despite his many virtues as a Navy combat pilot and former prisoner of war in Vietnam, was probably a decade in the past. The traditional determining factors of the economy were inarguable; McCain's reputation as the "un-Republican" could not lift his numbers past the dismal crises of banking, unemployment, and recession.

At the same time, 2008 demonstrated the powers of new media technologies, from blogging to Facebook and YouTube. Barack Obama's team was especially adept at adapting messages to reach younger voters and those seeking out information via social media as well. His traditional methods of get-out-the-vote, fundraising, and organization were all rated highly. The resulting lesson was that, for a good candidate running in favorable circumstances and employing with skill the old and the new persuasive mechanisms, a campaign could be formidable.

Andrea M. Weare and David D. Perlmutter

See also: Campaign 2008; Federal Matching Funds; Obama, Barack

Further Reading

Day, Jonathan. 2008. "Presidential Election of 2008." In Kenneth F. Warrren, ed. *Encyclopedia of U.S. Campaigns, Elections and Electoral Behavior*. Twin Oaks, CA: Sage Publications.

Johnson, Dennis. 2008. *Campaigning for President, 2008*. New York: Routledge.

Perlmutter, David D. 2008. *Blogwars: The News Political Battleground*. New York: Oxford University Press.

Candidates, Presidential Election 2012

The 2012 presidential season saw a crowded field of Republicans who vied for a chance to unseat incumbent Democratic President Barack Obama, America's first African American chief executive. Conservatives widely believed that Obama was beatable since the nation was still emerging from the so-called Great Recession, which was widely regarded as the worst economic downturn since the Great Depression of the 1930s. The recovery that began in earnest in 2010 had been ragged since unemployment numbers dropped infuriatingly slowly. Many of the new jobs that were being created in 2012 did not pay as well as the jobs that were lost in 2008 and 2009.

Republicans were especially irritated by Obama's big-government approach to problem solving, lashing out at his American Recovery and Reinvestment Act of 2009 which pumped an estimated $830 billion in mostly borrowed money to stimulate the economy through infrastructure investment, tax incentives, and increased unemployment benefits. Another sore point for the GOP was Obama's Patient Protection and Affordable Care Act signed into law on March 23, 2010, a program offering private insurance contracts directly overseen by the federal government which mandated coverage standards, eliminated "pre-existing conditions" as a reason to deny coverage, and created tax penalties for Americans who refuse to obtain insurance. It was the most sweeping reform of the U.S. health care system since 1965, when Congress approved the Medicare and Medicaid programs.

Because of the controversies created by Obama's initiatives, concerns over rapidly rising federal debt, and irritation over the slow economic recovery, the president's approval ratings were low. The Gallup Poll reported that more American adults disapproved than approved the job Obama was doing in office throughout much of 2011 and into January of 2012.

It is hardly surprising that many nationally prominent Republicans filed papers with the Federal Election Commission announcing their intentions to seek the White House that year. Among them were the following:

- Minnesota Rep. Michele Bachmann
- Georgia businessman Herman Cain
- Former House Speaker Newt Gingrich of Georgia
- Former Utah Governor and businessman Jon Huntsman Jr.
- Former New Mexico Governor Gary Johnson
- Texas Representative Ron Paul
- Texas Gov. Rick Perry
- Former Massachusetts Gov. Mitt Romney
- Former U.S. Sen. Rick Santorum of Pennsylvania

The official list is actually much longer if candidates who failed to mount a campaign in at least two states are counted. Among them was Andy Martin of Illinois, whom the national press dismissed as a "perennial candidate" who filed a lawsuit against the State of Hawaii to disclose Obama's birth records in his attempt to prove that Obama was not a U.S.-born citizen who lawfully could hold the presidency and that he was concealing his radical Islam ties.

The field of candidates had two ties to the Libertarian Party, which, like the GOP, generally prefers free-market solutions rather than actions by a large, central government. Gary Johnson withdrew his candidacy for the Republican nomination in December 2011 and successfully sought the Libertarian Party's nomination. Johnson won nearly 1.3 million votes in the general election, which represented 1 percent of the popular vote. Johnson's candidacy was the largest vote tally for any national Libertarian candidate, although his vote percentage trailed slightly behind former Libertarian candidate Ed Clark's 1.1 percent showing in 1980.

Also in the Republican field was U.S. Rep. Ron Paul, who had been the Libertarian presidential candidate in 1988 but received only about 0.5 percent of the popular vote. He had also sought the GOP nomination for president in 2008. A physician from Duke University's School of Medicine, Paul served as a U.S. Air Force flight surgeon before locating to Texas and serving several terms in Congress. Likeable, with a gentle and grandfatherly smile, Paul actually lasted the longest of all the Republicans who challenged Mitt Romney. Although he won the popular vote only in the U.S. Virgin Islands, Paul came in second place in a number of late-voting large state primaries, including California and New York. Since he never officially released his delegates in favor of Romney at the Republican National Convention, Paul technically came in second place at the convention with about 8 percent of the delegates.

One of the first candidates to drop from the race was Michele Bachmann, a favorite of the conservative Tea Party movement. Bachmann actually won the Ames Straw Poll conducted in August 2011, but her results in the official Iowa Caucus on Jan. 4, 2012 were quite different. Bachmann came in sixth place and immediately dropped her candidacy.

Georgia businessman Herman Cain, the only black candidate in the field, appeared briefly and surprisingly to be a rising star, coming in as a front-runner in national polls in late 2011 after doing well in debates hosted by a Tea Party group and Fox News. But his campaign quickly crumbled after female employees complained of "inappropriate behavior" during his tenure as head of the National Restaurant Association, forcing the association to make financial settlements. Allegations from other women quickly emerged, including one woman who said she'd had a 13-year-long affair with him. Cain and his wife vehemently denied the charges, but Cain suspended further campaigning on December 3, 2011.

Another businessman, former Utah Governor Jon Huntsman Jr., originally got attention from the national media as an important and rising voice in the GOP. Huntsman resigned as U.S. ambassador to China in 2011 to prepare exploratory efforts for a presidential run. But he rarely polled well in the critical early months of the campaign and shut down his candidacy in mid-January after coming in third in the New Hampshire primary.

A surprising failure came from Texas Governor Rick Perry, who was actually polling as the leading contender in late summer of 2011. He touted the very low unemployment rates in Texas as proof that he was the prescription that the ailing American economy needed. However, Perry's prospects dimmed quickly with his poor performance at televised candidate debates, including a disastrous flub in November when he couldn't identify the three federal agencies he intended to eliminate upon winning the White House. (He'd forgotten that he wanted to eliminate the U.S. Department of Energy.) Perry came in fifth place in the Iowa Caucus, skipped the New Hampshire Primary entirely, and then dropped out in mid-January after polls showed him trailing in South Carolina.

That left three serious Republican contenders who'd slug it out for several months: Newt Gingrich, Mitt Romney, and Rick Santorum. What followed was a lengthy, expensive, and protracted slugfest between three prominent conservatives who all had very negative political baggage. Many GOP political strategists have said the Romney-Santorum-Gingrich struggle doomed Republican chances to unseat Obama since the three men had to unload unflattering attacks against the other two for months.

Gingrich was once widely praised as the architect of the "Contract with America" campaign that brought Republicans to power in the House of Representatives in 1995 and made him Speaker of the House, a position third in line for presidential succession under the Constitution. But standoffs with President Bill Clinton prompted leadership mistakes that led to unpopular government shutdowns in 1995 and 1996. The resulting poor showing by Republicans in the 1998 midterm election and allegations of ethics violations forced Gingrich to resign both his speakership in late 1998 and his House seat in 1999. When Gingrich declared for the presidency in 2012, he performed poorly in both Iowa and New Hampshire but clung on until the Southern primaries. He won in South Carolina after strong debate performances but fell flat in Florida. He came in second place in five states and third in 11 more, but, financially stretched by Romney's well-funded campaign, Gingrich officially ended his campaign on May 2, 2012.

Rick Santorum's campaign posed the greatest threat to Romney even though Santorum had lost his Pennsylvania Senate seat in 2006 after having to defend many of his social conservative proposals and statements. A staunch abortion opponent, Santorum had written a book in which he compared pro-choice voters to "Nazi Germans" and denounced what he called "radical feminism." He also had proposed a 2001 amendment to the No Child Left Behind Act that would promote teaching "intelligent design" while questioning evolution. These positions probably helped him with many Republican primary voters in 2012. He won the Iowa Caucus and then went on to victories in Alabama, Colorado, Kansas,

Louisiana, Minnesota, Mississippi, Missouri, North Dakota, Oklahoma, and Tennessee. But, like Gingrich, Romney's relentless campaign wore down Santorum's hopes. Santorum suspended his campaign on April 10, about three weeks earlier than did Gingrich.

That Mitt Romney, an intelligent, well-spoken, and attractive Republican from Massachusetts had so much difficulty defeating baggage-laden opponents like Santorum and Gingrich is a testimony to one of his central problems: Conservatives suspected Romney was a closet moderate. The GOP's rank-and-file hated that Romney has signed into law the Massachusetts health care reform bill that Obama touted as the model for the Affordable Care Act. That he was a Mormon also didn't sit well with much of the party's white Protestant base in the South and Midwest. Nevertheless, Romney ran a disciplined, well-funded campaign that showed few missteps.

Romney mathematically clinched his party's nomination after he won in Texas on May 29. The New Englander had also carried primaries or caucuses in Alaska, Arizona, Arkansas, California, Connecticut, Delaware, Florida, Hawaii, Idaho, Illinois, Indiana, Kentucky, Maine, Maryland, Massachusetts, Michigan, Montana, Nebraska, Nevada, New Hampshire, New Jersey, New Mexico, New York, North Carolina, Ohio, Oregon, Pennsylvania, Rhode Island, South Dakota, Utah, Vermont, Virginia, Washington, West Virginia, Wisconsin, and Wyoming.

"Our party has come together with the goal of putting the failures of the last three and a half years behind us," Romney said after winning in Texas. "I have no illusions about the difficulties of the task before us. But whatever challenges lie ahead, we will settle for nothing less than getting America back on the path to full employment and prosperity."

But Romney went on to be defeated by Obama on November 6 in an election that, once again, demonstrated a Democratic advantage in presidential elections because of overwhelming support by women and racial and ethnic minorities.

Thomas K. Hargrove

See also: Campaign 2008; Campaign 2012; Federal Matching Funds; Obama, Barack

Further Reading

Balz, Dan. 2013. *Collision 2012: The Future of Election Politics in a Divided America.* New York: Viking.
Halperin, Mark, and John Heilemann. 2013. *Double Down: Game Change in 2012.* New York: The Penguin Press.

Catholic Voters

See Roman Catholic Voters

Censorship

A common misperception in the United States is that any obstruction to the publication of one's expression is "censorship." For example, if a newspaper removes a person's post to its online comments forum, some might call that an act of "censorship"—but that would be a gross exaggeration. In a free society, people and organizations have as much right to say "no" as they do to say "yes," and that of course applies to editorial decisions made by news media under the freedom-of-the-press protections granted by the First Amendment. Choosing not to publish, therefore, is not "censorship," but "choice." Actual censorship involves government restrictions on public communication.

Probably the most well-known form of legal censorship in the United States is classification of certain government documents. Classified information is not censored entirely—it can still be reviewed by individuals with sufficient security clearances, or "classification." (For example, the U.S. Secretary of State will have access to information that is not accessible by undersecretaries, who in turn will have access to some information not available to lower-level support staff in the same department.) The classification of specific information can be challenged via the Freedom of Information Act, or FOIA, and as such may eventually be released. At the federal level, the FOIA applies only to the executive branch of government, and documents held by members of Congress are essentially exempt from compulsory disclosure. A loophole of the law mandates that the government can only release documents that are known to exist; therefore, members of the public rarely are successful in obtaining top-secret documents via FOIA actions.

Another type of formal censorship in the United States is redaction. Redaction is used to black out passages in certain documents before the documents are released. Redactions typically obscure individual phrases or numbers, such as the Social Security numbers of citizens or the home addresses in personnel records of certain public employees, such as police officers. Typically, federal and state laws stipulate what information may be (or must be) redacted before documents are released to the public.

A third form of legal censorship in the United States is public-disclosure exemptions. Exemptions apply at both the federal and state levels, and are typically included in laws regulating the handling of public records. The federal FOIA enumerates exemptions, most of which relate to matters of national security, personal information of employees, and intellectual property. Individual states may have varied exemptions to public-records laws, although the general practice is that governmental records must be disclosed unless there is an enumerated exemption in the law. For example, personnel records of employees at public universities are considered "public records" in Ohio but not in Iowa. State-level exemptions may be expanded or reduced in response to federal laws (e.g., federal laws regarding health- care records or the academic records of college students) or as the outcome of lawsuits seeking to open or restrict access to records.

A fourth form of governmental censorship in the United States is regulation of content of certain media forms. In general, such censorship is reactive and punitive rather than proactive and restrictive—that is, the government does not block publication of the unlawful content, but rather can impose fines or other penalties on violators. Governmental regulation of content in the United States generally regulates only certain forms of commercial communication—specifically, advertising of certain products, such as tobacco, alcohol, and prescription medications—and certain forms of communication that are not considered "protected speech," such as pornography or threats of violence. In addition, the Federal Communications Commission (FCC) enforces laws aimed at curbing "obscenity, indecency and profanity" over public airwaves.

The fifth form of formal governmental censorship in the United States falls under the broad concept of "executive privilege." Whereas classification, redaction, exemption, and regulation are used, generally, to obstruct public and/or media access to information, executive privilege can have a direct effect on certain forms of media, particularly media produced under the authority of government agencies, such as branches of the military and public schools. In regard to the latter, high-school principals have the legal authority to censor the content of student-produced media produced in school classes, stemming from a 1988 Supreme Court case, *Hazelwood School District v. Kuhlmeier.* The authority has been diminished over time by changes in state laws granting "public forum" status to student publications and subsequent legal challenges to specific acts of censorship.

In addition to legally implemented censorship, authorities in the United States sometimes engage in various forms of so-called "soft censorship." Soft censorship occurs when government agencies impose political or financial pressure on individuals or groups in veiled attempts to discourage unfavorable coverage. For example, in 2012, the Student Activity Fee committee at the University of Memphis voted to slash the budget of the campus's student newspaper because committee members did not approve of some of the newspaper's journalistic decisions. A much more common form of soft censorship is when police obstruct or arrest journalists from doing their jobs. Even though the charges are typically dropped eventually, the short-term goal of censoring journalists is often accomplished. Just as with legally sanctioned censorship, improper or soft censorship can take moments to accomplish and years to overcome, which is why news media, professional journalism organizations, and civil-rights/government-accountability organizations in the United States routinely challenge even seemingly minor attempts by government to censor public information.

Bill Reader

See also: Freedom of Information Act

Further Reading

Brulote, Michael. 2013. *Censorship, Liberty and Truth.* Seattle: Amazon Digital Services.
Cohen, Nick. 2012. *You Can't Read This Book: Censorship in the Age of Freedom.* New York: HarperCollins.

Church and State

The American Constitution in upholding the principle of church/state separation provides a path to civic equality across society. Accordingly, no person is to be denied because of their religious beliefs the basic liberties guaranteed to all citizens.

The separation principle is discernible in America as early as the colonial period. Martha Nussbaum, a philosopher and legal ethics scholar at the University of Chicago, says that not all colonial governments established a government-backed religion. Those that did taxed citizens to support the established church and denied opportunities to hold public office to non-church members. Dissenters believed that these circumstances ran afoul of religious liberty and of the equal treatment of citizens.

This outlook set the stage for incorporating the separation principle into the United States Constitution and for the associated embrace of civic equality. Thus, the First Amendment says, "Congress shall make no law respecting an establishment of religion, or prohibiting the free exercise thereof." President Thomas Jefferson in his letter to the Connecticut Danbury Baptist Association in 1802 referred to this clause as the basis for the American people "building a wall of separation between church and state." The government is neither to establish a religion, nor to repudiate peoples' religious freedom. To do otherwise is to jeopardize the core freedoms that, along with religious liberty, are critical to the achievement of civic equality. These core freedoms, as specified in the First Amendment, are the freedoms "of speech" and "of the press" as well as the rights of "the people peaceably to assemble, and to petition the Government for a redress of grievances."

The separation principle is connected to civic equality not only through the freedoms just cited but also through what Nussbaum describes as an American tradition that houses a strong "argument for religious liberty and equality." This argument commences "from a special respect for" the mental faculty called conscience, which all possess. Conscience provides people an opportunity to "search for life's ultimate meaning" and thereby acquire a sense of substantive self-worth. So critical is this experience that it elicits an obligation to treat all individuals as equals, deserving the opportunity to pursue religious beliefs arising from conscience. A protective setting for conscience is secured through a government that guarantees each person religious freedom and equal status under law, key elements of civil equality.

A major challenge to the separation principle emerges here. Achieving equal status under law requires that the laws be applied to all citizens, without exception. Thus, it is not legitimate to receive an exemption from taxes because of one's distaste for certain government policies. Yet, people in the name of the First Amendment's separation principle often seek exemptions from laws said to cover all citizens.

Nussbaum says that the Supreme Court has not always agreed with this view. The Court rejected a request of a Native American group to use peyote in religious ceremonies on the grounds that if the government decides, as a matter of a "compelling state interest," that certain types of conduct should be proscribed then requests for exemptions based on religious beliefs are not justified.

Nonetheless, as Nussbaum makes clear, there is a tendency for the Supreme Court to protect individual observance of religious creeds, even when doing so requires exemptions from established laws. For instance, the Court upheld the view that school children whose religion requires that they not salute the American flag should not be forced to do so; that a person terminated for refusing work on Saturday, her Sabbath, was exempted on religious grounds from losing her job; that an exemption from New York state taxes for non-profit religious and non-religious organizations is permissible to treat both equally; and that for religious reasons parents can keep their children from attending the last two years of high school.

On what basis are exemptions granted in Court decisions? Nussbaum says the Court has ruled that the state may institute a "substantial burden" on the exercise of religious liberty only to serve a "compelling state interest," as opposed to a mundane one. Moreover, laws fashioned by this intent must be "narrowly tailored" to advance the state's interest in the "least burdensome manner possible." The Court provided further guidance in another case by ruling that statutes affecting religion should be shaped to promote a secular agenda both by not prohibiting or advancing religion and by not enmeshing the government in religion.

Despite these standards, the question of the conditions under which exemptions are legitimate remains. To explain why, start with the presumption that a decent society complies with high ethical principles like the advancement of social justice. Robert Bellah says that citizens' support for such principles and for the public policies based on them is motivated by a personal commitment to religious convictions common to all religions in American society. Bellah calls this relationship between religion and ethics a "civil religion," and in 1975 he wrote that the American civil religion was "an empty and broken shell." Given the contemporary absence of consensus on what constitutes the civil religion, the same claim can be made about today's society. Liberals seek a civil religion that incorporates the demands of minorities, gays, women, and immigrants for social justice. Conservatives worry that this agenda may forsake justice by overlooking what they perceive as morally justified restrictions on matters such as reproductive choice and same sex unions.

In this setting, even if it can be shown that many Americans from diverse religious traditions share overlapping religious convictions and a belief in the separation principle, political controversies on where to draw the line on exemptions will continue.

Steven M. DeLue

See also: Evangelicalism; Fundamentalism; Roman Catholic Voters

Further Reading

Bellah, Robert N. 1975. *The Broken Covenant: American Civil Religion in Time of Trial.* New York: Seabury Press.

Nussbaum, Martha C. 2008. *Liberty of Conscience: In Defense of America's Tradition of Religious Equality.* New York: Basic Books.

Class (Economic) Voting

How powerful are the influences of wealth, poverty, and social class upon how Americans vote and, ultimately, upon how political power is apportioned?

American political scientist Robert A. Dahl of Yale University laid down the question in his famous book *Who Governs?* which examined political power in the late 1950s in New Haven, Connecticut. He asked, "In a political system where nearly every adult may vote but where knowledge, wealth, social position, access to officials and other resources are unequally distributed, who actually governs?" Dahl concluded that power was surprisingly widely dispersed among a complex and sometimes counter-balancing series of coalitions throughout that city. He found pluralist leadership through what is sometimes called "polyarchy" or a "rule of many."

Larry Bartels of Vanderbilt University cited Dahl's work in his 2008 book, *Unequal Democracy,* even as he rejected many of its conclusions. "The political process has evolved in ways that seem likely to reinforce the advantages of wealth. Political campaigns have become dramatically more expensive since the 1950s, increasing the reliance of elected officials on people who can afford to help finance their bids for re-election," Bartels concludes. The rise of sophisticated lobbying efforts by corporations and professional organizations has outpaced the efforts of dwindling labor unions and public interest groups, he said.

The American Political Science Association in 2004 convened a Task Force on Inequality and American Democracy, which concluded that political scientists know "astonishingly little" about the effects of growing economic inequality upon democracy in the United States. But the group did express concerns that "rising economic inequality will solidify longstanding disparities in political voice and influence, and perhaps exacerbate such disparities."

At first glance, the impact of economic class upon voting behavior is enormous. In the 2008 presidential election, for example, only 52 percent of voters with family incomes of $20,000 or less cast a ballot while the voting rate among people with family incomes of $100,000 or more was 73 percent. People in the lowest economic cohort voted for the Democratic presidential candidate (Barack Obama) 64 percent of the time. But Obama's support fell to 49 percent among voters in the highest economic cohort, although he was tied with his Republican challenger among this group.

Economic class politics is often exploited by politicians (see Class Warfare Politics) when they make their appeals to voters by boasting of policies aimed at different class groups. But economic class is not always a simple explanation for how Americans actually vote. Emory University political scientist Alan I. Abramowitz used the 2012 American National Election Study of 4,000 voters to analyze the effects of class. He concluded that, "Upper and lower-income Americans did not differ very much in either their presidential voting decisions or their opinions on a variety of major policy issues including government spending. Other characteristics such as race, partisanship and religion had much stronger effects on American's political attitudes and behavior in 2012."

A voter's race seemed to be a much better predictor of voting behavior in 2012 than their economic status, Abramowitz found. Black voters overwhelmingly supported the reelection of President Obama, regardless of their economic status. White voters tended to support Republican Mitt Romney, with the highest level of support among white families in the lower (but not bottom) economic range. The only exception was among Hispanic voters, for whom support for Romney was nearly nonexistent among the poorest families and reached above 40 percent among the wealthiest.

Another big dividing line was religion. White voters who regularly attend religious services overwhelmingly voted for the Republicans in 2012, while whites who rarely or never go to church were likely to support Obama. These trends were not particularly influenced by economic class, however. Devout affluent white voters were generally less likely to support Romney than were less affluent devout whites. Obama did better among the most affluent non-observant voters than among middle-class non-observant voters. When issues like race and religion are taken into consideration, personal economics seems to play a much reduced role in determining how Americans vote.

There is not much doubt that income inequality has been increasing in the United States in recent decades as the so-called "super rich" possess a rising share of the nation's wealth. At the same time, much of the American middle class has felt an economic squeeze that threatens to bring them closer to the lower economic rungs. There is also general agreement that Americans are becoming more politically polarized, as voters who lean Democratic or Republican are becoming less likely to identify their political philosophies as "moderate."

But economic class is a poor predictor of voting behavior, especially when other factors like race and religion are considered. College graduates, especially young Americans who've attained advanced degrees, are becoming much more Democratic than Americans without a four-year degree.

"The clear implication of these findings is that growing income inequality cannot, as some have argued, explain growing partisan polarization in the American electorate," Abramowitz concludes. "Americans today are more deeply divided along party lines than at any time in recent history, but those divisions have little to do with social class."

Thomas K. Hargrove

See also: Class Warfare Politics

Further Reading

Abramowitz, Alan I. 2014 "The Minimal Class Divide in American Politics: Why Growing Economic Inequality Does Not Explain Partisan Polarization." University of Virginia's Center for Politics. http://www.centerforpolitics.org/crystalball/articles/the-minimal-class-divide-in-american-politics. Accessed October 13, 2014.

Bartels, Larry M. 2008. *Unequal Democracy: The Political Economy of the New Gilded Age.* Princeton, NJ: Princeton University Press.

Dahl, Robert A., and Douglas W. Rae. 2005. *Who Governs? Democracy and Power in an American City.* 2nd ed. New Haven, CT: Yale University Press.

Jacobs, Lawrence. 2004. "American Democracy in an Age of Rising Inequality." Published online by the American Political Science Association. http://oldapsa.apsanet.org/imgtest/taskforcereport.pdf. Accessed October 13, 2014.

Class Warfare Politics

Americans often divide along economic class lines on Election Day, when rich voters and poor voters frequently cast their ballots quite differently. But when politicians craft their appeals to voters in ways that target specific economic groups, such appeals can be criticized for engendering class warfare—an attempt to exploit the political tensions that occur between affluent and impoverished voters.

Defenders of class conflict rhetoric argue that politics offers disadvantaged voters a chance, perhaps their only chance, to seek redress for unfair conditions that ensure their impoverishment. Critics say class warfare rhetoric is essentially un-American since it urges voters to cast their ballots according to their economic status rather than their personal beliefs of governance.

The Founding Fathers recognized class struggles even in the earliest days of the Republic when the gap between rich and poor was not especially large, at least by modern standards. Thomas Jefferson famously wrote in 1787 that most European governments "under pretense of governing have divided their nations into two classes, wolves and sheep. . . . Experience declares that man is the only animal which devours his own kind, for I can apply no milder term to the governments of Europe and to the general prey of the rich on the poor."

Concerns about poverty can play a powerful role in American politics. "I pledge you, I pledge myself, to a new deal for the American people," Franklin D. Roosevelt said in 1932 when accepting the Democratic Party's nomination for president for the first time. The New Deal became an unprecedented attempt by the federal government to combat the poverty created by the Great Depression. FDR fashioned what political scientists have come to call the "New Deal coalition," in which people on government relief, blue collar workers, and racial and ethnic minorities coalesced with many others into a powerful voting bloc.

Class warfare politics drew new life in the 2012 presidential election in which President Barack Obama, America's first black chief executive, sought reelection over Republican former Massachusetts Governor Mitt Romney, himself a multimillionaire venture capitalist.

Obama took obvious glee in reminding voters early and often that he faced a very wealthy opponent during a campaign season when America was still recovering from the Great Recession of 2008 and 2009, the nation's worst economic downturn since the Depression. The president often focused his campaign on the different tax policies the two candidates espoused. "My opponent thinks that someone who makes $20 million a year, like him, should pay a lower rate than a cop or a teacher who makes $50,000," Obama told voters at a campaign stop in Virginia Beach.

Romney sought to undermine the class warfare debate in the early days of the campaign. "You know, I think it's about envy. I think it's about class warfare," Romney told the NBC *Today* show audience in January. "When you have a president encouraging the idea of dividing America based on the 99 percent versus 1 percent—and those people who have been most successful will be in the 1 percent—you have opened up a whole new wave of approach in this country which is entirely inconsistent with the concept of one nation under God. The American people, I believe in the final analysis, will reject it." He would go on throughout the campaign to complain about Obama's class warfare politics.

The president drew sharp criticism for another Virginia speech he gave in Roanoke on July 13, 2012, when he again asked rich Americans to pay higher taxes. "There are a lot of wealthy, successful Americans who agree with me—because they want to give something back. They know they didn't—look, if you've been successful, you didn't get there on your own. If you were successful, somebody along the line gave you some help."

Romney blasted back almost immediately. "I'm convinced he wants Americans to be ashamed of success," the Republican told a crowd in Pennsylvania. "I don't want government to take credit for what individuals accomplish."

If what became known as Obama's "You Didn't Build That" speech was a mistake, Romney would go on to make a much larger one of his own through a video that surfaced in late July of remarks he made in May at a private fund-raising even held in Florida.

"There are 47 percent of the people who will vote for the president no matter what. All right, there are 47 percent who are with him, who are dependent upon government, who believe that they are victims, who believe the government has a responsibility to care for them, who believe that they are entitled to health care, to food, to housing, to you-name-it. That that's an entitlement. And the government should give it to them," Romney said.

Romney was probably correct that a significant percentage of Americans are locked into their choices for president according to their political party inclinations. But he went on to describe nearly half of the nation as freeloaders. Worse, he was inciting the very class warfare politics he had criticized Obama for using.

Obama referenced the "47 percent" speech in the final minutes of the October 16 television presidential toward the end of the campaign. "When my grandfather fought in World War II and he came back and got a GI Bill that allowed him to go to college, that wasn't a handout—that was something that advanced the entire country," Obama said. "I want to make sure that the next generation has those same opportunities. That's why I'm asking for your vote and that's why I'm asking for another four years."

If the 2012 presidential campaign was a demonstration of class warfare, it clearly favored the Democrats. Republican candidates in the future will need new tactics when challenged by the politics of class.

Thomas K. Hargrove

See also: Class (Economic) Voting

Further Reading

Balz, Dan. 2013. *Collision 2012: Obama v. Romney and the Future of Elections in America.* New York: Viking.

Editorial Board of the *New York Times.* 2012. "Mitt Romney, Class Warrior." *The New York Times,* September 18.

Thrush, Glenn, and Jonathan Martin. 2012. *The End of the Line: Romney v. Obama: The 34 Days that Decided the Election.* New York: Random House.

Clear and Present Danger Doctrine

The Clear and Present Danger Doctrine introduced limitations on freedom of expression if they are necessary to prevent serious and imminent harm to society. The doctrine and its related progeny today provide guidelines about when and how government may restrict inflammatory expression, including written, spoken, broadcast, online, and even symbolic expression.

Since the passage of the Bill of Rights in 1791, the U.S. Constitution has contained basic guarantees for press, speech, and assembly, specifically as it relates to public discussion about political and social issues. However, as the nation has faced political and security crises, the highest court has supported limitations on expression when convinced that speech might harm social order or national security.

During World War I, Congress enacted the Espionage Act of 1917, which outlawed any attempt to "interfere with the operation or success of the military or naval forces or the United States . . . to cause insubordination . . . in the military or naval forces . . . or willfully obstruct the recruiting or enlistment service of the United States."

In 1919, the U.S. Supreme Court heard the first of challenges to the law in *Schenk v. United States.* Schenk was charged under the law because he had 15,000 pamphlets printed urging resistance to the draft. Justice Oliver Wendell Holmes wrote for the unanimous court that the government had a duty to restrict speech that represented a "clear and present danger" to the nation. Holmes's test is significant because it is one of the earliest examples of the court's willingness to recognize legitimate limits to free speech.

Justice Holmes wrote that Schenk had a right to distribute the pamphlets and say what he said "in many places and in ordinary times." However, he said circumstances dictate the limits of free speech.

Among the most-often quoted phrases from the decision is: "The most stringent protection of free speech would not protect a man in falsely shouting fire in a theatre and causing a panic." Justice Holmes compared that scenario to a nation at war. "When a nation is at war, many things that might be said in time of peace are such a hindrance to its effort that their utterance will not be endured so long as men fight and that no Court could regard them as protected by any constitutional right."

Holmes asserted that when the nation it as war the government should have the power to prevent speech that might harm military recruitment. Therefore, it also has the power to punish someone who uses speech to obstruct the draft.

"The question in every case is whether the words are used in such circumstances and are of such a nature as to create a clear and present danger that they will bring about the substantive evils that Congress has a right to prevent," Holmes wrote.

Uncomfortable with the standard, the court only employed Holmes's Clear and Present Danger Test in Schenk and another post-World War I case until retreating to a more regressive Bad Tendency Test. The test emphasized the defendant's intentions and the tendency of the potential expression to cause illegal actions.

In the 1940s, the court moved away from the Bad Tendency Test's focus on potential harm to society to "preferred freedoms," which weighted personal rights guaranteed in the Constitution and Bill of Rights. However, the Court has never gone as far to adopt a stance of First Amendment "absolutism," which reads the First Amendment as absolute "Congress shall make no law . . . abridging the freedom of speech, or of the press. . . ."

Absolutist Justice Hugo Black said that First Amendment freedoms could not be "balanced" against other governmental goals. He said that speakers should never be punished for what they say. They may, however, be punished for the place, time, or way in which they say it.

By 1951 the Supreme Court again modified the Clear and Present Danger Doctrine with the so-called Clear and Probable Danger Test. In *Dennis v. United States*, the court ruled "Whether the gravity of the 'evil,' discounted by it improbability, justifies such an invasion of free speech as is necessary to avoid danger."

First Amendment scholars have noted a correlation between the severity of a national crisis and the degree of restrictions the Supreme Court has imposed on freedom of expression. That comes despite strong language in many decisions advocating the preservation of a free marketplace of ideas and protecting a robust public debate.

In 1969, the court adopted the Brandenburg Test in *Brandenburg v. Ohio*. The decision drew a bright-line distinction between simply advocating violence or inciting imminent illegal or violent activity. The Brandenburg Test requires that the expression be directed toward inciting immediate violence or illegal action and is likely to produce that action. The case remains the guiding doctrine today.

Actions that may trigger government regulation of expression include violence, property damage, criminal speech, encroaching on the rights of others, burdens on government functions, trespassing, and forms of expression considered outside the scope of the First Amendment, including strictly defined libel and obscenity.

Joel J. Campbell

See also: Constitution, First Amendment

Further Reading

Hentoff, Nat. 2012. *First Freedom: The Tumultuous History of Free Speech in America*. New York: Delacorte Press.
Sunstein, Cass R. 1995. *Democracy and the Problem of Free Speech*. New York: The Free Press.

Climate Change

One of the more vexing political issues in the United States and in many other developed nations in recent decades has been the appropriate governmental response to the world's changing climate. The debate centers primarily on a simple statistical fact: the world is getting warmer.

The U.S. Environmental Protection Agency estimates the average temperature of the Earth has risen 1.4 degrees Fahrenheit over the last century and is projected to rise anywhere from 2 to 11 degrees Fahrenheit during the next 100 years. As a result, the world's ice caps are melting, sea levels are rising, and global weather patterns are changing with many areas experiencing increased rainfall and flooding while others experience droughts and severe heat waves.

What has been in dispute, however, is the cause of this change. A few scientists and many mostly conservative political leaders have said these changes may be the result of natural fluctuations in global weather. The preponderance of scientific thought and most liberal and moderate political leaders have come to believe that human activity is responsible for the atmosphere's measurable increase in carbon dioxide and other greenhouse gases produced, primarily, from the almost unrestricted burning of fossil fuels like coal and petroleum to produce energy.

The United States' National Research Council issued findings in 2010 after several years of review of the climate change issue. The group noted that there are still some uncertainties in understanding anything as complex as the Earth's climate. "Nevertheless, there is a strong, credible body of evidence, based on multiple lines of research, documenting that climate is changing and that these changes are in large part caused by human activities," the group said. "While much remains to be learned, the core phenomenon, scientific questions, and hypotheses have been examined thoroughly and have stood firm in the face of serious scientific debate and careful evaluation of alternative explanations."

The research council also warned that recognizing the human sources of climate change is "crucial because it allows decisions makers to place climate change in the context of other large challenges facing the nation and the world."

But taking action within a democratic government, almost any action, tends to elicit counter responses by opposing political parties. It has certainly been true for environmental policy. Since Democrats have become the pro-environmental party, the GOP has become advocates for protecting U.S. business interests from aggressive government regulation. The growing gridlock in Congress prevented U.S. ratification of the 1997 Kyoto Protocol on climate change, a result of the United Nations Conference on the Environment and Development held five years earlier in Rio de Janeiro.

Australian academic Clive Hamilton said that the failure to act on global warming results from campaigns waged by companies such as ExxonMobil and General Motors who are responsible for the "sustained and often ruthless exercise of political power by the corporations who stand to lose from a shift to low- and zero-carbon energy systems."

Republicans cried foul in 2009 when the EPA, under President Barack Obama, declared that it had found "compelling and overwhelming" scientific evidence that carbon dioxide and five other heat-trapping gases endanger public health and welfare, invoking its regulatory powers under the Clean Air Act. Many congressional Republicans accused the Obama administration of overreaching its constitutional authority and of following policies that would increase energy costs and kill jobs in an economy that was just beginning to emerge from the Great Recession.

The climate change issue was raised repeatedly during the 2012 Republican primary season when moderate former Massachusetts Gov. Mitt Romney had to fend off attacks from more conservative Republicans over his environmental policies. Romney wrote in his 2010 book *No Apology: The Case for American Greatness*, "I believe that climate change is occurring—the reduction in the size of global ice caps is hard to ignore. I also believe that human activity is a contributing factor. I am uncertain how much of the warming, however, is attributable to factors out of our control."

Former Republican Sen. Rick Santorum of Pennsylvania criticized Romney's positions for supporting a cap-and-trade policy in New England. "I've never supported even the hoax of global warming," Santorum said.

Romney had to tread a difficult verbal path on the environment during the latter phases of the presidential campaign. "Do I think the world's getting hotter? Yeah, I don't know that, but I think that it is. I don't know if it's mostly caused by humans," he said during a campaign event August 24 in Lebanon, New Hampshire. "What I'm not willing to do is spend trillions of dollars on something I don't know the answer to."

The 2012 Republican National Platform took a stronger stand on Obama's environmental policies. "We will end the EPA's war on coal," the platform proclaimed. It also lashed out at Obama's National Security Strategy which the GOP said "subordinates our national security interests to environmental, energy, and international health issues and elevates 'climate change' to the level of a 'severe threat' equivalent to foreign aggression. The word 'climate' in fact appears in the current president's strategy more often than Al Qaeda, nuclear proliferation, radical Islam, or weapons of mass destruction."

But the GOP's stand on the environment was clearly troubling to many conservatives. New York City Mayor Michael Bloomberg, who became a Republican in 2001 to run for mayor and then switched to independent status in 2007, surprised many New Yorkers when he announced a few days before the 2012 general election that he was endorsing Obama in the wake of Superstorm Sandy, which caused extensive damage in New Jersey and New York.

"Our climate is changing," Bloomberg said. "And while the increase in extreme weather we have experienced in New York City and around the world may or may not be the result of it, the risk that it may be—given the devastation it is wreaking—should be enough to compel all elected leaders to take immediate action."

By 2014 the Democratic president was feeling secure enough about his environmental policies to openly chide the GOP's opposition. "In Congress, folks will tell you climate change is a hoax or a fad or a plot. A liberal plot," he told the League of Conservation Voters meeting in June of 2014. "They say, hey, I'm not a scientist, which really translates into: 'I accept that manmade climate change is real, but if I say so out loud, I will be run out of town by a bunch of fringe elements that thinks climate science is a liberal plot so I'm going to just pretend like, I don't know, I can't read.'"

Thomas K. Hargrove

See also: Environmentalism

Further Reading

Hamilton, Clive. 2010. *Requiem for a Species: Why We Resist the Truth About Climate Change*. New York: Earthscan.

Hernandez, Raymond. 2012. "Bloomberg Backs Obama, Citing Fallout from Storm." *The New York Times*, November 1.
National Research Council. 2010. *America's Climate Choices: Panel on Advancing the Science of Climate Change.* Washington, DC: The National Academies Press.

Clinton, Hillary Rodham (1947–)

Attorney, former first lady (1993–2001), U.S. senator (2001– 2009), presidential candidate in 2008, and secretary of state (2009–2013), Hillary Diane Rodham was born on October 26, 1947, in Chicago and was raised in Park Ridge, a prosperous Chicago suburb. Her family was staunchly Republican, and during the 1964 presidential campaign, while still a high school student, she actively campaigned for Republican nominee Barry Goldwater. She entered Wellesley College in 1965, and by 1968 she had become disenchanted with Republican politics and the Vietnam War. In 1968 she supported the Democratic antiwar presidential candidate Eugene McCarthy; the following year she graduated with a degree in political science.

Rodham enrolled at Yale Law School, where she met fellow student Bill Clinton, whom she would later marry. Graduating in 1973, she took a position with a child-advocacy group. The next year she served as a staff attorney for the House Committee on the Judiciary during the Watergate Scandal that caused President Richard Nixon to resign in 1974. In 1975, she wed Bill Clinton.

In 1976, Bill Clinton launched his political career when he was elected attorney general of Arkansas. The next year, Hillary Clinton joined the Rose Law Firm, the premier legal firm in Arkansas, where she specialized in intellectual property law and continued pro-bono child advocacy legal work. Bill Clinton became governor of Arkansas in January 1979, the same year that Hillary Clinton became a full partner in the Rose Law Firm, the first woman to achieve such status. In 1980 Bill Clinton lost a reelection bid but was reelected in 1982; Hillary Clinton was again the first lady of Arkansas, an informal post that she would hold until her husband became president in January 1993. She continued her legal work and was active on several boards, including those of Arkansas-based Wal-Mart as well as Lafarge and TCBY.

Taking a leave of absence from the Rose Law Firm to help her husband campaign for the presidency in 1992, Clinton proved to be a formidable campaigner, repeatedly weathering allegations that her husband had engaged in extramarital affairs. After Bill Clinton upset incumbent president George H.W. Bush in the November 1992 elections, Hillary Clinton became first lady in January 1993. She was an activist first lady, certainly more so than any of her immediate predecessors. Some pundits likened her to Eleanor Roosevelt, but it quickly became clear that Clinton would be a far more influential first lady than even Roosevelt.

Hillary Clinton's role in White House policy-making was derided by the right wing of the Republican Party, and even some mainstream Democrats openly questioned her central role in decision making. In 1993 her husband named her chairperson of the Task Force on National Health Care Reform, a move that, in retrospect, was probably not wise. Many questioned Hillary Clinton's motives, and the secrecy in which she conducted much of the task force's business only added to the public's skepticism. In the end, her health care plan was deemed too bureaucratic and too burdensome for business. The plan died in Congress and became a major campaign boon to the Republicans in the 1994 elections, which saw the Democrats lose their control of Congress. Despite the setback, Hillary Clinton actively promoted certain national legislation, including the State Children's Health Insurance Program in 1997. She traveled widely, ultimately visiting 79 nations.

Clinton was at the epicenter of the fruitless Whitewater investigation, a Republican-inspired inquiry into a decade-old land deal in which the Clintons had been involved in Arkansas. As such, she became the only first lady to be subpoenaed by a federal grand jury. Although years of probing and $50 million of taxpayers' money went into the Whitewater inquiry, neither Clinton was found to have engaged in any illegal activity. Unfortunately, however, Whitewater revealed a sexual dalliance between Bill Clinton and a White House intern, Monica Lewinsky, that mortified Hillary Clinton and led to the president's impeachment in December 1998. While Mrs. Clinton's allegation that the persecution of her and her husband was the result of a "vast right-wing conspiracy" may have been hyperbole, there can be little doubt that the Clintons were subjected to endlessly harsh scrutiny and criticism, particularly by Republicans and other detractors.

In 2000 the Clintons purchased a home in New York, and Hillary Clinton ran for the state's senatorial seat being vacated by retiring U.S. senator Daniel Patrick Moynihan. Clinton was at first running against popular New York City mayor Rudolph Giuliani, and many believed that her chances of winning were not good. But after Giuliani dropped out of the race because of health problems, Clinton—now running against Rick Lazio, a relatively unknown congressman—was virtually assured a win. Clinton won the election by an impressive 12-point margin and took office in January 2001.

During her first term, Clinton maintained a relatively low profile but garnered high marks for her intellect, excellent grasp of issues, and willingness to work in a bipartisan manner. Following the September 11, 2001, terror attacks on the United States, Clinton strongly backed the George W. Bush administration's response, including Operation Enduring Freedom in Afghanistan and the 2001 Patriot Act. In October 2002, Clinton voted with the majority to grant the Bush administration authority to wage war in Iraq to enforce United Nations (UN) resolutions should diplomacy fail. She did not support an amendment that would have required another congressional resolution to invade Iraq. Meanwhile, Clinton visited both Afghanistan and Iraq to gauge the effectiveness of the U.S. war efforts there.

By 2005, already planning a run for the presidency in 2008, Clinton began to publicly criticize the Iraq war effort, noting the growing insurgency and the absence of firm plans to either extricate the United States from Iraq or quash the insurgents. She was careful to state, however, that a precipitous withdrawal was unwise if not dangerous, a position that chagrined many antiwar Democrats. Clinton did not back any of the Bush tax cuts, viewing them as economic grenades that would derail the economy, nor did she vote for Bush's two Supreme Court nominees, John Roberts and Samuel Alito.

In November 2006 Clinton, now quite popular with New York voters, won a landslide reelection. In early 2007 she began transferring leftover funds from her Senate race to her presidential campaign. On January 20, 2007, she announced her intention to form an exploratory committee for the 2008 presidential contest. That same year, she refused to support the Bush administration's troop surge in Iraq and backed unsuccessful legislation that would have forced the president to withdraw troops from Iraq based on a predetermined time line. Forced to deal with her affirmative vote for the Iraq War, Clinton now had to explain that she probably would have voted against the 2002 resolution had she been privy to accurate and reliable intelligence. Her position change left many wondering why she had taken so long to come to such a conclusion.

By the autumn of 2007, Clinton seemed the person to beat amid a large Democratic presidential field. Following a mediocre performance in a debate in October, Clinton's momentum began to slip. After placing third in the January 2008 Iowa caucus, Clinton's campaign began to slowly unravel as Senator Barack Obama made significant inroads with Democratic voters. After waging a well-run and valiant campaign, Clinton finally dropped out of the race on June 7, 2008, and endorsed Obama's candidacy.

In 2009, Obama nominated Clinton as secretary of state, and she was subsequently confirmed in that position by the Senate. Since assuming the office, she has widely traveled the globe and has been particularly active in initiatives to repair U.S. relations with Western Europe and Russia that had deteriorated since the 2003 invasion of Iraq. One of the worst crisis during her administration of the nation's foreign policy came on the evening of September 11, 2012, when Islamic militants attacked the U.S. diplomatic mission in Libya, killing Ambassador J. Christopher Stevens and three others. Republican critics on Capitol Hill questioned whether State Department officials were honest about the nature of the attack and had taken sufficient measures to strengthen security of Middle Eastern embassies.

Her four-year tenure as Secretary of State ended in 2013, when Clinton retired to private life to consider her future in American politics. She was widely regarded to be the leading contender for the Democratic presidential nomination in 2016.

Paul G. Pierpaoli, Jr.

See also: Campaign 2008; Candidates, Presidential Election 2008; Clinton, William Jefferson

Further Reading

Bernstein, Carl. 2007. *A Woman in Charge: The Life of Hillary Rodham Clinton*. New York: Knopf.
Clinton, Hillary Rodham. 2003. *Living History*. New York: Simon and Schuster.

Clinton, William Jefferson (1946–)

United States Democratic Party politician and president of the United States (1993–2001), William "Bill" Jefferson Clinton was born William Blythe in Hope, Arkansas, on August 19, 1946. His early life was characterized by hardships and struggles that formed his character and attitudes throughout his public life. His biological father, William Blythe III, was killed in an automobile accident prior to his son's birth, and young Blythe was raised by his mother, Virginia Kelley. His mother's marriage to Roger Clinton prompted William's adoption and the changing of his name to William Clinton just prior to starting secondary school.

Clinton was a bright and astute student who hoped to pursue a medical career until he met President John F. Kennedy on a Boys' Nation trip to Washington, D.C. This experience led Clinton to focus his future career aspirations on public service and politics. He received an academic scholarship to attend Georgetown University, where he earned a bachelor of science degree in international affairs. During his time at Georgetown, he spent a year assisting Arkansas senator J. William Fulbright. Clinton's credentials as a progressive Democrat and social liberal were further developed under the tutelage of this prominent senator. In 1968 as the United States was being transformed by social changes and wracked by protests against the Vietnam War, Clinton was selected as a Rhodes Scholar. He spent 1968 to 1970 studying at Oxford University. On his return to the United States, he enrolled in the Yale University School of Law.

While studying at Yale, Clinton met his future wife, Hillary Rodham, who shared many of the liberal and progressive ideas that would become the hallmark of Clinton's political career. They were married in 1975.

Clinton's initial foray into national politics occurred shortly after receiving his law degree. In 1974 he was defeated in a congressional race for Arkansas's Third District. After a brief career as a professor at the University of Arkansas (1974–1976), he was named state attorney general and was elected governor in 1978 at age 32, the youngest governor in the nation. In 1980 he suffered a humiliating reelection defeat, caused by widespread opposition to an automobile licensing tax. Clinton's resiliency and commitment were apparent when he successfully regained the Arkansas governorship in 1982, a post he held until his election as president in 1992.

In the summer of 1992, Clinton secured the Democratic Party nomination to run against incumbent president George Herbert Walker Bush, a Republican. Clinton was bedeviled, however, by questions regarding his marital fidelity and the emerging Whitewater real estate scandal in Arkansas. In the race, he benefited from an economic downturn and businessman H. Ross Perot's Independent Party candidacy.

Clinton won the November 1992 election with a minority of the popular vote. During his first term he balanced domestic issues and foreign policy in a highly effective manner. At home, he lobbied unsuccessfully for major health care reform. Clinton was successful, however, in raising taxes and reducing expenditures to reduce—and then eliminate—the federal deficit and in pushing through major welfare reforms. In foreign affairs, he promoted free trade agreements, brokered peace efforts in the Middle East, removed U.S. military personnel from Somalia, and restored diplomatic relations with the Socialist Republic of Vietnam.

The congressional elections of 1994, however, brought Republican majorities in both the House and Senate. The Republicans' "Contract with America," crafted chiefly by Republican congressman Newt Gingrich, called for reducing the role of government and continuing the conservative policies of Ronald Reagan and was a thorough repudiation of Clinton's presidency. A standoff between Clinton and congressional leaders led to a federal government shutdown in November and December 1995.

In the 1996 presidential campaign, Clinton promised a tough approach to crime, supported welfare reform, called for reducing the federal deficit, and insisted on the need to continue affirmative action programs. Robert Dole, a respected senator and World War II veteran, was the Republican Party candidate. The booming U.S. economy and suspicions regarding the Republicans' agenda ensured a respectable Clinton victory. He was the first Democrat to secure a second presidential term since Franklin D. Roosevelt.

In 1997, Clinton submitted to Congress the first balanced budget in nearly three decades. The cooperation of congressional Republicans and major compromises by Clinton generated significant budget surpluses during the remainder of his presidency. By decade's end, the American economy was more robust than at any time since the mid-1960s. Unemployment stood at a historic low, and the stock market had reached new highs.

In addition to significant domestic accomplishments, Clinton responded effectively to a series of international crises. In 1998 in response to Iraqi president Saddam Hussein's noncompliance with United Nations (UN) weapons inspections, Clinton authorized air strikes in Iraq (Operation Desert Fox), and sanctions significantly hurt Iraq's economy yet without producing any significant change in the Iraqi dictator's behavior. In 1999 Clinton prodded a North Atlantic Treaty Organization (NATO) military response to genocide conducted by Serbs against Albanians in Kosovo. He also worked mightily, but unsuccessfully, to secure a resolution to the Israeli-Palestinian conflict, a major Clinton administration goal.

The Clinton White House also faced several foreign-inspired terrorist attacks on U.S. soil and on U.S. interests, the most serious of them being the 1993 World Trade Center bombing, the August 1998 truck bombing of two U.S. embassies in Kenya and Tanzania, and the bombing of USS *Cole* in Yemen in October 2000. The last two incidents were specifically linked to Al Qaeda, and the earlier attack was more than likely tied to the terrorist group. In retaliation for the 1998 embassy attacks, Clinton ordered cruise missile strikes against suspected Al Qaeda posts in Khartoum, Sudan, and in Afghanistan. The strikes were largely ineffective and engendered significant controversy in the United States and abroad. After leaving office and after the September 11, 2001, attacks by Al Qaeda, Clinton was insistent that his administration was fully aware of the danger that Al Qaeda posed to the United States but that it could not move quickly enough because neither the Central Intelligence Agency (CIA) nor the Federal Bureau of Investigation (FBI) was certain beyond all doubt as to Al Qaeda's complicity in the earlier attacks. He claimed that battle plans were already in place for an invasion of Afghanistan and a massive hunt for Al Qaeda leader Osama bin Laden, but the clock on his administration ran out before the plans could be put into motion.

Clinton's second term was also marked by personal scandal and legal problems. Kenneth Starr, the independent counsel investigating Whitewater, leveled against the president charges of sexual misconduct and lying to a federal grand jury. He did not, however, ever find evidence of wrongdoing in the Whitewater deal. In September 1998 the U.S. House of Representatives passed two articles of impeachment against the president, but in early 1999 the Senate acquitted Clinton on both counts along party lines. To end the Whitewater investigation, Clinton agreed to a five-year suspension of his law license and a $25,000 fine.

After leaving the presidency, Clinton assisted his wife in her successful senatorial campaign in New York and in her failed bid for the presidency in 2008, opened his own office in Harlem in New York City, and established a presidential library in Little Rock, Arkansas. He has also traveled extensively abroad and raised significant sums of money for charitable causes, including AIDS and, with former president George H.W. Bush, tsunami relief. Clinton also helped form the William J. Clinton Foundation, a global outreach enterprise that has helped millions of people around the world, and wrote his memoirs.

James F. Carroll and Spencer C. Tucker

See also: Clinton, Hillary Rodham

Further Reading

Clinton, Bill. 2004. *My Life*. New York: Knopf.

Maraniss, D. 1995. *First in His Class.* New York: Simon and Schuster.

Posner, R.A. 1999. *An Affair of State: The Investigation, Impeachment, and Trial of President Clinton.* Cambridge, MA: Harvard University Press.

CNN (Cable News Network)

Cable News Network (CNN) is the first 24-hour news network. CNN is headquartered in Atlanta, Georgia, and was launched by cable television entrepreneur Ted Turner on June 1, 1980. The CNN brand has grown to include other news, talk, and information ventures, such as Headline News (HLN), CNN International, CNN Radio, CNN Newsource, CNN Airport Channel, CNN en Espanol, and various digital platforms including CNN.com and CNN Mobile.

Turner was not the first to consider starting an all-news television network, which by the late 1970s became possible with the growth of cable television and the development of communication satellites, computers, and videotape technologies. Turner's ability to make CNN a reality within two years is considered a brilliant achievement, especially in light of skepticism and obstacles he faced from cable executives and the major broadcast and networks, the latter which saw CNN as a poor-quality embarrassment to the news business—the "Chicken Noodle News."

In 1979, Turner hired television executive Reese Schonfeld, who ran a nonprofit television news syndication company for about 25 independent broadcast stations, to build what would become Cable News Network. CNN's first "name" anchor was Daniel Schorr, who had worked at CBS News and for Schonfeld's news syndication company. Schonfeld wrote in a 2001 memoir that CNN focused on four types of news genres: hard news, financial news, sports news, and news talk. CNN also counterprogrammed against broadcast network schedules as much as possible. A financial news show, *Moneyline*, for example, aired when most network stations aired their primary nightly news programs. Although CNN programming was mostly live, the network repeated shows in early mornings because it could not afford to staff a true 24-hour live format.

CNN did not make a profit until the second half of the 1980s after more U.S. homes subscribed to cable television. CNN was available to reach about 20 percent of American homes in 1980. By 1985, 40 percent of all U.S. homes had cable television service and CNN. Turner invested heavily in his news operations regardless, and launched Headline News in 1982 to vanquish an attempt by ABC and Westinghouse to launch their own headline service, the Satellite News Channel. He started CNN International in 1985 based on the suggestion of Cuban dictator Fidel Castro, who met with Turner in 1982. The English language service now reaches nearly every country in the world.

CNN's most impressive journalistic triumph came during the 1991 Gulf War. Unlike its competitors, CNN was determined to cover the war from Baghdad, the Iraqi capital, and spent a reported $22 million covering the war. CNN got permission from the Iraqis to set up a four-wire telephone connection that bypassed the usual switchboard. Thus, when American air attacks knocked out the Iraqi telephone system, CNN correspondents still had a working phone to use for live reports. CNN ratings rose dramatically, and the broadcast networks were forced to use CNN coverage for their own reports.

In 1995 Turner agreed to sell Turner Broadcasting, which included CNN and related brands, to Time Warner. Time Warner, in turn, was purchased by America Online (AOL), an internet software and content company, in 2000. AOL was spun off from Time Warner in 2009, but the Turner Broadcasting Division remains part of Time Warner. CNN's ratings declined, especially in primetime, throughout the 2000s as company executives were accused of focusing on generating profits and bolstering stock prices. CNN suffered its worst primetime ratings in 21 years during one quarter in 2012.

Moreover, cable television viewers had more sources for news and talk content, especially from the Fox News Channel and MSNBC (both launched in 1996). Although Fox presented a conservative view of the news and MSNBC eventually adopted a liberal viewpoint, CNN tried to remain nonpartisan. Even though CNN pioneered political debate on cable with *Crossfire*, a program that aired from 1982 to 2005 and from 2013 to 14, the network maintains that a major part of its brand and reputation are based on its commitment to a nonpartisan presentation of the day's news.

With CNN's ratings rising and falling based on breaking news events, executives have tried to find programming to maintain ratings when news is slower. Soon after Jeff Zucker, a former NBC executive, was hired as president of CNN Worldwide in 2013, CNN announced it had hired chef Anthony Bourdain to do a food-themed travel show for its primetime schedule titled *Parts Unknown*. The show was among the first of several "lifestyle" nonfiction programs Zucker hopes will attract viewers. Zucker is also putting more attention and resources on CNN.com as a way to reach a non-cable audience and also to learn audience preferences in the day's news. Despite all of the attention to its faltering primetime audience, CNN remains very profitable. In 2013, it made an estimated $340 million, not counting the revenue from CNN International or HLN.

Dale Zacher

See also: Ailes, Roger; Fox News; MSNBC

Further Reading

Auletta, Ken. 2004. *Media Man*. New York: W.W. Norton.

Flournoy, Don, and Robert Stewart. 1997. *CNN: Making News in the Global Market*. Luton, UK: University of Luton Press.

Goldberg, Robert, and Gerald Jay Goldberg. 2014. *Citizen Turner: The Wild Rise of an American Tycoon*. New York: Harcourt Brace.

Lafayette, John. 2013. "At Evolving CNN, Lifestyle is News." *Broadcasting & Cable* 143(11):14.

Schonfeld, Reese. 2001. *Me and Ted Against the World: The Unauthorized Story of the Founding of CNN*. New York: Harper Collins.

Cold War

The Cold War describes a 44-year period of military and political struggle between the United States and its Western allies against the Soviet Union and its Eastern European allies in the Warsaw Pact. It had a profound influence upon 20th century politics and policies in the United States that reverberates well into the 21st century.

It was called a "cold" war because the United States and the Soviet Union never directly engaged in full-scale combat. However, it produced a series of regional conflicts in places like Korea, Vietnam, and Afghanistan that cost millions of lives. It was also a truly global struggle that engulfed most of the world's nations.

The Cold War occurred from 1947 until the Soviet collapse in 1991. It resulted from the aftermath of World War II when Soviet leaders decided to retain military control of the Eastern Europe nations the U.S.S.R. had wrestled from Nazi Germany. The United States responded with a policy of containment—a military and political hardline stand against any further Soviet expansion. That policy was first outlined by diplomat and historian George F. Kennan, who was stationed in the U.S. Embassy in Moscow in 1944. Two years later, he wrote a famous dispatch to officials in Washington that eventually became known as "the Long Telegram" warning that the Soviets believed they were in a perpetual war against capitalism.

Kennan in 1947 published an article in the journal *Foreign Affairs* under the pseudonym "X" in which he urged that U.S. policy "must be that of a long-term patient but firm and vigilant containment of Russian expansive tendencies." The policy was embraced by President Harry Truman as the basis of the so-called "Truman doctrine" that prompted U.S. military and economic assistance to Turkey and Greece to prevent Soviet expansion.

Fear of Soviet growth was one of the prime causes of the Marshall Plan in which the United States contributed billions of dollars to rebuild Germany and much of war-ravaged Western Europe. The United States led a coalition of 11 other nations to form the North Atlantic Treaty Organization (NATO) in 1949, a military pact that assured the Soviets that aggression against any one member would be met by retaliation from the entire alliance.

Confrontations began almost immediately. Soviet leader Joseph Stalin in June of 1948 ordered closure of the supply route between Western Europe and West Berlin, an embargo that prompted a massive "Berlin airlift" to supply Berliners with food, fuel, and other necessities. Stalin backed down the following year after his policies were repudiated in anti-Communist elections throughout West Germany.

The Cold War led to dramatic policy and political changes in the United States, including creation of a unified Department of Defense, permanent worldwide espionage efforts through creation of the Central Intelligence Agency, and state-operated propaganda efforts through the Voice of America and Radio Free Europe. Cold War tensions also led to a domestically destructive anti-Communist movement generally called "McCarthyism" named after Sen. Joseph McCarthy of Wisconsin, who claimed that Communists had infiltrated the State Department and other federal agencies. Sometimes called the "Red Scare," McCarthyism led to blacklisting of Hollywood writers and artists suspected of pro-Soviet sympathies.

The Cold War turned bloody in June 1950 when the North Korean People's Army, with direct military assistance from the Soviets, invaded South Korea, prompting the United Nations to authorize military operations to stop the invasion. The ensuing war claimed an estimated 1.2 million lives, including more than 44,000 U.S. troop fatalities and missing in action. The bloody conflict ended in an armistice that created a demilitarized zone between North and South Korea in mid-1953.

President Dwight Eisenhower continued the policy of containment during the 1950s, developing a vast nuclear arsenal that assured a "massive retaliation" if the Soviets attacked the United States or its allies. The policy eventually became known as Mutually Assured Destruction (or M.A.D.) since the United States promised it would destroy the bulk of the Soviet civilian population even if most Americans were killed by a Russian first strike. The United States eventually amassed more than 10,000 nuclear warheads—a force that some scientists feared could have ended life on earth if fully employed.

The tensions continued into the 1960s with a failed attempt by the United States to topple the pro-Communist regime of Fidel Castro in Cuba with the 1961 military invasion at Cuba's Bay of Pigs. Castro defeated a CIA-backed invasion of anti-Castro Cubans, causing a major decrease in U.S. global prestige. The Soviets, in response to further invasion fears, installed intermediate-range missiles in Cuba capable of delivering nuclear warheads to the U.S. mainland. Discovery of Soviet missile sites just 90 miles from the coast of Florida prompted the Cuban Missile Crisis of 1962. President John F. Kennedy ordered a naval blockade of Cuba, putting both U.S. and Soviet nuclear forces on high alert. Soviet leader Nikita Khrushchev backed down in November, agreeing to remove the missiles. Khrushchev's decision contributed to his ouster from power by Soviet Communist hardliners in 1964. It was perhaps the closest the world came to a global nuclear conflict since Soviet military commanders had been authorized to use tactical atomic weapons if Kennedy implemented his preparations for a second military invasion.

It's hard to overstate the impact the Cold War had on American life. Even the so-called "space race" was a competition between the United States and Russia, a rivalry with early and stunning Soviet successes. The Russians shocked America by launching the world's first artificial satellite, called Sputnik, in 1957. Russian cosmonaut Yuri Gagarin became the first human to orbit the earth in 1961. But the United State proved its dominance in 1969 when astronaut Neil Armstrong became the first human to set foot on the surface of the moon.

The Cold War's bloodiest conflict occurred in Vietnam and much of Southeast Asia following the 1954 defeat of the French military by Communist forces. The Eisenhower administration ordered U.S. military advisors and economic aide to support the pro-Western regime in South Vietnam, setting the stage for a confrontation that escalated under President Lyndon Johnson in the mid-1960s. More than 58,000 American military troops perished in a war that sharply divided American public opinion. The North Vietnamese, with Soviet support, staged a major military counter-offensive in early 1968. By August, the Gallop Poll reported that 53 percent of Americans said it was "a mistake" to send U.S. troops into Vietnam. The United States didn't cease military operations until 1973, despite widespread antiwar demonstrations. The North Vietnamese defeated the South Vietnamese army in 1975 and created a unified government, which later estimated that the two-decade conflict cost more than 3 million Vietnamese lives.

Perhaps emboldened by the Communist victory in Vietnam, the Soviet Union orchestrated a Communist takeover in Afghanistan beginning in April 1978. What followed was a bloody nine-year confrontation between nearly 100,000 Soviet Red Army troops and a complicated alliance of anti-Soviet insurgents called the "Mujahedeen," who were given military assistance by the United States. President Jimmy Carter imposed embargoes on grain and technology shipments to the Soviet Union as well as a U.S. boycott of the 1980 Moscow Summer Olympics. Carter lost his reelection bid in 1980—at least partially due to his perceived weakness in Afghanistan—to Republican challenger Ronald Reagan. President Reagan in 1981 immediately began a major military buildup in response to the perceived threat of renewed Soviet expansionism. Reagan also ordered more aggressive assistance to anti-Soviet forces in Afghanistan, including delivery of "Stinger" anti-air missiles and other high technology weapons. The Russians found themselves embroiled in a holy war as Islamic Afghans, with support from the broader Muslim world, aggressively opposed their infidel invaders.

The Soviet regime, once termed an "evil empire" by Reagan, collapsed fairly quickly following the 1985 ascension of Mikhail Gorbachev as general secretary of the Soviet

Communist Party. The Communist economy had never worked particularly well, but a decline in worldwide oil prices in the 1980s sharply curtailed the Soviet's principal source of "hard currency" needed to purchase essential items worldwide. (Few global traders wanted payment in Russian rubles.) Gorbachev ordered a series of economic reforms he called "perestroika," which means "restructuring." He called for new freedoms in a process called "glasnost," or "openness," and began peace initiatives through Soviet treaties with the West that would have been unthinkable under Stalin. Gorbachev ordered the withdrawal of Soviet forces in Afghanistan in 1989, ending what had become the Soviet Union's equivalent of the Vietnam War.

The end of the Cold War came as a sudden surprise to most Americans. The Warsaw Pact eroded in 1989 when Poland and Hungary initiated the first free and open elections since World War II. The East German government announced in November of that year that its citizens could visit West Germany and West Berlin, leading to the rapid dismantling of the Berlin Wall, the most famous symbol of the Cold War. The Communist Party was quickly ousted from power in every Eastern Bloc nation. Gorbachev ceded control of Eastern Europe in hopes of retaining control of the Union of Soviet Socialist Republics, but that, too, was officially dissolved on Christmas Day, 1991, to be replaced by the Commonwealth of Independent States, a symbolic organization that attempts to coordinate trade and policy among the former Soviet states.

Thomas K. Hargrove

See also: Reagan, Ronald

Further Reading

Gaddis, John Lewis. 2011. *The Cold War: A New History*. New York: Penguin Group.
Judge, Edward H., and John W. Langdon. 2010. *The Cold War: A Global History with Documents*. 2nd ed. New York: Person.
Walker, Martin. 1995. *The Cold War: A History*. New York: Henry Holt and Co.

Congressional Black Caucus

The Congressional Black Caucus was established in 1971 with 13 black members of the House of Representatives who wanted to advance the civil rights agenda mainly through legislation and committee work in the House. Its creation was the result of an increase in African American congressional representation brought about by a combination of changes from migration, reapportionment, and guarantees resulting from the passage of the Voting Rights Act of 1965.

By the time of the formation of the CBC, the nation's population had shifted in such a way that approximately 70 percent of its African American citizens lived in major metropolitan areas. By contrast, only around a third of the white population lived in cities. However, in suburban areas, whites outnumbered blacks by a 35 to 1 ratio. But concentration of African Americans in central cities strengthened black representation in Congress, especially in districts that depended on the concentration of blacks in particular sections of cities. As a result, this concentration of African American voters led to increased opportunities for black representation on the House of Representatives.

In addition to the changes in demographics and population, reapportionment rulings that the Supreme Court enforced contributed to the increased electoral opportunities for blacks running for office. These Court decisions included barring state and local governments from altering district lines in a way that would disadvantage black voters, establishing redistricting as a judicial issue in which the courts had the authority to provide judicial solutions, ruling that congressional districts should be drawn in as equitable a manner as possible with "one person, one vote" as the central idea, and finally that the seats in both houses of Congress be allocated based on population. African Americans in urban districts were the main beneficiaries of the political changes wrought by these Court decisions, even as the decisions increased the number of white-majority districts in suburban areas. African American members of Congress who were elected in cities with districts having a high density of African American voters were among the legislators whose influence led to the creation of the CBC.

Most importantly, the passage of civil rights legislation—the Civil Rights Act of 1964 and the 1965 Voting Rights Act—created the conditions under which the aforementioned population and judicial changes could be taken advantage of by African American voters and those seeking political office. The legislation allowed for black voters to have the civil and political equality that was the focus of all civil rights activism. The achievement of political equality was especially important because it created a new electoral environment. This environment was one that saw a substantial increase in the number of registered African American voters, which resulted in an increase in the number of African American elected officials. Part of this increase came as a result of the Voting Rights Act's enfranchisement of Southern voters, who formed a significant voting bloc. This gave rise to an increase in black elected officials in the South.

The expansion of the number of African American delegates in Congress—along with the political backgrounds of the new members, the election of Richard Nixon as president in 1968, and the loss of leaders in the African American community after the civil rights activism of the 1960s—expedited the formation of the CBC. When the 92nd Congress convened in 1971, it did so with the largest number of African American delegates in the twentieth century, and at a time when promoting issues of concern among African Americans seemed to hold promise for the possibility of change. In addition, the backgrounds of the new black members of Congress who were Democratic and whose political styles had their origins in the struggle for civil rights—particularly William Clay from Missouri, Shirley Chisholm from New York, and Louis Stokes from Ohio—suggested that promotion of such issues would be possible.

Despite concerns that the CBC's political focus was too centered on matters of race, the 1968 election of Richard Nixon to the presidency proved to be a stimulant for the creation of the organization. Nixon's election signaled a national shift toward a more conservative stance that included moving away from focusing on the political and civil rights gains and other issues of importance to African American voters resulting from the activism of the civil rights era. This political change, coupled with the loss of public African American leaders like Martin Luther King Jr. and Malcolm X, among others, suggested that an organization like the Congressional Black Caucus was not only a good idea but also a necessary one. With the increased presence of black officials throughout government, African American voters expected more improvements in economic and political fortunes.

The members of the CBC understood that satisfying the expectations of their constituents required tangible, substantive evidence of their effectiveness in Congress. The Caucus provides an organizational framework through which its members could focus and document their efforts.

Today, the Congressional Black Caucus is among the oldest of the informal networks within the House of Representatives and remains a necessary institution because many African Americans, especially those living in the South, are represented by members of Congress whose policy aims differ from or are incompatible with the concerns of African American voters in their districts. The CBC serves as an important virtual representational body for the mass of African American voters whose needs are ignored by politicians whose political careers have been shaped by catering to the needs of white voters.

The CBC's agenda focuses on domestic policy issues pertinent to African Americans using a process of bill introduction distinct from both the entire Democratic caucus and Democratic liberals. The heart of the CBC political agenda includes advancing civil rights, community development, and public sector employment, issues that are of the most importance to the Caucus's constituents.

The CBC continues to advocate for changes to policies that negatively impact communities of color and their constituencies. Its initiatives include voter protection and empowerment, eradicating poverty and increasing access to economic opportunity by supporting policies that lead to job creation and protecting against reductions in social and economic programs, and advancing legislation and policies that contribute to immigration reform.

Calvin L. Hall

See also: African American voters; Jackson, Jesse; Obama, Barack

Further Reading

Berg, John. 1994. *Unequal Struggle: Class, Gender, Race and Power in the U.S. Congress.* Boulder, CO: Westview Press.

King, Marvin. 2011. "Bill Preference: The Continued Relevance of the Congressional Black Caucus," *Politics & Policy* 39(3): 421–439.

Singh, Robert. 1998. *The Congressional Black Caucus: Racial Politics in the U.S. Congress.* Thousand Oaks, CA: SAGE Publications.

Conservative Voters

More than a third of Americans identify themselves as politically conservative, according to polls conducted over many years. Conservatives generally represent a much larger component of the electorate than do self-described liberals. They are a powerful voting bloc that, generally, more reliably participates in elections than do liberals or moderates.

The editors of the Gallup Poll report that the rate at which Americans identify themselves as "conservative" has varied far less in recent decades than has self-identification for "liberal" or "moderate" political beliefs. According to interviews with tens of thousands of adult residents of the United States conducted from 1992 through 2012, Americans' self-identification as "conservative" kept to a tight range of 36 percent as a low to 40 percent as a high. The rate at which adults identify as "liberal" ranged from 16 percent to 23 percent, while self-described "moderates" ranged from 34 percent to a high of 43 percent.

What exactly is meant by "conservative" is a very difficult question, however. Conservatives are easily counted by pollsters, but their values and political beliefs are much more difficult to define by political scientists or journalists.

The word "conservative" generally invokes a desire to "conserve" traditional and longstanding political values. The term is often ascribed to French writer and historian François-René de Chateaubriand, a royalist during the Bourbon restoration, which installed a constitutional monarchy after the defeat of Napoleon. He founded the journal *Le Conservateur* in 1818, which urged conservative values in the aftermath of the bloody excesses of the French Revolution. Irish-born politician and writer Edmund Burke, often described as the father of British conservatism, also objected to the French Revolution but generally embraced American independence.

What Americans mean by "conservatism" has historically been at least as difficult to define as what we mean by "liberalism." The American Revolution was simultaneously a conservative and liberal movement. The Founding Fathers called for removal of the British monarchy in favor of a republic because, they said, King George III had violated the natural rights of American colonists by imposing taxes and other measures without granting them representation in Parliament, a "right" granted to other Englishmen. The Revolution was also quintessentially liberal since it rejected the ancient notion of the monarchist sovereignty in favor of democratic rule.

But from their earliest days, American conservatives have struggled with sometimes competing values. Conservatives usually take a high view of the rule of law, a belief that social order must extend from commitment to legal values that transcend transitory political power. The Bill of Rights is often viewed as a conservative contribution to the Constitution, even though it was passionately demanded by revolutionaries like George Mason of Virginia. Conservatives also tended to champion Christian religion and biblical values even as they supported a secular Constitution that banned an official state religion.

Historically, conservatives are suspicious of a strong central government. Ronald Reagan, who did more than anyone to define and popularize conservatism in the late 20th century, once famously noted that "The nine most terrifying words in the English language are, 'I'm from the government and I'm here to help.'" He concluded that the natural tenants of government are, "If it moves, tax it. If it keeps moving, regulate it. And if it stops moving, subsidize it."

But conservatism has become increasingly complex and contradictory in modern times since it's a coalition that includes Christian evangelicals, the anti-tax and anti-debt Tea Party, laissez-faire capitalists, global free traders, constitutional strict constructionists, national security militarists, and a growing libertarian movement that actually opposes many of these other values.

American publisher Henry Regnery, who would publish some of the nation's most important conservative authors, including William F. Buckley and Russell Kirk, once noted that "Conservatism is not a fixed and immutable body of dogma, and conservatives inherit from Burke a talent for re-expressing their convictions to fit the times." It has certainly become true for modern conservative politicians.

When trying to assess the four leading Republican presidential candidates during the 2012 general election, journalist Conor Friedersdorf devised a 21-point construct of quite different—and sometimes contradictory—worldview values that conservatives often profess. He concluded that Republican candidates like former Massachusetts Gov. Mitt Romney, former House Speaker Newt Gingrich, former U.S. Senator Rich Santorum of Pennsylvania, and Rep. Ron Paul of Texas ascribe to some, but never all, of these values:

1. An aversion to rapid social or moral change and a belief that tradition and prevailing social norms often contain "handed down" wisdom.
2. A desire to preserve the political philosophy and rules of government outlined in America's founding documents like the Declaration of Independence and U.S. Constitution.
3. An imperative to preserve traditional morality, usually as articulated in the Bible.
4. A willingness to preserve traditional morality, usually as articulated in the Bible by using cultural norms and the power of the state.
5. An embrace of free-market capitalism and a belief in the legitimacy of market outcomes.
6. Belief that America is an exceptional nation, a shining city on a hill, whose rightful role is leader of the free world.
7. A belief that America should export its brand of democracy through force of arms.
8. The conviction that government should undertake, on behalf of the American polity, grand projects that advance our "national greatness" and ennoble our characters.
9. An embrace of localism, community and family ties, human scale, and a responsibility to the future.
10. A belief that America shouldn't intervene in the affairs of other nations except to defend ourselves from aggression and enforce contracts and treaties.
11. A desire to return to the way things once were.
12. Affinity for, identification with, or embrace of Republican America's various cultural cues. For example, gun ownership, a preference for single-family homes oriented around highways rather than urban enclaves organized around public transit, embrace of country music, disdain for arugula and fancy mustard, etc.
13. Disdain for American liberalism, multiculturalism, identity politics, affirmative action, welfare, European-style social policies, and the left and its ideas generally.
14. A desire to be left alone by government, often viewed as a natural right.
15. A principled belief in federalism.
16. The belief that taxes should be lower and government smaller.
17. The belief that the national debt and deficits put America in peril.
18. The belief that, whenever possible, government budgets should be balanced.
19. Consciousness of the fallibility of man, and an awareness of the value of skepticism, doubt, and humility.
20. Realism in foreign policy.
21. Non-interventionism in foreign policy.

Shortly before his death in 2008, writer and television commentator William F. Buckley Jr. was asked to define the meaning of the word conservatism. Buckley is often described as one of the intellectual fathers of the modern conservative revolution that came to fruition under Ronald Reagan. "Conservatism aims to maintain in working order the loyalties of the community to perceived truths and also to those truths which in their judgment have earned universal recognition," Buckley said.

In this, perhaps surprisingly, conservatives share a value system with American liberals. Both believe they speak for universal truths that the world ignores at its peril.

Thomas K. Hargrove

See also: Liberal Voters; Polarization.

Further Reading

Friedersdorf, Conor. 2012. "What Americans Mean When They Say They're Conservative." *The Atlantic*, January 27.

Jones, Jeffrey M. 2014. "Liberal Self-Identification Edges Up to New High in 2013." January 10. Princeton, NJ: The Gallup Poll.

Muller, Jerry Z. 1997. *Conservatism: An Anthology of Social and Political Thought from David Hume to the Present*. Princeton, NJ: Princeton University Press.

Conspiracy Theories

What do the Watergate break-in, Hurricane Sandy, and the month of October have in common? They are all players in what some people see as nefarious attempts to illegally influence presidential elections, others see as examples of presidential election conspiracy theories that have no basis in reality, and still others see as coincidences.

All three of these—the break-in, the hurricane, and month preceding presidential election—are real people and thing, But here's where the conspiracy theory comes in: The Watergate break-in was part of an attempt to ensure the reelection of President Nixon in 1972. Hurricane Sandy was perhaps engineered by the government to influence the 2012 election, and October is a time of heightened conspiratorial activity, often referred to as the "October surprise."

The linkages, however, are confusing. It is undisputed that the hotel, Sandy, and increased electioneering in October are real, but are they part of real conspiracies, or are other evil forces *saying* they are part of a conspiracy (when they are not) to discredit the other side? Such operations are called "false flags," and are used to discredit the other side by attributing to them statements and actions they have not, in fact, made.

Perhaps the best way to understand the connection between conspiracy theories and presidential elections is to look at what may or may not be conspiracies that may or may not have influenced elections.

Watergate

The basic outline of Watergate is so well known, it need not be repeated here, but sorting fact from fiction is still something of a cottage industry. Here are some incidents that are still debated ranging from the silly to the serious:

* To disrupt campaign activities, Republican operatives, claiming to be Democrats, call venue managers to change the times of Democratic campaign rallies.

* Republicans planted agents at Democratic rallies. The agents were to engage in illegal activities so as to discredit Democratic candidates.

* Democratic front-runner Edmund Muskie allegedly made a disparaging remark about "Canucks." The comments were included in a letter sent to the Manchester Union Leader, but the letter was later shown to be a forgery. *Washington Post* reporter Marilyn Berger said deputy White House communications director Ken Clawson told her he wrote the letter, a statement Clawson later denied. The letter is often seen as leading directly to the implosion of the Muskie campaign.

It can safely be said there was a conspiracy (a group of people acting in concert in an illegal manner) to reelect President Nixon.

Hurricane Sandy

At the other end of the credibility scale is the idea that the Obama administration engineered Hurricane Sandy to influence the 2012 election. According to the websites InfoWars.com, TheIntelHub.com, and the ConsfearacyNewz blog site, shortly before the 2012 election, the government's High Frequency Active Auroral Research Program (HAARP) helped create and control Hurricane Sandy. Then, the theory goes, President Obama was able to act, well, presidential, and provide aid and comfort to stricken areas of the East Coast, thus assuring his election.

There is, in fact, a project HAARP facility, located in Alaska, designed to study radio communications and the ionosphere. The site's home page, complete with diagrams, photographs, and maps, says HAARP is "a premier facility for the story of ionospheric physics and radio science" (HAARP, 2013).

The October Surprise

The term "October surprise" came into popular culture during the 1972 Nixon-McGovern presidential campaign and generally refers to what are called "pseudo-events" especially created to influence the election. Since elections must occur between November 2 and 8, the events in question must occur in October to have any impact. Thus the term "October surprise."

It is important, however, to distinguish between two types of surprises. One involves news stories that contain derogatory information (drunk driving, trial verdicts, immigration status, etc.). This kind of information is fairly easy to check. The other October surprise involves events or allegations that are almost impossible to verify.

Nixon-McGovern (1972)

By 1972 the United States had been involved in Vietnam for 22 years, with the creation of the Military Assistance and Advisory Group. On the domestic front the war had led to the downfall of one president (Johnson), and in the late 1960s antiwar riots had spread across the country.

Negotiations to end the war had been conducted sporadically for four years, with little result. However, on October 26, 1972, a mere 12 days before the election, President Nixon's national security advisor and chief negotiator, Henry Kissinger, announced "peace is at hand." Nixon had, in fact, promised to end the war four years earlier, during the 1968 campaign, but no end of the war was in sight. Although Nixon was almost assured reelection in 1972, conspiracy theory advocates say the "peace is at hand" statement was mere rhetoric, especially since the last American troops were not withdrawn until 1975.

Carter-Reagan (1980)

In 1979 Iranian militants stormed the United States embassy in Tehran and took 52 American hostages. Negotiations over the next year to gain the release of the hostages were fruitless.

In this case there are two different conspiracy theories: in one scenario, President Carter had been planning a major military operation for October in an attempt to rescue the hostages. The other theory is that candidate Reagan was secretly negotiating with the Iranians to delay the release until after the election. The rescue attempt never materialized, leading to speculation that there never was going to be a rescue attempt but that word of an attempt was leaked to boost Carter's standing in the polls.

The Reagan conspiracy theory is bolstered by the fact that the hostages were released mere minutes after Reagan was inaugurated

Bush-Kerry (2004)

According to this theory, in late 2004 Saudi Prince Bandar cut the price of oil to help the George Bush campaign. *Washington Post* editor Bob Woodward said on the CBS news program *60 Minutes* that the prince wanted to cut, or at least maintain relatively low, oil prices to help the U.S. economy. This would, in turn, help the Bush campaign. This theory is bolstered by alleged close ties between the Bush family and the Saudi royal family.

Whence Conspiracy Theories?

So what is it that prompts large numbers of people to believe conspiracy theories? First, everyone likes to know a secret. Conspiracy theories thrive on the notion that the masses are brainwashed, and only a select few know the truth. The fact that the truth can't be supported by hard evidence doesn't seem to make any difference. Second, conspiracy theories seem to simplify a confusing, complex world. Conspiracy theorists take what appears to be conflicting data and reduce it to a simple narrative that is easy to understand but which almost always falls apart on closer analysis. Finally, conspiracy theories almost always divide the world between the forces of good and the forces of evil, again making the complex and confusing events simple. Then the forces of evil are traced back to a single source so well hidden that no one can find it, except those who have exposed the conspiracy.

Larry Burriss

Further Reading

Barkun, Michael. 2006. *A Culture of Conspiracy: Apocalyptic Visions in Contemporary America.* Berkeley: University of California Press.

Beglich, Nick, and Jeane Manning. 2013. "The Military's Pandora's Box." http://www.haarp.net. Accessed February 4, 2015.

Bernstein, Carl, and Bob Woodward. 1972. "FBI Finds Nixon Aides Sabotaged Democrats." *The Washington Post*, October 10, page A1.

Boorstin, Daniel. 1992. *The Image: A Guide to Pseudo-Events in America.* New York: Vintage.

HAARP. 2013. The High Frequency Active Auroral Research Program. http://www.haarp.alaska
.edu. Accessed January 30, 2015.

Katel, Peter. 2009. "Conspiracy Theories: Do They Threaten Democracy?" *CQ Researcher* 19:
885–908.

Martosko, David. 2012. "Conspiracy Theorists: Hurricane Sandy 'Engineered' to Affect Election."
http://dailycaller.com/2012/10/30/conspiracy-theorists-hurricane-sandy-engineered-to-affect
-election. Accessed January 12, 2015.

Pipes, Daniel. 1997. *Conspiracy: How the Paranoid Style Flourishes and Where It Comes From.* New
York: Free Press.

Schoen, John W. 2004. "Did Saudis Assure Bush On Oil Prices: Report Says Prince Pledged Reelection Support." http://www.nbcnews.com/id/4779686/ns/business-oil_and_energy/t/did-saudis
-assure-bush-oil-prices. Accessed January 12, 2015.

Ungar, Craig. 2007. *House of Bush, House of Saud: The Secret Relationship Between the World's Two
Most Powerful Dynasties.* New York: Scribner.

Constitution, First Amendment (1791)

The First Amendment is the constitutional authority that prohibits government from regulating freedom of religion and expression: "Congress shall make no law respecting an establishment of religion, or prohibiting the free exercise thereof; or abridging the freedom of speech, or of the press; or the right of the people peaceably to assemble, and to petition the Government for a redress of grievances." It is the legal basis for claims that government has unconstitutionally failed to separate religion from government or has violated the freedom of religion, belief, speech, press, assembly, association, or lobbying.

The framers of the U.S. Constitution defeated a proposal for a bill of rights at the constitutional convention in 1787, but pressure built during the ratification process to create one. In the first Congress in 1789, Representative James Madison introduced a package of amendments to the Constitution to protect civil rights, including freedom of expression. Although not controversial, Madison's plan was rewritten in the Senate. It passed after a House-Senate conference as thirteen amendments for ratification by the states. All but the first two were approved, and what had been the third amendment became the First Amendment, effective in 1791. These first ten amendments are called the Bill of Rights.

The framers seemed generally to understand that a legal right to freedom of expression meant that the government should not tax, censor, or license speech or press, principles that the Supreme Court eventually established as constitutional doctrine. The framers, however, did not object to legislation that punished seditious libel or criticism of authority. Congress passed the Sedition Act in 1798, which was used by the Federalists to fine and jail their Jeffersonian political opponents for criticizing President John Adams and Congress. The political reaction to the prosecutions led to the pardoning of those convicted, the election of President Thomas Jefferson, the demise of the Federalist Party, and a growing under- standing that seditious libel law is incompatible with democracy. Yet ever since, legislation that chills political dissent has sometimes been enacted by Congress and state legislatures, especially during times of crisis. The imprisonment of political radicals sometimes has generated Supreme Court elaboration on the meaning of the First Amendment.

Like the Bill of Rights more generally, the First Amendment was initially seen as more of a motto than the powerful legal instrument that it has become. It was not until the 20th century that the Supreme Court developed the political philosophy that is associated with the modern libertarian understanding of the First Amendment, such as the marketplace of ideas, the metaphor intended to represent the American system of freedom of expression. Seditious libel law was assumed to have been eradicated by 1964 when Justice William J. Brennan Jr. wrote for the Court that the First Amendment represented "a profound national commitment to the principle that debate on public issues should be uninhibited, robust, and wide-open, and that it may well include vehement, caustic, and sometimes unpleasantly sharp attacks on government and public officials."

Reluctantly, the Supreme Court has approved regulation of expression based on its content. The government, under certain circumstances, is permitted even to censor obscenity, threatening words, revelations of national security secrets, child pornography, copyright infringement, and false advertising. Broadcast indecency, non-obscene sexual expression, and expressive torts, such as defamation and invasion of privacy, are also subject to less than full protection by the First Amendment. But political expression is considered the least subject to control because it is at the heart of the First Amendment. "For speech concerning public affairs is more than self-expression," the Court said in 1964, "it is the essence of self-government." In 1966, the Court added, "Whatever differences may exist about interpretations of the First Amendment, there is practically universal agreement that a major purpose of that Amendment was to protect the free discussion of governmental affairs." The Court in 1989 maintained the "First Amendment 'has its fullest and most urgent application' to speech uttered during a campaign for political office."

The Court has shielded anonymous political speakers and members of political organizations when government has attempted to identify them and broadly protected political advertising, political communication by corporations, the right to receive political information, and political action such as burning flags, distributing literature, picketing, parading, and door-to-door soliciting.

Despite the Court's protectiveness of political communication, the justices have long been divided over the constitutionality of legislation meant to reform campaign corruption by limiting the amount and kind of political contributions and expenditures by individuals, campaigns, candidates, corporations, unions, and other sources. Acknowledging that money can be expression, the Court has upheld much of this legislation as constitutional but struck down almost as much as violating the First Amendment, resulting in a complicated process for determining whether, and under what conditions, state and federal government can regulate campaign financing.

The Court has permitted "reasonable restrictions" on contributions to federal campaigns but not regulation of campaign expenditures. Political parties are free to spend money on congressional campaigns but only if they act independently of the candidates. The Court upheld federal restrictions on "soft-money" contributions and political advertisements but struck down legislation that limited unions, corporations, and other organizations from spending money on campaigns as long as they did not contribute directly to the campaign and disclosed the sponsors of advertising. A significant part of the mission of the Federal Election Commission is the regulation of political communication.

The Supreme Court has made the First Amendment the acme of the Bill of Rights and the Constitution, offering continuing support for Justice Benjamin Cardozo's often-cited quotation: "Freedom of expression is the matrix, the indispensable condition, of nearly every other form of freedom."

Thomas A. Schwartz

Further Reading

Feldman, Stephen M. 2008. *Free Expression and Democracy in America: A History*. Chicago: University of Chicago Press.
Grossman, Mark. 2012. *Constitutional Amendments: An Encyclopedia of the People, Procedures, Politics, Primary Documents, Campaigns for the 27 Amendments to the Constitution of the United States*. Amenia, NY: Grey House Publishing.
Levy, Leonard W. 1985. *Emergence of a Free Press*. New York: Oxford University Press.
Lewis, Anthony. 2007. *Freedom for the Thought We Hate: A Biography of the First Amendment*. New York: Perseus Books Group.

Constitution, Twelfth Amendment (1804)

The Twelfth Amendment was passed in 1804 after the election of 1800 showed there was a major problem with the Constitutional provision for the election of the president. Article 2, Section 1 provided that each state would have a number of electors equal to the number of senators and representatives, and each elector would have two votes, one of which had to be cast for someone not from the same state as the elector. The thinking was that an elector might want to vote for someone from his state, and this provision would force the elector to cast at least one vote for a leading candidate.

The Constitution also said that to be elected the candidate had to have a majority of the electoral votes. If nobody did, or there was a tie, then the House of Representatives would pick the president. In that proceeding, each state would have one vote. The Constitution also said that the person with the second highest Electoral College vote total would be vice president.

There was no problem with this in 1788 and 1792 with George Washington getting all the electoral votes and John Adams being the clear choice for vice president. There was a problem in 1796 when Adams was elected, but electors divided their votes for vice president. The runner-up in the Electoral College was Thomas Jefferson, so Jefferson became vice president. Jefferson was a Republican, and Adams was a Federalist, so the president and vice president were of different parties. This was perceived at the time as a political inconvenience rather than a serial problem.

What happened in 1800 was a serious problem. With 52 percent of the electoral vote, Thomas Jefferson defeated Adams. However, Aaron Burr, the Republican vice-presidential candidate, had the same number of electoral votes as Jefferson did. The tie meant that the House of Representatives had to decide who would be president. The vote, of course, was by states, and on the first ballot Jefferson had 8 votes of a possible 16, and that was not a majority. The house went through 34 more ballots with the same result. On the 36th ballot, Jefferson got 10 votes and became president. Burr became vice president but served only one term.

A factor in the decision was the effort by Alexander Hamilton to discredit Burr. He wrote letters to members of the House saying Burr simply was not qualified and could not be trusted. That in part led to the duel in 1804 in which Burr killed Hamilton.

The 12th Amendment, passed in 1804, changed the election rules to prevent a repeat of the 1800. It kept many of the original Constitutional provisions, but provided that electors vote separately for president and vice president, with each elector having one vote for each office. If no candidate for president has a majority of the electoral votes, then the House of Representatives will choose the president. The stipulation that each state has one vote is retained. A new provision was that if no candidate for vice president has a majority of the electoral votes, then the Senate will select the vice president. The rationale was that the vice president presides over the Senate.

There has been only one other instance of the House selecting the president. In 1824 there were four candidates, none of whom had a majority of the electoral votes. The House chose John Quincy Adams despite the fact that Andrew Jackson led in both the popular vote and the electoral vote. Four years later Jackson defeated Adams and went on to win again in 1832.

Guido H. Stempel III

Further Reading

Berg, Al, and Lauren Sherman. 2004. "Pistols at Weehawken." The Weehawken Historical Commission. http://duel2004.weehawkenhistory.org/pistols.pdf. Accessed January 12, 2015.

Burgett, Robert. 2011. *1803: Constitutional Intent for Electing the Presidency: How the Twelfth Amendment Failed to Anticipate the Rise of Competing National Parties.* Parker, CO: Outskirts Press.

Grossman, Mark. 2012. *Constitutional Amendments: An Encyclopedia of the People, Procedures, Politics, Primary Documents, Campaigns for the 27 Amendments to the Constitution of the United States.* Amenia, NY: Grey House Publishing.

Constitution, Fourteenth Amendment (1868)

The Thirteenth, Fourteenth, and Fifteenth Amendments are frequently thought of as a package that was required to implement the Emancipation Proclamation issued by President Abraham Lincoln in 1863. Each, however, was a separate political action, and it took four years for all three to be ratified.

The Thirteenth Amendment, which simply outlawed slavery, was ratified December 6, 1865. This left the status of former slaves in doubt because Article 1, Section 2 of the Constitution said slaves should be counted as two-thirds of a person for determining the number of representatives in Congress and apportionment of taxes.

The Fourteenth Amendment addressed this head on, stating in its first sentence that "all persons born or naturalized in the United States . . . are citizens of the United States and the state in which they reside." It went on to say that no state could make or enforce any law that abridges the rights of any citizen. It also said that all citizens are entitled to equal protection of the law. The former slaves thus had the full rights of citizenship. Clearly this was needed to give the Thirteenth Amendment its full impact, but it was not ratified until July 9, 1868, two and a half years after the Thirteenth Amendment was ratified.

The Fourteenth Amendment went beyond the matter of the rights of former slaves. By the references to states, it extended the coverage of this amendment and the Bill of Rights to the states. The amendments that make up the Bill of Rights do not mention states except for the Tenth Amendment, which says rights not delegated to the federal government are reserved for the states. For example, the First Amendment begins "Congress shall make no law" and says nothing about the individual states.

Rep. John A. Bingham of Ohio, author of the amendment, said it was his intent that this amendment should extend the coverage of the Bill of Rights to the states. Sen. Jacob Howard of Michigan, who introduced the amendment in the Senate, agreed, but many in Congress did not agree. It would be more than half a century before the Supreme Court agreed. That happened in 1925 in *Gitlow v. New York* (268 US 652) when the Court ruled that a New York state law on anarchy violated the First Amendment. The First Amendment thus meant that states, and for that matter cities, must respect freedom of the press.

That ruling led to the Fourteenth Amendment becoming the most widely cited precedent in Supreme Court cases. Nothing else in the Constitution and its amendments made it clear that rights spelled out in the Constitution applied to the states. Furthermore, this interpretation kept states from justifying restrictions by citing the Tenth Amendment.

The Fourteenth Amendment has been applied to cases that had nothing to do with the rights of former slaves. It has been cited in cases involving voting rights, education rights, and rights of the accused as First Amendment cases. While the Supreme Court was slow to see the broad perspective of the Fourteenth Amendment, it is seldom questioned anymore.

The Fourteenth Amendment also contains some long forgotten provisions related to the Civil War. It said that persons who had engaged in rebellion or given aid and comfort to enemies of the United States could not hold state or federal office. It also provided that Congress could vote to "remove such disability." It also provided that any debts incurred by the Confederacy should not be assumed by the United States or any state.

Guido H. Stempel III

Further Reading

Curtis, Michael Kent. 1986. *No State Shall Abridge: The Fourteenth Amendment and the Bill of Rights*. Durham, NC: Duke University Press.

Grossman, Mark. 2012. *Constitutional Amendments: An Encyclopedia of the People, Procedures, Politics, Primary Documents, Campaigns for the 27 Amendments to the Constitution of the United States*. Amenia, NY: Grey House Publishing.

Constitution, Fifteenth Amendment (1870)

The Fifteenth Amendment may be the least effective of the 27 amendments to the United States Constitution. Passed in 1870, it was the third of three amendments meant to guarantee the rights of freed slaves. Its specific purpose was unmistakably clear. It was to prohibit preventing people from voting because of "race, color, or previous condition of servitude." That should have guaranteed blacks and other minorities the ability to vote, but it did not because segregationists in the South blocked that right. They refused to let blacks register. They enacted poll taxes. They required prospective voters to pass a knowledge test about government, but often there was one test for whites and quite another for blacks. The test for blacks was more difficult because it featured questions on obscure issues. The Ku Klux Klan terrorized, and in some instances killed, black citizens who attempted to vote. The net result was that by 1940, only 5 percent of blacks in the South were registered to vote.

Voting, rights became a major focus of the civil rights movement in the 1950s and 1960s. Activists from the North went south to help blacks register. They were often met by angry mobs that attacked them, and some were killed.

The Twenty-Fourth Amendment, which banned poll taxes, was ratified in 1964. At the urging of President Lyndon Johnson, Congress addressed the issue with the Voting Rights Act of 1965. The Fifteenth Amendment would be achieved.

It did not last. Those who wanted to restrict voting found new ways to do so. Some states passed laws requiring voters to have a picture ID. Members of the armed forces found their military ID card would not do because it did it have their address. Other picture IDs were rejected because of various technicalities. In some states, it had to be a card issued by a state agency.

Voters faced long lines because election boards did not provide enough voting machines. Some voters became discouraged and left, and others who waited were turned away when closing time came. There was some evidence that election boards deliberately shortchanged minority precincts in allocating voting machines. In some cases election boards made wholesale, arbitrary purges of registration lists. For example, lists of felons were compared with registration lists, and if a name appeared on both, it was dropped from the registration list without checking on the person registered. In some cases there were two people with the same name—one a felon and the other a legitimately registered voter.

In addition, the U.S. Supreme Court made it more difficult for the federal government to enforce the 1965 Voting Rights Act. In *Shelby County v. Holder* (570 US 1953), it ruled that the provision that governments with a history of racial discrimination must get approval from the federal government for changes in regulations was unconstitutional.

On the plus side, it became easier to vote absentee, and in some places voters could vote early at designated county offices. The battle to achieve what the Fifteenth Amendment promises seems unending.

Guido H. Stempel III

Further Reading

American Civil Liberties Union. "Voting Rights: Your Vote, Your Voice." www.aclu.org/voting-rights. Accessed January 12, 2015.

Grossman, Mark. 2012. *Constitutional Amendments: An Encyclopedia of the People, Procedures, Politics, Primary Documents, Campaigns for the 27 Amendments to the Constitution of the United States.* Amenia, NY: Grey House Publishing.

Constitution, Seventeenth Amendment (1917)

When the Seventeenth Amendment was ratified by the state legislature of Connecticut in 1913, it made the direct election of a state's senators by its people the law of the land. Its adoption replaced the mechanism for electing Senators originally outlined by the Constitution, shifting responsibility for the choice from a state's legislature to its citizens.

This replacement of an intentionally nondemocratic institution with one more directly beholden to the people is seen by some as a further realization of American democracy. But others, including some in the Tea Party movement, have criticized the amendment and called for its repeal, charging that it is a threat to federalism.

Writing as "Publius," James Madison carefully outlined the differences in design and purpose of the Senate and the House of Representatives. These differences were intentional because the new nation was to be a "compound republic, partaking both of the national and federal character, [one in which] the government ought to be founded on a mixture of the principles of proportional and equal representation." Federalist by design, this mechanism was ineffectual in practice, leading to gridlock within state legislatures, accusations of candidate bribery, and, ultimately, vacancies in the Capitol for Indiana and Delaware.

Many states responding to this gridlock—as well as populists calling for legislators to be more responsive to the will of the people—adopted more direct mechanisms for electing their own senators. In time, many of these newly elected legislators went on to support the proposed Seventeenth Amendment along its path to passage in 1912, first by the Senate and then the House. Connecticut provided the crucial three-fourths ratification vote, and in 1914, for the first time, every state's citizens chose who would represent their interests in the Senate. Nevertheless, many have found the Seventeenth Amendment controversial since its inception, with Utah refusing to ratify it, even symbolically. These critics protest the amendment on the grounds that it is an attack on the federalism protections enumerated in the Constitution, particularly states' rights.

As the issue of states' rights has grown salient again in recent years, so has displeasure with the Seventeenth Amendment; to some, the amendment is emblematic of the intrusion of the federal government into areas believed to be reserved for the states. Robert Welch, founder of the conservative John Birch Society, criticized the Seventeenth Amendment as early as 1966 as a concentration of centralized national power within the executive branch at the direct expense of state governments. This debate has persisted into the 21st century, suggesting that many view state rights as threatened, especially as the national government has grown.

In April 2004, Republican Senator Zell Miller of Georgia introduced a joint resolution aiming "to repeal the seventeenth article of amendment to the Constitution of the United States." While no other Senators signed on to Miller's bill and it died in committee, its introduction nearly a century after ratification is suggestive of the amendment's continued unpopularity with some citizens. While Miller's bill represents the most formal overture, the issue has been a popular one among Republican primary candidates for Congress in 2010 and 2012 and for at least two hopefuls for the Republican presidential nomination in 2012.

In a speech before the Conservative Political Action Conference in 2009 by Congressman Ron Paul of Texas, and in a newsletter distributed by his campaign again in 2012, he explicitly advocated for repeal. Another hopeful, Texas Governor Rick Perry, in a book published shortly before his entrance to the 2012 Republican primary, described the amendment as a mistake that has weakened the states' influence over the national government, signaling support but making no explicit call for repeal.

While calling for repeal seems unlikely from a mainstream presidential candidate, a 2010 congressional race in Idaho elected a pro-repeal candidate. Two Republican primary candidates spoke in favor of repeal, but one of them later withdrew his support after intense public scrutiny. Raul Labrador, the candidate who remained in favor of repeal, went on to win the primary and defeat Democrat incumbent Walt Minnick in a close race. Tea Party support may have been pivotal in the election, with one of its affiliates initially endorsing Minnick only to withdraw its support and endorse Labrador instead. This suggests a careful line that candidates who court the Tea Party's support must walk, not only advocating for important issues like supporting repeal of the Seventeenth Amendment, but also remaining undaunted in the face of public pressure.

Chris David Kromphardt

Further Reading

Grossman, Mark. 2012. *Constitutional Amendments: An Encyclopedia of the People, Procedures, Politics, Primary Documents, Campaigns for the 27 Amendments to the Constitution of the United States.* Amenia, NY: Grey House Publishing.

Madison, James. 1788. "The Senate." Independent Journal, February 27. United States Senate website. "Direct Election of Senators." http://www.senate.gov/artandhistory/history/common/briefing/Direct_Election_Senators.htm. Accessed on February 4, 2015.

Senate Joint Resolution 35, 108th Congress, 2nd Session. 2004. "To repeal the seventeenth article of amendment to the Constitution of the United States."

Constitution, Nineteenth Amendment (1920)

The Nineteenth Amendment to the United States Constitution grants women the right to vote. The amendment was first introduced in Congress in 1878 but was not ratified until August 18, 1920. The woman's suffrage movement began in earnest in the mid-19th century with marches, conventions, newspaper articles, and other means of protest. Most of the pioneers of the movement, including reformers Lucretia Mott (1793–1880), Lucy Stone (1818–1893), Susan B. Anthony (1820–1906), and Elizabeth Cady Stanton (1815–1902), did not live to see the victory of women's voting rights.

The text of the Nineteenth Amendment reads, "The right of citizens of the United States to vote shall not be denied or abridged by the United States or by any State on account of sex." The movement to grant women the right to vote began in earnest in 1848 with the first Women's Rights Convention in Seneca Falls, New York. Most progressive women who advocated for gender equality were also abolitionists. In 1840, Mott and Stanton had attended the Anti-Slavery Convention in London. Although allowed to accompany their husbands as delegates to the London convention, women were segregated from the men in the assembly hall and not allowed to speak. Prominent American abolitionist and newspaper publisher William Lloyd Garrison sided with the women, sitting with them in the rear balcony rather than joining the men.

Mott, a Quaker minister, and Stanton stood together in that segregated arena. Stanton later credited their conversations at the anti-slavery gathering as the genesis of the right-to-vote movement they later championed at Seneca Falls. Stanton, who had moved from Boston to Seneca Falls with her husband in 1847, organized a woman's rights convention the next year. Prior to the meeting, she and others authored a "Declaration of Sentiments," modeled on the Declaration of Independence.

In part it read, "When, in the course of human events, it becomes necessary for one portion of the family of man to assume among the people of the earth a position different from that which they have hitherto occupied, but one to which the laws of nature and of nature's God entitle them, a decent respect to the opinions of mankind requires that they should declare the causes that impel them to such a course. We hold these truths to be self-evident: that all men and women are created equal . . . The history of mankind is a history of repeated injuries and usurpations on the part of man toward woman, having in direct object the establishment of an absolute tyranny over her. To prove this, let facts be submitted to a candid world."

The two-day convention, advertised in the local Seneca Falls newspaper, was attended by some 300 people, male and female, black and white. Lucretia Mott, among others, worried the resolution would make the women subject to ridicule, which is what happened in the days following the Seneca Falls Convention. Former slave and abolitionist publisher Frederick Douglass was one of the most prominent attendees and supported Stanton's motion to demand the right to vote. The vote resolution passed, and was signed by 68 women and 32 men. Some, bowing to the public backlash, later asked that their names be removed.

Following Seneca Falls, regional conventions took place around the country. In 1851, a clergyman at a woman's rights meeting in Akron, Ohio, criticized women as being of the weaker sex and needing the aid of men. Former slave Isabella Baumfree (c. 1797–1883), whose self-chosen name after 1843 became Sojourner Truth, stood and gave a famous reply:

"That man over there says women need to be helped into carriages and lifted over ditches, and to have the best place everywhere. Nobody ever helps me into carriages or over puddles, or gives me the best place—and ain't I a woman?"

Anthony, daughter of a Quaker farmer, met Stanton in 1851. The two worked together for suffrage over the next 50 years. In 1890, suffragists Lucy Stone and Anthony put aside past differences and joined forces between their two organizations—the American and the National Woman Suffrage Associations—to form the National American Woman Suffrage Association, or NAWSA.

Individual territories and states offered some early victories. The Wyoming and Utah territories, for example, approved suffrage in 1869. Congress ended the female vote in Utah in 1887 over the issue of Mormon polygamy. The State of Washington approved suffrage in 1910.

State by state pushes for women's voting rights took place in the first two decades of the twentieth century. Before her death in 1906, Anthony handpicked Carrie Catt as her successor to head the NAWSA. Finally, on August 18, 1920, the Tennessee House of Representatives voted by a slim margin to ratify the federal suffrage amendment, when Catt was in her second term and Woodrow Wilson was president of the United States. On August 26 of that year, the U.S. Secretary of State signed the proclamation that the woman suffrage amendment had been ratified by the requisite 36 states. It was now the law of the land.

Anthony Hatcher

See also: Feminism; Gender Gap

Further Reading

Baker, Jean H., ed. 2002. *Votes for Women: The Struggle for Suffrage Revisited*. Oxford: Oxford University Press.

Cooney, Robert P.J., Jr. 2005. *Winning the Vote: The Triumph of the American Woman Suffrage Movement*. Santa Cruz, CA: American Graphic Press.

DuBois, Ellen C. 1998. *Woman Suffrage and Women's Rights*. New York: NYU Press.

Mead, Rebecca J. 2004. *How the Vote Was Won: Woman Suffrage in the Western United States, 1868–1914*. New York: NYU Press.

Constitution, Twenty-Fourth Amendment (1964)

The Twenty-Fourth Amendment, ratified January 23, 1964, banned poll taxes in federal elections. The Fifteenth Amendment gave former slaves the right to vote, so Southern states enacted poll taxes as a means to limit the voting of blacks. While every Southern state had enacted a poll tax, by the time this amendment was ratified only five states still had such laws on the books.

The Fifteenth Amendment, ratified in 1870, said voting rights could not be denied or abridged because of race. While a poll tax would not deny the right to vote, it would seem to abridge it, as voter turnout figures from Southern states make clear. Yet the U.S. Supreme Court ruled in *Bredlove v. Virginia* in 1937 that a poll tax was not unconstitutional.

The Twenty-Fourth Amendment was not the end of the issue. The amendment said voters who had not paid poll taxes could not be banned from voting in "any primary or other election for President or Vice President or electors for President or Vice President or for Senators or Representatives in Congress." Four Southern states then went before the Supreme Court claiming that poll taxes were still permitted for state elections.

In *Harper v. Virginia Board of Elections* two years after the Twenty-Fourth Amendment was ratified, the Supreme Court, drawing on the Fourteenth and Fifteenth amendments as well as the Twenty-Fourth Amendment overturned *Bredlove*. Any poll tax violated the Constitution.

That was the end of poll taxes, but some people suggested that requiring voters to buy an ID card from the state in order to vote was merely creating a different form of poll tax. The price of ID cards in some states was about the same as poll taxes were. The ID requirement, however, was not limited to Southern states the way poll taxes were.

The Twenty-Fourth Amendment, along with *Harper v. Virginia Board*, closes a gap left by the Fourteenth and Fifteenth amendments. States that seek to abridge voting rights of any citizens face a severe challenge in the Supreme Court.

Guido H, Stempel III

Further Reading

Grossman, Mark. 2012. *Constitutional Amendments: An Encyclopedia of the People, Procedures, Politics, Primary Documents, Campaigns for the 27 Amendments to the Constitution of the United States*. Amenia, NY: Grey House Publishing.

Constitution, Twenty-Sixth Amendment (1971)

Adult suffrage for American citizens became nearly universal (felons can still be denied the vote by the states) when the Twenty-Sixth Amendment was ratified on July 1, 1971, thereby extending the franchise to 18-year-olds. The amendment was a culmination of several years of political activism by young adults, which largely focused on debates over civil rights, the Vietnam War, and the draft; furthermore, the amendment's ramifications have shaped the current political environment, as politicians, such as Barack Obama in 2008 and 2012, try to energize a significant, "sleeping" portion of the electorate by emphasizing issues that are salient to young adults.

The rallying cry behind the Twenty-Sixth Amendment was quite simple: "Old enough to fight, old enough to vote." If an 18-year-old can die fighting for his country, he should be privileged to choose who makes the policy decisions to send him off to war. The draft, which from 1948 to 1973 enabled the federal government's conscription into the armed forces of men ages 18 through 26, led to some of those young men being required to fight against their will. Draft card burnings and public protests were common. Before it was changed, the minimum voting age was 21 years old. Historically, the Constitution coincided with British common law in this regard. However, as young adults and the issues they valued grew in salience throughout the 1960s, some politicians—somewhat ironically, given the patent inability of this particular constituency to support them at the ballot box—began to call for a change in policy.

Congress acquiesced in 1970, amending the Voting Rights Act of 1965 to allow for the provision, and Richard Nixon signed the bill into law; Nixon's prediction, however, that making such a change required not just a new law but a constitutional amendment proved to be correct, as the Court ruled the provision unconstitutional in *Oregon v. Mitchell* (1970). Congress quickly responded to the Court's ruling with the passage, on March 23, 1971, of what was to become the Twenty-Sixth Amendment. To the extent that young adults are different from the rest of the electorate, and are politically active in service of those issues important to them, the Twenty-sixth Amendment has altered the shape of American politics.

The Center for Information and Research on Civic Learning and Engagement (CIRCLE), a nonprofit institute that promotes research on youth issues and voting, publishes findings about youth demographics and voting patterns. CIRCLE reports that 18–29 year olds, some 46 million people, comprise 22 percent of all eligible voters. Additionally, young eligible voters are less likely to be white, non-Hispanics than older voters, and are almost twice as likely as older voters to be unemployed. CIRCLE also reports that, contrary to popular belief, the youth vote, historically, has not been a lock for the Democratic presidential candidate; in fact, while the youth vote has gone for the Democratic candidate since 1992, several Republican presidential candidates have captured a majority of it since 1972. Since 1984, the youth vote has predicted all but one presidential election.

A stark characteristic of registered voters younger than 30 is that they report a much lower rate of giving a lot of thought to an election and of planning to vote. The "enthusiasm" gap between older and young voters increased from 11 points in 2006 to 22 points in 2010, and the voting gap is even larger: 23 points in 2006 and 31 points in 2010 (Pew Research Center).

In 2010, the youngest group of registered voters were the most likely to approve of Obama's job performance and were the only age group to express the view that

Obama's policies had improved the economy as well as to express support for the Affordable Care Act and for a bigger government that provided more services. Despite the dismal enthusiasm and voting numbers they report, young adults are still courted by politicians.

During the 2012 presidential election, President Obama was a regular fixture on college campuses in swing states, rallying support for policies geared specifically toward the millennial generation, such as increased Pell grants, limits on college-loan rates, and, a hallmark of his signature Affordable Care Act, the ability for young adults to stay on their parents' insurance until they are 26.

While those enfranchised by the Twenty-Sixth Amendment are lumped into the larger 18–29 age group for polling purposes, their import to American elections is not to be understated. The youth vote is in many ways a sleeping one, and—as was demonstrated in 2008, when Obama defeated Senator John McCain by a margin of almost 34 points—a candidate can connect with this group to an impressive degree and shatter the illusion that young adults are politically apathetic.

Chris David Kromphardt

Further Reading

Calmes, Jackie. 2012. "Obama Courts the Votes of a Less-Engaged Youth." *The New York Times*, August 28.

Grossman, Mark. 2012. *Constitutional Amendments: An Encyclopedia of the People, Procedures, Politics, Primary Documents, Campaigns for the 27 Amendments to the Constitution of the United States.* Amenia, NY: Grey House Publishing.

Pew Research Center Publications. 2010. "Lagging Youth Enthusiasm Could Hurt Democrats in 2010." Pew Research Center for the People and the Press.

Contributions, Court Rulings on

Two court decisions in 2010 significantly reduced decades-old restrictions on political contributions. *Citizens' United v. Federal Elections Commission* dealt with the desire by the conservative nonprofit organization called *Citizens' United* to air on television a film that criticized Democratic presidential candidate Hillary Rodham Clinton during the 2008 primary season. The Federal Elections Commission had ruled that this would violate the McCain-Feingold Act of 2001, which prohibited such activity within 30 days of a primary election.

Citizens United appealed to the United States Supreme Court, arguing that this violated their First Amendment rights. The court agreed in a 5-4 decision. It ruled that part of McCain-Feingold was unconstitutional because organizations, including corporations and labor unions, have the same First Amendment rights as do citizens. Strangely, although there have been many recent cases in which the court ruled that an organization has the same right as a citizen, the court based this latest conclusion on a statement in an 1886 case, *Santa Clara County v. Southern Pacific Railroad*. Critics have objected that a corporation is not like a citizen in many ways. It cannot speak, vote, get married, serve in the military, or get elected to political office.

What has been overlooked in the often heated discussions that followed the ruling is that the court ruling left intact the prohibitions against contributions to political parties or candidates 30 days before a primary or 60 days before an election. Some observers warn that in the flurry of contributions that has followed, those restrictions have been overlooked and violated.

The Court also ruled that the dollar limits on contributions did not serve a justifiable governmental purpose and therefore also were in violation of the First Amendment. The Court rejected arguments that such contributions might enable donors to get favors from members of Congress and other government officials.

The other case was *SpeechNow.org v. Federal Elections Commission*. SpeechNow was an independent nonprofit organization that sought to make contributions to causes and to solicit funds for such purposes. It obtained an opinion, but not a ruling, from the Federal Election Commission that such activity would violate McCain-Feingold. SpeechNow then went to the Federal District Court to ask for an injunction against the Federal Election Commission. The Federal District Court ruled against SpeechNow, but SpeechNow appealed to the Federal District Appeals Court and won. That court agreed that dollar limits on contributions violated the First Amendment.

In both cases, the plaintiffs argued that the requirement that they report the source and amount of contributions was also a violation of the First Amendment. However, both courts rejected that argument and left reporting requirements of McCain-Feingold intact. It is because of this that we can say, for instance, that the multimillionaire brothers Charles G. and David H. Koch made political contributions totaling $416 million in 2012.

What is the effect of these two cases? First of all, they apply to political action committees, not to political parties or candidates. Limits on expenditures by, and contributions to, parties and candidates remain in force. However, political action committees are free to spend as much as they wish on political communication. For 30 days before America's rather lengthy primary period and during the primary period, they cannot focus on candidates. For 60 days before the election, again, they cannot focus on candidates. That leaves a little more than two months in between the end of primaries and the start of that 60-day period when they can advertise and televise their messages about specific candidates.

An ad or other paid communication can directly mention a candidate. For example, an ad that deals with an issue such as coal-fired power plants, pro or con, can name a candidate and that candidate's stand on the issue, so long as that is a minor part of the ad. There is nothing in the rulings to prevent a political action committee from running a series of ads on various issues with a mention of the same candidate in each ad. Yet, for all practical purposes, this is a political ad campaign.

There is an open question about how enforceable the provisions are that require mention of candidates not be the major point of an ad, and the volume of ads has become so great that enforcement of the Supreme Court's intention is difficult. Targeted ads for congressional candidates appear only in their districts, making national tracking especially hard.

It was anticipated that as a result of these two court decisions, expenditures would increase. It did in 2012, when the total for all elections was $6 billion, a billion more than in 2008. However, the 2008 total was a billion more than the 2004 total had been. In the presidential races, the results were about the same, with the major party candidates raising roughly a billion dollars in both 2008 and 2012. Preliminary analysis of the 2014 off-year election show that in dozens of Senate and House races, spending by outside groups surpassed spending by the candidates themselves.

Guido H. Stempel III

See also: Dark Money; Political Action Committees

Further Reading

Citizen United v. Federal Election Commission. 2010. (558 US 310).

Federal Election Commission. 2010. *SpeechNow.org v. Federal Election Commission.* http://www .fec.gov/law/litigation/speechnow.shtml. Accessed January 12, 2015.

Youn, Monica, ed. 2011. *Money, Politics and the Constitution.* New York: The Century Foundation Press.

Corporation for Public Broadcasting (CPB)

The Corporation for Public Broadcasting (CPB) is a private, nonprofit corporation whose primary function is to distribute federal money to 1,400 noncommercial radio and television stations and their programs without subjecting them to political influence. The CPB is governed by a nine-member board of directors. The president appoints each board member, subject to approval by the U.S. Senate, to serve a staggered six-year term. The CPB does not operate any stations. Instead, stations are controlled locally and can choose and schedule programs as they see fit.

The CPB began operating in April 1968 after President Lyndon Johnson signed the Public Broadcasting Act of 1967 the previous November. The creation of a private corporation to encourage the development of noncommercial broadcasting was the key recommendation of a private study commission funded by the Carnegie Foundation in 1965. The Carnegie Commission of Educational Television also urged Congress to implement a 2–5 percent excise tax on the sale of television sets to give the new corporation a source of stable, apolitical funding, but that aspect of the Commission's report was not adopted after equipment manufacturers fought the idea. The Carnegie Commission also focused on noncommercial television, but last-minute lobbying by educational radio supporters got radio added to the final bill. The Carnegie Commission also used the term "public" instead of "educational" broadcasting to show that the intended programming was aimed at a wider audience, and was not "appropriate or available" from commercial broadcasters or designed simply to support a teaching function.

The CPB started its own television network, the Public Broadcasting Service (PBS), in 1970. PBS puts together a recommended schedule and operates facilities to interconnect its member stations to programming sources, but PBS only distributes programs that other sources produce. Member stations pay dues based on the size of their market and their budget. PBS does not supply all national programming to local stations. Large amounts of content, including many pledge-drive specials, are supplied by various third-party sources,

The CPB created National Public Radio (NPR) in 1970 to interconnect member stations and also to produce its own programming, unlike PBS. CPB radio funds go to member stations directly, which in turn pay NPR for programs the stations use from the network. In addition to news programs such as *Morning Edition* and *All Things Considered*, NPR distributes a variety of cultural, talk, and information programs to its member stations. Since the 1980s, two major nonprofit distributors of content to public radio stations have emerged to compete with NPR, both based in Minnesota: American Public Media, which distributes *A Prairie Home Companion* hosted by Garrison Keillor, and Public Radio International, which produces *The Takeaway*. Like NPR, both receive CPB money indirectly, through the dues that member stations pay.

Historically, the argument in support of public broadcasting is that it serves groups not served by commercial broadcasting and offers programming not found elsewhere, but with increasing news and entertainment choices available on cable television, direct broadcast satellite, satellite radio, and the Internet, some have argued that the federal government's role in supporting public broadcasting needs to be reevaluated. Conservatives in Congress in 1994 and 2011 questioned the need for federal funds to support public broadcasting during times of budget deficits. Each time the CPB managed to retain most of its annual appropriation, which has steadily increased or remained stable most years since 1969.

In recent years the CPB has been re-emphasizing the educational mission of its member stations to help differentiate its offerings from its other choices in an increasingly crowded media universe. In January 2008 it released a survey, "Public Television Stations: A Trust Source for Educating America," which highlighted the "off-air educational services," the stations offered in their communities. The survey found that 76 percent were partnering with K–12 schools and 68 percent were working with higher education institutions. The CPB also increasingly uses the term "public media" instead of "public broadcasting" to describe the multiple platforms stations are using to reach diverse audience with their content.

Overall, about 15 percent of the total budgets of public radio and television stations in the United States come from money distributed by CPB. Membership contributions are the largest income source for public broadcasting—making up about 27 percent of the budgets of all public stations in fiscal year 2011. In June 2012, the CPB released a report conducted by the consulting firm Booz & Company that studied alternative ways to fund public broadcasting. The report found that alternative sources would not be enough: ending federal funding to the CPB would severely diminish or possibly end public broadcasting, especially at stations in rural or underserved areas. Usually funded for a two-year appropriation cycle, the CPB was requesting $445 million for fiscal years 2014 and 2016. The CPB is quick to point out that its annual appropriation costs each American about $1.35 per year.

Dale Zacher

Further Reading

Carnegie Commission on Educational Television. 1967. *Public Television: A Program for Action.* New York: Harper & Row.

Corporation for Public Broadcasting. 2012. "Alternative Sources of Funding for Public Broadcasting Stations."http://www.cpb.org/aboutcpb/Alternative_Sources_of_Funding_for_Public _Broadcasting_Stations.pdf. Accessed January 12. 2015.

McCauley, Michael. 2005. *NPR: The Trials and Triumphs of National Public Radio*. New York: Columbia University Press.

McGregor, Michael, Paul Driscoll, and Walter McDowell. *Head's Broadcasting in America: A Survey of Electronic Media*. Boston: Allyn and Bacon, 2010.

McLouglin, Glenn, and Mark Gurevitz. 2013. "The Corporation for Public Broadcasting: Federal Funding and Issues." *Journal of Current Issues in Media and Telecommunications* 5(4): 405–414.

Counterculture

The counterculture of the 1960s was a period that initiated a dramatic shift in society, marked by notable changes in music, art, drug use, political behavior, struggle for rights (through the civil rights movement, the women's movement, and the gay rights movement), and in fashion. Though the rebellion of the era is often simplified in the characterization of hippies and free love, the complexity and range of upheaval, both positive and negative, extends beyond such basic summarizations. The myriad of radical changes (some of them long-lasting) in culture that occurred during this period establishes the 1960s counterculture as one of the most historically memorable and culturally significant transition periods in the United States and much of the Western world.

Following the rather complacent and traditional 1950s, members of the counterculture in the 1960s reevaluated the world in which they lived and sought to challenge structures of oppression that relegated various groups powerless and immobile. The civil rights movement of the 1960s introduced both separationists—such as Malcolm X and the Black Panther Party—who endorsed the use of aggression by African Americans in retaliation for racism and assimilationists—such as Martin Luther King Jr. and Students for a Democratic Society—who advocated for peaceful protest against racial discrimination. The long-brewing racism, embedded in both the political and economic structure of the American South, erupted at the end of the decade, and cities across the Southern states experienced a surge of protests (many ending tragically in violence) against the Jim Crow laws that denied African Americans rights.

The women's movement also developed as part of the counterculture and embodied the general attitudes toward freedom and equality. The earlier publication of literary works, such as Simone de Beauvoir's *The Second Sex* and Betty Friedan's *The Feminine Mystique*, deemed provocative at the time, touted equal rights for women and endorsed the ideas that women could be liberated from the patriarchal structure that diminished their political, economic, and social status. More women began enrolling in higher education and securing jobs, not just marriages, following their college graduations. Body liberation was emphasized as well, and many women rebelled from the traditional clothing at the time that restricted movement and promoted certain feminine stereotypes. Hair and makeup likewise evolved from a very primped look to a more relaxed, natural look.

A third movement within the counterculture, also demanding more civil rights, was the gay and lesbian rights movement (now known as the LGBT movement). Beginning with the infamous Stonewall Riots following a 1969 police raid of a gay bar in New York's Greenwich Village, the public took notice of the rising prominence of homosexual individuals demanding civil rights. Though the movement was in its infancy, relative to its present achievements, the media and the masses began to notice the gay and lesbian community around them, and the community itself utilized the sweeping changes happening elsewhere in the counterculture to aid their cause.

The look and sound of the counterculture is often the most memorable aspect of the era, in part because of its lasting legacy on fashion and the arts today. Following the underlying ideals of equality and freedom, members of the counterculture slowly adopted a radical dress that separated them from those unaffiliated with the movement. Though the late 1950s and the early 1960s continued to uphold gender differences through fashion, the hippies of the counterculture promoted more equality between the sexes and was typified by bell-bottoms, jeans with extra fabric inserted past the knees to create a "bell" illusion, worn by both men and women. The general look of "unkemptness," abhorrent by traditional fashion standards of the time, raged within the counterculture, and long, flowing hair, adorned with braids and flowers; colorful tie-dyed shirts; buttons; and beads became popular signifiers of the hippie style.

Like the whimsical image of hippie fashion, the music also embodied a unique sound, with beatnik, earlier rock-n-roll, and folk influences. Singers Bob Dylan and Joan Baez were known for playing folk melodies on their guitars while singing poetic, and sometimes political, lyrics. Harder rock singers, such as Jimi Hendrix and Janis Joplin, incorporated the electric guitar and shocking rhythms into their songs. Both appeared at the now-famous farm concert, Woodstock, in which many facets of the counterculture experience were brought to life. Just as experimentation in fashion and music were frequent, so too was experimenting with drugs, as Timothy Leary's LSD, acid, and other illegal substances became more popular and available.

The music of the counterculture was deeply inspired by many of the political struggles of the times, including the United States' deepening commitment to South Vietnam as the small Asian nation struggled to fend off the Communist opposition. After World War II, many U.S. presidents gave money and sent troops to Vietnam, in hopes of staving off the spread of Communism and preventing the feared domino effect. President Johnson and President Nixon were highly criticized in their role, as was Secretary of Defense Robert McNamara. The increasing prominence of the counterculture demonstrated participants' anger with peaceful protests and marches opposing the American presence in such foreign affairs.

Laura Merrifield Sojka

See also: Baby Boom; Generation X

Further Reading

Gitlin, Todd. 1993. *The Sixties: Years of Hope, Days of Rage.* New York: Bantam.
Heath, Joseph, and Andrew Potter. 2004. *Nation of Rebels: Why Counterculture Became Consumer Culture.* New York: HarperCollins.

Culture Wars

Since at least the 1960s, nearly every political issue in the United States has been framed in terms of the "culture war," a struggle for hegemonic dominance between self-identified "conservative traditionalists" and "liberal progressives." The metaphor of "war" is apt because the cultural divisions are typically framed, not in terms of debating differences of opinion in the democratic tradition, but rather in terms of enmity, demonization, and a "win at all costs" zealotry. As in real wars, the culture war typically is fought between powerful minority groups, with the moderate majority of American voters caught in the crossfire.

The culture war statistically involves a relative minority of Americans, yet it dominates the public perception of the state of the nation. The culture war envelopes nearly every issue of public interest, from the very serious—such as environmental regulation and health care policy—to the patently silly (notable examples include the so-called "war on Christmas" and the "war on soda").

Rather than reflecting deep divisions in public opinion over specific issues, the culture war reflects a more or less generalized mood of intolerance from the ideological fringes. Both sides use radicalized rhetoric, emotional hyperbole, and pseudoscience to bolster their positions and rally their supporters. That intolerance is most clearly exhibited when "conservatives" use the word "liberal" as an epithet, and vice versa.

The term "culture war" is derived from the German word "Kulturkampf," meaning "culture struggle." The Kulturkampf was a period of secularization in Prussia during the 1870s, a movement that led to laws aimed to curb the political influence of Catholicism. Like the Prussian Kulturkampf, the American culture war of recent decades has strong religious-vs.-secular connotations. However, the American culture war was launched by the religious right against the secular left, not the other way around.

There is some debate about when the American culture war started, although many scholars suggest that open hostilities began in the 1980s with the mobilization of the religious right into national politics. Of course, the United States was built on a culture of discord, and it has experienced many periods of deep socio-political divisions from the very start (the bitter feuds between Federalists and Anti-Federalists during the constitutional conventions surely set a national tone). Obviously, the Civil War and the civil rights movement represent periods of intense cultural divisions. Those earlier divisions were over pre-existing issues, however. One aspect of the culture war of the late 20th and early 21st centuries is that it has created its own issues—that is, it is a cause of divisiveness, not a result.

In fact, considerable evidence suggests that the culture war itself is predicated on a myth that American voters are polarized on most issues, when in fact the majority of the electorate is in the ideological and political center. As such, the culture war has a disproportionate influence on politics and political campaigning compared to actual public opinion.

For example, with regard to abortion, factions on either side of the issue claim the moral high ground ("pro-life" vs. "women's rights," suggesting that their opponents are either "anti-life" or "pro-misogyny"), and each persistently argues that the other side poses a "threat" to society. The two movements tend to exhibit a general fanaticism that precludes reasonable compromise. Political candidates at all levels are often expected to pick sides; many eagerly and emphatically do so, especially during primary elections. However, reputable polls suggest that the two "sides" together make up a minority. Gallup polling from 2001 through 2012 showed that only about 20 percent of Americans wanted to ban abortion entirely and only about 25 percent wanted no legal restrictions on abortion whatsoever. The remaining 55 percent seem to prefer the moderated view that abortion should be "safe, legal, and rare." Despite the consistently moderate view held by most Americans, the "abortion issue" in politics is almost always framed in terms of all or nothing, and it has been one of the most divisive issues in state and national politics.

Such divisiveness is not just exhibited with regard to specific hot-button issues such as abortion, private gun ownership, same-sex marriage, and the like. The very concept of compromise is, itself, a casualty of the culture war. That was obvious in late 2012 and early 2013, for example, on the issue of the "fiscal cliff"— a months-long stalemate over funding federal programs and reducing national debt. Public opinion overwhelmingly favored a compromise involving limited tax-increases for wealthier Americans and spending cuts in federal programs, including social-welfare services. A *USA Today*/Gallup poll taken immediately after the November 2012 election found that two-thirds of all Americans wanted the two parties to compromise equally. Yet leaders of both parties stubbornly rejected compromise in favor of unyielding partisan gridlock.

Special-interest groups, professional pundits, and adjuncts to the political process have profited considerably from the culture war, using amped-up rhetoric (and often trumped-up charges) to solicit donations and enlist unpaid volunteers from their strongest supporters. The culture war also has been useful to deter moderate, compromise-minded politicians from seeking higher office, and many politicians with long, respectable careers as good-faith negotiators have resigned rather than compromising their principles. Fomenting an angry and fearful electorate, easily swayed by distorted truths and dubious "facts" was a way to win elections in the late 20th and early 21st centuries. As such, the culture war may never end.

Bill Reader

See also: Class Warfare Politics; Polarization

Further Reading

Abramowitz, Alan I. 2012. *The Polarized Public? Why American Government Is so Dysfunctional.* New York: Pearson.

Fiorina, Morris P., Abrams, Samuel J. and Pope, Jeremy C. 2010. *Culture War? The Myth of a Polarized America.* 3rd ed. New York: Pearson.

Gelman, Andrew. 2009. *Red State, Blue State, Rich State, Poor State: Why Americans Vote the Way They Do.* Princeton, NJ: Princeton University Press.

Cynicism in Politics and Media

Scholars commonly cite political disaffection (alienation) as the primary reason for a lack of citizen engagement and participation in public affairs. Cynicism is a primary aspect of disaffection, typically defined as a lack of confidence in, and a feeling of distrust toward, the political system, officials, and institutions. Some researchers suggest cynicism is the result of poor-quality news media reports about politicians and elections; others believe candidates' negative campaign tactics produce cynicism; still others blame a reliance on television.

In their well-received 1997 book *Spiral of Cynicism*, Cappella and Jameson suggest that news media seek to cover conflict, so politicians provide conflict to generate media coverage. This results in a mutually reinforcing spiral in which the media provide citizens with a relatively consistent stream of negative information, which ultimately contributes to greater voter cynicism and further distances citizens from the political process.

This process may be exacerbated by candidates' negative campaign tactics, which turn off potential voters and also produce citizen cynicism. This may be a particular concern for young voters who, according to some scholars, are more likely to get trapped in a cycle in which cynicism breeds low efficacy. Research indicates that cynicism negatively associates with external efficacy—citizens' sense that government is responsive and they can successfully influence governmental decisions and operations; efficacy has a positive relationship to voting intentions and related public-affairs behavior.

As efficacy falls, cynicism may increase, resulting in apathy, which is a lack of willingness to get involved in the public affairs process. The outcomes of an apathetic citizenry are evidenced by low voter turnout and a lack of public affairs media use. Empirical evidence to support this perspective is equivocal, however. While research indicates apathy and cynicism relate to efficacy independently, they do not appear to relate to each other. In addition, while citizens who are cynical tend to distance themselves from media and the government, research evidence indicates that purposeful use of the media associates with a low level of disaffection and a high level of involvement or engagement in public affairs. As a result, while there is an empirical basis for concerns regarding the media, candidates' election tactics, and political cynicism, research results indicate that political disaffection is multifaceted and that it is an oversimplification to blame the news media and candidates' negative campaign tactics for voter malaise.

To better understand political decision making and disaffection, it is useful to distinguish between healthy skepticism, which reflects a critical but open approach to the media and public affairs information, and unhealthy cynicism, which refers to a lack of confidence in and feeling of distrust toward politics and governmental institutions. While skeptical citizens may be critical consumers of both positive and counter-attitudinal election information, cynical citizens distrust the media and government, and purposeful, informed use of the media by these citizens is infrequent. This is because cynicism represents a distancing from the political process—essentially a closure to new information. It follows that when citizens feel alienated from politics and choose not to seek public affairs information in the media, they may be more likely to lapse into apathy and opt out of the political process altogether.

While cynicism and skepticism both represent a negative posture toward the political process and relevant media, they appear to operate quite differently in the political decision-making process. In particular, research indicates skeptical citizens may be critical of politicians, government institutions, and relevant public affairs media but still benefit from a strong connection to the political process. Evidence of this relationship is based on the positive association of skepticism to external efficacy and negative relationship to apathy. Skepticism may produce a somewhat critical perspective toward news media and other sources of public affairs information, but this does not mean skeptical citizens abandon the political process or relevant information sources altogether. Instead, skeptical citizens maintain a sense that their political participation makes a difference based on the link of skepticism to external efficacy.

For cynical citizens, the political process holds no promise of positive outcomes, and relevant public affairs media are not useful and perhaps are untrustworthy. For cynical citizens, the public affairs process is corrupt and unresponsive. Further, these citizens are unwilling or uninterested in consuming information that might help change their perspective and produce a stronger desire to engage in the political process. Even so, cynicism does not automatically produce apathy. When cynicism, skepticism, and apathy were included in a structural model of political decision making, cynicism had no direct relationship to apathy and a negative relationship to efficacy. As a result, citizens' cynicism shows strong potential to undermine civic health because trust and engagement are worn down, which appears to erode the skills and resources necessary to maximize the civic health of communities, even if does not produce apathy outright.

Bruce E. Pinkleton

See also: Conspiracy Theories; Polarization

Further Reading

Ansolabehere, S., and S. Iyengar. 1995. *Going Negative: How Political Advertisements Shrink and Polarize the Electorate.* New York: The Free Press.

Cappella, J.N., and K.H. Jamieson. 1997. *Spiral of Cynicism: The Press and the Public Good.* New York: Oxford University Press.

Dionne, E.J. 1991. *Why Americans Hate Politics.* New York: Simon and Schuster.

Moy, Patricia, and Michael Pfau. 2000. *With Malice Toward All? The Media and Public Confidence in Democratic Institutions.* Westport, CT: Praeger.

Pinkleton, B.E., E.W. Austin, Y. Zhou, J.F. Willoughby, and M. Reiser. 2012. "Perceptions of News Media, External Efficacy, and Public Affairs Apathy in Political Decision Making and Disaffection." *Journalism and Mass Communication Quarterly* 89: 23–39.

D

Damage Control

Damage control is the effort by a politician or political party to minimize or eliminate damage to their reputation. The damaging situation may occur in a number of ways. It may be the result of an ill-advised or unfortunate statement a politician makes in a speech. For example, the politician makes a speech in which he or she says that unions are out of control and then realizes that in the city in which he made the speech 70 percent of the workers are union members. What can he or she do?

The first possibility is to claim he was misquoted. In doing that, the politician is putting his credibility against that of the newspaper or broadcast station which reported the speech. That may be believed by some people, but not everybody. The second possibility is to issue a clarification, which in effect changes the politician's position through elaboration. Key phrase is "what I really mean . . ." The third possibility is not to say anything more on the issue with the hope that most will forget. Of course, the political opponent may make sure that the public does not forget.

The second possible source of damage is a natural event, such as a tornado, hurricane winter storm, or plane crash. The event is damaging to the politician because of a position he or she took earlier. For instance, if the politician voted against funds for flood control and a major flood occurs, that vote may come back to haunt the politician. The politician may respond by coming out strongly for emergency flood relief. If that happens, the earlier vote may be forgotten. Another approach is to try to shift blame. The state legislator will blame the U.S. Congress for failing to act, and the congressman will blame the state legislature. Perhaps the politician will blame a state or federal agency.

A third possible source of damage is a scandal involving a government agency. When President Harry Truman said, "The buck stops here," he had it figured out. When the Internal Revenue Service was found in 2013 to be singling out conservative groups for special attention when it reviewed their requests for tax exempt status, conservatives blamed President Barack Obama. Yet what was being done was not the president's policy or even the policy of the Internal Revenue Service. It was the interpretation of policy by a small Cincinnati office of the Internal Revenue Service. Yet the president had to deal with the damage.

When the scandal broke in 2014 about the state administration in New Jersey creating traffic jams for political purposes on the George Washington Bridge at Fort Lee, New Jersey, criticism was directed at Gov. Chris Christie. He maintained, however, that he knew nothing about it, and there did not seem to be conclusive evidence that he did.

In both these cases, damage control included press conferences in which charges were denied, and the issue was cast in a different light. The president did not approve of what the IRS had been doing, and the governor did not approve of creating traffic jams.

A fourth possible source of damage is a charge of sexual (or other personal) misconduct. For the politician so charged, there are really only two choices. One is to deny the charges. The other is to ignore the charges and hope the voters will do likewise. There certainly have been cases in which that is what has happened.

Any time a politician engages in damage control, he or she is running the risk that this will keep the issue before the public and perhaps make the issue and the damage worse. Furthermore, not all damage control efforts will succeed. Some efforts at damage control have done more damage than there was in the beginning, yet the temptation to respond can be very difficult for a politician to resist.

Damage control is an exercise in politics. While politicians might hope that an effort at damage control will convince everybody, they probably recognize that will not happen, nor is it really necessary. The politician's first concern is to convince those who favor him or her. It might be nice to cross party lines and bring more people over, but that is secondary to holding the supporters already won.

Guido H. Stempel III

Further Reading

Dezenhall, Eric, and John Weber. 2011. *Damage Control: The Essential Lessons of Crisis Management.* Westport, CT: Prospecta Press.

Lehane, Christopher, Mark Fabiani, and Bill Guttentag. 2012. *Masters of Disaster: The Ten Commandments of Damage Control.* New York: Palgrave MacMillan.

Dark Money

Politically active nonprofit organizations have a growing influence in American politics since they can spend so-called "dark money"—funds from undisclosed donors. These nonprofits can receive unlimited donations from corporations, unions, special interest groups, and wealthy individuals.

Donations to nonprofit groups are considered confidential by U.S. tax laws. The law also limits the amount of political activity nonprofit groups may engage in, although the issue has become politically charged and the Internal Revenue Service has done little to police political spending by these groups. Attempts to regulate dark money have been stalled by congressional gridlock.

Ann M. Ravel, the Democratic vice chairman of the Federal Elections Commission, testified before Senate Rules Committee on April 30, 2014 that "dark money networks are able to anonymously inject large amounts of money into our political process. Using shell corporate entities, wire transfers, and fund swapping with no apparent purpose other than to hide the sources of funds, these national networks skirt disclosure rules with relative ease."

The Center for Responsive Politics in Washington, D.C., estimates that dark money spending has grown from about $5 million in 2006 to more than $300 million in the 2012 election cycle. Precise accounting of these expenditures is difficult, however, since it is not always easy to determine the intentions behind nonprofit expenditures. In the 2014 election cycle, spending by outside groups using dark money outpaced the direct spending by dozens of congressional candidates.

The largest dark money expenditure in recent elections was made by the "twin" groups American Crossroads and Crossroads GPS, started by Republicans Karl Rove and Ed Gillespie, both political consultants to President George W. Bush. The Crossroads GPS group specifically was created, according to American Crossroads political director Carl Forti, because "some donors didn't want to be disclosed." The two groups raised more than $325 million during the 2012 elections. Other significant dark money groups include the U.S. Chamber of Commerce, Americans for Tax Reform, the League of Conservation Voters, and the National Rifle Association.

Thomas K. Hargrove

See also: McCain-Feingold Campaign Finance Reform Law

Further Reading

Center for Responsive Politics. "Political Nonprofits: Top Election Spenders." https://www.opense crets.org/outsidespending/nonprof_elec.php. Accessed July 26, 2014.
Ravel, Ann M. "Testimony of Ann M. Ravel, Former Chair, California Fair Political Practices Commission." April 30, 2014, posted by the Federal Election Commission. http://www.fec.gov /members/ravel/testimony/wr0itten_testimony_04302014.pdf. Accessed July 26, 2014.

Death Penalty

Few issues in criminal justice—and American politics—are as controversial as the death penalty. For most people who support the death penalty, the execution of convicted murderers (and people who commit other horrible acts) makes sense. Death penalty supporters frequently state that executions prevent those executed from committing heinous crimes again and that the example of executions prevents people who might contemplate committing appalling crimes from doing so. In addition, many death penalty supporters believe that people who commit such crimes deserve to die—that they have earned their ignominious fate.

For opponents, the death penalty issue is about something else entirely. For many opponents, the level of death penalty support in the United States is a rough estimate of the level of maturity of the American people. The not-so-subtle implication is that a mature, civilized society would not employ the death penalty. Opponents maintain that perpetrators of horrible crimes can be dealt with effectively by other means and that it makes little sense to kill some people, however blameworthy they may be, to teach other people not to kill. These opponents argue that although the perpetrators of terrible crimes may deserve severe punishment, that punishment need not be execution.

The first person executed in what is now the United States was Captain George Kendall, a counselor for the Virginia colony. He was executed in 1608 for being a spy for Spain. The fact that he was executed was not particularly unusual because the death penalty was just another of the punishments brought to the New World by the early European settlers.

Since Kendall's execution in 1608, more than 19,000 executions have been performed under civil authority. This estimate does not include the approximately 10,000 people lynched in the 19th century. Nearly all of the people executed during the past four centuries have been adult men; only about 3 percent have been women. Ninety percent of the women were executed under local as opposed to state authority, and the majority (87 percent) were executed prior to 1866. About 2 percent of the people executed have been juveniles—that is, individuals who committed capital crimes prior to their 18th birthdays. Most of them (69 percent) were black, and nearly 90 percent of their victims were white.

All of the significant changes in the practice of capital punishment in the United States—culminating in its complete abolition in some jurisdictions—are the result of abolitionist efforts. Those efforts created degrees of murder, which distinguish between murders heinous enough to warrant death and those murders that do not; a reduction in the number of offenses warranting the death penalty (except for the federal government and some states since 1994); the hiding of executions from public view; and a decreased number of annual executions. Although abolition of the death penalty has been their unremitting goal, abolitionists have been far more successful in reforming its practice.

Globally, the death penalty is trending toward abolition. More than half of the countries in the world—104 of them—have abolished the death penalty in law or practice. All of the major U.S. allies except Japan have abolished the death penalty. On the other hand, only 58 countries and territories have retained the death penalty and continue to apply it; 35 other countries retain it on paper but have not applied it in a decade or more.

In the United States, 14 jurisdictions do not have a death penalty, and among the 39 jurisdictions that do have one, only a handful use it more than occasionally and almost all of them are located in the South. The U.S. Supreme Court temporarily set aside death sentences in the 1972 landmark case *Furman v. Georgia* until states eliminated unfettered jury discretion in the application of capital punishment. More than 70 percent of all post-Furman executions have occurred in the South. Still, executions are more concentrated than the 70 percent figure suggests. Five states—Texas, Virginia, Oklahoma, Missouri, and Florida—account for 65 percent of all post-Furman executions; three states—Texas, Virginia, and Oklahoma—account for 53 percent of them; Texas and Virginia account for 45 percent of them; and Texas alone accounts for 36 percent of them. Thus the death penalty today is used more than occasionally in only a few nonwestern countries, a few states in the U.S. South, and two U.S. border states. This is an important point because it raises the question of why those jurisdictions need the death penalty, whereas the vast majority of jurisdictions do not.

The death penalty has proved stubbornly resilient and will probably remain a legal sanction for the foreseeable future. One reason is that death penalty support among the U.S. public, at least according to the major opinion polls, remains relatively strong. According to a 2009 Gallup poll, for example, 65 percent of adult Americans favored the death penalty for persons convicted of murder, 31 percent opposed it, and 5 percent did not know or refused to respond (Gallup 2010). It is unlikely that the practice of capital punishment could be sustained if a majority of U.S. citizens were to oppose it. However, in no year for which polls are available has a majority of Americans opposed the death penalty. (The first national death penalty opinion poll was conducted in December 1936.)

The abiding faith of death penalty proponents in the ability of legislatures and courts to fix any problems with the administration of capital punishment is another reason for its continued use in some places. However, the three-decade record of fine-tuning the death penalty process remains ongoing. Legislatures and courts are having a difficult time "getting it right," despite spending inordinate amounts of their resources trying.

Many people support capital punishment even though they are ignorant of the subject. It is assumed by abolitionists that if people were educated about capital punishment, most would oppose it. Unfortunately, research suggests that educating the public about the death penalty may not have the effect the abolitionists desire. Although information about the death penalty can reduce support for the sanction—sometimes significantly—rarely is the support reduced to less than a majority, and the reduction in support may be only temporary.

Politicians continue to use support for the death penalty as a symbol of their toughness on crime. Politicians who oppose capital punishment are invariably considered soft on crime. Criminal justice officials and much of the public often equate support for capital punishment with support for law enforcement in general. It is ironic that although capital punishment has virtually no effect on crime, the death penalty continues to be a favored political silver bullet—a simplistic solution to the crime problem used by aspiring politicians and law enforcement officials. In sum, although the global trend is toward abolishing the death penalty, pockets of resistance in the United States remain and will be difficult to change.

Robert M. Bohm

Further Reading

Bakken, Gordon Morris, 2010. *Invitation to an Execution: A History of the Death Penalty in the United States.* Albuquerque: University of New Mexico Press.

Banner, Stuart. 2002. *The Death Penalty: An American History.* Cambridge, MA: Harvard University Press.

Bohm, Robert M. 2007. *Deathquest III: An Introduction to the Theory and Practice of Capital Punishment in the United States.* 3rd ed. Cincinnati, OH: Anderson.

Sundby, Scott E. 2007. *A Life and Death Decision: A Jury Weighs the Death Penalty.* New York: Palgrave Macmillan.

Debates (Televised Presidential)

Debates between political candidates have a long history in the United States—Stephen A. Douglas and Abraham Lincoln met for a series of debates in 1858 when they were candidates for the U.S. Senate from Illinois, for example—but the first televised debate between presidential candidates wasn't held until Massachusetts Sen. John F. Kennedy and Vice President Richard M. Nixon debated on national television on September 26, 1960.

Scholars and politicians argue that the first of the four Kennedy-Nixon debates, staged at the CBS affiliate WBBM-TV in Chicago and viewed by 70 million people, irrevocably altered the relationship between politicians and the medium of television, as well as the effect—for better or worse—of television upon U.S. politics.

The political records of the candidates were markedly different. Kennedy, a Democrat, had little more than one unspectacular term in the U.S. Senate. Nixon, a Republican and a two-term vice president of the United States, also had a storied legislative career. But even at the time of the debate, the issues received far less attention from the public and the media than did the physical appearances of the candidates.

Kennedy, 43, was tanned, affable, and relaxed after spending the weekend before the debate rehearsing answers with his aides and resting. About a month earlier, Nixon, who was actually only a few years older than Kennedy, had bumped his knee on an automobile door and was hospitalized for 12 days for a staphylococcus infection in his knee. On the night of the debate, recovering from a bout of the flu, Nixon was ashen, sallow, exhausted, and 20 pounds underweight. He re-injured his knee getting out of an automobile at WBBM-TV. He told the president of ABC News that he had a 102-degree fever. Aides asked if he wanted to postpone the event, but he declined.

When Kennedy declined CBS's offer of stage makeup, Nixon did too, not realizing that Kennedy's aides had already intervened. Instead, Nixon opted to camouflage his typically heavy "five o'clock shadow" with drug-store quality makeup called "Lazy Shave," which melted under the hot lights of the television set. While Kennedy knew instinctively that televised images would forever alter the political landscape in the United States, Nixon had viewed the debate as nothing more than another on a long list of campaign stops—a decision he would later regret, writing in his memoir, *Six Crises*, "I should have remembered that a picture is worth a thousand words."

Scholars and political pundits have long asserted that people who watched the debate on television thought Kennedy "won," but students at Northwestern who listened on the radio in an experiment thought Nixon "won." Radio listeners in 1960 likely were disproportionately rural, conservative Protestants who had been suspicious of Kennedy, the first Catholic candidate for president. Nevertheless, the effect of television on American politics was unalterably changed by the first Kennedy-Nixon debate, as subsequent candidates and their teams would focus more on image than substance, eventually insisting that televised debates be controlled and choreographed with little left to chance.

Political candidates and their aides, having learned from the results of the first televised presidential debates in 1960, declined to debate in the 1964, 1968, and 1972 presidential campaigns. Gerald Ford was the first candidate to agree to a debate after the Kennedy-Nixon debates. In 1976, debating Gov. Jimmy Carter, Ford said, "There is no Soviet domination of eastern Europe," a statement that he declined to correct even after the incredulous debate moderator provided him with the opportunity. That statement, which may have cost Ford the election, also showed politicians and campaign aides the twin power of televised images and gaffes or, conversely, well-placed one-line zingers that become historical campaign sound bites.

For example, in 1980, Gov. Ronald Reagan, a former actor with a natural affinity for the camera, was credited with besting President Jimmy Carter when Reagan good-humoredly responded, "There you go again" to Carter's assertions. Four years later, Reagan, then 73, was asked if age was a detriment in the campaign, and he responded, "I am not going to exploit, for political purposes, my opponent's youth and inexperience." His opponent, former Vice President Walter Mondale, later said the quip effectively ended his campaign.

Debates have been conducted during every presidential campaign since, albeit with increasing insistence that candidates and aides be allowed to orchestrate even the smallest of details in hopes of preventing a costly error. The nonpartisan League of Women Voters had sponsored the debates since 1976 in an effort to promote a well-informed electorate, but in 1988 the organization withdrew its sponsorship, explaining in a news release that it had "become clear to us that the candidates' organizations aim to add debates to their list of campaign-trail charades devoid of substance, spontaneity and honest answers to tough questions." The then-new Commission on Presidential Debates, also nonpartisan, sponsored the 1988 debates and the debates in every presidential election since.

In recent years, debates typically have been held at universities, with each focusing on a different theme, such as domestic policy and foreign policy, with questions asked by a moderator or panel member, candidate responses, rebuttals, and closing remarks. A major breakthrough in the evolution of presidential debates occurred in 1992 with the implementation of the first "town hall" format during the second debate involving President George H. W. Bush, Bill Clinton, and Ross Perot. An independent polling firm selected about 200 uncommitted voters to ask the candidates questions of their choosing. In a variation on that format, the debate moderator has had the discretion to ask questions submitted by audience members online. As debates evolve further, it is likely that the public—ostensibly the reason for the debates but historically the least involved party in their execution—will play a greater role as media technologies allow and encourage interactivity between the public and the candidates.

Bonnie Bressers

Further Reading

Gordon, John Steele. 2015 "A Short History of Presidential Debates." *The Wall Street Journal*, October 15, 2012. http://online.wsj.com/news/articles/SB100008723963904437492045780529319035484420. Accessed January 11, 2015.

"The Kennedy-Nixon Debates." The History Channel. http://www.history.com/topics/kennedy-nixon-debates. Accessed January 11, 2015.

Kraus, Sidney. 2000. *Televised Presidential Debates and Public Policy*. 2nd ed. Mahwah, NJ: Lawrence Erlbaum Associates.

Schroeder, Alan. 2000. *Presidential Debates: Forty Years of High-Risk TV*. New York: Columbia University Press.

Declaration of Independence and Free Press

The most quoted part of the Declaration of Independence is the first sentence of the second paragraph. It begins:

> We hold these truths to be self-evident, that all men are created Equal, that they are endowed by their Creator with certain Unalienable rights, that among these are life, liberty and the Pursuit of happiness,

That is as far as most people go, or usually remember, but the next twenty words are at least as important:

> That to secure these rights, governments are instituted among men, deriving their just powers from the consent of the governed.

There's nothing here about the divine right of kings or presidents or the speaker of the House: it is the consent of the governed—of the people. The Declaration goes on to enumerate a long list of grievances the colonists had against their British rulers, but there is nothing more about free speech or censorship.

Eleven years later, Thomas Jefferson expanded on this when he wrote:

> The way to prevent these irregular interpositions of the people is to give them full information thru' the channels of the public papers & to contrive that those papers should penetrate the whole mass of the people. The basis of our government being the opinions of the people, the very first object should be to keep that right and were it left to me to decide whether we should have government without newspapers or newspapers without government, I should not hesitate to prefer the latter—but I should mean that every man should receive these papers and be capable of reading them. (Tebbel and Watts, 53)

This makes it clear that Jefferson wanted an informed public, people who would be able to give an informed consent. It should be noted that while part of this quote appears often, the last 17 words seldom are used.

The First Amendment came into being four years later, but it was threatened by the Alien and Sedition Acts of 1798. They were inspired by conflicts the new nation was having with the French. The acts defined sedition so broadly that the administration of President John Adams interpreted to mean that any criticism of the president was sedition. Fourteen journalists were prosecuted and convicted.

The acts became a central issue of the 1800 presidential election. When Jefferson won, the acts were allowed to lapse. However, Jefferson became very critical of the press during his presidency with some reason. Many newspapers of that era were the voices of political parties or other special interests. Their commitments were to those causes and not to truth. Their criticism of Jefferson was excessive and seldom based in fact.

Jefferson remained bitter about the press for a while after his presidency. In 1814, five years after he was out of office, he deplored "the putrid state to which our newspapers have passed, and the malignity, the vulgarity, and mendacious spirit of those who write for them" (Levy, 373).

Many have concluded from statements like these that Jefferson might have had second thoughts about the First Amendment and the press. However, he expressed very different thoughts in 1823, his presidency then 14 years behind him:

> This formidable censor of public functionaries, by arranging them at the tribunal of public opinion, produces reform peaceably, which otherwise must be done by revolution. It is also the best instrument for enlightening the kind of man and improving him as a rational, moral and social being. (Levy, 376)

Jefferson thus came back to the concept implied in his statement in the Declaration about consent of the governed.

Guido H. Stempel III

Further Reading

Levy, Leonard W. 1966. *Freedom: Zenger to Jefferson*. Indianapolis, IN: Bobbs-Merrill.
Tebbel, John W., and Sarah Miles Watts. 1985. *The Presidents and the Press*. New York: Oxford University Press.

Democratic Party

The Democratic Party is one of the two principal political parties in the United States. The Democratic Party, the oldest surviving U.S. political party, traces its origins to the anti-Federalists and other smaller groups opposed to centralized government during the 1780s and 1790s. The Democratic-Republican Party (the forerunner of the Democratic Party) was established in the early 1790s as a reaction to the Federalists, led by Alexander Hamilton, who believed in a strong central government, a national bank, and government support of business and industry. The anti-Federalists, represented most prominently by Thomas Jefferson and James Madison, helped form what would ultimately become the Democratic Party in opposition to the Federalist agenda. They believed that democracy was best served by a system in which the states and individual citizens held the majority of the economic and political power of the nation.

By the early 1800s the Democrats were known as the party of states' rights, which accounts for the party's great influence among Southern planters, who wanted as little interference as possible with slavery. Following the death of the Federalist Party in 1816, as a consequence of its opposition to the War of 1812, the Democratic-Republican Party split, with one faction favoring more positive federal government action to promote economic growth. War hero Andrew Jackson, elected to the presidency in 1828, then joined with Martin Van Buren to forge the modern Democratic Party.

The Panic of 1837 and the depression that followed prompted the formation of the Whig Party and the election of its candidate, war hero William Henry Harrison, as president in 1840. Democratic president James K. Polk's foreign and domestic policies, which included the Mexican-American War, huge territorial acquisitions in the West, and reduced tariffs, alienated many Democrats, who decided to form the Free-Soil Party.

By 1860 the Democratic Party had become so splintered over the issue of slavery that it nominated two presidential candidates, Illinois Senator Stephen Douglas, representing the northern states, and John C. Breckenridge, representing the South. This ultimately paved the way for Abraham Lincoln's election and the Civil War. By 1870 the idea took hold of the "Solid South," or a monolithic Democratic Party that predominated in the southern tier of states. This alignment would last for nearly a century.

In the pivotal 1896 elections, Democratic presidential nominee William Jennings Bryan, who championed free silver, lost to Republican candidate William McKinley. From 1900 until 1932 Republicans dominated the U.S. Congress, and there was only one Democratic president in this 32-year time span: Woodrow Wilson. He won the presidency in 1912 only because Theodore Roosevelt, in his attempt to win a third term as president, split the Republican vote when he ran against incumbent William Howard Taft. It would take the Great Depression and Franklin D. Roosevelt to remake the modern Democratic Party.

Roosevelt's appeal came not only in his call for national unity in the face of a grave economic crisis but also by his bold penchant for experimentation to help end the Great Depression. Thus, the mainstream Democratic Party cast aside entirely its former aversion to big, activist government.

Although Roosevelt's New Deal did not solve the economic problems of the depression (only World War II did so), his programs endeared millions of new voters to the Democratic Party, including African Americans, Asian Americans, urban laborers, farmers, and other groups that had heretofore voted Republican or had been fence-straddling independents.

Roosevelt's 1936 reelection further solidified what some historians have termed the New Deal Coalition.

Although the United States was staunchly isolationist during the 1930s, Roosevelt led the way gradually toward a more interventionist foreign policy in the late 1930s. The advent of World War II vindicated Roosevelt's outlook, and after the war was won, the Democrats asserted that there could be no turning back to the isolationism of old. As such, the United States led the way in organizing the United Nations (UN) and cobbling together international and regional economic arrangements that would ensure U.S. (and Western) predominance.

After Harry S. Truman became president upon Roosevelt's death in April 1945, the torch of New Deal liberalism was passed. But Americans had become more conservative, fearful of never-ending commitments abroad and a large, activist government at home. The Republicans won control of Congress in 1946 for the first time since 1928, but lost it two years later when Truman upset Republican Thomas E. Dewey. Although the conservative coalition in Congress assiduously blocked Truman's Fair Deal, Truman did bring together internationalist Republicans and Democrats into a bipartisan foreign policy consensus. However, the Republicans swept the 1952 election, proclaiming they would throw out the New Deal. Nevertheless, the changes that Roosevelt introduced beginning in 1933 not only had changed and reinvigorated the Democratic Party but also had shifted the U.S. political system to the left. Fifty years later, the Republicans are still trying to roll back New Deal programs.

After John Kennedy won in 1960 and Lyndon Johnson won in 1964, the Republicans won five of the next six elections but controlled Congress only briefly. With third-party candidate Ross Perot getting 19 percent of the vote, mostly from Republicans, Democrat Bill Clinton defeated Republican incumbent George H.W. Bush in 1992. However, Republicans won control of Congress in 1994 and kept in for 12 years, Clinton's effort to get universal government-supported health care was a major reason for that loss. When the Democrats elected Barack Obama and majorities in both houses in 2008, they passed universal health care, something they had been trying to do for 60 years.

Paul G. Pierpaoli, Jr.

Further Reading

Fisher, Murray, ed. 1992. *Of the People: The 200-Year History of the Democratic Party.* Los Angeles: General Publishing Group.

Fraser, Steve, and Gary Gerstle. 1990. *The Rise and Fall of the New Deal, 1930–1980.* Princeton, NJ: Princeton University Press.

Hamby, Alonzo. 1992. *Liberalism and Its Challengers: From FDR to Bush.* New York: Oxford University Press.

Deregulation of Broadcasting

Attempts by the U.S. government to lessen its control over broadcast radio and television moved the industry closer to having the same First Amendment rights as the Internet and the traditional print media. The campaign to deregulate broadcasting began in the 1980s during President Ronald Reagan's administration. The Federal Communication Commission, responsible for regulating every aspect of the broadcasting industry from technical oversight to programming content, began abolishing limits on what stations could show, such as the number of commercials, as well as requirements on what they had to broadcast, such as news coverage. While the broadcast industry began to experience less government control, it still was mandated by law to operate in the public interest, especially during elections.

Broadcast political ads have been effective and popular campaign tools for candidates seeking to gain votes. Understanding the critical role broadcast media play in the election process, Congress and the FCC have imposed specific obligations on broadcasters regarding political speech—regulations that would be unconstitutional if imposed on the print media.

Unlike newspaper publishers, broadcasters are required by federal law to provide access to legally qualified candidates for local, state, or federal office. Under the equal-time rule, broadcast stations are required to treat all candidates equally. If a broadcast station gives or sells airtime to a candidate for any office, that station must, in turn, provide the same opportunity for all opposing candidates who request it. A broadcast station can choose not to run any political ads for candidates for local or state office, but they cannot deny access to candidates for federal office. Under the equal access rule, a broadcast station would be in danger of losing its license if it refused to sell (at a reasonable cost) air time to a candidate running for Congress or the president of the United States. However, these political broadcast rules are not without some exemptions. Broadcasters are exempt from having to grant equal time to a candidate's opponents if that candidate's appearance is in a documentary, a bona fide news interview, regularly scheduled newscast, or a breaking news story. Political debates not hosted by the broadcast station are considered news events and are also exempt, which is why presidential and vice presidential debates include only the major-party candidates with no air time offered to minor-party or independent candidates.

Not only does federal law require broadcast stations to treat all political candidates equally in providing airtime for their campaign ads, but stations are also required to keep this information on file for public inspection. The stations' public inspection files include information about which political campaigns have purchased ads and how much they paid for them. In 2012, the FCC instituted new rules that required TV broadcast stations to upload their public inspection information into a central FCC online database, giving the public easier access to the stations' political files, which before could be viewed only by going directly to each TV station. While broadcasters were not happy about posting their public inspection files on the Internet, open-government advocates believed the centralized database would bring more transparency to the election process during a time when many broadcast political ads were being funded anonymously and were difficult to track.

Campaign spending reformers have sought to limit the influence of wealthy corporate interests by emphasizing the importance of maintaining a "level playing field." They fear that labor unions and corporations could influence the outcome of an election by dominating the airwaves with highly effective ads, thus corrupting the political process. Opponents of campaign reform believe that limiting the amount of money corporations can spend supporting or attacking a candidate is censorship and a violation of the First Amendment's guarantee of free speech. In 2010 the U.S. Supreme Court supported this position.

During the 2008 presidential campaign, an advocacy group, Citizens United, wanted to air on pay-per-view cable television a 90-minute documentary critical of then-candidate Hillary Rodham Clinton. The Federal Election Commission prevented Citizens United from airing *Hillary: The Movie*, along with all TV ads promoting the film, because it had determined that the movie was really a political ad disguised as a documentary and, therefore, subject to federal election laws. However, the U.S. Supreme Court in 2010 ruled that the federal law that gave the FEC the authority to control this form of corporate political speech was unconstitutional. This landmark 2010 decision essentially wiped out decades of laws designed to curb corporate influence on elections. Before the Court's ruling in *Citizens United v. Federal Election Commission*, political action committees were barred from advertising within 60 days of a general election or 30 days of a primary. Corporations and labor unions were now free to spend their own money to directly advocate the election or defeat of candidates for president and Congress right up through Election Day, which reshaped how campaigns were conducted in the 2010 midterm races that were already underway and triggered predictions of dramatic increases in unrestricted corporate spending on broadcast political advertising.

Eddith Dashiell

Further Reading

Citizens United v. Federal Elections Commission, 130 S. Ct. 876; 175 L. Ed. 2d 753 (2010).

Eisenach, Jeffrey, and J. Randolph. 2001. *Communications Deregulation and FCC Reform: Finishing the Job*. Dordrecht, The Netherlands: Kluwer Academic Publishers.

Federal Communications Commission (FCC). 2012. *Standardized and Enhanced Disclosure Requirements for Television Broadcast Licensee Public Interest Obligations; Extension of the Filing Requirement for Children's Television Programming Report (FCC Form 398)*, 77 FR 27631; 47 CFR Part 73 (May 12).

Fitzgerald, Thomas. 2012. "Justices Shift Campaign-Finance Rules." *The Philadelphia Inquirer*, January 22, Page A01.

McNulty, Timothy. 2012. "FCC Rule Would End Anonymity of Political Ads." *Pittsburgh Post-Gazette*, May 7, Page A1.

Diffusion

The classical definition of diffusion—that is, the meaning agreed upon prior to 1990—involved a step-wise spread of information from one point, either geographical or cultural (or both), to a multitude of other points, crossing political and semantic barriers. But everything changed after 1990. The way we measure information flow in the modern era involves more sociocultural barriers and few, if any, geographic challenges. This change has had a profound impact upon American politics.

Often in our new media age, diffusion of an idea (e.g., egalitarianism), a cultural artifact (e.g., Bob Dylan), or a political mantra (e.g., democracy) is posted on a one-to-many communication platform, skipping over such concepts as opinion leaders. This new media-created pattern of sharing information moves so quickly to affect human behavior and crowd information sourcing—seeming to jump past what communications researcher Everett Rogers described in *The Diffusion of Innovation*—that it would be easy enough to write off the theory as passé and useless in predicting information flow.

Yet in politics the need to influence a few at first—those that would then influence others—is still a valuable model to win elections. And for researchers the diffusion model proposed by Rogers remains a useful heuristic in explaining just how a uses b to influence c. The flow of information from one point to many is still very much present. Town hall e-meetings, online political blogs, and other new media platforms have not cancelled diffusion: the process simply moves so much faster and with different types of steps than those illuminated in Rogers's taxonomy. The various traditional checking devices included in most diffusion models are still present. They have merely been rendered part of the individual acting within a more public and more anonymous environment than that of the soapbox in St. James Square.

Perhaps one of the most cited researchers of information flow, J.W. Kingdon, considers the opportunity to share a function of "policy windows." These windows, largely based on the language of satellite technology, suggest that only at particular times within particular situations is information passed from one point to another. Those best adapted to taking advantage of the right time and right place are the most successful in sharing their information.

Some 25 years after Kingdon, both Heaney and McClurg described the impact of new media on the diffusion of ideas within the political landscape of the United States as requiring various elements, including "coordination, cooperation, or trust," as well as "multiple levels of trust." Indeed, Heaney and McClurg provide an excellent model for examining the role of social networks within political communities, whether these groups exist in online workspaces, informal blogs, or more formal sites such as Twitter and Facebook. As noted, "along these lines, social networks can be examined as readily as political attitudes, trust, or partisanship" (729). The motives for involvement are as classic as Rogers's original paradigm: "access to information, expertise, and status."

As noted earlier, the diffusion model remains a workable scheme for predicting how information, whether political or personal, moves through a social network via "posts" offered by online participants. The initial actor remains an individual compelled by a desire to affect an existing influence group, whether that be friends, associates, or even competitors. Two possible models emerge. The homogeneous "echo-chamber" group reinforces and supports proposals and offers the author (or poster) reassurance that he or she is thinking "correctly." On the other hand, communication may occur within a conflict environment, wherein the poster wishes to "win" or "convert" others to the "correct" view or stance.

It would be easy to suggest that social networks have somehow warped the Rogers model, especially with the introduction of anonymity. Lack of author identification may facilitate more dialogue, as well as the inclusion of bolder ideas. It may also result in a broader variety of ideas and, interestingly, broader diffusion of these related concepts. On the negative side, anonymity can easily result in more hostility, corrosive behavior, and a breakdown in the trust related to the transfer of information. The mere inclusion of an extreme adjective (or meme) reduces the social exchange to name-calling. But is this really that foreign to Rogers's model? Even within traditional diffusion studies, outliers were present. Perhaps all that online social networks provide are more of these extreme actors within a diffused network of more ideas and more players. All that has been increased is the amount of dialogue. Indeed, the ability to move fluidly among various boards and communities has been enhanced, thus reinforcing each author's ability to be heard.

Equally enhanced, however, is the ability of some readers to be exposed only to concordant ideas: the echo chamber. Such groups rarely permit ideas judged as "wrong" or "inappropriate," whether on a website or television/radio show. The relative ease with which these echo chambers can be established and sustained is certainly problematic when compared to what Rogers must have considered in 1983 or to what researchers Bernard Berelson, Paul Lazerfeld, and William N. McPhee encountered in the Erie County Study of 1940 or Lazerfeld, Berelson, and Hazel Gaudet in the Elmira Community Study of 1948. As noted by Michael T. Heaney and Scott McClurg in 2009, "the applicability of community-based [research] has come into question, as many scholars claim Americans are increasingly 'bowling alone' and replacing neighborhood social interactions with online social interactions" This new "place-less" idea exchange virtually eliminates the geographic component.

Ultimately, the impact of social networks on the diffusion of political ideas falls into two (at least) outcomes. Either the echo chamber becomes stronger, thus increasing the social and political distance between various groups, or the ability to easily share more ideas across disparate social and political groups enhances the political dialogue. It is not too far a reach to suggest that both of these outcomes are already happening and will continue to increase as engagement and isolation are enhanced via new online social network technologies.

Thomas H.P. Gould

Further Reading

Heaney, M.T., and S.D. McClurg. 2009. "Social Networks and American Politics: Introduction to the Special Issue." *American Politics Research* 37: 431–464.

Kingdon, J.W. 1984. *Agendas: Alternatives and Public Policies*. Boston: Little, Brown.

Lazerfeld, Paul F., Bernard Berelson, and Hazel Gaudet. 1948. *The People's Choice*. New York: Columbia University Press.

Rogers, E.W. 1983. *Diffusion of Innovation*. New York: Free Press.

Douglas, William O. (1898–1980)

Few members of the U.S. Supreme Court have had more influence on modern politics and the nature of political discourse than William Orrville Douglas, the longest-serving justice in Supreme Court history. A passionate advocate of First Amendment rights and individual sovereignty over governmental authority, Douglas famously observed in one ruling that "the Constitution is not neutral. It was designed to take the government off the backs of the people."

Douglas was born in rural Maine, Minnesota, but is generally associated with Yakima, Washington, and the Pacific Northwest. His family moved there after the death of his father. The family was poor, and as a child Douglas may have been afflicted with polio, although this claim has been challenged by biographer Bruce Murphy. To compensate for his affliction, Douglas became an outdoorsman and an avid hiker. His background instilled in Douglas a sense of individualism, a desire to protect the downtrodden, and a mistrust of governmental power. These principles would guide his judicial philosophy. Douglas graduated from Whitman College and Columbia Law School. He was at the center of the fledgling legal realism movement at Columbia and Yale law schools, where he taught. This movement challenged the conventional explanations for judicial decision making. Legal realists maintained that decisions reflected the attitudes and backgrounds of the judges as well as the social, political, and economic context of the times. They downplayed formalist adherence to legal principles and precedent.

Douglas was appointed to the Securities and Exchange Commission in 1936 and named its chairman in 1937. He was nominated to the Supreme Court by his friend President Franklin D. Roosevelt in 1939 to take the seat formerly held by Louis Brandeis. Roosevelt, fresh from a protracted battle with the Supreme Court over the constitutionality of New Deal legislation, felt Douglas's populist views on regulation would protect his economic recovery program. In 1944, Roosevelt initially considered asking Douglas to leave the Court to run as his vice presidential candidate but ultimately opted for Harry Truman of Missouri. Truman, who succeeded to the presidency following Roosevelt's death in April 1945, considered Douglas for the vice presidential nomination in 1948. Douglas was more interested, however, in seeking the presidential nomination himself and briefly considered, but later rejected, the idea of leaving the Court to enter the 1948 campaign.

Controversy surrounded Douglas as a consequence of his stands on many issues, his off-the-bench-writings, and his personal life (Douglas was married four times and divorced three times). Impeachment of Douglas was discussed in 1951 after the justice publicly advocated recognition of Communist China. Congressman Gerald Ford led a more serious attempt to impeach Douglas in 1970. While questions about a conflict of interest were the stated reasons for beginning impeachment proceedings, it is clear that Justice Douglas's liberal views and his lifestyle were the underlying motivation.

Douglas's judicial behavior characterized him as a moderate in his early years on the Court. Some claim that this was because he harbored political ambitions and wanted to appear palatable to the public. The evidence suggests, however, that Douglas's early behavior and that of his frequent ally on the Court, Hugo Black, was a function of the times (the early forties), the novelty of the issues before the Court, and his lack of prior judicial experience. By the early fifties, Douglas was espousing the liberal views that are typically associated with his name. As the Warren Court matured and ideological allies were appointed, Douglas's views were increasingly read into constitutional doctrine. He supported the incorporation doctrine, applying the Bill of Rights to the states through the Fourteenth Amendment; absolutism in First Amendment matters; greater protection of criminal defendants; and a broad view of state action to permit the government to attack discrimination. Douglas was a supporter of civil liberties and civil rights, upholding these values in approximately 90 percent of the cases decided during his tenure.

Douglas was the very epitome of the judicial activist. He was a result-oriented jurist, whose judgment was often not controlled by precedent or strict adherence to constitutional text. He supported open-ended theories of the law. His opinion in *Griswold v. Connecticut* (1965) was perhaps the best example of this activism, as Douglas helped create the right to privacy out of "the shadows and penumbras" cast by the First, Third, Fourth, and Fifth amendments as well as the long-dormant Ninth Amendment. The privacy doctrine would become the constitutional foundation for the effective legalization of abortion in *Roe v. Wade* (1973).

Douglas was criticized for his result-oriented jurisprudence. Critics claimed that his work was hastily constructed and his ideas underdeveloped, but defenders admired the passionate manner in which he decided the question in each case. He felt it was important to consider the social, political, and economic consequences of cases. While most members of the Court complained about the workload justices faced, this did not seem to bother Douglas, who wrote many opinions as well as numerous articles and some 30 books.

His opinions were characterized by a commitment to individual rights and a distrust of government power. He believed that the Constitution and the Bill of Rights were designed to take government off the backs of the citizens. Douglas did not write majority opinions in many of the landmark decisions that were issued during his lengthy tenure. He did, however, author many concurring and dissenting opinions, a sign of his fierce independence and a reflection of the fact that his position was often more liberal than the center of the Court.

Many adjectives have been used to describe the justice who served 36 years and 7 months. He was considered brilliant, eccentric, independent, iconoclastic, and controversial. Douglas was a legal pragmatist who did not have a broad theory of constitutional jurisprudence.

An ailing Douglas left the Court in November 1975, allowing his old nemesis, then president Gerald Ford, to nominate his successor, John Paul Stevens. Douglas died January 19, 1980.

Richard L. Pacelle Jr.

Further Reading

Ball, Howard. 1959. *Of Power and Right: Hugo Black, William O. Douglas, and America's Constitutional Revolution*. New York: Oxford University Press.

Douglas, William O. 1981. *The Court Years, 1939–1975: The Autobiography of William O. Douglas*. New York: Vintage Books.

Murphy, Bruce. 2003. *Wild Bill: The Legend and Life of William O. Douglas*. New York: Random House.

Simon, James F. 1980. *Independent Journey: The Life of William O. Douglas*. New York: Harper & Row.

E

Earmarking

The term "earmarks" typically refers to benefits that members of Congress secure for their own home states or districts, usually by a quiet, unnoticed process of adding specific items to comprehensive spending bills. These benefits can take many forms. For example, a representative might secure a federal research grant for his or her college alma mater or funding to improve an airport or build a road. Placing a federal program in a particular state is another form of earmark because it brings money and jobs to the location. Basically, any form of monetary benefit that a member brings home for a specific project can constitute an earmark, depending on how it is obtained.

Earmarks are derogatorily referred to as "pork" or "pork barrel spending," and the process of obtaining them is often called "bringing home the bacon." Some in Congress have proven very adept at securing money for their home states. Senator Robert Byrd (D-WV), who was the longest-serving member of the Senate before his death in 2010, had been called the "King of Pork" for securing over $1 billion (yes, billion) for the state of West Virginia. Representative John Murtha (D-PA), Senator Ted Stevens (R-AK) (both of whom also died in 2010), and others have been similarly labeled because of their success in securing hundreds of millions of dollars in federal funds for their respective states.

Many in Congress see earmarks as improper and harmful, viewing them as gifts secured irresponsibly by members to improve their chances for reelection. Arizona senator and former 2008 presidential candidate John McCain, for example, has consistently refused to engage in pork barrel spending, making earmarks a central issue in his 2008 bid for the presidency. The voters of Arizona have returned McCain to office despite the fact that he has brought zero dollars in pork spending to his state. But while many in Congress are willing to criticize earmark spending in principle, few are willing to completely refrain from it in practice.

There are two primary criticisms of earmarks. The first concerns the propriety of using earmarks to improve one's chances of being reelected to Congress. It is ironic that, at a time when Congress's approval rating is at an all-time low, public opinion polls show that Americans still positively view the job performance of their own representatives. That is, voters like their individual congressman or congresswoman but do not like Congress itself. How can this seemingly inconsistent attitude be explained?

Some scholars argue that individual members of Congress gain popularity because of the various favors and "perks" (perquisites) they undertake for constituents. An influential member of Congress can secure millions of dollars per year in special funding for his or her home state and district, a practice that does not go unnoticed come election time. In fact, voters overwhelmingly return incumbents to Congress at a rate of more than 90 percent. Save for a career-ending scandal or criminal indictment, it is rare for a sitting member to be removed from office. Knowing this, interest groups and lobbyists on all sides of the political spectrum tend to donate to the campaigns of incumbents because they know that the incumbents are mostly likely to win. Undoubtedly some of these donors expect their candidate to remember them and to find the federal money to fund their special projects.

The second complaint against earmarks is that members of Congress secure them secretly, without considering the interests of the nation as a whole—and specifically without considering their impact on the national budget. Typically, members of Congress will add language to a spending bill to fund their special projects. Because spending bills are often hundreds of pages in length, these last-minute additions go unnoticed. They are not discussed or debated and can be approved without anyone even knowing that they are included in the bill. The idea of "slipping in" a few million dollars in extra spending here and there might seem sneaky and outrageous, but it is such a common practice that members of Congress tend to look the other way when it happens. For that reason, earmark spending is largely unregulated and unrestrained. Members submit spending requests at will, and they add up. Over the past 40 years, this practice has contributed significantly to the national debt.

Many earmarks are approved for projects of questionable merit. The most infamous recent example is the 2005 approval of the "Bridge to Nowhere," a $225 million project proposed by Alaska Senator Ted Stevens and Congressman Don Young. The enormous bridge would link the small town of Ketchikan (population 9,000) with the Island of Gravina (population 50), where the Ketchikan airport is located. In addition to that bridge, Young secured another $200 million in funding for a bridge linking Anchorage to the tiny towns of Port McKenzie and Knik, which between them have about two dozen residents.

When news of the "Bridge to Nowhere" came out, embarrassed members of Congress found themselves suffering the ire of the American people, who could not understand why one of the least populous states in the nation received almost a quarter of the transportation funds in that year's mega transportation bill. Eventually Congress was forced by public pressure to withdraw the funding that it had previously approved, and the bridge project was abandoned. But this change of heart was far from typical. Each year Congress approves hundreds of millions of dollars in earmarks, many of disputed value.

Isn't it one of a member's duties to take care of the folks back home? Congress is, after all, made up of representatives of all 50 states and 435 individual legislative districts. One can legitimately argue that representation includes taking care of the spending needs of the citizens. The federal government spends billions of dollars on projects every year, and this money should be distributed among the states and various local constituencies. The allocation of these monies naturally becomes a political process, and some representatives prove better at it than others. What's wrong with that?

This argument is not without merit. The framers understood that representatives would indeed be responsible for representing the interests, and meeting the needs, of their constituents. In creating the Constitution, they favored a strong central government and strong Congress over the weak and ineffective legislature of the Articles of Confederation. The framers gave Congress the power to coin money, levy taxes, regulate interstate commerce, and make appropriations for all of the federal government's needs. They gave special power to the House of Representatives by requiring that all appropriations bills originate there. Representatives are well used to spending government money as part of their legitimate job duties.

However, earmarks are different. The political watchdog group Citizens Against Government Waste has identified seven criteria that distinguish earmarks from traditional government spending. Specifically, earmarks meet one or more of the following criteria:

- They are requested by only one chamber of Congress;
- They are not specifically authorized;
- They are not competitively awarded;
- They are not requested by the president;
- They greatly exceed the president's budget request or the previous year's funding;
- They are not the subject of congressional hearings; and/or
- They serve only a local or special interest.

The framers knew that political officials could be corrupt or corrupted, and they created a system of checks and balances to guard against the concentration of power in a few hands. What checks exist to stop the kings and queens of pork, who spend taxpayer money with reckless abandon?

Kathleen Uradnik

Further Reading

Mann, Thomas E., and Norman J. Ornstein. 2006. *The Broken Branch: How Congress Is Failing America and How to Get It Back on Track*. New York: Oxford University Press.

Savage, James D. 2000. *Funding Science in America: Congress, Universities, and the Politics of the Academic Pork Barrel*. Cambridge: Cambridge University Press.

Stein, Robert M., and Kenneth N. Bickers. 1997. *Perpetuating the Pork Barrel: Policy Subsystems and American Democracy*. Cambridge: Cambridge University Press.

Economic Stimulus Programs

An economic stimulus program generally refers to a government-led initiative to influence floundering or outright failing economies, usually through injection of public monies into the economy. In times of economic prosperity, the notion of direct government intervention into market-based economies is debated among economists and politicians. During economic crises, however, such criticisms recede amid public clamor for government intervention.

The global downturn of 2008–2009—often called the "Great Recession"—became a stunning experiment in Keynesian economics by many Western governments, especially by the United States. The bipartisan U.S. Financial Crisis Inquiry Commission issued a final report in January 2011 on the causes of the Great Recession, widely acknowledged as the worst global economic decline since World War II. The commission concluded that "the crisis was avoidable and was caused by: Widespread failures in financial regulation, including the Federal Reserve's failure to stem the tide of toxic mortgages; Dramatic break-downs in corporate governance including too many financial firms acting recklessly and taking on too much risk; An explosive mix of excessive borrowing and risk by households and Wall Street that put the financial system on a collision course with crisis; Key policy makers ill prepared for the crisis, lacking a full understanding of the financial system they oversaw; and systemic breaches in accountability and ethics at all levels."

Although there were many contributing causes, the economic crisis broadly resulted from a widespread reduction in the valuation of American homes resulting in millions of Americans experiencing, for the first time in their lives, "underwater" mortgages, in which the debts of recently financed homes were significantly greater than the actual market values of the properties. Many of these debts were in the form of "subprime" mortgages—loans made to people who had difficulty keeping to their repayment schedules because of growing unemployment or other economic problems. Wall Street compounded the crisis through the recent creation of "mortgage-backed securities" as investment instruments.

The unemployment rate—which began the 21st century at about 4 percent of the U.S. labor force and rarely rose above 5 percent—started to spike. By October of 2009, jobless-ness hit a peak of 10 percent, the worst since mid-1983. Thousands of businesses failed. Many Americans grew fearful the nation was facing another Great Depression that could last many years and result in widespread misery.

Federal Reserve Board Chairman Benjamin Bernanke had spent much of his academic life researching the economic and political causes of the Great Depression and concluded, as had economist Milton Friedman before him, that the United States made many signifi-cant errors in the late 1920s and 1930s that allowed that economic downturn to be far worse than it needed to be. That a recession was looming in 2008 became apparent early, thanks to a sophisticated monitoring system of economic indicators maintained by the Federal Reserve Board and other groups. Bernanke testified before Congress that quick action was needed to stimulate the economy with "targeted" government expenditures and tax incen-tives, resulting in the passage of the $152 billion Economic Stimulus Act of 2008, passed by the House and Senate and signed into law by President George W. Bush in February of that year. The program allowed taxpayers to receive tax rebates of at least $300 per person, $600 for married couples, and $300 for each dependent child. Families could receive up to $1,200 in rebates.

Although it was called a stimulus act, many economists said the program was much too small to influence the worsening recession. The economic crisis approached a panic on September 15, 2008, when Lehman Brothers Holdings Inc., the fourth-largest invest-ment bank in the United States, filed for federal protection from its creditors and became the largest bankruptcy filing in U.S. history. Many economists and policy experts now believe it was a mistake to allow Lehman Brothers to fail, since the destruction of one of the nation's largest banks caused an immediate liquidity crisis as other financial institu-tions became loath to lend money—especially to businesses and individuals who needed emergency funds in a time of economic crisis.

Bush approved the Emergency Economic Stabilization Act of 2008, passed in the final days of his administration, to authorize the U.S. Treasury to buy $700 billion worth of distressed financial instruments like mortgage-backed securities. That act, too, should be considered a stimulus initiative since it sought to protect the solvency of banks. Those institutions were needed to inject money into the economy through loans if the nation was to recover.

However, financial institutions became reluctant to make loans as the scope of the "lending crisis" became apparent. Banks' former easy-credit policies had permitted millions of subprime loans to homebuyers who could barely afford their mortgages even in a healthy economy. As a result, financial institutions were limiting the number and size of loans they made during the worst of the recession. This liquidity crisis threatened to force the economy into an ever-worsening downward spiral.

Newly elected President Barack Obama won congressional approval of the American Recovery and Reinvestment Act of 2009 to authorize even greater spending (estimated at more than $830 billion) to stimulate the economy through federal infrastructure investment, tax incentives, and increased unemployment benefits. The act included direct spending for state and local roads, bridges, and other transportation infrastructure construction, as well as spending for a variety of education, health, and energy programs. Obama also urged continued federal government program spending despite rapidly declining tax revenues. As a result of the massive government stimulus attempts during the Great Recession, the national debt grew from $10 trillion in early 2009 to more than $16 trillion four years later.

Did the stimulus programs work?

The United States experienced four consecutive quarters of declines in the gross domestic product (GDP) from the third quarter of 2008 through the second quarter of 2009. The GDP experienced one of its worst declines in history in the fourth quarter of 2008 when the economy shrank at an annual rate of 8.2 percent. It was unquestionably the worst downturn since World War II, but the economy was back in the black by the summer of 2009.

The nonpartisan Congressional Budget Office issued a report in August 2010 that concluded that the American Recovery and Reinvestment Act has "lowered the unemployment rate by between 0.7 percentage points and 1.8 percentage points" and "increased the number of people employed by between 1.4 million and 3.3 million." Much more difficult to know is whether stimulus spending changed the trajectory of economic decline, helping to prevent a very bad recession from becoming a global depression.

Conservatives complain that the stimulus programs caused dramatic increases in public debt and ask if any stimulus attempt was worth such a cost, which must be borne by future generations. They also decry a public policy mentality in which federal authorities take liberties in deciding which companies and financial institutions are "too big to fail" and therefore deserve bailouts from federal coffers. Public concerns about the size of federal stimulus and bailout programs were probably the largest factor in massive Democratic losses in the 2010 off-year election.

Economist John B. Taylor of Stanford University takes issue over claims that the American Recovery and Reinvestment Act had a significant impact on the economic turnaround since, at its maximum level of spending, federal purchases were no more than 0.2 percent of GDP in the third quarter of 2010, when the economy was already recovering. "Clearly these amounts are too small to be a factor in the economic recovery," Taylor concluded. The stimulus package "has not been effective in stimulating economic growth and job creation."

The debate over the effectiveness of federal spending initiatives during the 2008–2009 recession is expected to continue for decades as economists evaluate mountains of economic data assembled during the period.

Thomas K. Hargrove

See also: Campaign 2010; Keynesianism

Further Reading

Financial Crisis Inquiry Commission. 2011. "The Financial Crisis Inquiry Report." January. http://fcic.law.stanford.edu/report/conclusions. Accessed November 11, 2014.

Taylor, John B. 2012. *First Principles: Five Keys to Restoring America's Prosperity*. New York: W.W. Norton & Company.

Editorial Endorsements

While newspaper endorsements may be waning in impact, they are still a highly sought-after prize in most political campaigns, particularly in important presidential primary states. At the same time, many newspaper editors consider endorsing candidates and political issues part of a constitutional role in their communities.

It's difficult to say if there is any strong correlation between endorsements and how people vote. Every Republican presidential candidate from 1940 to 1984 had the largest percentage of newspaper endorsements, but 5 of the 12 lost.

With waning numbers of broadcast stations that air editorials, editorial endorsements remain largely the domain of newspapers. In 2012, of the top 100 U.S. newspapers (based on circulation), 77 endorsed presidential candidates. Forty-one newspapers endorsed President Barack Obama, while another 35 endorsed GOP candidate Mitt Romney, and one paper registered a split decision. A lone standout would not endorse either candidate. Another 23 papers did not endorse any candidates, including the two largest national newspapers, *USA Today* and the *Wall Street Journal*. In earlier studies, a minority of editors said they couldn't agree on a candidate to endorse or had nonendorsement policies. The *Wall Street Journal* hasn't endorsed a presidential candidate since 1928, when it endorsed Herbert Hoover.

Researchers have long seen a decline in the influence of newspaper endorsements. For example, Diana Owen, Georgetown University political science professor, told Bloomberg *Businessweek* that reduced faith in the media has made endorsements less relevant. For newspaper endorsements, the low level of trust is compounded by a declining number of people who rely on newspapers for their campaign information or who find newspapers helpful in making their voting decisions, she said.

Despite the waning influence of endorsements, some newspaper executives see it as their civic responsibility to continue to make them. According to a 2000 survey of 193 newspaper executives spread among small, medium, and large-circulation newspapers, most still believe in the value and importance of editorial endorsements. At least three out of four papers did make an endorsement in the presidential race that year.

Although there is no clear documentation on when political endorsements began in the United States, the *New York Times* made its earliest endorsement to 1860. The newspaper endorsed then-candidate Abraham Lincoln. The paper wrote, "Things will go on very much as they have hitherto—except that we shall have honesty and manliness instead of meanness and corruption in the Executive departments, and a decent regard for the opinions of mankind in the tone and talk of the Government on the subject of Slavery."

Endorsements have shifted from Republican to Democratic candidates since the middle of the 20th century. A 2006 study found that between 1940 and 2002, newspapers have shifted from strongly favoring Republican candidates in the 1940s and 1950s, to dividing their editorial endorsements about equally between the two major parties. In addition, Democratic candidates are about 10 percent more likely to receive an endorsement than Republican candidates five decades earlier. Second, newspaper editorials have come to favor incumbents. Incumbents today receive the endorsement about 90 percent of the time. In the 1940s, incumbents received endorsements only about 60 percent of the time.

Some political observers have raised ethical questions about whether news organizations should continue the practice of endorsements because it might bias the public's perception of the new organization's campaign coverage. That may be particularly true in the era of online information, where it is difficult to distinguish between opinion and fact on many news sites.

The Society of Professional Journalists Ethics Committee said in a position paper that it supports newspaper endorsements but warns reporters covering campaigns to keep their opinions private. "SPJ encourages editorial pages to promote thoughtful debate on candidates and politics; letting readers know through endorsements which candidates share the newspaper's vision is part of that discussion. Part of an editorial page's responsibility, though, [is] to take every appropriate opportunity to explain the firewall between news and opinion," wrote then Ethics Committee Chairman Fred Brown.

Most journalists insist on a wall of separation between editorial and news pages to prevent bias. Kahn and Kenney questioned those claims of unbiased coverage in a study of more than 60 senatorial campaigns. The researchers found that information on news pages is slanted in favor of the candidate endorsed on newspapers' editorial pages. They found that the coverage of incumbent senators is most affected by the newspaper's endorsement decision. Voters evaluated endorsed candidates more favorably than candidates who were not endorsed. Endorsements had the most powerful impact in races receiving heightened press attention and among daily newspaper readers. Numerous studies of presidential campaign coverage have found that, with a few exceptions, news coverage of campaigns did not seem to be related to editorial endorsements.

Joel J. Campbell

Further Reading

Ansolabehere, Stephen, Rebecca Lessem, and James M. Synder. 2006. "Orientation of Newspaper Endorsements in U.S. Elections, 1940–2002." *Quarterly Journal of Political Science* 1 (October): 393–404.

Brown, Fred. 2012. "Ethics Committee Positions Papers: Political Involvement." Society of Professional Journalists. http://www.spj.org/ethics-papers-politics.asp. Accessed January 2, 2014.

Huang, Jon, Singdha Koirala, and Ryan Smith. 2012. "New York Times Endorsements Through the AgesTInteractive Timeline." October 27. http://www.nytimes.com/interactive/2012/10/28/opinion/presidential-endorsement-timeline.html. Accessed January 2, 2014.

Kahn, Kim Fridkin, and Patrick J. Kenney. 2002. "The Slant of the News: How Editorial Endorsements Influence Campaign Coverage and Citizen's Views of Candidates." *American Political Science Review* 96(2): 381–394.

Woolley, John, and Gerhard Peters. 2012. American Presidency Project. "General Election Editorial Endorsements by Major Newspapers." http://www.presidency.ucsb.edu/data/2012_newspaper_endorsements.php. Accessed January 2, 2014.

Educational Attainment

The amount of education a voter has received can have a powerful influence on voting behavior. It certainly affects the rate at which Americans register to vote and actually cast ballots.

The decision to participate in elections is a complicated convergence of issues for most people. People must believe they will benefit personally or that society will be enhanced if they participate in voting. They also must believe there is a chance that their vote matters and that their participation will benefit the general social welfare or will further their own personal political views. Also, voters generally must believe they have a civic duty to vote or at least will achieve a personal or social gratification for their participation. All of these factors added together must overcome the not inconsequential issues of time, bother, effort, and cost involved in registering to vote and going to a polling place or arranging for alternative methods of voting like absentee balloting or advanced balloting.

Statistically, Americans have a much higher chance of winning a state lottery than actually participating in an election with a one-vote victory margin. It is believed by political scientists that the most powerful motivating force for voting is a sense of duty to the electoral process, a sense that appears strongest among well-educated people despite a nearly universal sense that "my vote doesn't really matter much."

The U.S. Census found that 50.5 percent of Americans who did not finish high school had registered to vote by the time of the 2008 national election for president, and 39.4 percent actually reported casting a ballot. Both of these statistics increase steadily with educational attainment. Among Americans who've attained post-graduate college degrees (master's degree, doctorate, or an advanced professional degree) 85.8 percent had registered and 82.7 percent reported casting a ballot.

Education is associated with many other socioeconomic factors. Better educated people are more likely to be affluent than less educated people, to own homes and live in the same city or suburb for many years and therefore feel rooted to their community. All of these factors are associated with increased voting participation, but education is generally regarded to have the strongest influence of any of these factors upon voting.

The decision of how to vote is a much more complicated matter. Democratic Party candidates tend to do better than Republican candidates among voters at the extreme ends of educational attainment. Because of the Democrats' advantages in appealing to racial and ethnic minority groups, they usually win solid majorities of voters who've received only a high school diploma or who did not graduate high school. Republican candidates do much better among voters who've attended some college and, especially, who've obtained a bachelor's degree from a traditional four-year institution. But support for the GOP falls off sharply among voters who've participated in post-graduate education.

In the 2012 reelection of President Obama, the Democrat received a majority of support among people with less than a high school diploma (64 percent) and among high school graduates (51 percent.) The vote among people who attended some college was nearly evenly divided between the two major parties. Republicans won 51 percent of the vote among college graduates. But Obama won 55 percent of the vote among people with post-graduate educations.

The popularity of the Democratic Party among the highest educated has been around at least since the days of Franklin Roosevelt, but the reason has often been a matter of speculation. Political author David Callahan, co-founder of the liberal public policy group

Demos, speculates that "super educated" voters are more liberal on social issues and, therefore, are drawn to the Democrats.

"Education tends to increase one's exposure to different viewpoints and kinds of people, fostering tolerance—a key basis for social liberalism," Callahan suggests. "In contrast, less educated voters—according to research—are more likely to embrace intolerant, authoritarian values when it comes to regulating social behavior and, in addition, are more likely to be distrustful of those who are different than they are."

Conservative authors and politicians have suggested the academic environment in most American institutions is biased considerably to the left. They accuse high-level instructors of political intolerance that makes academic life difficult for conservatives and right-leaning scholarship.

The issue took center stage during the 2012 primary season when Republican former Pennsylvania Sen. Rick Santorum addressed a Tea Party meeting in Troy, Michigan, about the policies of President Obama during his bid for reelection. "President Obama once said he wants everybody in America to go to college. What a snob," Santorum said. "I understand why he wants you to go to college. He wants to remake you in his image."

"There are good decent men and women who go out and work hard every day and put their skills to test that aren't taught by some liberal college professor trying to indoctrinate them," Santorum said. The *Washington Post* noted, however, that Santorum's remarks were curious since the Republican holds a bachelor's degree, a master's of business administration, and a J.D. degree.

Other Republicans cringed at the remark. "I wish he'd said it differently," Virginia Gov. Robert F. McDonnell said. "When you look at what's going on in other countries, China, India, the premium they put on higher education—we've got to do better if we still want to be the global leader we are."

Thomas K. Hargrove

Further Reading

Callahan, David. 2012. "Why Obama Won the Post-Grad Vote." *The Huffington Post*, November 11. http://www.huffingtonpost.com/david-callahan/why-obama-won-the-postgra_b_2093523.html#. Accessed on June 29, 2014.

Edsall, Thomas B. 2012. "The Politics of Going to College." *The New York Times*, April 1. http://campaignstops.blogs.nytimes.com/2012/04/01/the-politics-of-going-to-college. Accessed January 11, 2015.

Roper Center Public Opinion Archives. 2012. "How Groups Voted in 2012." Exit polling by Edison Media Research for the National Election Pool. http://www.ropercenter.uconn.edu/elections/how_groups_voted/voted_12.html. Accessed January 11, 2015.

Education Reform

Public education has become a significant national political issue. This may seem surprising since, when the United States was founded, education was thought to be a state and local responsibility and was funded accordingly. Even today, only 15 of the 50 states get more than 15 percent of their public education funding from the federal government, and only four states get more than 20 percent. States set general curricular standards, and local school boards set specific standards.

But national interest was roused by a decline in scores on the Scholastic Aptitude Test (SAT) that began in 1967. In the following decade, verbal test averages fell 38 points and the math score averages fell 24 points. The Educational Testing Service said its test was fine and the problem lay with the schools. Critics said this was misguided blame-gaming. Although the SAT was used by many colleges and universities to determine which students to admit, several studies found that high school grades were a better predictor of success in college than SAT scores. Furthermore, the main purpose of the tests was not to find out how much students knew, but to create a wide ranging array of scores so colleges and universities would have a basis for selecting one student and rejecting another.

But the declining test scores drew increasing attention, starting with the publication of "A Nation at Risk" in 1983. This was a report of the National Commission on Excellence on Education, which was appointed by Secretary of Education Terrel H. Bell during the Reagan administration. It pointed to the poor standing of the United States in international tests. The report said this showed the schools were doing poorly and were the reason the United States was losing steel and automotive business to other countries. Trade policies were not considered as part of the problem in that finding, although they obviously were involved. However, the report did not lead to immediate action by the federal government. Reagan and George H.W. Bush did not advocate any response. Bill Clinton wanted to, but when the Republicans took control of Congress, the opportunity was lost.

The next development was the growing number of charter schools authorized by states, with Minnesota being the first in 1991. The main reason was to provide choice, especially for pupils in poorly performing schools. Polls consistently showed a majority of Americans approve of charter schools, but students in these new institutions usually do not perform as well on state tests as do students at traditional public schools.

In 2002, the administration of George W. Bush did act, creating the No Child Left Behind (NCLB) Act. In his 2000 campaign, Bush spoke of the "Texas miracle" of improving education through expanded testing and using test results to increase accountability. Using Texas as a model, Congress passed a law requiring testing of every child annually from grades 3 through 8. States had to report test scores by race, ethnicity, income status, disability status, and English proficiency. Schools that failed to meet targeted scores faced penalties, including possible closure. The number of schools deemed failures rose, and by 2014 more than half the public schools in the United States had been declared failures. (In 2006, only 29 percent had been deemed failures.)

At the same time, other academic measurements were producing opposite results. Scores on the National Assessment of Educational Progress rose. On fourth-grade math, the national average was 64 in 2000 and 81 in 2011. On eighth-grade math, the national average was 65 in 2000 and 73 in 2011. On fourth-grade reading, the average rose from 58 in 1998 to 66 in 2011. On eight-grade reading, the average rose from 71 in 1998 to 75 in 2011. However, both SAT and ACT scores have declined slightly.

Federal funding in support of NCLB was not adequate, and schools had to dig into their budgets to find money to pay for tests and test preparation materials. Money that might have gone to support these went instead to suddenly formed tutoring organizations and consulting firms that would advise schools on how to meet NCLB standards.

When it came time to renew NCLB in 2007, there were a number of concerns. No consensus emerged in Congress, so the program was allowed to continue without change. In 2011, the Obama administration began its own "Race to the Top" program, which provided special funding for schools doing well on tests.

The debate over education reform put enormous attention upon the use of standardized academic testing. Teachers were obviously under pressure, many critics said, and were forced to a greater or lesser extent to start "teaching to the test." There were also concerns about the pressure that the testing put upon students. Parents began questioning if so much testing was necessary. Some also questioned whether results of a day or two of testing should count more than the results of 180 days of class work.

The advent of Common Core, which is intended to create a common national education, will raise more questions about testing. It will mean more testing, with national tests in English and math. Common Core is largely the brain child of David Wilhoit and David Coleman, administrators of various education organizations. In 2008 they went to see Bill and Melinda Gates about their idea. They were successful, and the Gates Foundation has put $280 million into the project. Much of this went into promotion, including grants to two major teachers' groups, the National Education Association and the AFL Teachers Union.

The English and math tests are likely to become controversial. Coleman played a major part in developing the English test. He wanted the English test and the supporting material to be nonfiction. That high school English or language arts should ignore literary giants like Shakespeare, Dickens, Faulkner, and Steinbeck was controversial, to say the least. The math test was largely the work of Jason Zimba, who was a partner with Coleman in Grow Network, an education consulting firm. He said the emphasis in math should be on finding different ways to solve a given problem. How these tests will work out has not yet been determined, although it is certain to increase revenues for the Pearson Corp., the world's largest producer of online education materials, which produced the new tests. Common Core has experienced challenges in half a dozen states. It was promoted as having been developed by experts from business and education, and the roles played by Gates, Wilhoit, Coleman, and Zimba are seldom mentioned.

A continuing concern has been the performance of U.S. students in international tests: U.S. high schools students rank in the 20s among the nations of the world in math, reading, and science. Yet scores for U.S. pupils from schools with less than 10 percent of pupils in poverty were higher than the overall scores for all other countries.

The impact of poverty on schools is a subject of controversy. Some say poverty is the reason for low test scores in the United States while others say it is the failure of the nation's schools that caused poverty. The scope of the issue is underscored by the fact that nearly 40 percent of school children qualify for subsidized lunches.

Guido H. Stempel III

Further Reading

Layon, Lyndsey. 2014. "How Bill Gates Pulled Off the Swift Common Core Revolution." *Washington Post,* June 7. http://www.washingtonpost.com/politics/how-bill-gates-pulled-off-the-swift-common-core-revolution/2014/06/07/a830e32e-ec34-11e3-9f5c-9075d5508f0a_story.html. Accessed January 11, 2015.

Ravitch, Diane. 2013. *Reign of Error.* New York: Alfred A. Knopf.

Electoral College

The United States Constitution provides that the president is selected not by the vote of the public, but by the vote of the Electoral College. The electors cast their ballots the first Monday after the second Wednesday in December, and the votes are counted January 6 in a joint session of Congress. Of course that is a formality. The electoral vote count is usually known Election Day or the day after.

Each state has an elector for each member of Congress, counting both representatives and senators. In addition, the 23rd Amendment provides that the District of Columbia shall have electors, and it currently has three. That makes a total of 538, and the Constitution requires that a candidate have a majority of the electoral vote to be the winner. This process does not guarantee that someone will emerge with a majority. In 1824, Andrew Jackson had a plurality of the popular vote and 99 of the 261 electoral votes (or 38 percent). That meant that the House of Representatives had to decide who would be president. John Quincy Adams, who was second in both the popular vote and the electoral vote, was chosen. Jackson later was elected president in 1828 and reelected in 1832.

In each state, the political parties pick a slate of electors. When a voter casts his ballot for a presidential candidate, he or she is automatically voting for that candidate's slate of electors. That means that if a candidate wins the popular vote in a state, the candidate generally gets all of that state's electoral vote no matter how small the winning margin is. Some have criticized this provision, saying that it puts the emphasis on winning states, not on the popular vote. Campaigning is adjusted accordingly. A case in point is California, which the Democrats have carried by more than 1.2 million votes in the last six presidential elections. In recent campaigns, Republican candidates for president have made only minimal efforts in California compared to their efforts in so-called "swing states," including Ohio and Florida. California's 55 electoral votes are simply out of reach, since gaining even a million votes there would not help the Republican presidential nominee.

The number of electors a state has is not exactly proportional to its population. The number of members in the House of Representatives is, and that number can change with every Census. But small states and big states alike have two senators, a fact that can cause mathematical distortions in how presidents are elected. There are six states that have three electors, six that have four electors and four that have five. That is a total of 62, which is seven more than California has. Yet California's population is almost twice as much as the combined population of those 16 states. Political leaders in those states do not want to do away with the Electoral College, nor do a number of slightly larger states which also are slightly overrepresented in the Electoral College.

Because the Electoral College deals with votes by states, not the national popular vote, it is possible for someone to be elected by the Electoral College even though he lost the popular vote. In the 2000 election, Democratic candidate Al Gore had 501,000 more votes than had Republican candidate George W. Bush, but Bush had a 271-266 margin in the Electoral College and became president.

It is usually the case that the winner's proportion of the electoral vote is higher than his proportion of the popular vote. In 2012, Barack Obama had 51 percent of the popular vote and 58 percent of the electoral vote. The difference has usually been even larger than that. In 1984, Ronald Reagan had 59 percent of the popular vote and 98 percent of the electoral vote. In 1936, Franklin D. Roosevelt also had 98 percent of the electoral vote and 63 percent of the popular vote.

Guido H. Stempel III

Further Reading

Article 2, Section 1, United States Constitution.
National Archives and Records Administration. 2013. "What Is the Electoral College?" www.archives.gov/federal-register/electoral-college/about.html. Accessed January 11, 2015.

Environmentalism

Rachel Carson's best-selling book *Silent Spring*, published in 1962, generated public awareness of the environment. She wrote alarmingly about the damage pesticides were doing to creatures of all kinds. Spring, some year, would be silent because there would be no birds left to sing. Fish also would be affected, as would air quality and water quality. The major concern then was DDT, which scientists had known for more than a decade did more than just kill insects. It would upset the balance of nature and had done so in some parts of the world.

Not using DDT became controversial. After all, it was the proven way to get rid of mosquitoes. Don't you want your hometown to kill mosquitoes? Chemical manufacturers joined the argument. The claims of Carson, already a distinguished biological scientist, were denied by people with little or no scientific background.

Paul Ehrlich's book *The Population Bomb*, published in 1968, also created environmental awareness. Ehrlich argued that the rate of population growth was such that it threatened the existence of the planet. This book was less controversial and had less political impact.

Concern about the environment led to the passage of the National Environmental Policy Act of 1969. The next year, President Richard Nixon drew up a plan to reorganize federal agencies dealing with environmental matters. Both houses of Congress approved the plan, and on December 2, 1970, the president issued an executive order creating the Environmental Protection Agency. The agency now has 10 regional offices and 17 research centers. It has more than 15,000 employees.

The function of the EPA is to perform research, make assessments, and provide education about the environment. Specifically, its activity is determined by acts of Congress. Subsequently, there have been 9 more air quality acts passed, plus 13 acts related to water, 11 related to land, 9 related to hazardous waste and 6 related to endangered species. Each of these acts changed rules and set criteria with regard to environmental concerns.

The EPA's enforcement capability is largely through censures and fines. The EPA also works with state environmental agencies and with businesses that volunteer to cooperate on environmental matters.

The EPA faces increasing challenges. On the one hand, as our society grows more complex and more densely populated, there are more activities recognized as raising environmental concerns. Such incidents as Three Mile Island and the Exxon Valdez Alaskan oil spill indicate how serious these concerns can be. Industrial waste is more hazardous, and it no longer is acceptable to dump it in the nearest body of water or bury it in the nearest vacant lot.

Natural disasters add to the problem. Hurricane Katrina was beyond the capability of the EPA and other government agencies. Hurricanes of this magnitude will occur again, and climate change may bring them more often. Science discovers new potential environmental problems, such as mercury and asbestos, which were not previously recognized as problems. Among other areas, the EPA has been involved with gas mileage in automobiles, detergents, pesticides, air quality, oil pollution, and drinking water safety.

Coal has been a continuing concern of the EPA. A major part of that has been pollution from coal-burning power plants. The EPA has mandated reducing that pollution by requiring filtering of smoke, improving efficiency, and encouraging cleaning of coal before it is burned. Politicians from the leading coal-producing states—Wyoming, West Virginia, Ohio, and Pennsylvania—are quick to protest restrictions that may reduce coal mining.

Much of what the EPA must do affects businesses, and businesses contribute to political campaigns. This has meant continued conflict between the EPA and politicians, especially members of Congress. This has limited what the EPA can do and arguably has meant that we have not been able to protect the environment as well as we could.

The EPA is not the only major player with regard to the environment. There are a number of public interest groups, some of which have been around for more than a century. Some of these groups have more than a million members and thus have potential political impact. They engage in a variety of activities.

- Friends of the Earth claims to have prevented construction of 150 dams they believed would have been harmful to the environment.
- The National Geographic Society, with more than four million members, provides environmental information far beyond what the mass media provide.
- World Wildlife Fund has five million members, including 1.2 million in the United States. It is committed to saving the planet by reversing the degradation of the environment. It operates in 100 countries.
- Audubon Society, one of the oldest conservation groups, was founded in 1886. It has 500 local chapters and 400,000 members. It is committed to protecting birds and other wildlife and their habitats. It is known worldwide for its annual Christmas bird count.
- Nature Conservancy was founded in 1971. It has become a highly effective green organizations. It employs 700 scientists and has sustained 117 million acres of land and kept 5,000 miles of rivers clean.
- Greenpeace, founded in 1971, has 2.5 million members. It has stopped whaling and nuclear testing and works to protect Antarctica.

Taken together, these organizations and others are leading the fight to protect nature and our environment. Already they have made a difference.

Guido H. Stempel III

Further Reading

Carson, Rachel. 1962. *Silent Spring*. Boston: Houghton Mifflin.

Madrigal, Alexis C. 2010. "Why Nixon Created the EPA." *The Atlantic*, December 2. http://www.the atlantic.com/technology/archive/2010/12/gallery-why-nixon-created-the-epa/67351/. Accessed January 11, 2015.

Equal Time Rule

The Equal Time Rule was part of the 1927 Radio Act and was included in the Communication Act of 1934 that created the Federal Communications Commission. It was created to prevent radio station owners from using their stations for political advantage. It provided that if a station permitted a candidate for political office to use the station then it must afford all other candidates for that office the same opportunity. This had the effect of discouraging stations from endorsing candidates as newspapers did, but a few stations did endorse candidates and then allow opponents to respond.

In 1959, Lar Daly, a third-party candidate for mayor of Chicago, complained to the FCC that he was not getting as much time on television news as the Democratic and Republican candidate. That led Congress to pass a law exempting news programs for the Equal Time Rule. However, another problem arose in 1960 when the networks decided to have debates between the Democratic and Republican candidates for president. Congress passed a law exempting those debates from the Equal Time Rule. This was only for the 1960 election, and that law was not renewed. For the 1964 election, the Democrats controlled Congress, and President Lyndon Johnson did not need or want to debate Barry Goldwater, the Republican candidate.

In 1968, there was a significant third-party candidate, George Wallace. There was discussion of having a debate with three candidates, but the Nixon campaign staff rejected that, saying that they did not want to give Wallace free air time. Wallace then said he would waive his right to equal time because he wanted Nixon to debate somebody. Nothing came of that. Nixon also refused to debate in 1972.

Presidential debates resumed in 1976 under the sponsorship of the League of Women Voters. That put them outside the jurisdiction of the FCC. This was something of a subterfuge because the league used the facilities and personnel of the networks. The moderator and the panelists were TV news people.

In 1980 a new issue came up. Movie actor Ronald Reagan ran for president. Would showing a Reagan movie cause the Equal Time Rule to be invoked? If so, what would be the equivalent that the opponent would be entitled to? Would it be the number of minutes that Reagan was shown in the movie, or something else? Would *Bedtime for Bonzo* or *Knute Rockne All American* really be a political statement? Nobody tested the FCC, and cable broadcaster Ted Turner poked fun at TV and the FCC by announcing that he would run Reagan movies election night, which he did.

In 1984, a federal district court ruled that the Equal Time Rule should not apply to debates. That decision was not appealed and left the door open for the TV networks to take over the debates again, which they promptly did.

For all practical purposes, that decision reduced the Equal Time Rule to applying only to broadcast advertisements. Stations must give all candidates equal opportunity in advertising, which means equally desirable time slots. Stations must give candidates their lowest rate, which is the discounted rate they charge frequent advertisers. Stations cannot control or censor the content of candidates' ads.

Third-party candidates would be on the outside looking in on debates and news coverage. However, the two most significant third-party candidates, John Anderson in 1980 and Ross Perot in 1992, were included in televised debates.

The Equal Time Rule also applies to all broadcast stations and all elections, whether local, state, or national. However, it does not apply to the content of news broadcasts or any program produced by a broadcast news department.

Guido H. Stempel III

Further Reading

Donahue, Hugh Carter. 1989. *The Battle to Control Broadcast News: Who Owns the First Amendment?* Cambridge, MA: MIT Press.

Klieman, Howard. "Equal Time Rule." Museum of Broadcast Communications. http://www.museum .tv/eotv/equaltimeru.htm. Accessed January 11, 2015.

Rowan, Ford. 1984. *Broadcast Fairness: Doctrine, Practice, Prospects: A Reappraisal of the Fairness Doctrine and Equal Time Rule.* New York: Longman.

Ethnocentrism

Originating in anthropology, ethnocentrism is thinking one's culture is the most important and that all others are inferior. When people grow up and are exposed to only one culture, they tend to believe that theirs is the standard of excellence against which other cultures are measured and found wanting.

The term "culture" refers to a people's ideas, clothing, language, customs, traditions, norms and values, art, philosophy, and so on. Cultures are often defined by their geographic location (a country or region) as characteristics of people (ethnicity, gender, or sexual orientation) and as types of social institutions (governments). For example, when people compare their religion or political party to another, they sense that theirs is normal and the other strange. The in-group feels natural and normal, whereas the out-group lacks validity and is judged as deviant.

American social institutions often encourage the idea of two opposed groups: rich and poor, white and black, gay and straight. In the American news media, traditional definitions of objectivity have included the coverage of "both sides." This assumes that there is a clear distinction between them and therefore encourages voters to take one or another side, thus increasing political ethnocentrism.

In U.S. politics with a two-major-party system, both parties benefit from narrowing their focus on their strongest opponent, thus discouraging third parties. Membership in a political party was once more important than it is now, defining who was in and who out. More recently some voters rejected both parties, calling themselves independents. These voters might be considered a third political group, but independents lack strong in-group solidarity and therefore are probably the least ethnocentric group of voters in the United States.

The 2012 presidential election is an example of the dangers of ethnocentrism: The Republican Party claimed the far-right position, whereas the Democrats built a coalition of those who didn't want the Republican candidate to win. When the Republican candidate lost, he and his supporters were astounded. They had assumed that their party was superior to the Democrats, perhaps because they communicated only with people like them. The conservative media reinforced Republicans' sense of superiority by emphasizing Republican ideas and by portraying the Democratic candidate as unworthy. This ethnocentric view of U.S. politics helped the Republicans lose the election because they saw people in their group as superior and failed to value candidates and voters in the diverse electorate. Republicans' predominantly well-to-do, older, white male supporters considered themselves superior to the Democrats, whose goals were the Republican antithesis—promising to help women, ethnics, the poor, and gays.

A phenomenon called "groupthink" explains how people in one political party can become convinced of their superiority. People of one ideology often fail to open clear lines of communication with others, such that the serious discussion of issues cannot take place. Those in the in-group talk only among themselves and circulate only in-group information, thus coming to believe that their ideas are the best. Groupthink influences the group's decision-making, behaviors, and relations with others. In-group information may encourage the assessment of dangers where there are none. They refuse to communicate with outsiders because they know that outsiders are wrong thinkers and dangerous. Groupthink can also apply to leaders of a country, thus influencing foreign policy.

One explanation for ethnocentricity comes from evolutionary psychology, which suggests that defining "us versus them" is a byproduct of human evolution. Our early ancestors fought each other for resources, and, simply stated, formed social groups of winners and losers. The formation of group attachments resulted from judgments of who could be in and who was out. Those in a more successful group were more likely to live long enough to procreate, passing their genetic profiles to future generations.

Another biological explanation for ethnocentrism comes from recent studies of the hormone oxytocin, which is released by the pituitary gland. It not only encourages human bonding, but it can also increase anxiety and aggression. Oxytocin bonds people to those most similar to them, and it also creates suspicion of strangers. Thus Democrats bond with Democrats and Republicans bond with Republicans. Each regards the other as the enemy.

After the turn of the century, changes in the media market—especially movement of many news organizations to the Internet—reinforced political ethnocentrism. Competition for the fragmented audience was fierce, and the surviving media organizations positioned their brand to reach the largest audience. Some news media retained the standard of neutrality, whereas others advocated more specific ideological positions. Some voters selectively exposed themselves to media messages that reinforced pre-existing ideological ideas. The media's tendency to make the story "us" versus "them" reinforced the political parties'—and audience's—ethnocentric views of the world.

Ethnocentrism has disadvantages, such as the in-group members ignoring possible improvements in their health, wealth, and other political variables. If they dealt on a neutral basis with those in the out-group, both groups could benefit. People's tendency to identify with the in-group encourages a psychological defense against out-group ideas.

Identification and ethnocentrism are related but not equivalent constructs. Whereas ethnocentrism describes identifying with one group and believing that it is better than any other, it is possible for a person to identify with people across many groups. For example, people may identify themselves as Texans or New Yorkers and have pride in their own state's accomplishments without rejecting those of the other state. Identification strays into ethnocentrism if Texans judge New Yorkers by Texas's own culture and traditions, concluding that New Yorkers are inferior.

From the 1960s forward, American social scientists decided that they could help "developing" nations join the "developed" world economic community by improving communication systems. This ethnocentric dichotomy encouraged the scientists to reject the local culture in favor of that of the United States and Europe. In its communication systems and content was embedded American culture, and things American—clothing, media and so on—became popular. This process was later termed cultural imperialism, an attack on U.S. cultural ethnocentrism.

Pamela J. Shoemaker

Further Reading

Butler, Judith. 2004. *Precarious Life: The Powers of Mourning and Violence.* New York: Verso.
DeDreu, Carsten K.W. 2011. "Oxytocin Promotes Human Ethnocentrism." *Proceedings of the National Academy of Sciences,* January 10.
Labidi, Imed. 2012. "Arabizing Obama: Media's Racial Pathologies and the Rise of Postmodern Racism." *Journal for Critical Education Policy Studies*10(2): 363–391.
Shoemaker, Pamela J., and Stephen D. Reese. 2014. *Mediating the Message in the 21st Century: A Media Sociology Perspective.* New York: Routledge.

Evangelicals

Although evangelical Christians have always existed within the U.S. electorate, only in the last 40 years has this group become an influential and measurable demographic to be courted and analyzed. From evangelicals' re-emergence to power in the late 1970s to now, this group has consistently numbered about one-fourth of the U.S. electorate and is steadfast in its support of mostly conservative Republican candidates and ballot initiatives. In fact, about four out of every five white evangelicals voted for the GOP presidential candidates in 2004 (George W. Bush) and 2012 (Mitt Romney). In 2008, 73 percent of evangelicals supported John McCain's failed presidency bid.

Evangelicals and their voting power are alternatively called the "Religious Right," "Christian Right," "Christian Conservatives," and "New Christian Right," although these terms have at times also encompassed socially conservative Catholics. Scholars generally define evangelicals as Christians who believe the Bible is the inerrant word of God; who choose and maintain an active, personal relationship with Jesus Christ; who believe in the centrality of Jesus Christ's crucifixion and sacrifice in securing eternal life; and who believe God commands Christians to evangelize to the world. Evangelicals dominated U.S. religiosity in the late 1700s and 1800s after a series of revivals but declined as a major cultural force within the U.S. population over the next 100 years, as immigration and cultural phenomenon brought more diverse religious thought. Although theologically, members of historically Black protestant denominations can be described as evangelicals, the voting demographic described here and in political polling is predominantly white. (Black evangelicals still vote overwhelmingly Democratic, supporting Barack Obama in the 2008 and 2012 elections at the highest percentage of any religious cohort.) The organizations and mobilization efforts aimed at evangelicals in the past 30 years have targeted white evangelicals almost exclusively.

Ronald Reagan is the first president to identify and court evangelicals as a key voting bloc, in part with the help of the Moral Majority, a conservative advocacy group founded by evangelical televangelist Jerry Falwell in 1979. Although the Moral Majority was first, dozens of other organizations emerged in the 1980s and 1990s aimed at electing evangelicals and fighting what was perceived as a growing secular culture. These groups, comprised largely of evangelicals, included the Religious Roundtable, James Dobson's Focus on the Family, Free Congress Foundation, Family Research Council, and Christian Coalition. The groups funnel money to causes framed as "pro-family," such as legal initiatives fighting abortion, stem cell research, gay marriage, and pornography. Likewise, these organizations support funding for Israel, charter schools, and the freedom to meet and worship in public spaces.

Such evangelical advocacy groups helped conservative Christians bridge denominational differences among evangelicals. They also positioned traditional beliefs and culture against modernist, secular trends as an effective strategy for transitioning evangelicals from voting primarily for Democrats to voting overwhelmingly as Republicans. Writing in the 2009 *Oxford Handbook of Religion and American Politics* on "Religion, Parties, and Voting Behavior: A Political Explanation on Religious Influence," researchers John M. McTague and Geoffrey C. Layman analyzed National Election Survey results to show that in the 1960s, more than 50 percent of evangelicals who identified as "frequent attenders" of church services voted Democratic, with about 25 percent voting Republican. By the 2000s, those totals had flip-flopped. Even among infrequent church attenders, although a plurality now identify as independents, a similar migration toward the Republican party has occurred. The salience of social-moral issues in guiding voting decisions seems clear.

Evangelical activists worked to influence GOP platforms and candidate nominations beginning in the 1980s at the most local levels—causes and school boards—so that it took years before a clear and consistent succession of evangelical candidates existed. By 2004, political strategist Karl Rove had deemed evangelicals as the most reliable and loyal electoral base in President George W. Bush's reelection campaign. Rove engaged voters at the grassroots level, including within churches. Although clergy are limited as to how much they can advocate for specific candidates, clergy can freely advocate for social and moral issues. As opposition to abortion and gay marriage became entrenched as standard GOP rhetoric, the ability of clergy to steer churchgoers toward specific candidates grew. In fact, the coziness of some evangelical clergy with candidates led to an increase in challenges and complaints to the IRS about evangelical-leaning nonprofits violating IRS no-politics rules for religious nonprofits.

The future of the Evangelical vote will be affected by two key patterns. First, younger evangelicals tend to be culturally more liberal than the baby boom generation and they shun religious messages laden with strong anti-gay or even anti-abortion rhetoric. Second, the U.S. Supreme Court's 2010 *Citizens United v. Federal Election Commission*, which extended First Amendment rights related to political expenditures to corporations and nonprofit organizations, gave wealthy evangelical business owners the ability to leverage significant dollars in support of, or opposition to, issues and candidates. How these contradictory trends play out throughout the 21st century will be one of the most interesting and likely heavily researched movements in the future.

Debra Mason

Further Reading

Eisenstein, Maria. 2009. "Religion and Political Tolerance in the United States: A Review and Evaluation." In Corwin E. Smidt, Lyman A. Kellstedt, and James Guth, eds. *The Oxford Handbook of Religion and American Politics*. New York: Oxford University Press.

McDermott, M.L.2009. "Religious Stereotyping and Voter Support for Evangelical Candidates." *Political Research Quarterly* 62: 340–354.

McTague, John M., and Geoffrey C. Layman. 2009. "Religion, Parties, and Voting Behavior: A Political Explanation on Religious Influence." In Corwin E. Smidt, Lyman A. Kellstedt, and James Guth, eds. *The Oxford Handbook of Religion and American Politics*. New York: Oxford University Press.

Pew Research Center. 2012. "Election 2012 Postmortem." December 7. http://www.pewforum.org/2012/12/07/election-2012-post-mortem-white-evangelicals-and-support-for-romney/. Accessed November 3, 2014.

Wilcox, Clyde, and Gregory Fortelny. 2009. "Religion and Social Movements." In Corwin E. Smidt, Lyman A. Kellstedt, and James Guth, eds. *The Oxford Handbook of Religion and American Politics*. New York: Oxford University Press.

Executive Privilege

Executive privilege is the right of the president and the executive branch to withhold information. In most instances it is exercised in response to requests from the Congress, although it sometimes is in responses to requests from a federal court. The Constitution does not provide for it, but some scholars have argued it is implied in Article II, which defines the authority and responsibilities of the president.

It was first exercised by George Washington in response to a request from the House of Representatives for information concerning the negotiation of the Jay Treaty with Great Britain. He refused on the grounds that the Constitution does not provide a role for the House in regard to treaties. It does specify a role for the Senate, and when the Senate made the same request, Washington honored it.

Thomas Jefferson refused a request for papers about Aaron Burr when Burr was being tried for treason. The refusal was challenged in court, and Chief Justice John Marshall ruled that the president had no more right than any other citizen to refuse the request.

Executive privilege has led to a court proceeding infrequently. Two more recent situations did end up in court with the same outcome as in Jefferson's case. One came from the Watergate investigation in 1974. Special Prosecutor Archibald Cox requested tapes of conversations Nixon had in the White House with persons suspected of illegal activity.

The case went to the U.S. Supreme Court, which ruled that executive privilege did not apply in a criminal investigation. A federal district court came to the same conclusion when President Bill Clinton refused a request by a congressional committee investigating his personal and sexual relationship with White House intern Monica Lewinsky.

While refusal by the executive branch to provide information or documents has gone on since the time of Washington, the term "executive privilege" was not used until the administration of Dwight Eisenhower. Eisenhower is known to have used executive privilege 44 times, which appears to be the most any president has sought to invoke it. The main reason was the activity of Sen. Joseph McCarthy, who claimed there was extensive Communist infiltration of the federal government. He would subpoena supposed Communists to testify before his Senate committee. At one point McCarthy claimed there were more than 200 Communists in the State Department. Eisenhower issued a statement that any member of his administration who testified before McCarthy would be fired.

There is no accurate record of how often presidents have used executive privilege. When executive privilege is used, it may go unnoticed if the person making the request does not go public with it. Published estimates have placed the number of times President George W. Bush used executive privilege in a range from 6 to 43, although neither figure can be documented.

Two statutes have some bearing on executive privilege. One is the Freedom of Information Act of 1968. There are nine exemptions to the act. Three would seem to relate to executive privilege. Exemption 1 says matters of national security can be kept secret. Exemption 5 says interagency or intra-agency memos can be kept secret. Exemption 6 says personnel matters, including medical records, can be kept secret. Presumably the president or any members of the executive branch can use these exemptions rather than claiming executive privilege.

The other relevant statute is the Presidential Records Act of 1978, which provides that the papers of a president shall become public 12 years after he leaves office. It is not clear whether or not executive privilege can be exercised at that point.

It would seem that executive privilege has been used for four reasons:

- Protecting confidential presidential communication
- Protecting private deliberative processes involved in policy making
- National security
- Protecting ongoing law enforcement investigations

More than two centuries after President Washington's first use of executive privilege, it is still not fully defined. To an appreciable degree, separation of powers is involved. Any time Congress and the president are not on the same page, executive privilege may be invoked. That, of course, means it is more likely to happen when the president and one or both houses of Congress are not of the same party.

Guido H. Stempel III

Further Reading

Rozell, Mark. 2012. "The Constitution and Executive Privilege." Library of Law and Liberty. http://www.libertylawsite.org/2012/07/12/the-constitution-and-executive-privilege/. Accessed January 11, 2015.

U.S. v. Nixon 418 US 682 (1974).

F

Fairness Doctrine

The Fairness Doctrine is a controversial Federal Communications Commission policy—in effect from 1949–1987 and officially eliminated in 2011—that required TV and radio stations holding FCC-issued broadcast licenses to cover issues of community importance in an honest, fair, and balanced manner. Broadcasters were required to cover any issue that was deemed important to their communities and to allow the airing of opposing views on those issues.

The Fairness Doctrine gave broadcasters wide latitude in deciding which subjects qualified as issues of public importance; how much time should be devoted to replies; when replies should be scheduled; what format those replies should use (news segments, public affairs shows, or editorials), and who should speak for the opposing viewpoints. The Doctrine did not require equal time for opposing views but only required that contrasting viewpoints be presented. This made the Fairness Doctrine distinct from the "equal time" rule, which is still in effect and requires broadcasters to grant equal time to qualified candidates for public office. Additionally, the doctrine mandated that broadcasters notify anyone subject to a personal attack in their programming and give them a chance to respond, and required any broadcasters who endorsed political candidates to invite other candidates to respond.

The FCC created the Fairness Doctrine because it believed broadcasters had an obligation to ensure that their listeners and viewers were exposed to a diversity of viewpoints during a time when there was a limited number of broadcast channels. Broadcasters, however, argued that the doctrine infringed on their First Amendment rights. As a result, the Fairness Doctrine faced a series of legal challenges. In 1969 a unanimous U.S. Supreme Court upheld the constitutionality of the Fairness Doctrine. In *Red Lion Broadcasting v. Federal Communications Commission*, the U.S. Supreme Court ruled that while broadcasters did have First Amendment speech rights, the fact that the spectrum was owned by the government and merely leased to broadcasters gave the FCC the right to regulate news content. The landmark Red Lion decision upheld the FCC's right to enforce the Fairness Doctrine, but the decision did not obligate the FCC to do so.

President Ronald Reagan's administration during the 1980s ushered in an era of government deregulation of big business—including the broadcast industry—and the need for the Fairness Doctrine once again came under scrutiny. After reconsidering the Fairness Doctrine, the FCC ultimately revoked it in 1987, nearly 40 years after it began enforcing it. The FCC decided that the Fairness Doctrine did violate the free speech rights of broadcasters. Instead of providing a diversity of viewpoints, the FCC found that the doctrine actually had a "chilling effect" on the coverage of important public issues because many broadcasters avoided covering controversial topics altogether. Also, the FCC determined that increased competition from cable, satellites, and low-power TV in the electronic "marketplace of ideas" made "spectrum scarcity" obsolete. The public now had access to various viewpoints by sampling several stations instead of relying on just one station to provide all sides of an issue, thus making government intervention and the Fairness Doctrine unnecessary.

The repeal of the Fairness Doctrine, however, did not end the debate among lawmakers, scholars, and public advocacy groups about the need for the government to require broadcasters to provide public access to a diversity of viewpoints. Shortly after the FCC repealed the Fairness Doctrine, Congress tried to elevate the Fairness Doctrine from simply being a FCC policy into a federal law, but the law was vetoed by President Regan and never went into effect. Legal challenges to the repeal of the Fairness Doctrine resulted in court decisions that actually gave broadcasters more speech rights than the landmark Red Lion decision.

The repeal of the Fairness Doctrine also led to the creation of conservative talk radio and cable outlets to combat perceived liberal bias in the media. During the 1990s, Congressional liberals had sought to revive the Fairness Doctrine as conservative talk shows and networks gained leadership in listener and viewer ratings, but they were unsuccessful. Religious and conservative broadcasters continued to oppose the restoration of the Fairness Doctrine or any policy that would have a similar effect.

While the FCC had stopped enforcing the Fairness Doctrine in 1987, the rule still technically remained on the books. As a part of the President Barack Obama administration's broader efforts to revamp federal regulation, the Fairness Doctrine was among the more than 80 outdated and obsolete media-related rules deleted by the FCC in August 2011, nearly a quarter of a century after it stopped enforcing the controversial policy.

Eddith Dashiell

See also: Equal Time Rule

Further Reading

Ammori, Marvin. 2008. "The Fairness Doctrine: A Flawed Means to Attain a Noble Goal." *Administrative Law Review*. 60(4) (Fall): 881–893.

Federal Communications Commission Media Bureau. 2011. "FCC Eliminates Out-Dated Media Related Rules." Commission Document released August 24, 2011. http://www.fcc.gov/document /fcc-eliminates-out-dated-media-related-rules. Accessed January 11, 2015.

Friendly, Fred W. 1976. *The Good Guys, The Bad Guys and The First Amendment: Free Speech vs. Fairness in Broadcasting.* New York: Random House.

Red Lion Broadcasting Co. v. FCC, 395 U.S. 367 (1969)

Federal Election Commission (FEC)

The Federal Election Commission was created by Congress in 1975 as a post-Watergate reform intended to provide independent oversight of the financing of federal elections. The six-member commission, who historically have been evenly divided as Democrats and Republicans appointed by the president and confirmed by the Senate, was specifically tasked to enforce the Federal Election Campaign Act. Under its charter, the commission is an independent regulatory agency that works to ensure that campaign finance information is disclosed to the American public, that statutory limits and prohibitions on political contributions are enforced, and that public funding of presidential campaigns is managed according to law.

Each commissioner serves a six-year term. At least two seats must be appointed every two years. No more than three commissioners may be members of the same political party. At least four votes are required for any action by the commission, a provision "created to encourage nonpartisan decisions." The commission chairmanship rotates among the members each year with no member serving as chairman more than once.

The FEC has created a sophisticated website allowing the public to review financial statements filed by all candidates to federal office: www.fec.gov. The commission allows the public to make bulk downloads of all campaign donations over $200 and access to records relative to commission actions and complaints. The databases maintained by the FEC go back to 1980 and are widely used by news media and watchdog groups to monitor campaign spending and fundraising.

Critics, including members of the commission, have increasingly voiced their concerns that the FEC has become a toothless regulator since it frequently deadlocks along party lines. They warn the commission also has been stripped of much of its regulatory authority by the U.S. Supreme Court in rulings such as *Citizens United v. Federal Election Commission* issued in 2010 that held the First Amendment prohibits restrictions on political spending by corporations, nonprofit groups, and unions. The justices, however, upheld requirements for public disclosure of the sponsors of such spending.

A growing number of political groups have incorporated as nonprofit organizations that are not required, by law, to release the names of donors. The FEC deadlocked over proposals to tighten disclosure requirements for independent groups like Crossroads GPS, created by Republican political strategist Karl Rove, or Priorities USA created by Democratic supporters of President Obama. As a result, spending by independent nonprofit political organizations skyrocketed from $300 million in 2008 to $1 billion in 2012, according to the Center for Responsive Politics, an independent research group that tracks federal campaign spending.

"The commission was created after the Watergate scandal to ensure that money given and spent in federal elections is disclosed so voters know who is trying to influence the outcome. This transparency is vital to our democracy," Commissioner Ann M. Ravel wrote in an Op-Ed column for the *New York Times* in 2014. "The FEC is failing in its job to ensure that voters know who is behind the rapidly proliferating political advertisements made possible by this extraordinary spending."

The Supreme Court in 2014 ruled 5-4 in *McCutcheon v. Federal Election Commission* that the First Amendment invalidates "aggregate contribution limits." The case was brought by Shaun McCutcheon, a conservative businessman from Alabama, who objected to the federal limits on individual contributions, which, at that time, were set at $2,600 per candidate per election up to an aggregate total of no more than $48,600. Chief Justice John Roberts wrote for the majority in the case that the government's interest in "combating corruption and its appearance . . . must be limited to a specific kind of corruption—quid pro quo corruption—in order to ensure that the government's efforts do not have the effect of restricting the First Amendment right of citizens to choose who shall govern them."

Critics, including the Democratic-appointed minority on the court, warned that the effect of the two rulings undermined much of America's campaign regulation. "Taken together with *Citizens United v. Federal Election Commission,* today's decision eviscerates our nation's campaign finance laws, leaving a remnant incapable of dealing with the grave problems of democratic legitimacy that those laws were intended to resolve," wrote Justice Stephen Breyer for the court's minority.

The FEC also has effectively lost the impact of its role as overseer of public contributions to the major parties' presidential candidates during general elections, another reform made following Watergate. In 2012, neither President Barack Obama nor Republican challenger Mitt Romney accepted the millions of dollars of public money available to them from the FEC because they did not want the associated $91 million spending cap required under law. Each candidate spent many times that amount in the campaign. Obama, in 2008, became the first major presidential candidate to refuse public financing in a general election. "The public financing of presidential elections as it exists today is broken, and we face opponents who've become masters at gaming this broken system," Obama said then.

Meanwhile, FEC investigators have increasingly been thwarted when they seek details about the increasingly off-books nature of federal campaign spending by independent groups. When the commission's staff asked for details about funding within the Crossroads GPS group, a spokesman for the organization replied such inquiries "are unnecessary." The commission deadlocked on whether to demand greater accounting.

"It is an open scandal in Washington that the Federal Election Commission is completely ossified as the referee and penalizer of abuses in national politics," wrote the editors of the *New York Times* in a 2013 editorial.

Thomas K. Hargrove

Further Reading

Dowling, Conor M., and Michael G. Miller. 2014. *Super PAC!: Money, Elections, and Voters after Citizens United.* Routledge Research in American Politics and Governance. New York: Routledge
Ravel, Ann M. 2014. "How Not to Enforce Campaign Laws." *The New York Times*, Op-Ed page, April 2.
Salant, Jonathan D. 2013. "Will the Federal Election Commission Ever Work Again?" *Bloomberg Businessweek,* May 2.

Federal Matching Funds in Presidential Campaigns

In an attempt to reduce the influence of special interest money upon presidential elections, Congress created a Presidential Election Campaign Fund in 1971 and invited American taxpayers to indicate whether they wanted to support the fund by checking a box on their annual income tax statements. The program was the result of a Congressional initiative first passed in 1966 that invited taxpayers to designate that $1 of their income tax would be designated for the public presidential fund. By checking the box, taxpayers did not increase their actual taxes; they were only designating that $1 of the taxes they already paid would go to the election fund rather than to the U.S. Treasury for the operation of the federal government.

The Presidential Election Campaign Fund was an experiment in public financing of the political process. It appears to have failed, however, since recent major presidential candidates have opted not to take public monies so they would not face limitations in their campaign spending.

"It has long been suggested that government should find some way to help finance the cost of these campaigns," Democratic Sen. Russell B. Long of Louisiana said in 1966 when announcing the compromise bill that would create the Presidential Election Campaign Fund. "Theodore Roosevelt suggested nearly 60 years ago that this should be done with public funds."

The Senate's Special Committee to Investigate Campaign Expenditures for presidential and senatorial elections concluded in 1938 that private contributions to federal campaigns should be entirely prohibited, opting instead for use of public funds. Such a policy, the committee concluded, would reduce campaign spending excesses and leave politicians more beholden to the general election and less dependent upon special interests.

After decades of debate, Congress enacted a compromise fund in 1966 but later repealed it in favor of the Federal Election Campaign Act on 1971 that would invite taxpayers to designate $1 per year to the public fund. Another amendment in 1974 set spending limits for publicly financed campaigns. Congress in 1994 increased the check-off amount to $3. The program is overseen by the Federal Election Commission, which determines a candidate's eligibility to receive public monies for either the primary election or for the general election.

The campaign act allowed presidential candidates to receive public funding for primary elections in the form of federal matching payments. Candidates would qualify if they raised at least $5,000 in each of 20 states. Only contributions from individuals—and only contributions up to $250—were deemed to be "matchable." In exchange for the public monies, candidates must agree to limit overall spending and to spending limits within each state. The overall spending limit was capped to no more than $10 million, plus a cost-of-living adjustment calculated to 1974. That meant the primary election spending limit in 2012 was $45.6 million. However, since the law exempts some fundraising expenses, the actual spending limit in 2012 was $54.7 million. The presidential nominee of each major party was also eligible for up to $91.2 million that year.

Neither Democratic President Barack Obama nor Republican challenger Mitt Romney took any public monies from the presidential election fund in 2012. The available public monies amounted to small potatoes compared to the enormous expenditures going into presidential elections. Obama spent $722 million for his reelection, while Romney spent $447 million. Neither candidate thought he could afford to take public money since the law required spending caps that would have given his opponent an enormous advantage.

Obama declined to take federal matching funds in either the 2008 or 2012 general elections. Romney, during the campaign, said Obama's choices forced him to follow suit. "To be competitive, it means a lot more fundraising than I think I would like," Romney told voters in Denver in late September. "I'd far rather be spending my time out in the key swing states campaigning, door-to-door if necessary, in rallies and various meetings, but fundraising is a part of politics when your opponent decides not to live by the federal spending limits."

Historically, every major presidential candidate from 1976 through 2004 accepted federal matching dollars and abided by the required spending limits. Obama was the first to refuse the public match in 2008, overwhelming the spending by Republican Sen. John McCain, who accepted $84.1 million in public funds that year. As a result, Obama outspent McCain by nearly two-to-one.

The Federal Election Commission distributed just $1.4 million in 2012 to third-party candidates for the Reform, Libertarian, and Green parties. It was the lowest amount ever paid out by the fund. In fact, the only major distribution that FEC made that year was $36.5 million distributed evenly to the Democratic and Republican parties for the operation of their presidential nominating conventions. Even that expenditure of public monies appears to be doomed in future election cycles.

Obama in 2014 signed into law the Gabriella Miller Kids Research First Act, a bipartisan bill that dedicates public monies that used to go to defray the cost of national presidential nominating conventions be diverted to the National Institutes of Health to be earmarked for pediatric medical research. The bill was named for a 10-year-old Virginia girl who died of an inoperable brain tumor.

The American public has noticed that the Presidential Election Campaign Fund has become an anachronism, no matter how well intentioned. At the height of its popularity in 1980, nearly 29 percent of American taxpayers checked the box on their income tax forms to make a small donation to the fund. That percentage declined regularly until, as of 2013, just 6 percent indicated they wanted to donate to the fund.

Thomas K. Hargrove

Further Reading

Federal Election Commission. "Presidential Election Campaign Funds." http://www.fec.gov/press/bkgnd/fund.shtml. Accessed November 8, 2014.

Haake, Garrett. 2012. "Defiant Romney Says Obama Is Trying to 'Fool' Voters." NBCNews.com, September 23. http://firstread.nbcnews.com/_news/2012/09/23/14051304-defiant-romney-says-obama-is-trying-to-fool-voters?lite. Accessed February 5, 2015.

Filibuster

The filibuster is a parliamentary procedure in which a single legislator or a minority group of lawmakers use oratory and other legislative procedures to stall or block legislation. It also describes parliamentary measures taken by a minority to thwart the goals of a majority group. The practice has an especially rich tradition within the United States Senate, where it has been used to protect the interests of an individual or of the minority party from domination by the majority party. The filibuster has had a profound impact upon Senate deliberations.

The Senate—in the glossary of legislative terms it made public on its website—offers this definition: a filibuster is an "informal term for any attempt to block or delay Senate action on a bill or other matter by debating it at length, by offering numerous procedural motions, or by any other delaying or obstructive actions." The only procedure to overcome a filibuster, under Senate Rule 22, is through a vote for "cloture," which the Senate defines as a motion to "limit consideration of a pending matter" to 30 additional hours, but only by vote of three-fifths of the full Senate, normally 60 votes. Senate Rule 22 has often been described as mandating a "super majority" to end debate, unlike most procedures in the House of Representatives requiring only a simple majority. Since it is historically rare for either the Democrats or the Republicans to control 60 or more of the 100 Senate seats, the filibuster frequently has forced senators to seek accommodations with the minority party. Many commentators have praised the filibuster as a leavening influence upon Congress, but as legislative gridlock became more common in recent years, both Democrats and Republicans have considered (and sometimes implemented) changes in how the filibuster may be employed. Critics, especially minority senators, have described these rule changes in dire terms as a "nuclear option" that would end comity and cooperation between the major parties. However, polarization in Congress has prompted both parties to consider reducing the application of filibusters to achieve essential legislative business.

Sarah A. Binder, a senior fellow at the Brookings Institution, was asked to testify on the history of the filibuster before the U.S. Senate Committee on Rules and Administration in 2010. She concluded that there are many popular myths and misunderstandings about the procedure, including a belief that filibusters were enshrined by the Founding Fathers so that the Senate would be "a slow-moving, deliberative body that cherished minority rights." But Binder said rule books written by the House and Senate in 1789 were "nearly identical" in that both required only a simple majority to cut off debate. "It seems the filibuster was created by mistake," she said.

Binder said the filibuster was born out of a recommendation in 1805 by Vice President Aaron Burr, who'd been recently indicted for the murder of Treasury Secretary Alexander Hamilton during an illegal duel, to simplify the Senate rules by eliminating the "previous question" motion to cut off debate. Many of the Senate rules, Burr noted, were redundant and unnecessary. "And so when Aaron Burr said: 'Get rid of the previous motion question,' the Senate didn't think twice," Bender said. "When they met in 1806, they dropped the motion from the Senate rule book."

Although deletion of the rule made filibusters possible quite early in federal history, the first actual filibuster wasn't held until 1837. It gradually became more popular in the following decades and became increasingly disparaged by frustrated majority politicians as "obstructionism" by the minority. The motion for cloture entered the Senate rules in 1917 after President Woodrow Wilson objected to a Republican filibuster against his proposal to arm merchant ships in the outset of World War I. Wilson chided the obstructionists as a "little group of willful men" and succeeded in winning the cloture rule, which was dubbed as a "war measure" by the press.

"Adoption of Rule 22 occurred because Wilson and the Democrats framed the rule as a matter of national security. They fused procedure with policy and used the bully pulpit to shame senators into reform," Binder testified. Despite the adoption of Rule 22, the filibuster enjoyed robust use in the Senate. The longest one-man filibuster in modern times was conducted by Sen. Strom Thurmond of South Carolina, who held the Senate floor for 24 hours and 18 minutes to protest the Civil Rights Act of 1957. Thurmond, an avid segregationist, read into the Congressional Record the complete text of the Declaration of Independence, the Bill of Rights, and George Washington's Farewell Address. Although his filibuster was unsuccessful at stopping the civil rights measure, it helped make Thurmond enormously popular with his South Carolina constituency. Thurmond served in the Senate for 48 years, becoming its oldest serving (he was 100 years old when he left office in 2003) and one of its longest serving members.

Many of the Senate's most famous and flamboyant members have employed long-winded filibusters, including Democrat Huey Long of Louisiana in 1935 and Republican Robert La Follette in 1908.

Republicans and Democrats each seriously entertained suggestions to outright end or sharply curtail the effectiveness of filibusters as the Senate became increasingly polarized in the early 21st century. When the GOP controlled the Senate in 2005, majority senators considered requiring a simple majority to overcome Democratic filibusters to prevent judicial nominees by President George W. Bush from coming to floor votes. Republican Sen. Trent Lott of Mississippi termed this procedure as a "nuclear" option.

The filibuster debate over executive appointments waged for several more years, coming to a head under President Barack Obama who also was frustrated by delaying tactics by the minority for his judicial nominations. In 2013, the Democratic-led Senate voted 52-48 to eliminate use of filibusters to stop floor votes for the president's nominations to judicial or executive branch positions. Voting against the measure were all 45 Republicans and three Democrats. At that time, Republicans had forced delays in floor votes for 17 federal judgeships and 59 executive appointments.

"You think this is in the best interest of the United States Senate and the American people?" asked Sen. Mitch McConnell, Senate minority leader. "I say to my friends on the other side of the aisle, you'll regret this. And you may regret it a lot sooner than you think."

Thomas K. Hargrove

Further Reading

Binder, Sarah A. 2010. Senate Testimony. http://www.brookings.edu/research/testimony/2010/04/22-filibuster-binder. Accessed January 11, 2015.

Binder, Sarah A., and Steven S. Smith. 1997. "Politics or Principle? Filibustering in the United States Senate." Washington, DC: Brookings Institution Press.

Peters, Jeremy W. 2013. "In Landmark Vote, Senate Limits Use of the Filibuster." *The New York Times*, November 21.

527 Organizations

Taking advantage of a loophole found in Section 527 of the Internal Revenue Code of the United States, special interest groups have created politically active nonprofit and tax-exempt groups that became known as 527 Organizations. According to the Federal Election Commission, these groups are "organized and operated primarily for the purpose of influencing the selection, nomination or appointment of any individual to any federal, state or local public office, or office in a political organization."

These groups enjoy an enormous advantage over traditional political action committees in that there are no limits on who may contribute to them or how much they may receive. Donors may include individuals, labor unions, corporations, and even other nonprofit organizations. There are no specific prohibitions on foreign contributions. The 527 Organizations also have no spending limits. They must, however, register with the Internal Revenue Service and file periodic reports of their contributions, expenditures, and the identities of their donors.

Among the top grossing 527 Organizations are the Republican Governors' Association; the Democratic Governors' Association; the American Federation of State, Country, Municipal Employees; and EMILY's List, a political action committee founded by Ellen Malcolm in 1984 to elect pro-choice female Democratic candidates.

One of the best known of these organizations is the Swift Boat Veterans for Truth, organized in 2004 in opposition to Democratic presidential candidate John Kerry. Kerry, a U.S. senator from Massachusetts, campaigned on his record as a retired U.S. Navy officer who was awarded three Purple Heart medals for injuries he sustained during the Vietnam War. Houston attorney John O'Neill, also a Navy veteran during the war, organized the Swift Boat group under Section 527. The group said Kerry was "unfit to serve" as president because of his "willful distortion of the conduct" of American servicemen during the war. The group funded a series of devastating television ads during the critical early months of Kerry's national campaign, accusing the Democratic candidate of lying about his war record.

Former White House political strategist Karl Rove and former Republican National Committee Chairman Ed Gillespie founded American Crossroads, a 527 Organization that was influential in the 2010 Republican Party takeover of the U.S. House of Representatives. The group was less successful in the 2012 elections.

The IRS has set reporting standards that require 527 groups to file statements of organization (Form 8871) and to make periodic reports of contributions and expenditures (Form 8872). The filing schedule is roughly similar to FEC schedule: quarterly or monthly during even-numbered election years and quarterly, monthly, or semi-annually in odd-numbered nonelection years. During election years, the committees also file pre-general election and post-general election reports.

Thomas K. Hargrove

See also: Dark Money

Further Reading

Dwyre, Diana, and Victoria A. Farrar-Myers. 2007. *Limits and Loopholes: The Quest for Money, Free Speech, and Fair Elections.* Washington, DC: CQ Press.

O'Neill, John E., and Jerome R. Corsi. 2004. *Unfit For Command: Swift Boat Veterans Speak Out Against John Kerry.* Washington, DC: Regnery Publishing.

U.S. Government. 2012. *Internal Revenue Code Title 26.* Washington, DC: Government Printing Office.

Flag Burning

Flag burning is a controversial form of symbolic speech in which the U.S. flag is burned as an act of nonviolent political protest both inside the United States and abroad. The phrase "flag burning" typically refers only to burning a flag as a way to express an opinion that is critical of the government. However, the United States Flag Code allows for the burning of the U.S. flag in a dignified manner, "when it is in such condition that it is no longer a fitting emblem for display."

Repressive nations—such as Iran, China, Cuba, and Iraq under Saddam Hussein—have outlawed the burning of their national flags. As a democratic nation, the United States, in the view of many Americans and the U.S. Supreme Court, should be a country where all forms of nonviolent dissent are allowed, including the burning of the U.S. flag. However, many argue that flag burning is unpatriotic, un-American, and should be illegal.

In fact, there was a time in the United States when the act of burning a flag to protest the government was a crime. In the 1980s, 48 of the 50 U.S. states had laws that banned the desecration of the U.S. flag, but the U.S. Supreme Court ruled in two separate decisions that flag burning was protected symbolic speech under the First Amendment of the U.S. Constitution.

In 1984 Gregory Lee Johnson was among a group of political protestors at the Republic National Convention in Dallas, Texas, who marched through the streets and held signs that criticized the policies of President Ronald Reagan, who was running for reelection. As the demonstrators chanted "America, the red, white, and blue, we spit on you," Johnson poured kerosene on an American flag and set it on fire. No one was hurt, but some witnesses said they were extremely offended by Johnson's burning of the U.S. flag. Johnson was charged with violating a Texas law that prohibited the desecration of a venerated object. He was convicted, sentenced to one year in prison, and fined $2,000. Johnson appealed his conviction, arguing that his First Amendment right to freedom of expression had been violated. The state of Texas, however, argued that its interests in preserving the flag as a symbol of national unity and maintaining order were more important than Johnson's free speech rights.

In a 5-4 decision, the U.S. Supreme Court overturned the Texas law as unconstitutional, ruling that Johnson's burning of the U.S. Flag during the Republican National Convention constituted expressive conduct that was protected by the First Amendment. The Court concluded, "If there is a bedrock principle underlying the First Amendment, it is that the government may not prohibit the expression of an idea simply because society finds the idea itself offensive or disagreeable." As a result of its 1989 *Texas v. Johnson* decision, the U.S. Supreme Court had not only overturned the Texas desecration law but also invalidated all state laws that made flag burning a crime. Many Americans expressed disappointment, and even outrage, at the Court's decision.

In an attempt to bypass the U.S. Supreme Court's decision, the U.S. Congress in October 1989 passed the Flag Protection Act, a federal version of the already-struck state flag desecration statutes. The act stated that "whoever knowingly mutilates, defaces, physically defiles, burns, maintains on the floor or ground, or tramples upon any flag of the United States shall be fined under this title or imprisoned for not more than one year, or both." (However, this new federal law did not prohibit the disposal of an American flag when it had become worn or damaged.)

Thousands burned flags in protest of the new law, and when two protesters were arrested, the Supreme Court was asked again to review the constitutionality of flag burning. With its 1990 *U.S. v. Eichmann* decision, the same 5-4 majority affirmed its previous ruling and struck down the federal anti-flag burning law as violating the First Amendment.

Congress made seven attempts between 1990 and 2006 to overrule the U.S. Supreme Court by passing a constitutional amendment that would allow the government to ban flag desecration. In 1990, when the Flag Desecration Amendment was first brought up, it failed to achieve the necessary two-thirds majority in the House. In subsequent attempts, the amendment usually passed the House of Representatives but was always defeated in Senate. The most recent attempt to amend the U.S. Constitution to ban flag burning failed by one vote on June 27, 2006. More than two decades after the *Texas v. Johnson* decision, flag burning as a form of protected symbolic speech has remained a controversial issue in the United States.

Eddith Dashiell

Further Reading

Luckey, John R. 2008. "The United States Flag: Federal Law Relating to Display and Associated Questions." *Congressional Research Service Report for Congress.* http://www.senate.gov/reference/resources/pdf/RL30243.pdf. Accessed January 11, 2015.

Portland Press Herald (Maine). 2006. "Old Glory and the First Amendment: Wrapped in False Patriotism, Protecting the Flag Has Become a Political Bludgeon." Editorial, June 29, p. A12.

Texas v. Johnson, 491 U.S. 397 (1989).

United States Congress. Flag Protection Act of 1989, P.L.101–131, 103 Stat. 777.

Flat Tax

A flat tax is a type of taxation in which all contributing participants must pay the same amount as a method to generate government revenue. The constant marginal rate applies to all affected citizens. Unlike progressive taxation, which impacts citizens differently based on disparities in income and other traits that might influence one's ability to pay, flat taxes are considered regressive due to their indiscriminate impact on those affected. As their name indicates, flat taxes are levied across the board at the same flat and constant margin.

A citizen who earns $100,000 in total household income and another citizen who earns $25,000 are both taxed at the same percentage, or marginal rate, regardless of the income disparities. In a progressive tax, levels are created to distinguish high earners from lower ones and tax them at separate rates, traditionally resulting in the most affluent paying the most in taxes. Flat taxes affect everyone equally in terms of the marginal rate. Though the percentage taken out of the $100,000 income compared to the $25,000 is equal, the tax is less burdensome for the person with the larger income.

The most recognizable application of flat tax in the United States is its frequent use in sales taxes, which help support state and local governments. Sales taxes, like other forms of flat tax, leverage one uniform amount across all individuals so that the product or service being taxed is the only component that can fluctuate, not the consumer purchasing the goods.

States and local governments leverage a small percentage of tax upon the sales of these products and services; though this type of flat tax is often applied to sales in general, various categorizations distinguish how heavily an item is taxed. Sin taxes are utilized as a method to discourage the purchase of certain items deemed unhealthy (such as cigarettes or alcohol) or to penalize those who choose to purchase them by levying a higher tax percentage on these items. They serve as both governmental regulation and a method for collecting a larger percentage of tax for the ascribed items.

Flat taxes can also take shape in the forms of licenses or fees, as they all follow a similar underlying premise. Licenses, such as fishing licenses or driving licenses, are leveraged on those who wish to have access to their privileges and are uniform in their cost. Portions of the revenue generated through the collection of licensing and fees are redirected back to benefit the services from which they originated, such as funding improved roads or wildlife preserves.

The role of social equality and equitable distribution has brought the concept of flat taxation to the forefront of economic policy. Proponents argue that they are efficient and equitable in that they treat everyone the same, but critics argue that flat taxes disproportionately burden individuals of lower socioeconomic status. Their efficiency is demonstrated by the focus on the product or service and not on the consumer, which differs from the sometimes tedious and confusing income reports and exceptions through tax reporting necessary for progressive taxation. Using them can lead to unfair burdens on the poor, however, as a higher proportion of their overall net income must be used to pay for the tax in comparison to individuals with higher incomes.

This argument is illustrated in the reliance of some Southern states on sales tax to generate sufficient funds for their state budgets, including Alabama and Mississippi, who employ a grocery tax. The grocery tax acts as a sales tax that applies to food consumed in personal households. Unlike most sales taxes, which can be avoided by not purchasing the accompanying products or services, a sales tax on food is not avoidable because food is a necessary component to every household and thus an unavoidable expenditure. Seven other states, including Colorado, Illinois, Indiana, Massachusetts, Michigan, Pennsylvania, and Utah, institute a state flat tax for income (separate from the federal income tax, which follows a graduated, progressive structure), though these are rather small (around 5 percent on average) compared to international flat taxes. This necessitates that citizens pay the same marginal rate of tax on their income, regardless of the actual level of income they have.

Outside the United States, a number of countries use flat taxes as their primary mode of generating revenue for public services. The marginal rates range from as low as 5 percent up through 45 percent, though most average around the 20 percent range. Nations with larger flat taxes tend to be located in the Middle East and also states that were formerly a part of the Soviet Union. The effect of the flat income tax on the national economy, particularly on the eastern European countries, remains controversial, as the inconsistent economic growth can be attributed to a number of factors in addition to the implementation of the flat tax. Though the use of the flat tax can be controversial in its application with regards to equity, it remains a popular method for securing the necessary revenue for public works.

Laura Merrifield Sojka

See also: Tax Reform

Further Reading

Boortz, Neal. 2005. *The Fair Tax Book: Saying Goodbye to the Income Tax and the IRS*. New York: HarperCollins Publishers.
Hicko, Scott E. 1969. *The Flat Tax: Why It Won't Work for America*. Omaha, NE: Addicus Books.

Fox News

The Fox News Channel (FNC) was created in 1996 by Australian-born U.S. media entrepreneur Rupert Murdoch. He appointed Roger Ailes, a former media strategist for the Republican Party who personally directed Richard Nixon's 1968 media campaign, as the chief executive officer of the cable and satellite all-news channel. Created to compete with cable-based CNN and MSNBC, Fox News has become America's top-rated cable news channel. The channel has been widely criticized as showing a conservative bias despite its slogan of "fair and balanced" reporting.

Murdock built a news empire that began with newspapers in Australia and New Zealand in the 1950s and 1960s, expanded to Britain with the acquisition of the prestigious *News of the World* and tabloid *The Sun* in 1969, and eventually world-famous *The Times* of London in 1981. He became a naturalized U.S. citizen in 1985 when he purchased Twentieth Century Fox, followed by HarperCollins publishers in 1989 and *The Wall Street Journal* in 2007.

Murdock's News Corporation began operating Sky News in 1989, the first 24-hour news operation in Europe. Although the British cable operation was not exceedingly profitable, Murdock wanted to challenge America's Cable News Network and lured Ailes away from the "America's Talking" cable channel, which eventually became rival MSNBC. The channel began live cable feeds on October 7, 1996.

According to its mission statement posted online for many years, the Fox News Channel "is a 24-hour all-encompassing news service dedicated to delivering breaking news as well as political and business news." The channel in 2014 said it has been "the most watched news channel in the country for more than eleven years" and is "the most trusted television news source in the country," available in more than 90 million homes.

Cable operators did not immediately accept Fox News, which was available to only 17 million homes on its debut, absent from top markets like New York City and Los Angeles. But through aggressive marketing and occasional litigation challenging CNN's cable news "monopoly" in key markets, Fox rapidly expanded its reach.

Fox News is headquartered at 1211 Avenue of the Americas on Manhattan, although some of its studio broadcasts come from Rockefeller Center. From the beginning, Fox featured news opinion shows like *The O'Reilly Report* (later renamed *The O'Reilly Factor*) and *Hannity & Colmes*, which featured conservative Sean Hannity and liberal Alan Colmes, an on-air rivalry that lasted 13 years.

Prominent Democrats have long claimed that Fox News is unfair. Democratic presidential candidates Barack Obama and John Edwards objected to a proposal in 2007 that Fox host a Democratic debate. "There's just no reason for Democrats to give Fox a platform to advance the right-wing agenda while pretending they're objective," said Edwards's deputy campaign manager Jonathan Prince. Former Democratic National Committee chairman Howard Dean called Fox a "right-wing propaganda machine."

In 2004 O'Reilly told a national radio audience that Fox News "does tilt right" but denied that the network was "trying to help" President Bush's reelection. "It's not like the Bush administration is cozying up" to Fox, he said. Several media critics noted that the Bush administration made sure top policy makers appeared early and often on the cable network, and the White House gave an unofficial endorsement, of sorts, to Fox. The advance team for Vice President Richard Cheney in 2006 gave written instructions to hotel staff that the vice president, when traveling, requires that his hotel rooms should have "all lights turned on," the thermostat set to 68 degrees, and "all televisions tuned to Fox News."

Despite a "tilt right" to Fox's coverage, Republican leaders said they have just cause to be wary of the cable giant. Fox was instrumental in promoting what it called "FNC tax day tea parties" in early 2009, local protests that helped promote development of the tea party movement that directly challenged the GOP hierarchy.

David Frum, former speechwriter to President George W. Bush, complained the following year that Fox News had made it politically impossible for Republican lawmakers to negotiate with Democrats on health care reform in 2010. "Conservative talkers on Fox and talk radio had whipped the Republican voting base into such a frenzy that deal making was rendered impossible," Frum wrote on his blog. "Republicans originally thought that Fox worked for us and now we're discovering we work for Fox. The thing that sustains a strong Fox network is the thing that undermines a strong Republican Party."

Los Angeles Times columnist Jonah Goldberg, a conservative, agreed that Fox has a decidedly right lean. But that doesn't translate to lock-step loyalty to any party or ideology. "It's worth remembering that Fox is less a bastion of ideological conservatism and more a populist, tabloid-like network," Goldberg said.

Thomas K. Hargrove

See also: Ailes, Roger

Further Reading

Collins, Scott. 2004. *Crazy Like a Fox: The Inside Story of How Fox News Beat CNN*. New York: Penguin Group.

Frum, David. 2010. "Waterloo." Posted March 21 on his "Frum Forum" blog. http://www.frumfo rum.com/waterloo. Accessed February 5, 2015.

Sherman, Gabriel. 2014. *The Loudest Voice in the Room: How the Brilliant, Bombastic Roger Ailes Built Fox News and Divided a Country*. New York: Random House.

Fracking

Fracking is a means of extracting natural gas that has become widespread in recent years. Oil and gas business interests and environmentalists are in conflict about it. Like any mining or mineral extracting activity, it has to be regulated, with rules and procedures spelled out. This makes it a political issue, and an important one at this time.

Fracking involves drilling vertically until one reaches shale and then drilling horizontally to the natural gas. Liquid then is used to force the gas into a well. Oil and gas industry people say fracking has been going on for more than 60 years and that there have been more than a million fracking wells created; however, what they are referring to may not be the fracking procedure used today but a process involving only vertical drilling.

The appeal of fracking is that there is a lot of natural gas in the shale area. While setting up a fracking well is somewhat costly, the well typically lasts 20 to 40 years. Land owners in rural areas are compensated for leasing the rights to the gas, and they thus have a long-term source of income. Fracking also means jobs, and in the current era of high unemployment many government officials tend to support fracking because of that.

There are, however, some concerns about fracking. One is that the horizontal drilling may cause earthquakes. There is some anecdotal evidence of this; however, if one fracks somewhere and there is an earthquake nearby two or three days later, it does not necessarily follow that the fracking caused the earthquake. It is not unreasonable to wonder, but some of the supposed incidents have happened in areas that are prone to earthquakes and had the same amount of earthquake activity before fracking was done.

A second concern is contamination of drinking water. The liquid that is used to force the gas out is mostly water, but there are some chemicals. Companies that do fracking maintain that the composition of the fracking liquid is a trade secret and refuse to disclose it. This issue is compounded by the fact that tests of some fracking compounds have shown extremely high levels of radioactivity. It may be natural radioactivity, but the refusal of companies to disclose what they are mixing with the water raises suspicions.

Whatever the composition of the fracking compounds, there is concern that they may pollute underground water. Fracking occurs much further underground than water is usually found, but there is a risk, however small. Again, there is some anecdotal evidence of fracking apparently polluting water. Part of the concern is the huge volume of water that is used in each well. A larger concern is what is done with the fracking fluid after it has been used. It usually is put in leak-proof wells, but sometimes a well leaks, and the fracking compound gets mixed with the water we drink. It is hard to track this because sometimes the water polluted by fracking compound looks and smells no different from clean water.

Regulation of fracking is done at both the state and national level. The Clean Water Act and the Clean Air Act give the Environmental Protection Agency (EPA) responsibility for preventing fracking from polluting air and water. Each state has its own regulations, and they vary widely. In general state permission is required both to start a fracking well and to start a fracking waste disposal site. Inspection of both wells and disposal sites is usually called for, but the rigor varies.

The EPA has authorized and funded 18 studies dealing primarily with the effects of fracking on water supplies. A preliminary report was issued in 2012, but it offered no suggestions or conclusions. A final report was scheduled for 2014. Before the report was issued, something happened that raised concerns. In 2011 the EPA issued a report suggesting a connection between fracking and water pollution in a study in Wyoming. In 2014 the EPA backed out of that study. Some felt this was an indication of political pressure.

The reality is that the oil and gas industry gives far more money to political candidates than do environmental groups. This seems to create some reluctance for members of state legislatures and the U.S. Congress to push regulation of fracking.

Another concern about fracking exists not at the state or national level, but at the county level. Fracking usually occurs, not in urban areas, but in rural areas. Moving equipment in to set up fracking and moving the large quantity of fracking fluid puts heavy trucks on rural roads not designed for that. Some frackers agree to pay for road repairs, but some do not. Some counties cannot afford to repair the roads.

Concerns about fracking have led 250 communities to ban it. That, of course, is less than 1 percent of the communities in the country. Environmental groups want regulation increased, and one—Food and Water Watch—is arguing that all fracking everywhere in the United States should be banned. New York State did ban fracking in June 2015 after seven years studying it. Vermont also has banned fracking.

There obviously are some unanswered questions about the effects of fracking on the environment. The answers will not come easily. The 18 studies the EPA is sponsoring will provide some of those answers; however, the oil and gas industry is eager to push ahead without further delay. Decisions by legislative bodies will be crucial. Those also will not come easily, and final answers will not be found soon.

There certainly is evidence that fracking can be done safely by companies that know what they are doing, that understand the risks, and that exercise appropriate caution. It probably takes appropriate government regulation to make this commonplace.

Guido H. Stempel III

See also: Climate Change; Environmentalism

Further Reading

Food & Water Watch. "Fracking: What Is Fracking and Why Should It Be Banned." www.foodand waterwatch.org/water/fracking. Accessed January 11, 2015.

Gold, Russell. 2014. *The Boom: How Fracking Ignited the American Energy Revolution and Changed the World.* New York: Simon & Schuster.

Zuckerman, Gregory. 2014. *The Frackers: The Outrageous Inside Story of the New Billionaire Wildcatters.* New York: Portfolio/Penguin.

The Freedom Forum

Through the 1990s and until its attentions shifted almost exclusively to its lavish Newseum in Washington, D.C., the Freedom Forum was the nation's largest, most affluent (and beneficent) foundation dedicated to the press. At its headquarters in Arlington, Virginia, the Freedom Forum frequently played host to conferences and panels featuring leading U.S. and international political leaders and media professionals and scholars. Just across the Potomac from the White House, the Freedom Forum was often the venue for programs and meetings on the press and the U.S. political scene, hosting presidents, Senate and House leaders, and cabinet officers, as well as the ruling media elite of D.C. and the East Coast. For over a decade, conferences and—especially—publications and original research on the media and politics were a staple of the foundation, whose avowed focus on "Free speech, free press, free spirit" made it an attractive venue for Washington's and the East Coast's political and media leaders.

In addition to the regular political focus of programs at the Arlington center, the most important original research and publications on American politics and the media, especially during campaign seasons, came from the Freedom Forum's Media Studies Center, which was housed in the Journalism Building at Columbia University from 1984–1996 and directed by prolific and respected scholar Everette E. Dennis. The Center was a "think tank" in the most honorable and substantive sense of the term, an incubator for leading professionals and scholars to come and think, research, write, discuss, and explore the changing role of the press, new media technology, and the mass media's role in politics and society.

Its flagship publication, *Media Studies Journal*, was an accessible quarterly collection of original essays and research by scholars and media decision-makers on themes ranging from the presidency to new media to race and gender to foreign policy. Examples of entire issues of the *Media Studies Journal* dedicated to domestic and foreign political issues, campaigns, voting, and governance include "Campaign 2000" (2000), "Covering the 1996 Presidential Campaign" (1997), "The Media and Democracy" (1995), and "The Presidency in a New Media Age" (1994). In addition, the Center authored its own studies of press performance during campaign cycles, such as a multivolume *The Media and Campaign '92*, released through that presidential campaign, as well as regular examinations of the media and foreign affairs, diplomacy, presidential governance, and an exhaustive range of white papers. The Center also was home to residential fellows from the mass media and journalism education, who were underwritten for a year of original study and research that frequently led to books and other publications by some of the top names and thinkers of the profession and the academy.

What is striking about The Freedom Forum these days is how difficult it is to find information about what was once the nation's premier foundation dedicated to the study and improvement of journalism. Once an international leader in studying, supporting, and upholding journalistic freedoms, the foundation fell on hard economic times in 2008 and focused nearly exclusively on its crown jewel, the opulent Newseum on Pennsylvania Avenue in Washington, the world's only museum dedicated to the press.

Falling by the wayside were the elements of the Freedom Forum that, for more than a decade, made it a leading player among journalism researchers, media professionals, and educators in the 1980s and 1990s. The Media Studies Center closed in 1996. An ambitious program to support international press freedom with centers in London, Johannesburg, Hong Kong, and Buenos Aires closed in 2002 in favor of funding the Newseum. Many of the Foundation's wide-ranging independent and traveling programs at colleges and universities faded out by the end of the 1990s. The First Amendment Center and its Diversity Institute at Vanderbilt University in Nashville continued programs until the death of its patron and namesake, former Gannett editor and Freedom Forum officer John Seigenthaler, in 2014. The Al Neuharth Media Center at the University of South Dakota in Vermillion, South Dakota, houses the Freedom Forum's Diversity Institute. Another offshoot, the Overby Center for Southern Journalism and Politics at Ole Miss, named and run by former FF chairman and CEO Charles Overby, continues in Oxford, Mississippi.

Founded in 1991 by newspaperman and *USA Today* founder Allen H. Neuharth (1924–2013) on his retirement from Gannett, the Freedom Forum was successor to the old Gannett Foundation, created by Frank Gannett in 1935. At its peak in the late 1990s, the Foundation had $1.1 billion in assets that supported worldwide initiatives. By 2001, economic downturns had dropped the assets to around $700 million, and then-chairman and CEO Overby announced program cuts and deep staff layoffs to permit the foundation to focus on the Newseum (Baker, 2002).

Today, aside from the three named centers in Tennessee, Mississippi, and South Dakota, the Freedom Forum consists pretty much of the Newseum, whose programs and exhibits include plenty of attention to the intersection of press and politics. Some of these include the daily array of current events (including the popular and useful daily online collection of hundreds of newspaper front pages) as well as historical documentation of the press and the presidency, such as the recent exhibit and documentary film commemorating the 50th anniversary of the assassination of President John F. Kennedy. A 2012–2013 exhibit, "Every Four Years: Presidential Campaigns and the Press," "explored how media coverage of presidential campaigns has evolved from William McKinley's 1896 front porch campaign to Barack Obama's 2008 and 2012 Internet campaigns."

The Newseum aside, however, little of the Freedom Forum's authoritative voice on issues of the future of the press—free speech, free press, free spirit—endures.

Ted Pease

See also: Press Council; Presidents and the Press

Further Reading

Baker, Russ. 2002. "Cracks in a Foundation: The Freedom Forum Narrows Its Vision." *Columbia Journalism Review*, January/February. http://www.russbaker.com/archives/CJR%20-%20Freedom%20Forum%20Narrows%20Its%20Vision.htm. Accessed January 11, 2015.

Dennis, Everette E., and David L. Stebenne. "Requiem for a Think Tank: The Life and Death of the Gannett Center at Columbia, 1984–1996." *The International Journal of Press/Politics* 8(2): 11–35(2003).

Freedom of Information Act

The Freedom of Information Act was passed by Congress in 1966. It was a response to increased governmental secrecy in the years after World War II. Secrecy in wartime was usual, but it normally lessened after the war was over. However, the United States immediately went from a hot war to the Cold War with the Soviet Union. In response, President Harry Truman instituted, by executive order, the classification system that labeled some government documents secret and more sensitive ones top secret. Before long more than 10,000 government employees had the authority to classify documents, and they classified millions.

The initial intent of Congress was to give the public access to all the documents the government creates. That was not quite achieved. There are nine exceptions:

- national security
- internal agency rules
- information exempted by federal statutes
- trade secrets
- internal memoranda
- personal privacy
- investigative records
- financial institution records
- oil well information

Most important of these is national security. By the time the Freedom of Information Act was passed, there were millions of classified documents, many of which did not really involve national security. They were political secrets, not military secrets. This was illustrated in the Pentagon Papers case in 1971 when the government sought an injunction to prevent publication of those classified documents. Eight of the nine U.S. Supreme Court justices said they found no threat to national security in publishing the papers.

The act provided that a person wishing to see a document should make a request to the federal agency that created the document. The agency is required to respond to the request in 20 business days. Some agencies interpreted that to mean that all they needed to do was acknowledge receipt of the request until the Federal District Court of Appeals ruled in 2011 that a yes-or-no decision was required in 20 days. The only basis for refusal was that the documents in question were covered by one of the nine exceptions, and the agency must say which one and how it qualifies for the exception.

If a request is refused, the person making the request may file an appeal to the agency. If that appeal is refused, then the person making the request can go to federal court. That provision, however, has turned out not to be very helpful because it typically takes a year and a half—even two years—to get a ruling. That leads some journalists to seek leaks from agency officials rather than going to court.

The Freedom of Information Act disposition summaries by the Justice Department reported that in 2013 there were 237,682 requests. Forty-nine percent were granted entirely, 42 percent were granted in part, and 9 percent were refused. We do not know how much was deleted from those that were granted in part or whether what was left was really useful, and while refusing only 9 percent sounds small, it represents more than 20,000 documents.

The United States used to classify almost a million documents a year, but in the aftermath of 9/11, the number increased markedly. William Leonard, director of the Information Security Oversight Office, estimated in 2006 that there had been 15 million documents classified in 2004. It is doubtful that classification has kept up at that pace. In 2009, the Bush administration carried out an executive order by President William Clinton that declassified most documents that were 25 or more years old. That covered documents classified before 1984 but still left many millions of classified documents. There is, of course, no exact count—just estimates by various public officials. The Freedom of Information Act thus has had some effect on government secrecy, but clearly it has not ended it.

The future of the Freedom of Information Act is far from clear. Edward Snowden's hacking of the files of the National Security Administration signaled that the game has changed. This should have been a wake-up call, but there has been little activity beyond charging Snowden with espionage and making claims of harm done by him. The problem goes far beyond Snowden. China has admitted hacking some U.S. government documents. So has Syria. Only an optimist would suggest that is has been only those two. The need goes far beyond having 10,000 government officials with "secret" or "top secret" stamps to press on documents. However, the advent of new technology should not be allowed to diminish the public's right to know what the government is doing.

Guido H. Stempel III

Further Reading

Gellman, Barton. 2013. "Edward Snowden, After Months of NSA Revelations, Says His Mission Accomplished." *The Washington Post*, December 2.

Northam, Jackie. 2005. "Government Documents Increasingly Classified." National Public Radio, September 8. http://www.npr.org/templates/story/story.php?storyId=4837061. Accessed January 11, 2015.

Friendly, Fred W. (1915–1998)

Few broadcasters set the tone of how television news challenges and interacts with American politics more than network news executive Fred Friendly. From his early days challenging Senator Joseph McCarthy's anti-Communist campaigns to his final days as a fierce proponent of First Amendment rights for the press, Friendly set standards to which 21st century broadcast journalists must try to live.

Friendly was born in New York City in 1915 and spent much of his younger life in Providence, Rhode Island. There he began his career in broadcasting in 1937 as a local radio producer-reporter shortly before serving in World War II as a military newspaper correspondent in the Information and Education section of the China-Burma-India Theater.

Friendly's first real claim to fame came in 1947 when he explained his idea for an album of recorded history of the years 1933 to 1945. He intended to collaborate with Edward R. Murrow, who had achieved fame broadcasting shortwave reports from London during World War II. Murrow narrated scripts written by Friendly. The result was the album *I Can Hear It Now*, released in 1949, which achieved impressive sales. This was to be the beginning of several successful efforts of the "Murrow-Friendly partnership," as it became known. The next year, they produced volume two. Shortly thereafter, Friendly produced *The Quick and the Dead*, a four-part NBC radio documentary about the birth of the atomic bomb. By then, CBS management was attracted to the idea of a permanent Murrow-Friendly partnership.

The first regular series of the pair was *Hear It Now*, a weekly, one-hour news-documentary series produced about the time of the volatile Korean War, the threat of Chinese Communism, and the introduction into America of the medium of television. After one year, the radio series was replaced with a television series, *See It Now*, one of the first television documentaries and one that earned both Murrow and Friendly the respect of being part of a new breed—"broadcast journalists"—able to deal with news and public affairs in both radio and television.

The partnership was to last until the end of the decade and was a formidable combination. During their work together in 1953, they explored the dismissal of Milo Radulovich, who was stripped of his commission in the U.S. Navy because of an alleged connection of a family member to Communism. This and similar charges of Communist alliances were being made by a junior U.S. senator from Wisconsin, Joseph R. McCarthy. In the minds of Friendly and Murrow, the charges were unfair and bypassed the American justice system. In 1954, the two decided to air a *See It Now* program on McCarthy by revealing his own words that were instilling fear in the hearts of the common man in America. It took courage, for it was likely the pair would be branded Communists themselves, a disgrace in that era. Murrow and Friendly both decided to strike on the side of courage and justice. McCarthy's subsequent attempts to disgrace them went unbelieved by viewers who had seen and heard the senator's own words.

Friendly continued to work with Murrow throughout that fateful decade of the 1950s. Toward the end of their partnership, they produced a *CBS Reports* program, "Harvest of Shame," documenting the plight of migrant farm workers in the United States. The program aired in 1960 and left the impact that Friendly and Murrow intended—federal legislation was initiated to protect such workers. The broadcast followed the migrant laborers to their jobs and showed the subhuman living, working, and traveling conditions many endured on a daily basis, reflecting the callous view of some growers that it was far better for the laborers to have some limited income through periodic work than to be unemployed throughout the year. The children of the migrants were shown living in unsupervised squalor, and their lack of educational opportunities was also addressed in the program.

From 1959 until 1964, Friendly was executive producer of *CBS Reports*, extending past the time when Murrow left to become director of the U.S. Information Agency in 1961. In 1964, Friendly became the president of CBS News. After two years in that position, he again displayed his courage in a quarrel over the airing of the Senate Foreign Relations Committee hearings on Vietnam. The network television head, John A. Schneider, had decided to have the network carry reruns of *I Love Lucy* and *The Real McCoys* in place of hearings that proved to be vital information for the United States and its citizens. Friendly pleaded and tried to work with CBS CEO William Paley and CBS Chief Frank Stanton. But the decision had been made, primarily for monetary reasons, since the carrying of Congressional hearings was sustaining programming at the time—not commercially supported. Friendly, already known for his temper, resigned in a fit of anger. He reported in his letter of resignation that when he saw the reruns rather than the important news coverage he wished his news division to carry, he wanted to report, "Due to circumstances beyond our control, the broadcast originally intended for this time will not be seen." News judgments had been superseded by business decisions, a perspective that was not acceptable to Friendly. He subsequently wrote in detail of the experience in his book *Due to Circumstances Beyond Our Control*.

After CBS, Friendly was appointed to a named professorship, becoming the Edward R. Murrow Professor at the Columbia School of Journalism, where he served for three decades. He was also active as the Ford Foundation Advisor on Communication, where he etched out "News and the Law" seminars. The seminars, held at various venues around the country, used a Socratic method of posing ethical dilemmas to those in journalism, law, and communication education. Friendly was fond of quoting to practicing journalists the Socratic notion that "an unexamined life is not worth living." He continued to shift his focus to training journalists and future journalists to think about the difference they could make, both mutually and separately in their communities, in matters of public affairs coverage, international affairs, civil rights, and equal justice.

Friendly died of a stroke at his home in New York on March 3, 1998, at the age of 82.

Val E. Limburg

Further Reading

Friendly, Fred W. 1967. *Due to Circumstances Beyond Our Control . . .* New York: Alfred Knopf.
Konner, Joan. 1998. "Fred Friendly, 1915–1998." *Columbia Journalism Review*, May/June.

Fundamentalism

The term "fundamentalism" stems from a series of pamphlets that appeared between 1910 and 1915 called "The Fundamentals." These booklets represented an attempt on the part of conservative Protestants to counteract what they saw as a drift toward liberal theology or modernism in mainline Protestant denominations early in the twentieth century. Subtitled "Testimony to the Truth," these pamphlets contained articles on doctrinal matters written by respected evangelical theologians from North America, Australia, and Great Britain. The idea came from Lyman Stewart of Union Oil Company of California; he and his brother, Milton, financed their publication and set up a fund to distribute the booklets to Protestant pastors, Sunday school superintendents, and other religious leaders throughout the English-speaking world.

Out of the 90 articles contained in the pamphlets, approximately one-third addressed the contested issue of biblical inspiration, arguing that the Bible is divinely inspired and utterly without error in the original manuscripts. Other articles voiced conservative positions on such issues as the virgin birth of Jesus, the authenticity of miracles, the resurrection, and the Genesis account of creation. Those who subscribed to these doctrines became known as fundamentalists, and the term "fundamentalism" came to refer to the entire movement.

Although the term has since been applied more generally to conservative movements in other religious traditions—Islamic fundamentalism, Hindu fundamentalism, Jewish fundamentalism, and others—the term properly belongs to a movement within North American evangelicalism, which is characterized by a belief in the Bible as God's revelation to humanity, the centrality of a conversion experience, and the impulse to evangelize or bring others into the faith. Fundamentalism differs from the longer tradition of evangelicalism primarily in the demands on the part of its leaders for separatism, sectarianism, and militancy.

The Scopes trial of 1925 illustrates the tensions that emerged in the 1920s between Christian fundamentalists and mainstream U.S. society, including Christian modernists who accepted evolutionary teaching. At this trial, attorney Clarence Darrow and politician William Jennings Bryan squared off in the Rhea County courthouse in Dayton, Tennessee, over the teaching of evolution in public schools. Bryan, a fundamentalist and three-time Democratic nominee for president, feared that the teaching of evolution would lead to a kind of social Darwinism and thereby threaten traditional values and democratic principles. Although Bryan won his case—John T. Scopes was convicted of violating the state's Butler Act (1925), which forbade the teaching of evolution in public classrooms—the press contingent, led by H.L. Mencken, succeeded in painting Bryan and, by extension, all fundamentalists as backwoods country bumpkins who were averse to science and threatened by modernity. The hostility was so intense that many fundamentalists separated from the mainstream, creating new institutions, such as separate schools, and refusing to vote in popular elections.

Whereas evangelicalism historically has sought to be as winsome as possible to attract nonbelievers to the faith, fundamentalists have emphasized the importance of purity in doctrine and lifestyle, even to the point of separating from those who, in the judgment of fundamentalist leaders, fail to adhere to those standards. Fundamentalists, more often than not, wear their sectarianism as a badge, evidence that they have not succumbed to the allure of false doctrine or cultural blandishments.

Fundamentalism has also been described as a militant anti-modernism, but that characterization must be qualified. Fundamentalists are not opposed to modernism in the sense of being suspicious of innovation or technology; indeed, fundamentalists (and evangelicals generally) have often been in the vanguard of technology, especially communications technology, including radio and television. Fundamentalists have an aversion to modernity only when it is invested with a moral valence, that is, when modernity appears to authorize a departure from orthodoxy or traditional values.

Because of the movement's emphasis on biblical literalism, fundamentalists have devoted much attention to the prophetic passages in the Bible, especially the book of Daniel in the Hebrew Bible and the book of Revelation in the New Testament. Drawing on a 19th-century mode of biblical interpretation called dispensationalism, or dispensational premillennialism, fundamentalists—especially in the early decades of the movement—looked for the imminent return of Jesus. According to this dispensationalist scheme, the true believers (those who have been converted and who remain faithful) would be raptured, or taken directly into heaven, at the second coming of Jesus. Those outside of the faith, including those associated with theological liberalism, would face divine judgment. Because of this emphasis on the imminent return of Jesus, fundamentalists were adamantly apolitical for much of the 20th century. If Jesus was coming at any moment, they reasoned, why concern yourself with earthly matters?

From the end of the Scopes trial in 1925 until the late 1970s, many fundamentalists refused to participate in the political process; many were not registered to vote. That changed after 1976, however, when the Internal Revenue Service revoked the tax-exempt status of Bob Jones University, a fundamentalist school in Greenville, South Carolina, because of its racially discriminatory policies. Various fundamentalist leaders banded together to resist that ruling, thereby sowing the seeds of political activism that germinated into the Religious Right. By the time of the 1980 presidential election, the Religious Right included family values and opposition to homosexuality and abortion in its political agenda. In 1979 the political advocacy group called Moral Majority was organized by Jerry Falwell. Falwell, pastor of the Thomas Road Baptist Church in Lynchburg, Virginia, called on his fellow fundamentalists to register and vote in the 1980 election, many of them for the first time.

Finally, fundamentalism can be characterized as confrontational, at least as it has developed in the United States; Falwell, for example, insisted that he was a fundamentalist, not an evangelical. This militancy—on matters of doctrine, ecclesiology (church order), dress, personal behavior, or politics—has prompted George M. Marsden, the preeminent historian of fundamentalism, to remark that the difference between an evangelical and a fundamentalist is that a fundamentalist is "an evangelical who is mad about something."

Randall Balmer

Further Reading

Ammerman, Nancy Tatom. 1987. *Bible Believers: Fundamentalists in the Modern World.* New Brunswick, NJ: Rutgers University Press.
Carpenter, Joel A. 1977. *Revive Us Again: The Reawakening of American Fundamentalism.* New York: Oxford University Press.

G

Gallup, George (1901–1984)

George Gallup was a pioneer in public opinion research and the person most responsible for bringing it into the field of mass communication. He helped transform both political science and the American political process. The Gallup Poll remains a powerful force into the 21st century in how it assesses public opinion and informs policy makers.

Gallup's career in polling began when he was a graduate student at the University of Iowa. His doctoral dissertation was a personal interview newspaper readership study. After finishing his work at Iowa in 1928, he became head of the Department of Journalism at Drake. Three years later he went to Northwestern as professor of advertising and journalism. He left a year later to become director of research for Young and Rubicam, a New York advertising agency. In 1935, he and Harold A. Anderson formed the American Institute of Public Opinion. That same year he started a column called "America Speaks," which reported survey results. The name of the column was changed to the Gallup Poll in 1940.

The defining moment for Gallup was the 1936 presidential election. The magazine *Literary Digest*, which correctly predicted the outcome of five previous presidential elections, predicted that the Republican candidate Alf Landon would get 57 percent of the vote and win the election. Gallup, on the other hand, predicted that Roosevelt would win with 56 percent of the vote. Roosevelt actually got 61 percent of the vote, while Landon got only 37 percent. Roosevelt carried 46 of the 48 states and had 523 electoral votes.

It is widely said that the problem with the *Literary Digest* poll was that it was a mail survey of people who had telephones and owned cars. In the Depression year 1936, that left a lot of people out. However, a bigger problem was that only 24 percent of the 10 million people who received the questionnaire returned it. The 2.4 million did not constitute a representative sample. Gallup, using a much smaller but scientific sample, was much more accurate in predicting who would win.

The result put the *Literary Digest* out of business and increased the prestige of the Gallup Poll considerably. Gallup had shown what could be done, and that led other polling organizations to develop. In an expanding field, Gallup was the leader.

Gallup and most other pollsters missed the call in the 1948 election, predicting that Thomas Dewey would defeat President Harry Truman. Gallup had Dewey winning by 5 percent. Truman, with a whistle-stop campaign featuring attacks on the "do-nothing" 80th Congress and the "one-party press," defeated Dewey by 4 percentage points.

Gallup, after much study of his failure, determined the problem was that pollsters were so certain that Dewey would win that they stopped interviewing in mid-October and missed a pro-Truman surge. That answer satisfied many critics, but there was skepticism as the 1952 presidential election approached. This time Gallup correctly predicted the winner but underestimated the Eisenhower margin by 5 percent.

The next big problem came in 1968. In September the Gallup Poll showed Nixon ahead by 16 percent. Other polls had similar results, but the word was out that in a year of urban unrest interviewers were having difficulty completing interviews in center cities. Gallup's final poll had Nixon ahead by 1 percent, which was correct. How much this was the result of adjustments by Gallup and how much it was the result of the ineffectiveness of Nixon's campaign is anybody's guess.

The Gallup Poll continues to do surveys during presidential campaigns, but it no longer is the leader in election polling. The field it once dominated now has a couple of dozen other players.

Presidential election polls were only a minor part of Gallup's business; however, the presidential polls were important as validation. If you do a survey to find out whether people prefer mint-flavored or lemon-flavored toothpaste, it is difficult to prove that your findings are correct. With a presidential election poll, the election itself proves whether the poll was right or wrong.

While its headquarters are in Washington, D.C., the Gallup Organization has offices in 28 countries in North America, South America, Europe, Asia, and Africa. It has an estimated 2,000 employees and conducts a thousand interviews a day. While its fame rests substantially on its success in political polls, this is only a minor concern today. Gallup specializes in management consulting and leadership development. It publishes the online *Gallup Management Journal* and offers daily news about political, social, and economic issues. It has come a long way from the organization a young University of Iowa alumnus started 80 years ago, yet we should remember that it was Gallup who demonstrated the role that scientific polling could play in our political process. Others carry that legacy forward today.

Guido H. Stempel III

Further Reading

Gallup, George Horace. 1973. *The Gallup Poll: Public Opinion, 1935–1971.* 3 vols. Westport CT: Greenwood Press.
The Gallup House. George H. Gallup Biography. http://www.thegalluphouse.com/georgegallupbiography.html. Accessed January 11, 2015.

Gatekeeping

Gatekeeping represented one of the central functions of the modern mass media during much of the second half of the 20th century. The rise of Internet-based media, such as blogging and Twitter, challenges the traditional notions of media "gatekeepers" and raises questions about how much authority gatekeepers still hold. Still, "gatekeeping" is a significant idea in helping understand the role of media in politics and culture today.

Though the concept can be applied to many areas of social life, in journalism and the media in general, gatekeeping refers to the routines and decisions made by reporters, editors, producers, and others involved in the production of content to control the information that flows through the media to their various audiences, determining what is included and what is kept out. Gatekeeping theory is an effort to understand how, out of all the millions of discrete events that take place every day, a small subset is selected to be transmitted to the public as news. By controlling the flow of information, ideas, and opinions that enter public discourse, media gatekeepers can have an enormous—if sometimes unseen—impact on public discussion and debate. As the media scholar Ben Badikian once put it, controlling the flow of information to society can play a major role in controlling the political and social choices people make.

The metaphor of a media gatekeeper was first proposed by David Manning White in an article he wrote in 1950. The concept was based on an idea of Kurt Lewin, a prominent social psychologist, who observed as an aside to a study about food choices that news traveling through communications channels passed through areas that could be understood as "gates." White studied the activities of a wire service editor at the *Peoria Star*. He asked the wire editor, whom White dubbed "Mr. Gates," to document how he determined which of the wire service stories would be published in the newspaper and which would be cast aside. For a week in February, 1949, "Mr. Gates" retained all of the wire service copy he received and noted the reasons for his decisions. In the end, White found that Mr. Gates rejected nearly 90 percent of the wire copy he received, offering reasons that ranged from not having enough space to the personal or political preferences of the editor. The editor's judgments were shaped by professional, institutional, personal, social, and cultural considerations.

While White's study focused on the actions of one person, other researchers pointed out that a wire copy editor represented only one gatekeeper in the long chain from a potentially newsworthy event to the publication of a news story in a specific medium. From the widest perspective, those who initially bring an activity to the attention of reporters, including public relations practitioners, reporters themselves, and then nearly everyone involved in the editorial or content creation process can be thought of as gatekeepers. That is, they decide what content continues on its path toward the audience and what does not.

Of course, individual gatekeepers do not work in isolation. In most cases, news production is a complex, collaborative process, and the decisions of one person are frequently predicated on the anticipated responses of others involved. For example, public relations practitioners try to anticipate the needs of reporters, and reporters try to write stories that will win the approval of their editors as well as meet professional standards. All of those considerations can dictate what information will be included in a particular publication. Along the same lines, media organizations are alert to their audiences and their markets, as well as other cultural considerations that shape judgments about news content. In fact, gatekeeping can be studied at the individual level, as White did, the institutional level, or even at the societal level.

In the nearly 50 years following the publication of Manning's study, gatekeeping seems to explain part of the enormous influence that some of the news media played in political and social life. By largely controlling the flow of information, to a certain degree, the news media set the political and social agenda for the country. If a political candidate for a major party, for example, could not garner campaign coverage by the media, the candidate would be labeled as "fringe" and would be hard pressed to gain supporters. As the number of urban newspapers shrank and the audience of the national television networks grew in the 1960s and 1970s, it appeared that the gates to reaching a large national audience were narrowing. More and more, the gatekeepers at the newspapers with national impact, such as the *New York Times* and the *Washington Post,* as well as the network news programs seemed to be in a position, within limits, to control the national debate.

But in the same way that Internet-based media have threatened what is now called the mainstream media economically, they have posed a challenge to the media's gatekeeping function as well. First, people who wish to thrust themselves onto the public stage or publicize a particular activity or event are no longer as dependent on traditional media as before. They have a range of channels of communication through which to make their voices heard. Established newsmakers can communicate directly to the public via Twitter and blogs. In 2012, for example, President Obama had 25 million followers on Twitter, a substantially larger audience than any single media outlet could offer. Even Pope Benedict XVI had a Twitter feed. Anybody can post a video of an event on YouTube that could go viral at any time, attracting tens of millions of views. The Internet has swept away many of the barriers to potentially communicating with millions of people.

But gatekeeping still remains a significant social function for the media. Though mass media, like television, no longer exercise the same control of information to the public, they can amplify specific content circulating across the Internet. Many YouTube videos that go viral, for example, get a boost of publicity through what some people now call the megaphone media; that is, television and newspapers. An opinion, news report, or other mediated content may be first available on an Internet-based outlet, but it has a much greater chance of receiving widespread attention if it passes through major media gatekeepers.

Gatekeeping has always been a double-edged sword. On the one hand, it can keep content from the public. On the other hand, it insures that much of the content that does reach the public meets some implicit and explicit standards. As the influence of particular gatekeepers fades, information can flow in an unimpeded way, but the quality may be suspect.

Elliot King

Further Reading

Berkowitz, Dan. 1997. *Social Meanings of News*. London and Thousand Oaks, CA: Sage Publications.
Shoemaker, Pamela J., and Tim P. Vos. 2009. *Gatekeeping Theory*. New York and London: Routledge.
Sorokam, Stuart. 2012. "The Gatekeeping Function: Distributions of Information in Media and the Real World." *The Journal of Politics* 74(2): 514–528.

Gay Voters

The lesbian, gay, bisexual, and transgender (LGBT) community's struggle for civil rights has included policies and decisions that are both pro- and anti- at all levels of government. Debate over the rights of this community have included referenda at the local and state level, proposals to extend or limit rights in Congress, executive orders, and, perhaps most anticipated, decisions by state and federal courts and the U.S. Supreme Court.

Major civil rights struggles for this community include, but are not limited to, fairness in hiring and firing in employment, nondiscrimination policies in government, protection of LGBT youth in schools, transgender health care access, hate crimes recognition and prevention, and equal marriage (sometimes referred to as gay marriage or marriage equality). Marriage equality has been the most contentious national issue that has come before voters that impacts the LGBT community. Presidential candidates are often asked to take a stand on marriage equality, and the issue has been used as a wedge issue in national elections.

The LGBT community is estimated to be between 3 and 5 percent of the population, although some estimates go up to 10 percent of the American public. The LGBT community gained political power and visibility after the Stonewall Riots following a police raid on a largely gay and transgender bar in Greenwich Village in New York City in 1969. Power and visibility of the community increased following the disproportionate impact that the HIV/AIDS epidemic had on the community in the early 1980s.

The first national LGBT advocacy groups were founded in the 1970s, including Lambda Legal and the Task Force (formerly the Gay Task Force). These organizations aimed to build community among LGBT people, expand civil rights of the LGBT community, and raise awareness of the community's needs and discrimination that it faced. The first legal challenges to same-sex marriage bans were in the 1970s, including *Baker v. Nelson* (1971), and *Jones v. Callahan* (1973), both of which ruled that same-sex couples were not entitled to equal protection and the right to sue for equal marriage.

Backlash by conservative voters against the increasing visibility of the LGBT community has been swift since the 1970s, including proposals to ban LGBT individuals from the teaching profession in California, anti-gay votes against marriage equality passed by voters and written into state constitutions in thirty-one states, and the passage of the Defense of Marriage Act (DOMA) through Congress in 1996. DOMA allowed states to refuse to recognize same-sex marriages performed in other states and also defined marriage as being between one man and one woman. This policy effectively prevented same-sex couples from receiving federal tax and related marriage benefits.

Anti-LGBT legislation has also impacted adoption of children by same-sex couples, the ability of LGBT people to become foster parents, and the ability of educators to discuss LGBT health issues in school. Several organizations, including the National Organization for Marriage, have organized constituencies and encouraged anti-gay votes at the polls. White evangelical Protestants, according to Pew Research, are most likely to oppose same-sex marriage. At the federal level the Employment Non-Discrimination Act (ENDA), which would prevent discrimination in hiring and firing based on sexual orientation and gender identity, has been introduced in every Congressional session since 1994. It has also been defeated each time, largely attributed to legislators' opposition to the protections it offers to the LGBT community and the pressure of anti-gay constituents.

One of the most noteworthy aspects of pro-gay and anti-gay voting behavior lies with the rapid change of public opinion. In a study conducted in consecutive years by Pew Research since 2001, polling data show an almost exact flip in pro-gay vs. anti-gay marriage support over time. In 2001, when the research was first conducted, 57 percent of Americans opposed gay marriage and 35 percent supported it.

In 2014, at last count, 54 percent of Americans supported gay marriage and 39 percent opposed it. This is a substantial shift in public opinion, which impacts voting behavior. This rapid change is due in large part to a generational shift on the issue, with younger Americans being more likely to support same-sex marriage. Most Republicans polled by

Pew opposed same-sex marriage, two-thirds of Democrats support same-sex marriage, and support is rising for same-sex marriage across race and gender lines.

It is likely that the fight over pro- and anti-gay equality will be played out in the U.S. count system, although this does not guarantee the end of this issue. In early 2011, U.S. Attorney General Eric Holder announced that the Obama administration would not continue to enforce DOMA. In 2013, in the case *United States v. Windsor*, DOMA was struck down as unconstitutional, stating that singling out same-sex couples and restricting their rights and benefits violated the Fifth Amendment. Pending and resolved litigation is taking place in state courts, with an overwhelming number of decisions being in favor of marriage equality.

Sarah R. Young

Further Reading

Rimmerman, C.A. 2008. *The Lesbian and Gay Movements: Assimilation or Liberation? Dilemmas in American Politics*. Boulder, CO: Westview Press.
Sullivan, N.R. 2014. *The Marriage Equality Movement: A Brief History of (some) U.S. Social Movements*. Philadelphia: Lifting Consciousness Press.

Gender Gap

The gender gap refers to the differences in voting between men and women. This applies both to the rate at which the two sexes participate in elections and differences in how women and men support particular candidates and political parties. In recent years, the gender gap generally is used to describe how female voters are more likely than males to vote for Democratic candidates, a growing trend that has had enormous consequences upon the political balance of power in the United States.

In every presidential election from 1964 onward, more women have cast ballots than have men. The gap went from 39.2 million voting women versus 37.5 million voting men in the election between Democrat Lyndon B. Johnson and Republican Barry Goldwater to 71.4 million women versus 61.6 million men in the race between Democrat Barack Obama and Republican Mitt Romney. There are many reasons for this trend, including, of course, that women live longer than men and significantly outnumber them, especially within the subset of the population that is of voting age.

The Gallup Poll reports that the gender gap in 2012 was the largest ever recorded by the organization using data that reliably go back to the 1952 election. Gallup estimated that 56 percent of women voted for Obama while 44 percent supported Romney. The organization's estimate for men was reversed, with 54 percent of males voting for the Republican while 46 percent supported the Democrat. If this gender difference is added—women preferring the Democrat by 12 points and men rejecting the Democrat by -8 points—then there was a 20 percentage-point gender spread in 2012.

Gallup analyst Jeffrey M. Jones wrote that there are many possible issues-based reasons that the gender gap in the 2012 race was the largest on record. "For example, Romney's business background may have been more appealing to men than to women," he said. "Obama's campaign stressed maintaining the social safety net, raising taxes on the wealthy, maintaining abortion rights, and requiring health care coverage for contraception—all in contrast to Romney's more conservative positions on these issues of potential interest to women."

The Gallup Poll estimates that a majority of women supported the Democratic nominee in every presidential election from 1992 on. The second largest gender gap was recorded in Republican Ronald Reagan's landslide reelection in 1984, when former Democratic Vice President Walter Mondale selected a woman, Geraldine Ferraro, as the first woman to be a major party's nominee for vice president. Reagan was enormously popular that year, carrying every state except Mondale's home of Minnesota. But male voters preferred Reagan over Mondale by an enormous 28-precentage point advantage (the largest pro-GOP margin among men on record) while women supported Reagan by a much narrower 10-point margin. "It is unclear to what extent the presence on the Democratic ticket of Geraldine Ferraro, the first woman to be a major party's nominee for vice president, had on the vote of women that year," Jones said. It's also unclear if men were more likely to vote for GOP because the Democrats had nominated a woman on the ticket.

Here are Gallup's gender gap estimates over six decades. These data show the Democratic lead (or deficit in the case of negative values) among men and women and the estimated spread of the difference between the genders:

Election	Men	Women	Difference
2012	-8	12	20 pts.
2008	0	14	14 pts.
2004	-12	4	16 pts.
2000	-7	8	15 pts.
1996	1	15	14 pts.
1992	4	8	4 pts.
1988	-12	-4	8 pts.
1984	-28	-10	18 pts.
1980	-15	-5	10 pts.
1976	8	-3	11 pts.
1972	-26	-24	2 pts.
1968	-2	2	4 pts.
1964	20	24	4 pts.
1960	4	-2	6 pts.
1956	-10	-22	12 pts.
1952	-6	-16	10 pts.

Although the gender gap has reliably favored Democrats in recent elections, women were actually more likely than men to vote for Republicans during the 1950s and early 1960s. Women shifted toward the Democrats in 1964 when they solidly rejected Goldwater in

1964, although it should be noted that their pro-Republican skew was extremely small in 1960 when charismatic Democrat Robert F. Kennedy narrowly defeated Republican Vice President Richard Nixon.

Republicans nominated a woman as vice president in 2008; although, again, the effect may have been more profound upon male voters. Woman solidly rejected the GOP ticket of John McCain and Sarah Palin, but normally pro-Republican male voters were about evenly divided between the Democrats and Republicans that year.

The shifting pattern of how women vote in the United Sates mirrors a similar trend worldwide. Historically, over many decades and in many countries, women have tended to vote more conservatively than men. But this changed starting in the early 1980s, with "women moving toward the left of men throughout advanced industrial societies, though not in post-Communist societies or developing countries," according to a large review of polling data by political scientists Ronald Inglehart and Pippa Norris.

Thomas K. Hargrove

Further Reading

Inglehart, Ronald, and Pippa Norris. 2013. "The Developmental Theory of the Gender Gap: Women's and Men's Voting Behavior in Global Perspective." Center for Political Studies, University of Michigan and Steering Committee for the World Values Study.

Jones, Jeffrey M. 2012. "Gender Gap in 2012 Vote is Largest in Gallup's History." November 9. The Gallup Poll. http://www.gallup.com/poll/158588/gender-gap-2012-vote-largest-gallup-history.aspx. Accessed January 3, 2015.

Generation X

U.S. elections in the early 21st century have been dominated by "swing states" and "swing votes." Generation X can be considered the "swing generation," as that generation has been more evenly divided during U.S. elections than earlier and subsequent generational cohorts like the baby boom and millennials. That trend is likely to continue as generation X moves into middle age.

"Generation X," or simply "gen X," refers to the cohort born after the baby boom ended and before the start of the "millennial" generation. It includes U.S. residents born between the early-mid 1960s and the early 1980s (roughly 1965 to 1982, although the precise start and end points vary according to different scholars). In the 2010 census, that age group accounted for about 82 million Americans, or about 26 percent of the population.

The generation has been labeled as one of ambiguity and lacking in a cohesive generational identity (hence the "X" designation). Although the term "generation X" had been applied by some to the earlier baby boom generation, the current usage was cemented in the early 1990s, largely due to Douglas Coupland's novel *Generation X: Tales for an Accelerated Generation*. The novel focuses on a group of young adult friends trying to eke out a living from "McJobs" (slang for low-paying service jobs that offer little chance for advancement). Other pop-culture depictions of gen X include the television shows *Melrose Place* and *Friends*; films such as Spike Lee's *Do the Right Thing*, Richard Linklater's *Slacker*, and John Hughes's *The Breakfast Club*; and a number of nihilistic musical anthems across multiple musical genres (from hip-hop to alt-country), perhaps most notably Nirvana's 1991 hit "Smells Like Teen Spirit" (and its signature lyric, "I feel stupid. And contagious. Here we are now. Entertain us."). The generation's affinity for popular culture has led to its other moniker, "the MTV generation."

Most in the generation were children or young adults during pivotal political moments of the late 20th century—the launch of the "War on Drugs," the collapse of the Soviet Union, the Gulf War, the rise of the Internet, and presidential scandals such as the Iran-Contra affair faced by President Ronald Reagan and the sex-scandal impeachment of President Bill Clinton. Their young adulthoods have been markedly affected by two major events—the 9/11 terrorist attacks in 2001 and the Great Recession of 2008–2009. The generation endured two previous economic downturns and in 2014 faced long-term projections of a financially tenuous era. In 2011, the Pew Research Center found that "gen Xers" were less satisfied with their financial situations than any other living generation, including the younger millennials. Another study, produced in 2013 by The Urban Institute, found that generation X had accumulated about 7 percent less wealth by their 30s than had their parents and grandparents, that their financial success had stagnated through the early 21st century (those aged between 29 and 37 saw an average 21 percent decline in net worth by 2010). Despite feeling more pinched financially than previous generations, gen Xers were far more likely to say life in the United States has gotten better since the 1960s: 45 percent of gen Xers said that, compared to just 29 percent of baby boomers and 31 percent of the silent generation. Gen X is surprisingly upbeat despite its uncertain financial future.

The basis for gen X's financial anxiety is owed to a mix of factors. A 2013 survey conducted by the MetLife Mature Market Institute found that half of gen Xers reported they were behind on their retirement investments, mostly due to job insecurity and a lack of sufficient income. Most (70 percent) did not feel Social Security would provide them with full benefits as received by previous generations. About 42 percent believed they would have to work well past the standard retirement age of 65. Three-fourths did not believe they would receive any inheritance from their parents (largely because of expectations that parents' assets would have to go toward elder care, health care, assisted living, etc.). A large majority, 78 percent, expected to have to care for their parents, compared to 52 percent of baby boomers.

The mortgage crisis that began in 2008 and triggered the Great Recession had a disproportionate impact on generation X—about 82 percent had purchased homes, mostly during the pre-crisis "bubble," therefore gen Xers were much more likely to have homes that were "underwater" than previous generations (about one in five were in homes that were less valuable than their mortgage).

The majority of gen Xers live in dual-income households (about 65 percent). Gen Xers tended to marry later in life than previous generations but through 2014 had lower divorce rates. About three-fourths of gen Xers have children, many of whom were entering young adulthood and post-secondary education in 2014.

Facing tenuous personal finances, the high costs of elder care, and the very high costs of helping their millennial children launch into adulthood (particularly covering the rising costs of post-secondary education amid reduced government support), gen X voters are keenly focused on economic issues and policies in the early 21st century. In 2012, 50 percent of gen Xers agreed that they often do not have enough money to make ends meet, according to Pew Research data.

Politically, research suggests that generation X is bifurcated by age, with older gen Xers aligning more with the voting patterns of baby boomers and younger gen Xers aligning more with millennials. Gen Xers who began voting under the Ronald Reagan and George H.W. Bush administrations tended to vote Republican in the early 21st century, while those who reached adulthood during the two terms of Bill Clinton's presidency tended to vote Democratic. That split helps explain the generation's divisiveness in elections. The generation was evenly divided in the 2012 presidential election.

Generation X's partisan views vary by topic. Pew research found that gen X voters in 2011 favored Democrats with regard to health care policy and abortion laws, but favored Republicans on immigration laws and dealing with the federal deficit. About half—51 percent—said Democrats were "more concerned with people like me," compared to 36 percent who stated that about Republicans, and 52 percent viewed Republicans as "more extreme in its positions" compared to 37 percent who said that about Democrats. Only one in five gen Xers in 2011 supported the libertarian "Tea Party" movement, far below the rates of support of older generations, yet two in five gen Xers in 2014 identified as politically independent. Leading up to his reelection in 2012, President Barrack Obama had a 45 percent unfavorable rate among generation X voters, having lost the stronger support he had from the generation in 2008.

As with previous generations, gen X has grown more ideologically conservative than liberal as it has entered middle age (about 36 percent to 21 percent in 2011, compared to 30 percent conservative and 24 percent liberal in 2000), but it is slightly more liberal than previous generations on many social issues. Gen X is more racially diverse than the baby boomers but slightly less so than millennials (about 38 percent diverse, compared to 27 percent of baby boomers and 41 percent of millennials). That correlates with the generation's strong support for interracial marriage (92 percent). The generation is also leaning liberal on a number of social issues. A 2011 survey found that about 50 percent of gen Xers supported same-sex marriage, 55 percent believed immigration strengthened society, and about 20 percent did not identify with a specific religion. Later surveys by Pew showed gen Xers in 2012 slightly favored gun control over gun rights (53 percent to 46 percent); they were split on the perceived harms of government regulation (50 percent said regulation does more harm than good, the lowest level among all concurrent generations); and they were more favorable toward increased environmental-protection regulation than other generations (79 percent, compared to 77 percent of millennials). More than three-fourths of gen Xers in 2012 believed that, in the United States, "the rich get richer and the poor get poorer."

As a smaller demographic caught between the baby boomers and millennials, and largely bifurcated into camps that more closely align with those "bookend" generations, generation X is unlikely to become a cohesive block of voters. It is, however, clearly a bellwether age group, one whose political views most closely match the outcomes of elections. That group's voting through 2014 was trending conservative on fiscal matters, liberal on social issues, and not overly loyal to either major U.S. political party. Whether that trend toward moderation will hold is anybody's guess. Generation X has been, and likely will continue to be, the biggest X factor in generational politics of the early 21st century.

Bill Reader

Further Reading

Goyer, Amy. 2013. "The Me Life Study of Gen X: The MTV Generation Moves into Mid-Life." The Mature Market Institute, April. http://www.metlife.com/assets/cao/mmi/publications/studies/2013/mmi-gen-x.pdf. Accessed March 13, 2014.

Pew Research Center. 2011. "Angry Silents, Disengaged Millennials: The Generation Gap and the 2012 Election." http://www.people-press.org/files/legacy-pdf/11-3-11%20Generations%20Release.pdf. Accessed March 13, 2014.

Steuerle, Eugene, Signe-Mary McKernan, Caroline Ratcliffe, and Sisi Zhang. 2013. "Lost Generations? Wealth Building Among Young Americans." Urban Institute, March. http://www.urban.org/UploadedPDF/412766-Lost-Generations-Wealth-Building-Among-Young-Americans.pdf. Accessed March 13, 2014.

Gerrymandering

Gerrymandering (technically pronounced with a hard "g" sound, but popularly mispronounced as "jerry-mandering") is a long-standing but controversial method of reapportioning legislative districts into highly irregular shapes. It is an oft-used political tactic that gives one political party advantage over another during redistricting. In the United States, remapping of legislative districts takes place every 10 years based on the results of the Constitution-mandated census. That redistricting is done to apportion each state's legislative and congressional districts so they are essentially the same size in total population.

Gerrymandering prioritizes demographics over geography, such that a district sprawls across vast territory so that it contains a majority of people (and, by extension, registered voters) who are likely to support candidates and causes of a particular party. As a result, a "gerrymandered" district often has convoluted borders and a serpentine shape, sometimes with many thin tendrils reaching out to encapsulate and/or isolate certain communities.

The practice is often derided as a means for elected officials to choose their voters rather than the other way around, but gerrymandering also can be used to provide representative districts that are culturally homogenous or to ensure certain minority groups are not disenfranchised, in compliance with the Voting Rights Act. However, the practice can result in lopsided partisan representation both in statehouses and the U.S. Congress, such that a "swing state" with relatively equal numbers of Republican and Democratic voters could have disproportionate representation in statehouses and the U.S. House. For example, in the gerrymandered swing state of Ohio, the electorate voted in 2012 to reelect Democratic President Barrack Obama and Democratic incumbent U.S. Sen. Sherrod Brown. But the voting in gerrymandered congressional districts, Republicans won 12 seats compared to the Democrats' four. The ability of gerrymandering to essentially rig the outcome of elections is evident when considering Ohio's electorate was much more narrowly divided when voting for representation in the U.S. House, with 2.54 million voting for GOP candidates for the U.S. House compared to 2.30 million for Democrats, a 52-48 split.

Although the practice predates 1812, that is the year it was given a name. Gov. Elbridge Gerry of Massachusetts, a signer of the Declaration of Independence, approved a bill that allowed one of the state-senate districts in Essex County to be drawn in a serpentine shape, forming a narrow band along the northern and western borders of the county. It was an obvious attempt to give political advantage to Gerry's Democratic-Republican Party over its rival, the Federalist Party, as the other districts in the country were more-or-less polygonal in shape. Critics of Gerry's plan noted that the new district was shaped like a salamander, and to ridicule both the practice and the governor who signed it into law, they coined a portmanteau name for the district, "The Gerry-Mander."

There are two primary approaches to gerrymandering. The first, called "packing," draws districts in an effort to concentrate certain demographic groups, often racial minorities, into a single or a few districts (often called "minority-majority districts"). The second, called "cracking," dilutes regional majorities by breaking them up and adding those apportionments to nearby districts.

One of the most extreme examples of "packing" has been the 4th Congressional District of Illinois, west of Chicago. The district, drawn after the 2010 census, has been described as an "earmuff-shaped" gerrymander that connects two Democratic strongholds of mostly Hispanic voters via a narrow border drawn along the berms of Interstate 294 (the road surface is in the district, but properties on either side of the highway are in other districts). Other examples of "packing" include the 12th Congressional District of Pennsylvania, which was redrawn in 2002 with a long, multi-branched shape to include the neighborhood of a long-time Democratic congressman into a new, predominantly Republican district (effectively unseating the congressman); the 12th District of North Carolina, which since 1992 has snaked along Interstate 85 from Winston-Salem in the north to Charlotte in the south, packing into one district numerous African American communities that mostly vote Democratic; and Arizona's 2nd District drawn after the 2000 census, which was heavily gerrymandered from the western part of the state to include the reservation of the Hopi tribe of Native Americans in the northeast (but not the reservation of the Navajo tribe, which surrounds the Hopi reservation on all sides).

The other approach, "cracking," was most famously used in the controversial 2004 redistricting of Texas, which occurred shortly after the Republican party gained control of the state legislature for the first time in more than a century. The new Republican majority quickly moved to redraw districts to try to unseat 10 white Democratic members of the U.S. House. One of the most controversial aspects was the "cracking" of Travis County, where the state capital of Austin is located; the redistricting cut the Democratic stronghold into smaller sections that were added to more Republican-leaning rural districts. Before that mid-decade gerrymandering, Texas' congressional delegation was 17 Democrats and 15 Republicans; after the gerrymandering, the Republicans won 21 seats, and Democrats won 11.

Gerrymandering may be unseemly, but it is typically not illegal. In 2006, the U.S. Supreme Court upheld the legality of all but one of the gerrymandered districts in Texas. That ruling came two years after the 2004 ruling in *Vieth v. Jubelirer*, in which the court found that gerrymandered districts in Pennsylvania had not violated the U.S. Constitution's "one person, one vote" and "equal-protection" guarantees. The rulings in both the Texas and Pennsylvania cases bolstered gerrymandering efforts in other states, such as the Democrat-led effort in Maryland to gerrymander a number of districts in 2012, most notably the 3rd District that sliced through several counties and the city of Baltimore to eliminate a district held by a Republican incumbent.

Some scholars argue that the very high rate of incumbent seat retention in modern U.S. elections (typically, 95 percent or more) may be attributable to factors other than gerrymandering. Moreover, several efforts to limit gerrymandering have failed when put to the electorate via ballot referenda. In 2012, Maryland voters approved the above-mentioned gerrymandering that favored Democrats, while Ohio voters rejected a plan that sought to curb gerrymandering there that heavily favors Republicans in the otherwise bipartisan state.

A few U.S. states have attempted to limit partisan gerrymandering by taking that role away from state legislatures and giving it to different types of committees or commissions, most of them requiring bipartisan compositions. By 2012, six states prohibited elected officials from serving on such commissions. A notable example was California: In 2008, California voters approved the Voters First Act, which established a bipartisan commission to handle redistricting. The California Citizens Redistricting Commission's first maps went into effect in 2012 and largely avoided the heavy gerrymandering implement by legislature-drawn maps in previous decades. Montana traditionally has too few residents to have more than one congressional district, but its constitution requires state legislative districts to "consist of compact and contiguous territory" and to be drawn by "a commission of five citizens, none of whom may be public officials." Iowa's system, enacted in 1980, has a committee of nonpartisan legislative support staff members draw the maps, and state law requires that districts follow county lines, thus effectively preventing gerrymandering in that state.

The long-term future of gerrymandering in the United States remains uncertain. Computer-assisted analysis can produce redistricting maps that have no gerrymandering at all; for example, the process of "splitline districting" would use a population-based algorithm to divide states into tidy triangular and rectilinear districts. Absent widespread public demand or political will of incumbents and party leaders, however, it seems as if gerrymandering, a practice as old as the republic itself, will become an increasingly more complicated, nuanced, and often devious tool of partisan politics well into the 21st century.

Bill Reader

See also: Polarization

Further Reading

Bullock, Charles S. 2010. *Redistricting: The Most Political Activity in America*. Lanham, MD: Rowman & Littlefield.

Dodd, Lawrence C., and Bruce I. Oppenheimer. 2012. *Congress Reconsidered*. 10th ed. Washington, DC: CQ Press.

Get-Out-the-Vote Efforts (Mobilization)

Republican political strategists were astonished in 2012 when President Obama again carried Florida in what turned out to be an easy reelection. The GOP believed Obama could be beaten in a swing state like Florida since he carried significant political baggage after four years of governance. His health care reforms and promise of immigration reforms were especially unpopular with conservatives in the Sunshine State, but the president ended up narrowly carrying Florida by 74,000 votes, making him the first

Democratic presidential candidate to enjoy back-to-back Florida victories since Franklin D. Roosevelt.

The key—agree Republican leaders and political scientists—was Obama's remarkable get-out-the-vote effort, which politicians sometimes refer to by the acronym "GOTV" or by the descriptive phrase "ground game."

The president spent many millions of dollars in campaign funds to establish hundreds of local field offices in key counties in the dozen so-called "battleground" states that decide the winner in presidential elections. "Those counties in which the Obama campaign had established field offices during the general election saw a disproportionate increase in the Democratic vote share," concluded political scientist Seth Masket who analyzed Obama's 2008 campaign. "Furthermore, this field office-induced vote increase was large enough to flip three battleground states from Republican to Democratic."

Voting has never been mandatory in the United States, which means that only a fraction of the eligible population will go to the polls on Election Day, request an absentee ballot, or apply to vote in advance of Election Day. Even in presidential elections—which historically enjoy much higher turnouts than most local, state, and off-year national elections—only about 60 percent of people of eligible voting age participate. The kinds and numbers of voters who turn out usually decide the balance of power between Democrats and Republicans.

GOTV tactics have become highly sophisticated in recent years. The major political parties have established extremely detailed databases of most American households, listing the names of adult voters and demographic information such as age, marital status, number of children, employment, educational backgrounds, religious preferences, and the charitable activities of each household. The parties have calculated the likelihood that voters in each household are sympathetic to their candidates and causes.

Modern campaigns involve door-to-door canvassing of neighborhoods by paid workers and volunteers who carry handheld electronic devices (sometimes no more complex than a smartphone) that inform them of the names and past voting behaviors of each home's occupants even before they knock on the door. Campaigns will make targeted direct mailings espousing issues deemed important to carefully selected households. They also employ automated telephone messages, often with personalized audio messages, in the final days of the campaign urging sympathetic voters to go to the polls. Highly organized transportation networks are established to provide rides to polling places for the elderly, infirmed, or disadvantaged voters who don't own a vehicle.

Television advertising is also getting more sophisticated, although that may not seem obvious to viewers who complain of highly negative "attack ads" that seem to cheapen democratic dialogue. Well-funded campaigns will cast dozens of different ads using a variety of themes that resonate with specific voter groups and then air them as television (and some radio) spots during specific programming times known to be favored by targeted audiences. Young people and the elderly watch and listen to entirely different programming, as do men and women or people of different races and ethnicities. The structure of the audience for each major program and broadcast time slot has been identified and targeted.

So enormous has campaign advertising spending become that communication companies that own TV stations eagerly look forward to even-numbered years when political advertising will flood their broadcasts and significantly increase their profit margins. (These companies often tell their stockholders to be patient about diminished profits during the odd-numbered years.) Television stations in swing states like Ohio and Florida are significantly more valuable and have higher sale prices than stations located in states that rarely decide the outcome of elections.

The proliferation of so-called "smart" TVs will allow even more carefully targeted get-out-the-vote campaigns, which will be able to broadcast targeted advertisements to specific homes. It is not impossible that political advertising content will become so intensely personal that TV campaigns may be able to address members of a household by name in the not-to-distant future.

The 2000 presidential campaign's disputed Florida vote demonstrated that tiny shifts in voter turnout can decide who controls the White House. Democratic Vice President Al Gore knew the vote was so close in the Sunshine State that he made it his last campaign stop late election eve, hoping to win just a few more voters who watched the 10 o'clock news that night. He ended up losing the state, officially, by just 537 votes. But Florida demonstrated that small shifts in voter turnout can—and do—decide elections. "A new era of statistical accountability has been introduced," concluded political reporter Sasha Issenberg in his study of modern GOTV methods. "It has become impossible to correctly interpret campaign strategy without understanding the revolution in tactics."

Thomas K. Hargrove

Further Reading

Green, Donald P., and Alan S. Gerber. 2008. "Get Out the Vote: How to Increase Voter Turnout." Washington, DC: Brookings Institution Press.

Issenberg, Sasha. 2013. "The Victory Lab: The Secret Science of Winning Campaigns." New York: Broadway Books.

Masket, Seth E. 2009. "Did Obama's Ground Game Matter? The Influence of Local Field Offices During the 2008 Presidential Election." *Public Opinion Quarterly* 73(5): 1023–1039.

Graber, Doris Appel (1923–)

Doris Appel Graber is a luminary in both communication and political science. Undoubtedly one of the foremost figures in the area of political communication research, she has addressed fundamental questions about the role of the media in political processes. Ultimately, her work has helped to establish an agenda for political communication research. As a result, she has frequently been called upon to assess the status of current knowledge in political communication. When *Political Communication*, a journal co-sponsored by the American Political Science Association and the International Communication Association, was inaugurated in 1992, Graber was a natural choice to be the first editor. She has also been elected president of the Midwest Political Science Association and the Midwest Association for Public Opinion Research (MAPOR). She was recognized as a MAPOR fellow in 1988 and received awards from the American Political Science Association, including the Mentor Award in 1991 and the Edelman Career Award in 1992. Doris Graber's voluminous accomplishments place her among the giants in both communication and political science.

Graber received a Ph.D. in international law and relations from Columbia University. Both her M.A. and B.A. degrees were in political science from Washington University in St. Louis. As a high school freshman, Graber felt that her schoolwork was not challenging enough, so she took and passed the high school admission test to Washington University in St. Louis. Not only was she one of the youngest students on campus, but she finished her coursework in less than four years and graduated second in her class. She majored in political science with a minor in economics.

The Ph.D. dissertation stage of Graber's career provided the toughest test of her academic resolve. Originally, her doctoral adviser at Columbia University was Professor Charles Cheney Hyde, a leading authority on international law. Under his direction, Graber prepared a dissertation on the legal aspects of war crimes trials. Sadly, Professor Hyde died before the completed dissertation was defended. A political scientist with no expertise in international law was assigned to advise Graber. He argued that her dissertation was a work of "legal fiction" and voted not to accept it on the dubious grounds that war trials were political events devoid of substantial legal issues. Because the University required a unanimous committee, Graber had to return to the drawing board to draft a new dissertation.

Graber describes her career as a "multicolored braid." She says that "different strands came into prominence depending on the opportunities of the moment, on the need to balance marriage demands and children's upbringing with career demands, and on my eagerness to meet new and different challenges." In addition to her family roles as wife, mother, and homemaker, Graber says she has five other career strands—the journalist, the researcher, the teacher, the editor, and the officer for professional associations.

Graber's career as a journalist began as a feature writer at the *St. Louis County Observer* while she was an undergraduate. She covered issues related to the St. Louis County juvenile court system, local media ethics, and occupational hazards in the construction industry. She also worked for a weekly newspaper, the *University City Tribune*. Graber's journalistic career continued after she finished her Ph.D. coursework. She worked for the Commerce Clearing House of Chicago in charge of two publications, the U.S. Supreme Court Digest and the Legal Periodical Digest.

As a researcher, Graber has written 11 books, edited 2 others, and published 25 book chapters and 35 journal articles. Since 1970, she has presented 93 conference papers and has made 89 colloquium presentations on five different continents. In the process, she has played a major role in surveying the past and charting the future of political communication research. Graber has written five reviews of the current state of research in political communication. Her book *Mass Media and American Politics* (about to come out in its fifth edition) provides an important compendium of current knowledge.

Graber also served as a research associate at the Center for the Study of American Foreign and Military Policy at the University of Chicago. It was here that she did the work for Public Opinion, the President and Foreign Policy (1968).

Graber has taught at Northwestern University, the University of Chicago, North Park College, and the University of Illinois at Chicago, where she has been a full professor of political science since 1970. For eight years, she served as Harper and Row's social science college textbook editor.

Graber's involvement in professional service was initially motivated by the need to redress the absence of women in leadership positions of professional organizations. She served as president of academic organizations, including the Midwest Association for

Public Opinion Research, the Midwest Political Science Association, and the Illinois chapter of Phi Beta Kappa. She will also serve as the president of the International Society for Political Psychology. She is a past vice president of the American Political Science Association and has been the head of both the Political Communication section of the American Political Science Association and the Political Communication division of the International Communication Association. She has been on the editorial board of eight social science journals and served as an officer or committee member for numerous other professional organizations and associations.

In surveying Graber's research, we are immediately struck by the volume and breadth of her contributions. Her work has been eclectic and interdisciplinary in its approach to theory construction. Graber has addressed many of the major questions in the field of political communication.

Graber and her husband managed to balance their careers and parenting obligations through "teamwork" and "careful time management." Having two professional parents brought Graber's children unique opportunities to travel and to meet interesting people. Be it by nature or nurture, all of Graber's children have gone on to their own professional careers. As an outstanding academician and successful parent, Graber is an excellent role model and proof that a career and a family are not mutually exclusive.

Nancy Signorielli

Further Reading

Graber, Doris A. 2002. *The Power of Communication: Managing Information in Public Organizations.* Washington, DC: CQ Press.
Graber, Doris A. 2009. *Mass Media and American Politics.* Washington, DC: CQ Press.
Graber, Doris A., Denis McQuail, and Pippa Norris, eds. 1998. *The Politics of News: The News of Politics.* Washington, DC: CQ Press.

Green Party

The U.S. Green Party traces itself to the European Greens, who first organized as an anti-nuclear, pro-peace movement at the height of the Cold War. It was the German Greens, organized by Petra Kelly, who were most specifically influenced by the U.S. environmental movement of the early 1970s. The U.S. Green Party convened in 1984 in meetings that focused on local elections. By organizing itself at the local level, the Greens first influenced policy and government in towns, cities, and villages. The first Green Party candidate appeared on the ballot in 1986. In 1990, Alaska became the first state to grant the Greens full ballot status. California followed in 1992.

During the 1990s, the Green Party went through internal changes. Some Greens grew impatient with the strategy of radical, slow, long-term organizing. These Greens called for the immediate creation of state Green parties and some for a national Green party. Their calls created internal division, and two distinct factions took shape within the party. The first division believed that the Greens were a social movement that should work up from the grassroots; the second urged the party to pursue national power and to challenge the American two-party system.

In 1991, the groups changed their names, respectively, to The Greens and Green Party USA. The Greens would remained an activist party based on dues-paying members, whereas the Green Party USA sought national stature. The emergence to the national scene came quickly when, in November 1995, well-known activist Ralph Nader initiated the Green Party's first presidential campaign by officially entering the California Green primary. Nader's unconventional campaign aroused Green Party activity in states that up this point had little activity. By election eve, the Greens had placed Ralph Nader on twenty-two ballots nationwide, with another twenty-three states qualifying him as a write-in candidate. In August 1996, state Green parties held their first national Nominating Convention in Los Angeles, California. The party chose a ticket of Nader and Native American Winona LaDuke, a well-known activist for causes related to environmental and indigenous women's issues.

The Nader-LaDuke campaign challenged the candidates and platforms of the Democrats and Republicans and forced the parties to discuss issues that were important to the Green Party. The success of the campaign spurred many additional Green political efforts throughout the United States. In the end, the Nader-LaDuke campaign came in fourth place after that of Ross Perot. They garnered more than 700,000 votes, which accounted for approximately 1 percent of the vote nationwide. The single best state performance came in Oregon, where the Green Party earned 4 percent of the vote.

Although the Greens focused on local and state politics, some Greens continued to believe in a presidential run. In the 2000 presidential election, Nader ran for president again as a member of the Green Party with a platform against development, large corporations, and in support of environmental causes. Although polls suggest about 70 percent of Americans call themselves environmentalists, Nader's campaign garnered less than 5 percent of the national vote. However, genuine pockets of such sentiments were seen in states such as Wisconsin, Florida, Oregon, and California. A growing percentage of Americans appeared willing to entertain radical political change in the best interests of environmental causes.

The Green Party is organized around "Ten Key Values": ecological wisdom, grassroots democracy, decentralization, community-based economics, feminism, respect for diversity, personal and global responsibility, and future focus/sustainability. By forcing politicians to consider their stands on these issues, members of the Green Party have altered the national landscape of American politics. Throughout the nation, however, Green Party members elected to state and local office have initiated basic changes to the planning and environmental issues that concern Greens.

Often, the American public financially supports organizations that argue for their particular perspectives. Even traditional environmental organizations such as the Sierra Club (1892), National Audubon Society (1905), National Parks and Conservation Society (1919), Wilderness Society (1935), National Wildlife Federation (1936), and Nature Conservancy (1951) took much more active roles in policy making. The interest of such organizations in appealing to mainstream, middle-class Americans helped to broaden the base of environmental activists. However, it also contributed to the formation of more radical-thinking environmental nongovernment organizations (NGOs) that disliked the mainstream interests of the larger organizations. In fact, many devout environmentalists argued that some of these NGOs were part of the "establishment" that they wished to fight.

One of the first grassroots anti-pollution movements that gained national political traction was the Love Canal Homeowners Association (LCHA), which, in 1978 because of concerns raised by Lois Gibbs, focused on the dangers of toxic materials buried near the city of Niagara Falls, New York. Gibbs lived in the neighborhood, and her children attended the 99th Street School located on toxic ground. She told the group that her family had never been warned about the chemical dump that was buried before developers constructed the residential neighborhood and school. When she learned of the existence of the chemical waste from newspaper articles describing the contents of the landfill and its proximity to the 99th Street School, she grew particularly concerned because her own sickly child attended the school.

Gibbs became convinced that the waste may have poisoned her child, so she approached the school board with notes from two physicians who recommended that her son be transferred to another school for health reasons. The board refused on the grounds that it could not admit that the health of one child had been impacted without first admitting the possibility that the entire school population had been affected as well. Enraged, Gibbs began talking with other parents in the neighborhood to see if they were having problems with their children's health. After speaking with hundreds of people, she realized that many in the community were concerned about the potential problems from having their children interact with toxic waste. The parents wanted definitive answers.

From this start, the LCHA took shape and committed itself to alerting the entire nation, if necessary, to the dangers of chemical waste. Members of this grassroots organization came from approximately 500 families residing within a 10-block area surrounding Love Canal. Ultimately, the Green Party movement embraced LCHA as a model for countless similar organizations that gave voice to individual claims of environmental carelessness and injustice.

Brian C. Black

See also: Climate Change; Environmentalism

Further Reading

Black, Brian C. 2006. *Nature and the Environment in Twentieth-Century American Life.* Westport, CT: Greenwood Press.

Stephens, Jennie C., David M. Hassenzahl, Gary Weisel, Brian C. Black, and Nancy Gift. 2013. "Greenwashing." In *Climate Change: An Encyclopedia of Science and History.* Santa Barbara, CA: ABC-CLIO.

Gun Control and Gun Rights

The political struggle between proponents of gun control and defenders of Americans' right to bear arms has been fierce in modern times. Some politicians have come to regard the gun issue as a "third rail" —a reference to electrified rails that power light rail trains in many cities: "Touch it and you'll die."

Polling data in recent decades consistently show that about half of American households have at least one firearm on the premises. Gun control advocates believe the easy availability of guns, especially rapid-fire automatic and semi-automatic weapons, has contributed to an extremely high homicide rate in the United States when compared to murder trends in other developed nations. But gun rights advocates believe, often passionately, that the right to bear arms is essential to American freedom. They note that the American Revolution began when British Army troops marched to a colonial militia armory at Concord, Massachusetts, on April 19, 1775, to seize a stockpile of patriot weapons.

The nation's first Congress was certainly aware of the complexities of the issue when it struggled to create the Bill of Rights, a series of legal limits upon federal power that had been promised by the participants of the Constitutional Convention who created and won passage of the national charter. After considerable amendment between the House and Senate in 1789, the Second Amendment was adopted with this language: "A well regulated Militia, being necessary to the security of a free State, the right of the people to keep and bear Arms, shall not be infringed."

In the centuries that followed, Americans have debated the intent of the Second Amendment. Gun control advocates maintain gun ownership was intended to be linked to the operations of lawful state militias, which are referenced first in the amendment. They have noted that the references to gun ownership and militia operations are separated only by a comma.

But gun rights advocates cite the original wording of the Second Amendment as proposed by James Madison: "The right of the people to keep and bear arms shall not be infringed; a well armed and well regulated militia being the best security of a free country but no person religiously scrupulous of bearing arms shall be compelled to render military service in person." Here the right to bear arms is listed first and separated from the reference to militias by a semi-colon.

Passions certainly run deep if advocates on both sides argue sharply over the meaning of punctuation used by the Founding Fathers. The debate has grown increasingly fierce in recent decades following federal gun control proposals usually offered in response to sensational acts of violence.

One of the most important gun restriction laws of the 20th century was the National Firearms Act of 1934, which followed the Saint Valentine's Day massacre of 1929 (when Chicago gangster Al Capone's men brutally executed members of a rival crime group) and other uses of the so-called "Tommy gun" or Thompson submachine gun by mobsters. The new law gave federal regulatory power over sale and ownership of machine guns, shotguns, and short-barreled rifles favored by mobsters.

The Gun Control Act of 1968 came during an era of assassinations of public officials and celebrities like President John F. Kennedy, Sen. Robert Kennedy, civil rights leader Martin Luther King Jr., and black Muslim leader Malcolm X. The legislation placed restrictions on interstate firearms transfers except by licensed manufacturers, importers, and dealers.

Following the 1981 attempted assassination of President Ronald Reagan and the 1980 murder of former Beatle John Lennon, Congress passed the Firearm Owners Protection Act, which banned ownership of fully automatic rifles while reversing some of the restrictions imposed by the Gun Control Act.

That legislation was supported by the National Rifle Association, a group founded in 1871 to teach firearm competency and safety after Union officers were appalled by the lack of weapons skill of incoming Union troops during the Civil War. The NRA has proven to be a powerful lobby group as has the Gun Owners of America, founded in 1975 following attempts in California to ban handguns. Both groups have generally opposed more recent efforts to restrict gun ownership.

Following the 1989 Cleveland School Massacre in which a gunman used a Chinese variant of the AK-47 assault rifle to kill 5 school children and wound 30 other people, Congress enacted the Federal Assault Weapons Ban of 1994. The law restricted the manufacture and transfer of "semiautomatic assault weapons" and "large capacity" ammunition clips. The law expired in 2004 because of a sunset provision that required renewal. But by that time, pro-gun ownership groups had become much more organized and vocal in opposing federal restrictions.

President Barack Obama proposed a new gun control package following the 2012 mass shooting at Sandy Hook Elementary School in Newton, Connecticut, that killed 20 children and six adults. Adam Lanza, 20, used a Bushmaster XM15-E2S semi-automatic rifle to commit the mass killing of the young children. However, despite the intense emotions following the mass murder, Congress passed no new legislation. Obama had sought renewal of the assault weapons ban and more stringent background checks required to purchase firearms.

The Pew Center for the People and the Press for many years has asked the question: "What do you think is more important—to protect the right of Americans to own guns or to control gun ownership." Despite sensational mass killings in recent years, American public opinion has started to favor the rights of gun ownership over gun control. In 1994, the poll found that 35 percent reported that protecting gun rights should be the priority. That statistic generally rose through ensuing polls and reached 50 percent in early 2014. Forty-eight percent favored gun control that year.

The issue has become intensely polarized by political party. Among Republicans polled in 2014, 76 percent said it is more important to protect gun rights and 22 percent favored gun controls. Among Democrats, only 28 percent favored gun rights and 69 percent favored gun controls.

The dynamics of the issue were summarized by Wayne LaPierre, executive vice president of the NRA, who held a press conference shortly after the Sandy Hook mass murders in which he said, "the media demonize lawful gun owners, amplify their cries for more laws, and fill the national media with misinformation and dishonest thinking that only delay meaningful action." LaPierre famously concluded that "the only thing that stops a bad guy with a gun is a good guy with a gun."

Thomas K. Hargrove

Further Reading

Cornell, Saul. 2008. *A Well-Regulated Militia: The Founding Fathers and the Origins of Gun Control in America.* New York: Oxford University Press.

Pew Center for the People and the Press. Polling Data. http://www.people-press.org. Accessed February 5, 2015.

Shear, Michael D. 2013. "N.R.A. Leader Denounces Obama's Call for Gun Control." *The New York Times*, January 22.

H

Health Care Reform

The United States spent an average of $8,915 per person on health care in 2012—a total of $2.8 trillion—making the nation's health system the most expensive in the world. In all, health care spending accounted for 42 percent of federal revenues and 6 percent of household income. Yet for all of that, the United States often ranks last or near the bottom in international studies of health performance measures such as infant mortality or life expectancy. The United States also lags behind most developed nations in health coverage since many nations mandate universal coverage under the "single payer" system, in which governments directly administer health programs or cost reimbursement.

For these reasons, health care reform has been a major political issue for many years in America. These policy reform considerations have included debates over how to increase health care coverage for most Americans either through private insurance or government-run programs, how to reduce the spiraling costs that most Americans face, and how to improve the quality of care.

The federal government became directly involved in health care policy in 1965 when President Lyndon Johnson approved Title XVIII of the Social Security Act, which created the Medicare program to provide health coverage for people 65 or older. At the same time, Title XIX was added so that federal funds were provided in a matching program to assist states in providing medical assistance to economically disadvantaged people who could not afford basic health care.

What to do about health care costs for most working Americans remained an open debate for many years. President Bill Clinton asked his wife, Hillary Rodham Clinton, to develop a health reform plan when he first took office in 1993. She assembled a task force of experts who largely deliberated in secret before announcing a proposal of universal coverage for all U.S. citizens and legal resident aliens through mandatory corporate-sponsored health provider alliances. President Clinton campaigned aggressively for its passage.

But the Clinton reform plan drew well-organized opposition from conservatives and many health insurance organizations. The Health Insurance Association of America devised a devastating series of national television ads featuring actors playing fictitious characters named "Harry and Louise" who represented everyday middle-class Americans who were becoming skeptical of the impact and costs of the Clintons' proposal. The Health Security Act failed in Congress in 1994 and became a campaign issue that helped drive stunning Republican victories in the off-year Congressional elections.

Nevertheless, the public grew increasingly discontent with how much health care coverage was costing them. The Medicare program was amended in 2003 when Republican President George W. Bush approved a Democratic-led initiative to expand coverage to include most drug costs.

The largest and most controversial expansion of government-administered health care since the 1960s occurred during the administration of President Barack Obama, who signed into law the Patient Protection and Affordable Care Act on March 23, 2010. The program was immediately nicknamed "Obamacare" by its many conservative detractors. There were some popular provisions in the bill, including prohibition against insurance companies from refusing coverage based upon a patient's previous medical history. Refusal to pay for "prior medical conditions" had forced many Americans to declare bankruptcy after their health care expenses became untenable. The Affordable Care Act also expanded Medicaid eligibility for more low-income Americans whose income reached up to 133 percent of the federal poverty level.

But Obama's reform measure had many provisions that were unpopular with conservatives. The act required most employers to provide health coverage for their workers or face tax penalties—a government mandate Republicans said was especially hard on small businesses. As health costs increased, companies would be forced to rely more upon part-time labor, they said. Obamacare also required almost all Americans to enroll in a qualifying health insurance program or face income tax penalties. This provision was mandated on the theory that the nation's health system would only be financially viable if everyone participated, including young, healthy persons who were unlikely to need health care.

As a result, the Affordable Care Act became a central issue in both the 2012 and 2014 elections. Most of its provisions had not taken effect when Obama faced reelection in 2012. Republican criticism was also blunted in that election because Obama's challenger was former Massachusetts Governor Mitt Romney, who signed into law a similar health reform measure in his state that the president said was the model for Obamacare.

But the conservative drumbeat against the Affordable Care Act continued even after Obama's reelection. Economic data supported concerns that some employers were challenged by the growing costs of mandatory coverage for their workforce. Republicans scored sweeping gains in the 2014 election, nearly running the table of attainable Senate seats and capturing control of the upper body of Congress. Exit polls of voters in the off-year election found that 47 percent said Obamacare "went too far," while 25 percent said the law "didn't go far enough," and only 22 percent said the law was "just about right."

A trend study of polls sponsored by the Kaiser Family Foundation found that Americans have been deeply divided over the Affordable Care Act ever since it was passed. The first poll conducted in May of 2010 found 41 percent favored the health reform bill while 44 percent opposed it. Five years later, the poll estimated that 40 percent of Americans still favored Obamacare while 46 percent opposed it.

Despite recent victories by Republicans who campaign fiercely against Obamacare, the president trumpeted the successes of his program during his 2015 State of the Union address before Congress. "In the past year alone, about 10 million uninsured Americans finally gained the security of health coverage," Obama told the joint session of Congress, a slight majority of whom maintained a stony silence. "At every step, we were told our goals were misguided or too ambitious; that we would crush jobs and explode deficits. Instead, we've seen the fastest economic growth in over a decade, our deficits cut by two-thirds, a stock market that has doubled, and health care inflation at its lowest rate in 50 years. . . . This is good news, people."

Thomas K. Hargrove

See also: Clinton, Hillary; Obama, Barack

Further Reading

California HealthCare Foundation. 2014. "Health Care Costs 101: Slow Growth Persists." Oakland, CA. www.chcf.org. Accessed February 7, 2015.

Jacobs, Lawrence R., and Theda Skocpol. 2012. *Health Care Reform and American Politics: What Everyone Needs to Know.* New York: Oxford University Press.

McCalmont, Lucy. 2014. "Exit Polls: Don't Care for Obamacare." Politico blog posted November 4. http://www.politico.com/story/2014/11/exit-polls-dont-care-for-obamacare-112510 .html. Accessed February 7, 2015.

Reid, T.R. 2010. *The Healing of America: A Global Quest for Better, Cheaper and Fairer Health Care.* New York: Penguin Books.

Hispanic Media

The growth in Hispanic media parallels the increase in the Hispanic people. The 2010 Census found that there were 50 million Hispanics living in the United States, more than twice as many as there had been in 1990. The Census projects there will be more than 65 million in 2020.

The first Spanish-language newspaper in the United States was *El Misisipi,* founded in 1808 in New Orleans. Today there are 26 dailies, 428 weeklies, and 352 newspapers published less than once a week. Total circulation has been fairly constant at about 18 million the last decade, with dailies having five million, weeklies having more than 11 million, and papers published less than once a week having two million. The largest daily is *Hoy Chicago*, published by the Tribune Company, which also has weeklies of more than a hundred thousand circulation in Los Angeles, Fort Lauderdale, and Orlando. Total advertising revenue for Spanish-language newspapers is about $800 million a year, divided equally between dailies and weeklies. Revenue of dailies dropped more than a third during the 2008 recession, but weekly revenue stayed constant.

While Hispanic newspapers were the first medium and now are available in every city with substantial Hispanic population, television has become the major Hispanic medium. Univision is the largest Hispanic television network and the fifth largest of all U.S. TV networks. It is available in 94 million homes. While the four major networks—Fox, CBS, ABC, and NBC—have larger audiences than Univision, a Pew Research study found that in some of the 22 evenings in the sweeps period in winter of 2011, Univision had larger primetime audiences among 18–34 and 18–49 age groups than at least one of the English-language networks. Furthermore, Univision had larger primetime audiences than NBC for a week in April and larger audiences than both CBS and NBC for a week in May. Cesar Conde, the former president of Univision, has said he expects Univision to become the top network in the United States. Part of the strategy to achieve that is a greater investment in news. The network carries six national newscasts on its main channel. It also offers local newscasts in 18 cities.

Another Hispanic network, Telemundo, has almost the reach of Univision but its audiences are a third smaller. It is available in 93 million homes in 210 markets and has local stations in 15 major U.S. cities.

Spanish language radio began in the 1930s, and there are more than 1,300, including 18 clear channel stations. An analysis in 1941 found that 88 percent of the programming was music. Music remains the main programming, but news and information have become a much more significant part of Hispanic programming. The news and talk formats are used by about 100 stations. Univision is also a major player in radio with 79 stations.

While there are a hundred Hispanic magazines, only a handful actually provide a substantial amount of news. The magazines with the greatest revenue are women's and entertainment-related publications.

Pew Research, in a 2010 study, found a digital divide remains for Latinos. Hispanics use the Internet and cell phones slightly less than do whites or African Americans, and they use home broadband substantially less.

The most important political issue for Hispanics is immigration, and the Hispanic media pay considerable attention to it. This issue is probably the main reason Hispanics favor Democrats over Republicans by a 2-to-1 margin in recent elections. Hispanic media coverage of immigration probably offers a different slant than that provided by mainstream media.

Growing numbers of Hispanics were born in the United States and grew up in homes where both English and Spanish were spoken. Surveys indicate that people in such families continue to make some use of Spanish-language media. Some Hispanic media are becoming bilingual in recognition of this, and this may be the wave of the future for Hispanic media.

Guido H. Stempel III

Further Reading

Albarron, Alan, and Brian Hutton. 2009. "A History of Spanish Language Radio. Arbtron. www .arbitron.com/download/mcl_unt.history-spanish-radio.pdf. Accessed February 5, 2015.

Guskin, Emily, and Monica Anderson. 2014. "Developments in the Hispanic Media Market." Pew Research Center, 2014. http://www.journalism.org/2014/03/26/developments-in-the-hispanic-media-market/. Accessed February 5, 2015.

Guskin, Emily, and Amy Mitchell. 2011. "Hispanic Media Faring Better than the Mainstream Media."

Rosenstiel, Tom, and Amy Mitchell. 2011. "The State of the News Media, 2011." Pew Research Center. http://www.stateofthemedia.org/2011/hispanic-media-fairing-better-than-the-mainstream -media/. Accessed February 5, 2015.

Hispanic Voters

Hispanics are one of the fastest-growing voter groups in the United States. The number of ballots cast by Latinos more than doubled from 2000 to 2012, rising from 5.9 million ballots cast in 2000 (or 5.4 percent of the electorate) to nearly 11.2 million ballots in 2012 (or 8.4 percent of the electorate). This growth is largely fueled by the even more rapid expansion of the Hispanic population through a higher-than-average birth rate and through immigration.

The Census Bureau estimates that less than half of eligible Hispanics vote in major elections, although the rate of their participation in elections rose from 45.1 percent in 2000 to 49.9 percent in 2008 and then fell to 48.0 percent in 2012. Of the 23.3 million Latinos who were eligible to vote in 2012, 17.6 million were born in the United States, and 5.7 million were naturalized after immigrating.

Hispanic voting strength lags behind the ethnicity's share of the U.S. population, which was estimated at 17 percent in 2012. This is partially caused by a population bulge of young Hispanics. About 33 percent of Latinos in the United States in 2012 were under the age of 18, compared to less than 20 percent of non-Hispanic whites. For this reason, the Hispanic share of the electorate is expected to grow faster than any other major voter group as young Latinos mature.

Hispanics have become an important force in national elections. Although they lean Democratic, the degree of the lean can determine the outcome in presidential elections. President Bill Clinton enjoyed support from 73 percent of Hispanics in 1996 and easily won reelection. But Texas Gov. George W. Bush, who openly courted Hispanic voters and looked kindly upon immigration reform, was able to cut Latinos' Democratic lean to 62 percent in 2000 and even down to 53 percent in 2004. Barack Obama, who also pledged to fight for immigration reform, won back much of the Latino vote by garnering 67 percent in 2008 and 71 percent in 2012.

The Gallup poll in 2013 estimated that Latinos identify as Democrats by a margin of 2-1 over Republicans, although more than a fifth of younger Hispanics identify themselves as independent of either party.

Hispanics in America are entirely a self-identified group. The Census Bureau defines a Hispanic as "a person of Cuban, Mexican, Puerto Rican, South or Central American (except for Brazil), or other Spanish culture or origin regardless of race." The word comes down from the ancient Roman province of Hispania which comprised modern day Spain and Portugal. Since Hispanics are an ethnicity and not a race, they remain a political and social entity only as long as they choose to identify themselves as Hispanic. It is not clear how strong this self-identity will hold among third- and fourth-generation Hispanics. A growing number of Hispanics do not speak Spanish.

Hispanic leadership in the United States rose quickly as Hispanics became a growing voting bloc. Five Latino members of the House of Representatives formed the Congressional Hispanic Caucus in 1976. Thirty-eight years later, the CHC had grown to 26 House members and one senator, Robert Menendez of New Jersey. The first Hispanic politician to run for president was Bill Richardson of New Mexico, who was defeated by Obama for the Democratic nomination in 2008. Richardson had served as U.S. ambassador to the United Nations and as secretary of the Department of Energy during the Clinton administration. Sonia Sotomayor became the first Hispanic member of the U.S. Supreme Court in 2009.

Perhaps the most iconic Latino leader in the United States is labor leader and civil rights advocate Cesar Chavez, 1927–1993, who founded the National Farm Workers Association, later called the United Farm Workers. Hundreds of schools, parks, streets, and public buildings are named in his honor. His birthday, March 31, is a state holiday in California, Colorado, and Texas. Chavez often campaigned for unionism and civil rights for immigrants with a slogan "Sí, se puede," which is Spanish for "Yes, it can be done." Obama, acknowledging that slogan, shortened it to "Yes, we can" in his first presidential campaign in 2008.

Thomas K. Hargrove

See also: African American Voters; Asian Voters

Further Reading

Census Bureau. 2013. "The Diversifying Electorate—Voting Rates by Race and Hispanic Origin in 2012 and Other Recent elections." May. http://www.census.gov/prod/2013pubs/p20-568.pdf. Accessed October 11, 2014.

Lopez, Mark Hugo, and Ana Gonzalez-Barrera. 2013. "Inside the 2012 Latino Electorate." June 3. Pew Research Hispanic Trends Project. http://www.pewhispanic.org/2013/06/03/inside-the-2012-latino-electorate/. Accessed October 11, 2014.

Newport, Frank, and Joy Wilke. 2013. "Hispanics of All Ages Tilt Democratic." July 15. Princeton, NJ: The Gallup Poll.

Homelessness

Since the earliest days of the American Republic, lawmakers have struggled over how to treat homeless citizens. Many communities and states passed anti-vagrancy ordinances that criminalized activities associated with homelessness, including panhandling and trespassing (by sleeping on land homeless people do not own.) These laws may have seemed tame compared to anti-vagabond measures taken in Europe, in which homelessness was regarded in many nations as sufficient for imprisonment. Nazi Germany punished so-called "work-shyness" (arbeitsscheu) with forced labor in concentration camps.

American courts gradually came to look upon vagrancy laws as unconstitutional. The Supreme Court struck down Florida's vagrancy law in the 1972 case *Papachristou v. Jacksonville* since the statute was unconstitutionally vague and granted enormous and completely arbitrary latitude to police. That being said, however, anti-panhandling and anti-loitering laws are still widely enforced throughout the nation.

Homelessness has become a growing political and social issue in America. The U.S. Census Bureau in recent decades has made considerable efforts to count as many homeless persons as possible on the official Census Day for the decennial enumeration. The U.S. Department of Housing and Urban Development also conducts a series of "Point-in-Time Estimates of Homelessness," which found that there were 610,042 homeless persons living in the United States in January 2013. The estimate concluded that 65 percent of these persons were living in emergency shelters or transitional housing programs and 35 percent were living in unsheltered locations.

The Point-in-Time studies documented why homelessness should be a major issue for local, state, and federal officials. Nearly a quarter of the homeless persons in the 2013 estimate were children under the age of 18 (the exact count was 138,149.) About 36 percent of the homeless were people in families, of whom a majority were children. Individuals living alone accounted for 64 percent of all homeless persons.

The Point-in-Time studies have also concluded that homelessness is gradually declining, down from 671,888 homeless people counted in 2007.

Should homeless people be allowed to vote? The Founding Fathers at the Constitutional Convention in 1787, after considerable debate, decided not to set a national standard for voting rights, allowing individual states to set and regulate their own voting laws. That effectively meant that—in most places—voting was limited to white male landowners. Voting rights gradually expanded to include former black slaves, women, and eventually people of any creed or national origin.

But the homeless faced many formal barriers to voting remarkably late in American history. In the 1984 case *Pitts v. Black*, a federal court in New York explicitly found that homeless persons could not be denied the right to vote just because they did not live in a traditional residence. The New York State Election Law had forbidden people who live in the streets from registering to vote. The court found that people need only have "a specific location that they consider their 'home base'—the place where one returns regularly, manifests an intent to remain, and can receive messages and be contacted." A 1987 ruling in Alaska found that homeless people when registering to vote "may designate a shelter, park, or street corner as their residence." And the courts in 1992 took issue with New York's registration rules that subjected "groups likely to include transients" to more extensive inquiry to determine voting eligibility. The New York Supreme Court, Appellate Division, ruled in that case that state election officials improperly rejected 240 ballots by failing to "take reasonable, good-faith steps to determine the true residency of the individuals who were homeless."

It took more than 200 years, but American courts have accepted a legal presumption that the burden is upon local election officials to determine whether homeless persons are ineligible to vote for failing to meet residency requirements. Simply being homeless is no longer sufficient.

The Washington, D.C., based National Coalition for the Homeless has concluded that homeless people are entitled to register to vote if they are a citizen of the United States; are a legal resident of the state in which they wish to register; are at least 18 years old; are not in prison, on probation, or on parole; and have not been declared mentally incompetent by a court of law.

"Equal access to the right to vote is a crucial part of maintaining a true democracy," the homeless coalition said in its ongoing "You Don't Need a Home to Vote" campaign. "Voting allows people to play a part in deciding the direction of their communities by voicing their opinion on issues that are important and relevant to their lives."

Voting studies over many years have found that affluent people are much more likely to cast a ballot than are the economically disadvantaged, even when legal barriers are removed. The Census Bureau estimates that only about half of the nation's poorest income cohort (those earning less than $20,000 a year) cast ballots in the 2008 presidential election, as did only about a third of people who did not obtain a high school diploma. There are no reliable estimates on voting rates among the homeless, but it seems certain that most homeless do not vote even though many local policy decisions, such as initiatives to provide affordable housing or how to set property tax rates, directly affect the poor.

"Each election, low income and homeless individuals vote at a lower rate than people with higher incomes," the National Coalition for the Homeless has concluded. "Many homeless and low-income individuals may not have the appropriate identification documents required by some states to register or to vote. Furthermore, many individuals who are experiencing homelessness may lack the resources to educate themselves about candidates or may not be able to get to the polls on Election Day."

Thomas K. Hargrove

See also: Class Voting; Class Warfare Politics

Further Reading

Henry, Meghan, Alvaro Cortes, and Sean Morris. 2013. "The 2013 Annual Homeless Assessment Report to Congress." U.S. Department of Housing and Urban Development, Office of Community Planning and Development.
National Coalition for the Homeless. "Voting Policy Statement." http://nationalhomeless.org /campaigns/voting/. Accessed June 1, 2014.

Hutchins Report (1947)

The report issued in 1947 by the Hutchins Commission, officially titled the Commission on Freedom of the Press, was the result of a landmark inquiry into the role of news media and mass media in a modern democracy. This was not a commission created by the government but rather one created by two Yale classmates in 1942: Henry Luce, publisher of *Time* magazine, and Robert Hutchins, president of the University of Chicago. It was funded by Luce.

Never before in America had a group like this assembled to examine the function of the press, nor has another been formed since. It is still regarded as an important description of the function of media in a free society.

Hutchins was chair of the 16-member commission, and the brief summary report of their extensive work became known as the Hutchins Report. The commission met 17 times over four years. The commission interviewed 56 witnesses, and the commission staff spoke to 225 people. The staff prepared 176 documents. The report was revised nine times before it was published in 1947.

The report said the media should provide the public with the following:

- a truthful account of the day's events in a context that gives them meaning
- a forum for the exchange of comment and criticism
- a representative picture of constituent groups in society
- the presentation and clarification of the goals and values of society
- full access to the day's intelligence

The publication on the report in 1947 produced a firestorm. The media took the five recommendations as criticisms rather than suggestions. They pointed out that the members of the commission were all academicians with little direct knowledge of journalism. Some feared that emphasis on press responsibility and self-regulation would lead to government control of the press. In time, it came to be recognized that the five points constituted a reasonable set of goals for the press and that these goals were not being met by all of the press. Bias and sensationalism compromised the truthfulness and meaningfulness of the news. The Op Ed page, commonplace now, was not then, and the editorial page was not a forum. The failure of the press to represent all groups in our society would become a major concern of the Kerner Commission two decades later. Societal values were not a major concern of the press, and while the *New York Times* could proclaim in a front-page slogan that it offered "All the News That's Fit to Print," that did not fit the press as a whole.

Now, nearly three-quarters of a century later, the Hutchins Report is recognized as an important statement on the role of the media because there has never been anything like the commission in the subsequent years. It introduced the concept of social responsibility into the dialogue about media.

At the time the commission was formed, there was concern that the government might attempt to regulate media because it was happening in so many countries. The commission probably deserves some credit for preventing that from happening in the United States.

In addition to the Hutchins Report, there were six books written by members of the commission. The most significant was the two-volume *Government and Mass Communication*, by Zechariah Chafee. A ground-breaking work at the time, it remains a definitive statement on the subject.

Guido H. Stempel III

See also: Presidents and the Press; Press Council

Further Reading

Blevins, Fred. 1997. "The Hutchins Report Turns 50: Recurring Themes in Today's Public and Civic Journalism." http://mtprof.msun.edu/Fall1997/Blevins.html. Accessed January 12, 2015.

Commission on Freedom of the Press. 1947. *A Free and Responsible Press*. Chicago: University of Chicago Press.

Immigration and Reform

One of the most contentious national issues in the United States during the 20th and 21st centuries has been how a self-described "nation of immigrants" will police its international borders; regulate lawful requests for immigration and asylum; and treat the millions of workers who enter the country illegally or who stay in America after their lawful work or education visas expire.

At the end of the first decade of the 21st century, the United States had an estimated 11 million illegal residents who, themselves, were increasingly regarded as an important source of labor and economic growth. At the same time, the pool of lawful immigrant voters had grown dramatically, prompting increasingly strident calls for reform. The issue of how—or even whether—to reform immigration laws has become a fierce point of contention between Democrats and Republicans.

The political struggle over whom to allow into the United States resulted in a series of quota laws in the 1920s that sought to regulate immigration in such a way that the existing ethnic composition of the American population would not be changed. The 1921 Emergency Quota Act set immigration limits to no more than 3 percent of the number of foreign-born persons from each nation already living in the United States as of 1910. This law was thought by Congress to be too generous, and immigration was further limited in the National Origins Act of 1924 to 2 percent of the total number of residents from each nation living in the United States as of 1890. Although the primary intent of these laws was to reduce undesirable immigrants from Eastern and Southern Europe, it effectively banned Asians, Middle Easterners, and immigrants from India while having little impact upon Latin Americans, who already resided in Southwestern states in significant numbers.

The Civil Rights era brought a backlash against the use of the National Origins Formula that, critics argued, showed a racist preference for white immigrants from Northwestern Europe. The result was the Immigration and Nationality Act of 1965, which eliminated a quota system based upon the existing ethnic composition of the U.S. population. President Lyndon Johnson signed the new immigration bill into law on October 3, 1965, in a ceremony at the foot of the Statue of Liberty in New York City harbor. Johnson said the old quota system was "un-American in the highest sense, because it has been untrue to the faith that brought thousands to these shores even before we were a country."

The effects of the new policies were gradual but profound. In 1970, the Census Bureau estimated there were 9.6 million foreign-born residents of the United States, who accounted for 4.7 percent of the population. Both figures grew substantially in the following decades until, by 2010, the foreign-born population had swollen to 40 million persons representing 12.9 percent of the population. The U.S. Department of Homeland Security reports a similar increase in the numbers of foreign-born persons obtaining legal permanent status, rising from 361,972 in 1967 to more than 1 million in 2007 and reaching a zenith at 1.1 million in 2009. Demands for immigration and permanent legal status declined slightly in the aftermath of the Great Recession, but generally about 1 million green cards have been issued each year.

As a result, the national ethnic composition has been changing. The Census estimated in 2012 that by 2043, non-Hispanic whites will account for less than half of the U.S. population. The biggest cause of this change will be immigration, especially the millions of immigrants from Mexico, China, India, and the Philippines—the four biggest sources of foreign-born population according to the 2010 census.

Such significant population changes can hardly occur without political rancor. The 1965 reform act prompted other attempts at reform. The Immigration Reform and Control Act of 1986 was signed into law by President Ronald Reagan as a compromise. The law was intended to crack down on employers' hiring of illegal immigrants and tighten border controls while offering amnesty to three million illegal workers. The law is widely regarded to have failed because illegal immigration actually increased in the ensuing years. Little changed during the administration of President Bill Clinton, although under conservative pressure Clinton authorized increased border security and made it harder to obtain emergency asylum.

The first significant attempt at immigration reform during the 21st century came from Republican President George W. Bush, who had learned the sobering realities of immigration politics while he was governor of Texas. (Many Lone Star State politicians realized their future hopes rest with convincing the growing number of Hispanic voters to support them, or at least, not oppose them in overwhelming numbers.) Bush lost the popular vote in 2000 when he gained only 35 percent of the Hispanic vote. He began calling for a "guest worker program" in 2004. As a result of that, and because of the national security concerns raised by the War on Terrorism, Bush was able to win reelection decisively in 2004 by gaining 44 percent of the Hispanic vote. The president continued to push for reform.

"We're a nation of laws, and we must enforce our laws," Bush said in 2006 in what he touted as the first prime-time presidential television address on immigration. "We're also a nation of immigrants, and we must uphold that tradition, which has strengthened our country in so many ways."

Bush, to the astonishment of many conservatives, called for a five-part program of reform that included a "temporary worker program," which required a "tamper-proof identification card" and a "rational middle ground" between granting an "automatic path to citizenship" and "a program of mass deportation." The president kept the final point vague, but nothing he could say could stop other Republicans from lashing out at his program because it amounted to "amnesty" to illegal immigrants. Opposition from conservative talk radio was unrelenting, as was growing criticism from members of his own party.

President Barack Obama has consistently promised he'd support immigration reform and was awarded twice with solid support from the nation's growing Hispanic voters. But reforms were generally opposed by an unlikely marriage of GOP and the AFL-CIO, which did not want to see an influx of suddenly legal immigrant workers who'd take non-union jobs at lower wages than usually offered to U.S. citizens. Obama delayed several attempts at contentious reforms as the 2010, 2012, and 2014 elections approached.

"The progress we've made has been hard, sometimes it's been slower than we want, but that progress has been steady and it has been real," Obama assured a meeting of the Congressional Hispanic Caucus late in 2014. "I want to make something clear: Fixing our broken immigration system is one more big thing that we have to do and that we will do."

Thomas K. Hargrove

See also: Asian Voters; Hispanic Voters

Further Reading

Borjas, George J. 1999. *Heaven's Door: Immigration Policy and the American Economy.* Princeton, NJ: Princeton University Press.

Weiner, Rachel. 2013. "How Immigration Reform Failed, Over and Over." *The Washington Post,* January 30. http://www.washingtonpost.com/blogs/the-fix/wp/2013/01/30/how-immigration-reform-failed-over-and-over/. Accessed November 1, 2014.

Impeachment

From time to time, politicians talk about impeaching the president. There have, in fact, been three attempts to impeach a president. Presidents Andrew Johnson and William Clinton were impeached. Impeachment proceedings were in motion against President Richard Nixon, but he resigned before there could be an impeachment vote.

Impeachment is not merely something that applies to presidents. Article 2, Section 4 of the Constitution reads, "The President, Vice-President and all civil Officers of the United States, shall be removed from Office on Impeachment for and Conviction of, Treason, Bribery, or other High Crimes and Misdemeanors."

Note the distinction between impeachment and conviction, two separate processes. At the federal level, charges go to a committee of the House of Representatives, usually the Judicial Committee. If the committee agrees, it passes a resolution on to the House. If the House approves the resolution, it goes to the Senate for trial. If the Senate convicts, the official is removed from office.

States also can impeach state officials, and each state has its own procedures, but they do tend to resemble the federal procedures.

The House has approved impeachment 19 times. Impeachment of Johnson was approved, 252-61. Conviction failed in the Senate by the smallest possible margin. It takes a two-thirds vote for conviction, and the vote was 35-19 to convict—just one vote short.

The Johnson impeachment was strictly political. Johnson was a senator from Tennessee, and when that state joined the Confederacy, he refused to resign from the Senate. President Lincoln chose Johnson, a Democrat, to run as vice president in 1864 to attract Democratic voters. After the Civil War was over, radical Republicans pushed harsh measures of reconstruction. Four times Johnson vetoed such measures, and four times Congress overrode the vetoes. That set the stage for the impeachment effort.

The House approved impeachment of Clinton, 258-176. The vote in the Senate was a 50-50 tie, so Clinton was not convicted. The impeachment effort followed four years of investigation, first of a land transaction, which became known as Whitewater and then of sexual encounters with Monica Lewinsky, a White House intern.

The House Judiciary Committee recommended impeachment of Nixon, but Nixon resigned as president before the entire House could vote.

There have been 17 other impeachments—15 federal judges, one senator, and a lone cabinet official. Eight of these resulted in convictions and removal from office.

Guido H. Stempel III

Further Reading

Gavin, Philip. 2000. "Presidential Impeachment Proceedings." The History Place. http://www.historyplace.com/unitedstates/impeachments. Accessed January 12, 2015.

Library of Congress. 1868. "The Congressional Globe: The Impeachment Trial of President Andrew Johnson." http://memory.loc.gov/ammem/amlaw/lwcg-imp.html. Accessed January 12, 2015.

Income Gap

The income gap—also often called "income inequality"—describes a growing economic trend in which affluent Americans own an increasing share of the nation's wealth. At the same time, the Americans who are calculated by the federal government to be living in poverty have been increasing. Simply put, the rich have been getting richer, and the poor have been getting poorer.

The nonpartisan Congressional Budget Office studied the distribution of household income from 1979 to 2011 and concluded that wealth grew at "significantly different rates" for Americans at different points along the income scale. For households in the top 1 percent of income (the nation's richest families) after-tax, inflation-adjusted income increased an average of 3.5 percent per year. Over the 33-year period CBO analysts studied, the inflation-adjusted income for the nation's wealthiest households increased 200 percent. In contrast, Americans living in households in the bottom 20 percent of income experienced inflation-adjusted income growth of 1.2 percent per year. Consequently, Americans living near the bottom of wealth experienced only a 48 percent growth in income.

As a result of this inequity, households in the top 20 percent received slightly more than half of America's income in 2011 while poor households in the bottom 20 percent of income received just 5 percent of earned income.

If there was any good news in the CBO study, it was that the nation's progressive tax structure continued to place the greatest tax burden upon the wealthy. Households in the top 20 percent of income paid more than two-thirds of all federal taxes in 2011, while households in the bottom 20 percent paid less than 1 percent of the nation's taxes. When examined over time, the tax rate upon the poor has gradually declined for both the poorest households and for middle class households. Taxes for the wealthy have fluctuated considerably, but, taken at a three-decade average, have held relatively stable.

But the proportion and raw number of Americans living in poverty rose dramatically since 1999, especially through the Great Recession of 2008 and 2009. By 2013, more than 45 million people were living below the poverty line, up from 32 million in 1999. The actual rate of poverty rose from 11.8 percent of Americans in 1999 to a modern high of 15.0 percent in 2012, followed by a small decline to 14.5 percent in 2013.

The Congressional Budget Office concluded that "the precise reasons for the rapid growth in income at the top are not well understood." There are a host of well-documented contributing factors, however. Well-paying manufacturing jobs have generally declined in the United States as an increasingly globalized economy shifted many assembly lines to developing countries with relatively low-wage workers. Labor unions also declined, reducing their influence to improve wages for blue-collar work. Many of the production jobs that remained became increasingly technological, requiring good wages for only a handful of extremely well-trained and educated workers who could use automation on the assembly line. At the same time, pay for corporate CEOs skyrocketed as social norms for what boards of directors would perceive as appropriate compensation changed.

Attitudes over income inequality and what to do about it have become a bright dividing line between Democrats and Republicans. Liberals, historically, argue that government must be a moderating force to offset social and economic disparities that can resort from unchecked free market capitalism. Conservatives, however, argue that any government attempt to "fix" the naturally uneven distribution of wealth would amount to forced redistribution that stifles free enterprise and American individualism.

The issue became a central theme in President Barack Obama's administration. Alan B. Krueger, the chairman of the White House Council of Economic Advisors, addressed the Center for American Progress in early 2012 in a speech that focused on the issue: "The rise in inequality in the United States over the last three decades has reached the point that inequality in incomes is causing an unhealthy division in opportunities, and is a threat to our economic growth," Krueger said. "Restoring a greater degree of fairness to the U.S. job market would be good for businesses, good for the economy, and good for the country."

Obama, himself, made economic inequality the centerpiece in his 2015 State of the Union address, delivered after Democrats' resounding defeats a few months earlier that gave the GOP control of both houses of Congress. Obama called for new taxes on wealthy Americans and new tax breaks for the middle class for education and child care. "Will we accept an economy where only a few of us do spectacularly well?" he asked the mostly Republican assembly.

But Republicans have also been considering the problem of growing inequality. It was a major issue in the Republican National Committee's "Growth and Opportunity Project" report, which examined lessons the GOP should learn following Obama's 2012 reelection. "If we are going to grow as a Party, our policies and actions must take into account that the middle class has struggled mightily and that far too many of our citizens live in poverty," the report concluded. "To people who are flat on their back, unemployed or disabled and in need of help, they do not care if the help comes from the private sector or the government—they just want help."

Thomas K. Hargrove

See also: Class (Economic) Voting; Class Warfare Politics

Further Reading

Congressional Budget Office. 2011. The Distribution of Household Income and Federal Taxes. Washington, DC. https://www.cbo.gov/publication/49440. Accessed January 24, 2015.

Jacobs, Lawrence. 2004. "American Democracy in an Age of Rising Inequality." Published online by the American Political Science Association. http://oldapsa.apsanet.org/imgtest/taskforcereport.pdf. Accessed October 13, 2014.

Krueger, Alan B. 2012. "The Rise and Consequences of Inequality." Speech to the Center for American Progress. January 12. Posted on the White House blog. http://www.whitehouse.gov/blog/2012/01/12/chairman-alan-krueger-discusses-rise-and-consequences-inequality-center-american-pro. Accessed January 24, 2015.

Nather, David. 2014. "The GOP's Confused Inequality Message." *Politico*. February 14. http://www.politico.com/story/2014/02/repulicans-gop-inequality-103239.html. Accessed January 24, 2015.

Taibbi, Matt. 2014. *The Divide: American Injustice in the Age of the Wealth Gap.* New York: Spiegel & Grau.

Independent Voters

Independent voters express no affiliation with a political party. In a multiparty system such as France, this definition holds up fairly well, but in a two-party system, such as the United States, independent voters are usually defined as those who do not identify with either major party. Typically, respondents are asked a question like, "In politics today, do you consider yourself a Republican, a Democrat, or an independent?" Independents then are asked whether they "lean more to" one party. These are labeled Democrat or Republican "leaners," as opposed to pure independents. Since the turn of the century, Democrats have held a steady advantage among leaners. In 2012, 48 percent have affiliated with that party or leaned Democratic, compared to 40 percent for the GOP. According to Pew poll study in 2012, "That is little changed from recent years." Since leaners tend to differ little from partisans in political cognitions, attitudes, or behaviors, they tend to be considered "shy" or "hidden" partisans and are lumped together with partisans. True independents, in contrast, tend to differ from partisans in meaningful ways.

In this century, pure independents have been steadily increasing. According to Pew (2012), more than a third of Americans described themselves as independents in 2012, up from 32 percent in 2008 and 30 percent in 2004. "Looking back even further, independents are more numerous than at any point in the last 70 years," Pew reported. Gallup (2012) paints much the same picture. Gallup tracked party affiliation in 74 polls up through 2012, and in only three were independents outnumbered (by Democrats), and those differences were slight. There also is an inverse relationship between age cohort and party independence, suggesting that independents are likely to continue to increase.

Of those born before 1945 (the silent generation), only 27 percent in 2012 described themselves as independent, unchanged from 2008. In contrast, the three younger age cohorts have moved further away from the parties. Of those born 1946–1964 (baby boomers), independents rose from 31 percent to 34 percent from 2008 to 2012. Of those born 1965–1980 (generation Xers), 42 percent describe themselves in 2012 as independent, a jump of eight points. Among those born 1981–1994 (millennials), 45 percent said they were independent, up from 39 percent four years earlier (Pew, 2012).

Gender and race differences also exist. More men (43 percent) than women (33 percent) say they are independent. Independent women increased 4 percent from 2008 to 2012, but independent men increased twice as much, with defections among females coming about equally from both parties while among males coming mostly from Democrats. Nearly half (46 percent) of Hispanics and 38 percent of whites describe themselves as independent, pluralities in both cases. However, only 22 percent of African Americans identify as independents, due to their overwhelming identification as Democrats (69 percent). These numbers has remained fairly stable in recent years (Pew, 2012).

Interestingly, U.S. independent voters do not differ markedly from partisans (and leaners) in their positions, usually falling somewhere between Republicans and Democrats, depending upon the issue. Where they do differ, not surprisingly, is in their favorability toward the political parties and Congress. However, attempts to treat independent voters as a monolithic bloc are destined to mislead because those who choose not to identify with a party do so for different reasons.

Some voters do not identify with a party because they are what political scientists call "cross pressured," meaning they find distinct aspects of different parties appealing and cannot steadfastly support a single one. Some cross-pressured voters hold consistently middle-of-the-road views and see the parties' positions as more extreme. They feel more comfortable supporting moderate positions and candidates, regardless of party.

Some cross-pressured voters, however, are not centrists. They hold immoderate views on a number of issues, but these views cut across party lines. Such voters, for example, might hold views regarding social issues that align them clearly with one party but also hold views regarding economic issues that align them clearly with another party. Unable to reconcile their views with either party, they choose not to identify with either.

For some citizens, party independence seems to signify disinterest. Among registered voters in each biannual election between 1976 and 2008, independents were significantly less likely to have reported voting (an average of 59.8 percent across all 16 elections) than either Democrats (82.4 percent) or Republicans (84.6 percent). Independents also participate less politically in other ways, and are less politically knowledgeable (American National Election Studies, 2010). Independents, though, are equally as likely as partisans to hold political opinions (Pew, 2012).

Some independent voters hold a general hostile attitude toward the major parties and party system, which they view as ineffectual, even dangerous. They believe that elected officials fail to represent them and that "party politics" routinely lead to poor decisions. Some favor the cultivation of additional parties while others regard any party loyalty as problematic. These voters see the act of identifying themselves as independent as a strategic decision to help delegitimize the existing party system.

Finally, some view political independence as the ideal political state, one in which voters eschew all party lines and make political decisions based solely on merit. Indeed, this is the conception of political independence promulgated by those who created the United States. The newfound republic based on democratic governance seemed to necessitate a system by which popular support could be roused, herded, and crystalized, and the party system eventually emerged as the most practical way to accomplish this (Nichols 1967). However, the Constitution makes no mention of political parties, and when it was forged in 1787 political parties did not exist. In the *Federalist Papers*, Alexander Hamilton and James Madison warned against political parties. Throughout his presidency, George Washington did the same (Hofstadter, 1970; see also Washington's Farewell Address). At least some current-day political independents are descendants of such deep-rooted sentiments.

Dominic Lasorsa

Further Reading

The American National Election Studies. 2010. "The ANES Guide to Public Opinion and Electoral Behavior: Voter Registration: 1952–2008." http://www.electionstudies.org/nesguide/text/t6a_1_2. Accessed October 30, 2012.

Gallup Poll. 2012. "Party Affiliation: Trend Since 2004." http://www.gallup.com/poll/15370/party-affiliation.aspx. Accessed October 30, 2012.

Hofstadter, Richard. 1970. *The Idea of a Party System: The Rise of Legitimate Opposition in the United States, 1780–1840.* Berkeley: University of California Press.

Nichols, Roy Franklin. 1967. *The Invention of the American Political Parties.* New York: Macmillan.

Pew Research Center for the People & the Press. 2012. "Trends in American Values: 1987–2012." Washington, D.C., June 4.

Internationalism and Isolationism

The stress between the dueling notions of "internationalism" and "isolationism" has had a significant impact upon America's historical events, international relations, and public policies. This dualism can be traced to independence and geographic isolation of the United States from the Old World and the ideals of the country—to embrace and advocate freedom, democracy, and peace for human beings. The U.S. involvement in world affairs generally has been reluctant since the founding of the country. Founding Fathers advised Americans to pursue "peace, commerce and honest friendship with all nations; entangling alliance with none."

Naturally, Americans tend to want to pay more attention to their domestic concerns and not get involved in conflicts in other parts of the world. This is exactly why Americans resisted being involved in the First World War. When addressing the Congress, President Woodrow Wilson on April 2, 1017, emphasized that the German's warfare was against all nations and the challenge was to all mankind; he warned repeatedly that armed neutrality was impracticable. It was precisely for the ideal of isolationism that Americans waited till it became inevitable (the Pearl Harbor attack) to formally declare war against the Japanese during World War II.

Isolationism runs deep in Americans' psyche. Being separated by vast oceans on both sides of the United States proper from Asia and Europe, it has developed the idea of being safe from the old conflicts. The fact that the U.S. continent had never been directly involved in warfare since the War of 1812 strengthened this mentality of indifference to world affairs. Also, research shows that Americans are less interested in learning about world affairs and have been notoriously mediocre in knowledge tests of world geography and history. This seems particularly ironic given that the majority of Americans are descendants of immigrants from all over the world. American opposition to being involved in overseas warfare can be illustrated by a continuous Senate investigation (the Nye Committee) about the alleged influence from weapons' suppliers and manufacturers on public opinion and subsequent foreign policy to enter the war in 1917. It was reported that the ammunition industry raked in enormous profits during the First World War.

Isolationistic mentality took center stage when the United States initially faced the aggression from Japan and Germany before World War II. The Stimson Doctrine, named after the then Secretary of the State, Henry Stimson, allowed the United States to express concern but not to commit the country to direct involvement or action against the aggressors that illegally occupied territories in various parts of the world. Later, the Neutrality Acts in 1935 further demonstrated the country's desire to avoid the war. The ideas of isolationism and neutrality seem to be based on the conservative ideology, so it is not surprising that most of the isolationistic supporters are Republican lawmakers. Some well-known figures were also avid supporters (e.g., Charles Lindbergh and E.E. Cummings), which increased isolationism's popularity.

As the United States became more influential at the end of the 19th century, thanks to rapid industrialization and modernization, its earlier isolationist stance shifted to reflect the new status on the world stage. The decisions to be engaged (militarily or otherwise) with other nations often had to do with America's national interests at the time. To enhance world stature, many possible routes for the United States included expanding territory, colonizing like the Europeans, and competing with other world powers such as France, Germany, and Great Britain. Despite the seeming lack of intent, many argued that the United States had all the components of an imperial power.

"Internationalism" defies easy definition. The term essentially means that a country should interact and engage with other countries or groups of countries to achieve common economic and political goals, which may advance mutual interests, preserve peace, and/or uphold its core values. One of the natural corollaries of internationalism is the advocacy of international nongovernmental organizations to pursue the shared interests and objectives across national boundaries (such as climate change and terrorism). Also, internationalists may believe the most effective way to solve many problems is to pool all resources and effect transnational cooperation, rather than through individual countries' unilateral efforts.

From the U.S. perspective, internationalism often is translated to mean leading the international community to repel acts of aggression, to defeat terrorism and violation of human rights, and to promote democracy and world peace. There are, of course, debates about the role the United States should play (whether to lead and/or act in accordance with other nations); the circumstances and rationale to act; and realistic assessments (whether the action might lead to success and whether the American public would support it). A power with world recognition and global interests cannot avoid interaction with other nations. Several U.S. presidents are well known for their internationalist visions and policies, including Theodore Roosevelt, Franklin Roosevelt, and Woodrow Wilson.

Internationalism ought to be differentiated from globalization, a term that emerged at the end of the 20th century to emphasize the highly intertwined, intricate interaction among nations and also to underscore the organic interdependence between different parts of the world thanks to free trade and extensive transmission of cultures across national borders. Internationalism has more to do with a single nation's objective and orientation with other nations while globalization deals with the complex and interconnected phenomena that involve the whole world with or without the nation's intention.

The internationalist perspective may appear to be in stark contrast to the isolationist counterpart, but these two philosophies can coexist simultaneously in Americans' mentality. In other words, Americans may desire to be left alone from the rest of the world, but the country's prominent status on the world stage may still drag it to the center, expecting it to be a leader in thorny affairs. The most recent example is the Ukrainian crisis in 2014: most surveyed Americans did not want the government to be directly involved in the conflict even though diplomatic elites called for a much harder stance against Russia as the U.S. government sought a peaceful resolution.

H. Denis Wu

Further Reading

Goldstein, Joshua S., and John C. Plevehouse. 2012. *International Relations.* 10th ed. New York: Pearson.

Morrison, Samuel Eliot. 1965. *The Oxford History of the American People.* New York: Oxford University Press.

Internet for Political Movement

The phrase "political movement" is associated with the ideas of civic engagement, activism, and the public sphere. But in the context of political movement over the Web, Internet users do not need an event happening physically at a certain time. Like offline movements, political activism or engagement online can be issue-based, which can build up over a period of time. Issue-oriented social media pages, also known as issue communities, can engage citizens in social or political movements and promote political discourses.

When the Internet was first introduced in the early 1990s to the global citizens, there was a hope and expectation around the democratic potentials of the technology. As the Web and other digital delivery platforms (e.g., smartphone or tablet) are evolving with user-generated applications, there is a reason to expect that the constantly changing Internet will offer more control of content creation to the users. Social media, such as Facebook and Twitter, and blogs are easy to use for receiving and generating content on multiple platforms. The Internet users can post comments about a story from any of these device screens. In such an environment, there is hardly any distinction between content producers and consumers. All these changes in communication brought by the Internet are also shaping the methods of political communication and the practice of civic engagement, according to studies by communication scholars Lance Bennett and Robert Entman.

In U.S. society, we see a growing trend in the use of social media and mobile-connected Internet for the consumption of political information. According to a Pew Internet study, about two-thirds of adult social media users in the United States were engaged in some type of political engagement/activities through Twitter and Facebook. What's more, 36 percent of U.S. social media users consider these sites "very important" or "somewhat important" as sources of political news and discussion, according to a 2012 Pew study.

In the backdrop of a growing number of Internet and smartphone users, there should not be any doubt that the virtual world offers great potential for political groups. It has been suggested that the development of social media is geared toward advancing civic and political engagement among Internet users, mainly among the young. Chris Martin of Coldplay led the Oxfam's Make Trade Fair campaign. Martin's website promoted web links to the fair trade campaign materials. Sites like MySpace, Facebook, and Twitter created arenas for youth to organize political movements or political campaigns online in addition to their activities offline. Seeing the reach of these sites, many governmental organizations decided to ensure their presence there. During the Free Burma campaign in 2007 and 2008, the Free Burma Movement created a global community for Burma's freedom on Facebook and Twitter. An activist group against the World Trade Organization in 1999 used open source software to create "indymedia" for exchanging youth activist-generated content to share among them or within an anti-WTO community.

Online activism does not replace offline activities. The Internet has added a new option for organizing political movements or campaigns, but these campaigns must still facilitate an offline movement. Virtual worlds should not be dissociated from the real offline world. During civil uprisings in Africa and Middle East, popularly known as "Arab Spring," Twitter and Facebook pages were able to fill the void of information from local, independent news sources during the peak period of revolutions with the help of tech-savvy citizens, journalists, and expatriates living in Europe and North America. Nevertheless, it would be incorrect to describe the Arab Spring as a direct outcome of social media activism. A study by Philip N. Howard, Duffy Aiden, and Deen Freelon examined the roles of social media during civil uprising in Mideast and North African countries and came to three conclusions: (1) social media played a central role in shaping political conversations in the Arab Spring, mainly among young, urban, educated, and expatriates of the country in question; (2) online conversations on revolutions were more nuanced—full of political interpretations; and (3) social media helped spread democratic ideas across international borders.

Critics of online civic engagement would argue that there has been a decline in the quality of civic engagement. Some fear that certain online communities lack diverse viewpoints and may end up becoming an echo chamber. In contrast, advocates of the Internet for political communication would say that the Internet and social media are empowering citizens by giving them a voice and helping them build a community of ideas and campaigns.

Social or online media-based activism is neither changing the world nor making a revolution happen, but it is helping youth get a better understanding of a political phenomenon or an ongoing activism or movement. Media literacy and social capital are inevitable for effective civic activities online. Citizens need to be prepared through educational institutions and other intellectual forums so that they can improve and sustain the quality and diversity of political discussion online.

Masudul Biswas

Further Reading

Alterman, Jon B. 2011. "The Revolution Will Not Be Tweeted." *The Washington Quarterly* 34(4): 103–116.

Bennett, Lance, and Robert Entman, eds. 2001. *Mediated Politics: Communication in the Future of Democracy*. Cambridge, MA: Cambridge University Press.

Dahlberg, Lincoln. 2001. "The Internet and Democratic Discourse: Exploring The Prospects of Online Deliberative Forums Extending the Public Sphere." *Information, Communication & Society* 4(4): 615–633.

Howard, Philip N., Duffy Aiden, and Deen Freelon. 2012. "Opening Closed Regime: What Was the Role of Social Media During the Arab Spring?" University of Washington: Project on Information Technology and Political Islam. http://pitpi.org/wp-content/uploads/2013/02/2011_Howard-Duffy-Freelon-Hussain-Mari-Mazaid_pITPI.pdf. Accessed February 5, 2015.

Rainie, Lee, Aaron Smith, and Key Schlozman. Social Media and Political Engagement. Pew Internet & American Life Project. http://pewinternet.org/Reports/2012/Political-engagement/SummarThomas. Accessed February 5, 2015.

Iowa Caucus

The Iowa Caucus held in early January of presidential election years is the first widely watched voter selection process to choose Democratic and Republican presidential nominees. The first distinction to be made is the difference between the Iowa Caucus and the Ames Straw Poll, which is held in late summer before the caucus and primary season begins. Because of media coverage during presidential elections, voters outside of Iowa tend to confuse the two.

The Iowa Caucus is statewide and helps elects delegates to presidential conventions. The Ames (Republican) Straw Poll, typically held at Iowa State University a few months before the state Caucus, is more of a fund-raising event to gauge candidate and party strength. It has been compared to the Iowa State Fair with a political rather than agricultural theme. The Iowa Caucus dates back to 1972; the Straw Poll was started by the GOP in 1979. (There is no Democratic Straw Poll.)

There is little correlation between the two events other than the attention from media and each being an early indicator of candidates with possible front-runner status. Rules of the Iowa Caucus and the Ames Straw Poll differ. For the Straw Poll, Iowa's GOP headquarters identifies candidates and allows each to speak briefly before the poll is taken.

Rules of the state caucus are arcane. Iowa has 1,774 precinct caucuses that tend to follow their own procedures. Some caucuses are huge; others are half a dozen folks in a meeting place such as a library or even a private home. Those attending discuss the candidates. Ballots eventually are collected, and winners of each caucus are announced and duly reported. Results of all precincts are tabulated. Thereafter, delegates are chosen in a complicated process.

Historically, the Iowa Caucus has been the first test of front-runner status. In 1972, few people or media paid attention to the caucus, focusing instead on the New Hampshire primary. Democratic Senator Edmund Muskie of neighboring Maine was leading the polls in New Hampshire at the time, but challenger Senator George McGovern focused on the Iowa Caucus and had a surprising showing of 23 percent. This was the earliest sign that Muskie's campaign was weaker than projected with McGovern later becoming the eventual Democratic nominee. Since then, the Caucus has commanded national media attention, with candidates reluctant to skip the event.

In 2008, that almost became a reality for one major candidate. Hillary Clinton's campaign manager, Mike Henry, wrote a memo that asked, "What is the cost relative to the benefit of dedicating significant funding and other resources to Iowa?" Clinton rejected this and campaigned vigorously in Iowa. She congratulated her rivals on caucus night, including the one who came in second: John Edwards.

Political blogger Andrew Malcolm, writing in the *Los Angeles Times*, noted in this 2008 post that Edwards would likely have been the nominee if Clinton had bypassed the state. In hindsight, his extramarital scandal could even have put Republicans John McCain and Sarah Palin in the White House. This is the subtle power of the Iowa Caucus in shaping political coverage.

Media also bring in state revenues. According to one estimate, state revenue from the 2012 Caucus was $17,594,397 spent on TV spots, radio promos, newspaper ads, and campaign headquarters' costs for hotels, food, car rentals, and other transportation costs, such as buses and flights.

In 2012, two Iowa State University researchers—Dianne Bystrom and Daniela Dimitrova—conducted a study to ascertain the main sources of media information about candidates leading up to the Caucus. They conducted two telephone surveys of registered Republicans and independents, with 1,256 respondents surveyed in November 2011 and another 940 in December. They found that political predispositions influenced whether a person would participate in the event, with television remaining the primary medium of information. Surprisingly, social media played no significant factor.

Bystrom concluded, "Our study shows that social media does not appear to have played a large role in turning out participants in the 2012 Republican Party caucuses. Previous studies showed that the use of social media among Iowans prior to the 2008 caucuses was fairly high, leading us to speculate that Democratic caucus-goers may rely more on social media for campaign information than Republican caucus-goers."

The study found that pre-Caucus visits played a significant role in whether a person would participate in the process. That supports the conventional wisdom that candidates participating in the Caucus are tested interpersonally rather than through media in visiting all of Iowa's 99 counties and hundreds of individual precincts.

Mickey Bugeja

See also: New Hampshire Primary; South Carolina Primary

Further Reading

Iowa State University. 2012. "Iowa State Research Determines Political Information Sources of Iowa Caucus-goers." Iowa State News Service. http://www.news.iastate.edu/news/2012/06/27/caucus media. Accessed January 12, 2015.

Malcolm, Andrew. 2008. "What if Hillary Clinton Had Treated Iowa Like Barack Obama has Ky. and W. Va.?" *Los Angeles Times*, May 19. http://latimesblogs.latimes.com/washington/2008/05 /what-if-hillary.html. Accessed January 12, 2015.

Republican Party of Iowa. 2011. "What Is the Iowa Straw Poll?" http://theiowastrawpoll.org /strawpoll.php. Accessed January 12, 2015.

Issue Advertising

Most issue advertising is on television, but some is on radio and some is in print media. Little is done by political candidates. Their advertising is focused on their political opponents rather than issues and is negative. Issue advertising is done by advocacy groups. Because they have 501(c)(4) classifications from the Internal Revenue Service, they cannot attack political candidates directly. Their ads must deal with issues of social importance. However, an analysis of broadcast ads after the 2012 election until mid-2014 by *Huffington Post* found that 63 percent that mentioned a candidate mentioned one who was facing a serious challenge in 2014.

At the heart of the concern is Internal Revenue regulations. The 501(c)(3) category is for religious, social welfare, and educational organizations. Those with this designation cannot engage in any political activity. They are tax exempt, and contributions to such organizations are deductible.

The 501(c)(4) designation is for organizations working for social causes. They can engage in political activity, but the preponderance of their effort must be related to their social cause and not be political. A 501(c)(4) is tax exempt, but contributions to it are not. The tax exempt status saves the organization money, and naturally organizations want to take advantage of that. That is why conservative groups, especially the Tea Party, have been critical of how the IRS has handled 501(c)(4) applications. Part of the problem was that in the wake of the Citizens United decision, in which the Supreme Court ruled that corporations had the same First Amendment rights as a person, the number of 501(c)(4) applications increased dramatically. That slowed processing down, and understandably some groups felt the delay reflected bias.

Determining whether an organization has spent more of its time, money, and energy on political matters is difficult because some organizations mix politics and social issues. The *Huffington Post* analysis found that two senators facing serious challenges in 2014, Lindsey Graham, R-SC, and Mark Begich, D-Alaska, had been mentioned in issue ads of seven organizations. Most, but not all, mentions were unfavorable. They were not the only candidates treated this way. Organizations will argue that the mention of the politicians is incidental and that the main purpose of the ad was to advance the issue. This is a matter of judgment, and it requires looking at more than one ad to make a fair ruling. The IRS cannot review all the ads by 501(c)(4) groups, and that means some are more political than issue oriented.

The technique is as simple as it is unfair. Senators, in the course of six years, cast hundreds of votes. Out of this one can generally find as least one on a recurring issue, like immigration or taxation, that is unpopular with constituents. This may or may not be an accurate representation of that senator's position on the issue. Furthermore, a number of other senators may have voted the same way. Why was Senator X put in this ad? Was Senator X put in this ad because of this vote or for purely political expediency? Was the purpose of the ad to state a position on an issue or to influence a specific senatorial race?

There are, of course, many groups with 501(c)(4) status that do not touch politics. They recognize that taking a political stand will please some people and annoy others. They do not feel that helps their cause, and they are committed to that cause more than to a political party or candidate.

Political parties and candidates are not eligible for 501(c)(4) status, but they are free to buy advertising and to include issues in their ads. However, few ads by parties or candidates are about issues. Most broadcast ads are 30 seconds long, which does not permit an explanation of what the issue is about or why the candidate believes what he or she does. Conventional wisdom says that negative ads are more effective. The evidence on this is mixed. Some candidates have won with negative ads, but there are many campaigns in which both sides have used negative advertising. The candidate's main concern is for the ad to attack his or her opponent. Issues are irrelevant. The evidence on this is mixed. Some candidates have won with negative ads, but now there are many campaigns in which both sides use negative ads, which means the loser has used them as well.

For the public the message is be wary of issue advertising. Consider the source.

Guido H. Stempel III

Further Reading

Brennan Center for Justice, New York University Law School. "Express Advocacy and Issue Advocacy: Historical and Legal Evolution of Political Advertising." http://www.brennancenter.org/sites/default/files/legacy/d/download_file_10667.pdf. Accessed January 12, 2015.

Overby, Peter. 2012. "Why Political Ads in 2012 May All Look Alike." National Public Radio, June 1. http://www.npr.org/2012/06/01/154160392/political-ads-2012-a-reason-they-all-look-alike. Accessed January 12, 2015.

J

Jackson, Jesse (1941–)

Civil rights activist Rev. Jesse Jackson Sr. served as the loudest and most public voice for the concerns of African American voters for three decades from the 1970s through 2000s. Yet even in 2014, Jackson, a dynamic public speaker, was still rallying the public against injustices on issues such as police shootings and voting rights. His campaigns for the presidency in the 1980s paved the way for Barack Obama's election two decades later, but Jackson himself remained largely on the fringe of the national power circle throughout his career. In 1984, Jackson, an ordained Baptist minister, received more than 3 million votes, or about 18 percent of the electorate, during the Democratic primaries; in 1988 he received 6.8 million, or 29 percent of vote. When he ran in 1984, Jackson was only the second African American to run nationally for America's highest office in the 20th century (following Shirley Chisolm, who ran unsuccessfully in 1972). From 1991 to 1997, Jackson also was elected to represent the interests of Washington, D.C., as a lobbyist or "shadow senator" to the U.S. Senate, where the nation's capital has no formal voice.

Regardless of his waning political influence and other controversies, including an illegitimate child and financial debts within his organizations, Jackson was still highly recognized among the public. Two years before Barack Obama was elected president, Jackson was voted the "most important black leader" in an AP-AOL February 2006 poll.

Jackson was known as a smart organizer who created a number of prominent campaigns and organizations that remained active from the 1970s through today. He was savvy about galvanizing the power of the black church to support causes framed as moral injustices.

Jackson was born October 8, 1941, in Greenville, South Carolina, to a 16-year-old high school student and an older married neighbor (Noah Robinson). Jesse Jackson was adopted by his stepfather, Charles Henry Jackson, when his mother married a year later. Jackson grew up with segregated busses, bathrooms, and drinking fountains. He attended a racially segregated high school, where he was elected class president and graduated in 1959. He became active in local civil rights protests as a college student at the historically black North Carolina A&T, where he graduated in 1964.

Jackson was among the youngest people in Martin Luther King Jr.'s inner circle of rising stars during the 1960s civil rights movement. Jackson participated in several key historic protests, including the marches in Montgomery, Alabama, in 1965. Jackson was tasked with creating a key field office for the Southern Christian Leadership Caucus

(SCLC) in Chicago, where Jackson's "Operation Breadbasket"—boycotts of white business owners who didn't hire blacks—drew national attention. It would be the first a many successful campaigns for Jackson throughout his career.

Eventually, however, Jackson sought to recast and broaden the argument for black civil rights into campaigns for economic and class parity. As a result, he increasingly clashed with the most prominent civil rights groups that focused on race, including the SCLC where he worked. Although some black leaders saw Jackson as the successor to Martin Luther King Jr. after King's 1968 assassination, by 1971 Jackson had split entirely from the SCLC. Over the next few decades he focused on creating a number of prominent campaigns and organizations, including Operation PUSH (PUSH stands for People United to Serve Humanity) and the Rainbow Coalition. PUSH and the Rainbow Coalition merged in 1996 and still exist as RainbowPUSH (See www.rainbowpush.com). Boycotts of businesses for jobs, expanding voter's registrations, and social services such as housing were the mainstay of Jackson's work in the 1970s through 2014.

Jackson sought to play a role internationally, too, especially in the latter half of the 20th century and early 21st century, when he was instrumental in the release of numerous U.S. hostages held by foreign powers. He was first recognized for his international diplomacy in 1983, following successful negotiations to release a captured U.S. pilot from the Syrian government. A year later Cuban president Fidel Castro invited Jackson to negotiate the release of nearly two dozen U.S. prisoners. Just before the start of the Persian Gulf Ward in 1991, Jackson secured the release of British and American citizens held by Iraqi leader Saddam Hussein. President Bill Clinton sent Jackson to Kenya in 1997 to promote fair elections. Jackson also negotiated the release of three prisoners of war captured from a UN peacekeeping unit in 1999, during the Kosovo War. Jackson spoke out against the invasion of Iraq at a large antiwar demonstration in London in 2003 and over the next two years held high-level discussions with political leaders in Northern Ireland and Venezuelan President Hugo Chavez as well.

Jackson was caught more than once exercising strong opinions at moments when he didn't realize he was being taped. One such comment cost him close ties with the Jewish community during his 1984 presidential campaign, and another profanity critiqued then-candidate Obama in 2008. Regardless, Jackson has shown a strong ability to bounce back from adversity, including after the 2013 felony conviction of son Jesse Jackson Jr., who resigned from his U.S. House of Representatives seat in 2012 and later admitted to spending campaign funds for personal use.

Debra Mason

Further Reading

Brown, Khari R., and Ronald E. Brown. 2003. "Faith and Works: Church-Based Social Capital Resources and African American Political Activism." *Social Forces* 82(2): 617–641. Doi 1353/sof.2004.0005.

Gonzalez, David. 2005. "From Margins of Society to Center of the Tragedy." *The New York Times*, September 2.

Remnick, David. 2006. "The Joshua Generation." *The New Yorker*, November 17.

Walker, Felicia R., and Deric M. Greene. 2006. "Exploring Afrocentricity: An Analysis of the Discourse of Jesse Jackson." *Journal of African American Studies* 9(4): 62–71.

Washington, James Melvin. 1985. "Jesse Jackson and the Symbolic Politics of Black Christendom." *Annals of the American Academy of Political and Social Science* 480: 89–105. Doi 10.2307/1045337.

Jamieson, Kathleen Hall (1946–)

Kathleen Hall Jamieson is a leading authority on political communication and presidential campaigns. She is author or co-author of at least major 18 books, including *The Obama Victory: How Media, Money and Message Shaped the 2008 Election*, one of the most thorough studies ever made about a presidential election.

A rhetorical scholar by training, Jamieson has contributed to media studies, political history, and contemporary feminist thought. The quality, consistency, and sheer volume of her work has earned a wide, interdisciplinary audience. She finds frequent voice in the media as a source for journalists working on campaign communication and as a guest on television news programs. She has testified before Congress on communication issues and advises organizations funding studies in communication. While maintaining an active research program, since 1989 she has been dean of the Annenberg School for Communication at the University of Pennsylvania.

Kathleen M. Hall, the oldest of five children, grew up in the small town of Waconia, Minnesota. Educated in Catholic schools, Jamieson became active in interscholastic debate at the insistence of Sister Anne Rose while she was a student at St. Benedict's, an all-girls high school in St. Joseph. Graduating as the class valedictorian, she accepted a full scholarship to Marquette University, where she continued to debate. She completed her undergraduate degree in rhetoric and public address in 1967.

She went on immediately to graduate school. Her doctoral studies at the University of Wisconsin, Madison, led to a dissertation on *Humanae Vitae*, the 1968 papal encyclical on birth control, which won her the Speech Communication Association's Award for Outstanding Doctoral Dissertation in 1972.

She taught in the Department of Speech Communication at the University of Maryland from 1970 to 1986. While at Maryland she received grants from Lilly (1976), Fulbright (1980), and Mellon (1982), as well as an East-West Center fellowship (1985). Political communication occupied most of her scholarly attention during her last years at Maryland, during which time she released Packaging the Presidency (1984).

Jamieson left the University of Maryland in 1986 to become the G.B. Dealey Regents Professor of Communication and Chair of the Speech Communication Department at the University of Texas, Austin, a position she occupied until 1989. During this period, she also served on the Twentieth Century Fund's Task Force on Presidential Debates. Her research in political communication continued, marked by publication of *Eloquence in an Electronic Age* (1988), a revision of *Interplay of Influence* (2nd ed., 1988), and *Presidential Debates* (1988), co-authored with David S. Birdsell.

In 1989, Jamieson became dean of the Annenberg School for Communication at the University of Pennsylvania. She has continued to conduct research and teach during her tenure as dean, releasing over six years *Deeds Done in Words* (1990), co-authored with Karlyn Kohrs Campbell; *Dirty Politics* (1992); and *Beyond the Double Bind* (1995), as well as revised editions of *Packaging the Presidency* (2nd ed. 1992) and *Interplay of Influence* (3rd ed. 1992).

She continued to author and co-author widely read books into the new century with *Everything You Think You Know About Politics . . . and Why You're Wrong* (2000), *The Press Effect: Politicians, Journalists, and the Stories that Shape the Political World* (2003), and *Echo Chamber: Rush Limbaugh and the Conservative Media Establishment* (2008).

A frequent commentator on issues in political communication for print and broadcast outlets since the release of *Packaging* in 1984, Jamieson became a regular guest on Bill Moyers' *Listening to America* in 1992. Her commentary on that year's presidential campaign provided the PBS audience with a sustained, academically grounded critique of political communication. She continued her appearances on other programs as well, serving so frequently as a media commentator that she has been dubbed "Queen of Quotes" by several publications.

Jamieson and her colleagues founded two important research tools: the National Annenberg Election Survey and Factcheck.org. Both are research platforms, albeit quite different from one another and targeted toward difference audiences and purposes. The website factcheck.org—which calls itself a "consumer advocate for voters"—is routinely consulted by journalists and consumers of political news. The NAES is a longitudinal platform for scholarship on "political attitudes about candidates, issues, and the traits Americans want in a president. It also has a particular emphasis on the effects of media exposure through campaign commercials and news from radio, television, and newspapers." Factcheck.org takes assertions seriously and weighs the evidence offered, if any, and the quality of the evidence that might have been brought to bear; it is widely cited in the press and has many imitators (e.g., PolitFact.com and the *Washington Post's* "Fact Checker").

Jamieson's most important contributions fall into four broad and closely related areas: (1) developing rhetorical theory relating to institutions and genre; (2) advancing the field's understanding of the nature and influence of political media, particularly of the possible relationships among media; (3) developing programs for improving public discourse (Each category ties to the other across her teaching, research, and public activities.); and (4) developing tools and methods for assessing the impact of political communication on voters' beliefs and behaviors.

Jamieson's public activities evidence at the very least a nonacademic audience for her ideas. Her success in getting networks first to listen to and then to adopt the results of the adwatch studies credentials the practicality of attempts to shape discourse in the public sphere. Her ability to take complex ideas and distill them into a palatable form for television makes publicly available exactly the kind of sustained, careful analysis that she has championed in her academic writing.

David S. Birdsell

Further Reading

Jackson, B., and Jamieson, K.H. 2007. *unSpun: Finding Facts in a World of Disinformation*. New York: Random House.

Jamieson, K.H. 1988. *Eloquence in an Electronic Age*. New York: Oxford University Press.

Jamieson, K.H. 1992. *Dirty Politics: Deception, Distraction and Democracy*. New York: Oxford University Press.

Jamieson, K.H., and Waldman, P. 2003. *The Press Effect: Politicians, Journalists, and the Stories that Shape the Political World*. New York: Oxford University Press.

Kenski, K., B.W. Hardy, and K.H. Jamieson. 2010. *The Obama Victory: How Media, Money, and Message Shaped the 2008 Election*. New York: Oxford University Press.

Judicial Activism

How one defines judicial activism necessarily coincides with one's views on the judiciary's proper role. In an American context these views tend to fall into two distinct camps—those who favor a strict constructionist approach to interpreting the Constitution, maintaining that judges should weigh a law's constitutionality against the text of the Constitution's plain meaning; and those who believe that the Constitution's meaning evolves in the same way the political context in which cases are decided does, that the document is a "living Constitution." As one might expect from an issue where there exist significant differences between popular viewpoints, debates over the proper role of the American judiciary have energized citizens and politicians alike in recent elections.

Judicial activism may have existed for nearly as long the American republic, with perhaps the most famous exercise of such being Chief Justice John Marshall's "invention" of judicial review in the case *Marbury v. Madison* (1803). Scholarly work attributes the first written use of the term to an article written in 1947 by historian Arthur Schlesinger Jr. In that piece, Schlesinger contrasts activism with judicial restraint, a distinction that continues to shed some light on what the term means. However, no consensus yet exists as to the precise meaning of judicial activism despite the longevity of its use.

While the question remains as to what exactly qualifies as judicial activism and, indeed, whether it is a good or bad thing, there is no question about the political volatility of the issue. Ronald Reagan's nomination of Robert Bork in 1987 to fill a vacancy on the Supreme Court was an early landmark in an ongoing partisan feud in Congress over activist judges. Bork, who was rated highly by the American Bar Association and had served six years as federal appellate court judge, saw his confirmation denied by a vote of 42-58, with all but two Democrats voting Nay. Just one year earlier, Antonin Scalia, a judge with a similar ideology as Bork, had been easily confirmed by a 98-0 vote. The difference between the two nominees was that Bork had an extensive paper trail, including having written about cases he would vote to strike down and having served as Richard Nixon's Attorney General for the "Sunday Night Massacre." Apparently, Bork's views were viewed as extreme enough to warrant such a high-profile rejection.

The Bork nomination hints at the consequences of ambiguous definitions of judicial activism. To Bork's critics, his expressed views signaled that he was not sufficiently respectful of precedent; to his supporters, they signaled that he was a principled jurist who sought to rectify previous jurisprudential wrongs. Speculation about whether Bork would be an activist justice depended not on objective evaluation of his judicial competence but on the level of support for his policies. This implies that judicial activism might be a term devoid of meaning, a catchall term used by critics for judicial decisions with which they disagree.

This partisan tit-for-tat has become an issue in recent elections, as well. Phyllis Schlafly, founder and president of the conservative interest group Eagle Forum, declared judicial activism to be the biggest issue in the 2002 congressional elections. Schlafly explained that the impetus behind her statement was delaying tactics by Senate Democrats in confirming

George W. Bush's judicial nominees. The politicization of the judiciary has become an issue debated not just by elites in Congress and in the media but by the public as well.

States with merit selection, a feature of some state judiciaries that requires judges to stand for periodic retention elections, have been an empowering venue for a public disgruntled with activist judges. Merit selection is an institution that creates public accountability for state judges from which their federal brethren, who once confirmed hold their positions for life, assuming "good behavior," are exempt. A controversial instance of the public reacting to what it deemed activism was Iowa voters' removal of three state Supreme Court justices who were part of a unanimous panel that voted to strike down a law stipulating marriage as between a man and a woman. This removal, like the failed Bork confirmation, signals a politicization of the American judiciary that may cause judges to weigh public opinion, and thus hamper courts' ability to make important decisions that are unpopular with a majority of the public.

Unsurprisingly, where there is controversy there is opportunity for politicians to seek the spotlight. The 2012 Republican presidential primary gave occasion to a high-profile denunciation of activist judges: former Speaker of the House and presidential hopeful Newt Gingrich argued that Congress ought to be empowered to subpoena activist judges—for Gingrich, those who were focused more on achieving the correct results than following the plain meaning of the law—to testify about their indiscretions. Commentators from both sides of the ideological spectrum pegged this dramatic statement as an effort by Gingrich to appeal to voters—possibly in Iowa, home of the first nominating caucus—who feel that traditional values are being eroded by judicial overreach. However, Gingrich failed to gain political support for his positions, which again speaks to the difficulty in identifying activism and how to respond to it.

Whereas Gingrich sought to gain political support by making the judiciary an issue, Barack Obama has taken the opposite tack. Not wanting to expend political capital that could be used pursuing his domestic policies, Obama has nominated fewer and more moderate candidates during his first years as president. Even so, his nominees have often been met with vociferous opposition by Senate Republicans; the failed nomination of Goodwin Liu is illustrative. Liu, a young Asian-American law professor unanimously deemed well qualified by the A.B.A., nevertheless failed in his confirmation bid. Like Bork, Liu had a paper trail stating his opposition to cases, and some observed that Liu might make a strong Supreme Court nominee for a Democratic president in the future. Clearly, partisan battles over judicial nominees remain a symptom of a broader debate about judicial activism taking place in multiple arenas of American politics.

Chris David Kromphardt

See also: Bork, Robert

Further Reading

Kmiec, Keenan D. 2004. "The Origin and Current Meanings of 'Judicial Activism.'" *California Law Review* 92: 1441–1477.

Savage, Charlie. 2012. "Obama Lags on Judicial Picks, Limiting His Mark on Courts." *New York Times,* August 17.

Sulzberger, A.G. 2010. "Ouster of Iowa Judges Sends Signal to Bench." *New York Times*, November 3.

K

Kennedy-Nixon Debates (1960)

The series of four televised debates between presidential candidates Richard Nixon and John F. Kennedy during the 1960 election was a watershed event, marking the first time two presidential candidates appeared in such a televised format. Each of the debates was watched by an audience estimated at about 70 million viewers, the largest broadcast audience in American political history. More significantly, the debates permanently changed the face of politics, cementing a relationship to television that has weakened the power of political parties and hastened the use of campaign media advisers.

By 1960, television had come to 90 percent of American homes. To encourage interest in debates, the three television networks offered free time for the four debates, and both parties accepted the offer. Congress suspended the "equal time" rule so that air time would not have to be given to the 14 minor party candidates. No one knew how much effect a political debate would have, but after election day, in which Kennedy won the popular vote by only 113,000 votes of the 68.8 million cast, there was little question that the debates, most notably the first one (held on September 26, 1960), influenced the public's perception of the candidates. The outcome would set a standard for future candidates on how to orchestrate such events.

The four appearances actually were more like joint press conferences than classic "debate" confrontations. In a traditional debate, opponents talk to each other; in this debate, it was the candidate who spoke to the audience who turned out to be the winner. The first debate occurred at the studios of Chicago's CBS station WBBM-TV and was hosted by Howard K. Smith and produced by Don Hewitt. The focus was to be domestic policy, but the issues were subsumed by the images of Nixon and Kennedy. Before the debate, representatives of both candidates negotiated rules, lighting, camera angles, types of chairs, and even the color of the paint of the set. Although Nixon was considered by many to be an expert debater, his advisers were worried about how he might appear on camera. They were concerned because he had suffered a knee injury shortly before the debate and had lost weight and not fully recovered. Nixon's facial appearance also looked dour because of his pale skin. In what would become a major error, Nixon declined the services of a makeup artist.

Kennedy's staff had fewer concerns. He was tanned from campaigning in California and had rested on the day of the debate while Nixon had campaigned earlier in the day. By the time the candidates arrived at WBBM, Nixon, wearing a gray suit, looked tired.

Kennedy wore a dark suit, which complemented his features. An aide, noticing Nixon's five-o'clock shadow, went to a drugstore and bought a container of Lazy Shave to cover the candidate's stubble. As viewers would later see, it did not help.

What the candidates said would be overshadowed by their appearances. Nixon spoke well but looked haggard. Kennedy maintained steady eye contact with the camera; when he did not, he appeared to be listening intently, but calmly, to Nixon. Nixon followed a traditional debate style. When speaking, he looked at Kennedy. When not speaking, he looked around the studio. The debate featured a number of candidate "reaction shots." Kennedy had 11 such shots, taking 118 seconds; Nixon had 9, totaling 85 seconds. Nixon's aides criticized the type and timing of shots of him as unflattering—either they were too "tight" or they showed him favoring his sore knee. What also affected Nixon's appearance were the hot camera lights, including spotlights his advisers recommended to help his appearance, but by the end of the debate, Nixon seemed to be sweating profusely.

The Cold War and the fight against Communism was the focal point of the debates. Even though the first debate was devoted to domestic policy, Kennedy tried to include a discussion of the Cold War and economic issues. The first debate featured a question from NBC's Sander Vanocur about a remark President Eisenhower had made regarding the importance of Nixon's role as vice president. The question called for specific ideas Nixon had provided the administration during Eisenhower's presidency. Nixon's advisers felt that question was unfair.

The second debate, held in Washington, D.C., and hosted by NBC's Frank McGee, focused on foreign policy. Attitudes toward Cuba and the U-2 incident (when a U.S. spy plane was shot down by the Soviets, forcing the cancellation of a summit meeting between Soviet Prime Minister Khrushchev and President Eisenhower) were considered. Also, a dispute over two small islands, Quemoy and Matsu, between Communist China and For- mosa, was discussed. In the last two debates, more questions arose about China policy, labor unions, nuclear testing, and education. In the latter three debates, Nixon wore darker suits, stood in front of more appealing backgrounds, and had regained his normal weight. He looked more confident and appealing than in the opening debate, in part because he used the services of a theatrical makeup artist.

But it was the first debate that would have the most impact. Although it would not be known or fully appreciated right away, it appeared that Kennedy was a confident chal- lenger. His crowds grew, and he started to attract independent and undecided voters; public opinion surveys consistently reported that a majority of viewers felt the debates influenced their decision. In a Roper poll, 72 percent of those who were influenced by the debates voted for Kennedy. Even though Nixon was more poised in later debates, as he learned afterwards, the first impression on television had devastating consequences. Interestingly, students at Northwestern who had listened to the radio rather than watching the televised version (as part of an experiment) thought Nixon won the first debate.

Mark Conrad

Further Reading

Ambrose, Stephen. 1987. *Nixon—The Education of a Politician*. New York: Simon and Schuster.
White, Theodore H. 1961. *The Making of the President 1960*. New York: Atheneum.

Kerner Commission

The Kerner Commission, also known as the National Advisory Commission on Civil Disorders, was a landmark study into the causes of the mid-1960s race riots. The group concluded that the primary reasons for wide civil unrest in many of America's minority communities were poverty and the white establishment's indifference to suffering. The commission created a standard against which future investigations of social problems and injustices might be judged. Since poverty is again increasing in the United States, the half-century-old findings of this commission may again prove valuable.

Since the beginning of the U.S. republic, various committees and commissions have investigated both official and unofficial actions by the three branches of the government. Indeed, one of the first congressional investigations occurred even before the nation was fully established, when the Continental Congress investigated leaks of secret government information to Philadelphia newspapers by the secretary of the foreign affairs committee, Thomas Paine.

Later commissions investigated military operations in Ohio (1792), the Kennedy Assassination (1963), and the events surrounding 9/11 (2001). Some of these investigations (generally conducted by senate or house committees) were carried out by commissions comprising senators and representatives, while others were independent commissions made up of nongovernment experts and nonfederal public officials.

The years following World War II are often seen as a time of unparalleled prosperity in the United States. There was, however, an undercurrent of dissatisfaction, graphically described by writers such as Michael Harrington in 1962 in his classic book *Other America*, in which he described the new slums of the nation. "Its citizens are the internal migrants, the Negroes, the poor whites from the farms, the Puerto Ricans. They join the failures from the old ethnic culture and form an entirely different kind of neighborhood. For many of them, the crucial problem is color, and this makes the ghetto walls higher than they have ever been," Harrington wrote of the rising rage.

While the government began to focus efforts on relieving poverty in the cities, the 1960s were also a time of dramatic social change in middle class America. The environmental movement was questioning the sustainability of the planet. The women's movement was demanding equal pay for equal work. The war in Vietnam was causing a plethora of questioning, soul searching, and political turmoil. These and numerous other issues were polarizing the young and the old, liberals and conservatives, blue collar and white collar. A whole generation seemed to be turning on, tuning in, and dropping out, much to the chagrin of everyone from parents to politicians.

Also in this mix was a series of riots in the summers of 1965, 1966, and 1967, the last seeing more than 150 riots across the United States and attaining the name of the "long, hot summer." Serious riots occurred in Nashville, Jackson (Mississippi), Tampa, Cincinnati, Atlanta, Newark, and most significantly, Detroit, where President Johnson sent federal troops to restore order.

On July 28, 1967, while rioting was still occurring in Detroit, President Johnson appointed the Kerner Commission to explore and report on why the riots occurred and what could be done to prevent future disturbances. The members of the commission were the following:

- Otto Kerner, Governor of Illinois and chair
- John Lindsay, Mayor of New York and vice chairman

- I.W. Abel, President of United Steelworkers of America
- Edward W. Brooke, U.S. Senator
- James Corman, U.S. Representative
- Fred R. Harris, U.S. Senator
- Herbert Turner Jenkins, Police chief, Atlanta, Georgia
- William McCulloch, U.S. Representative
- Katherine Graham Peden, Former Commissioner of Commerce, Kentucky
- Charles Thornton, Chairman of the Board and CEO, Litton Industries
- Roy Wilkins, Executive Director, NAACP

Far from being an impartial report on the civil disturbances, the report had, according to Tom Wicker of the *New York Times*, a specific target audience: white America. President Johnson was severely criticized for the Commission's moderate character. Where were Stokely Carmichael, Floyd McKissick, Martin Luther King Jr., such white radicals as Tom Hayden, or such fiery evangelists as James Baldwin?

"[But] a commission made up of militants . . . could not conceivably have spoken with a voice so effective, so sure to be heard in white, moderate, responsible America. And the importance of this report is that it makes plain that 'white, moderate, responsible' is where the trouble lies," Wicker concluded.

After seven months of investigation, the commission released its report on February 29, 1968, and to the surprise of many, it became an instant best seller, with more than 2 million copies of the 426-page document sold.

In appointing the Commission, President Johnson sought the answers to three questions: What happened? Why did it happen? What can be done to prevent it from happening again? The "what happened" in 1965, 1966, and 1967 was clearly evident, but the Commission also presented a detailed history of racial prejudice and disquiet going back to the colonial era.

Indeed, one of the witnesses in the hearings, psychologist Kenneth B. Clark, testified about a sense of déjà vu regarding both the events and the resulting investigations and reports: "I read that report . . . of the 1919 riot in Chicago, and it is as if I were reading the report of the investigating committee on the Harlem riot of '35, the report of the investigating committee on the Harlem riot of '43, the report of the McCone Commission on the Watts riot. I must again in candor say to you, members of this Commission, it is a kind of Alice in Wonderland with the same moving picture reshown over and over again, the same analysis, the same recommendations and the same inaction."

In addition to its lengthy narrative, the Commission presented detailed statistical analyses relating race, age, education, and income to levels and locations of destruction. The Commission also concluded that most of the riots were not strictly "racial" in nature. That is, there was no black-on-white or white-on-black violence. In most instances black rioters targeted and looted black-owned businesses. In response, black business owners, trying to protect their property, actually fought rioters and defended firefighters. Their efforts, however, were generally unsuccessful, as evidenced by the amount of destruction.

As for the reasons for the riots, the Kerner Commission was quite explicit: "Certain fundamental matters are clear. . . . the most fundamental is the racial attitude and behavior of white Americans toward black Americans. Race prejudice has shaped our history decisively in the past; it now threatens to do so again. White racism is essentially responsible for the explosive mixture which has been accumulating in our cities since the end of World War II."

One must be careful, of course, in ascribing "results" to the publication of the Kerner Commission report. There have, however, been some statistical studies showing correlations (rather than causations) between social conditions in 1968 and the present. In addition, one has to be careful in how results are interpreted: raw numbers, percentages, or comparisons across groups. Nevertheless, positive trends can be seen. A report by Reynolds Farley with the Population Studies Center at the University of Michigan in 2008, for examples, notes that the gap between blacks and whites has significantly narrowed in a number of areas, including occupational prestige, elected and appointed public officials, poverty rates, and residential racial segregation.

However, the report also notes that although the status of blacks on other social indicators has improved, the status of whites has also increased, thus leaving a racial gap that is as large as it was in 1968. These indicators include high school completion, median household income, and home ownership.

The National Advisory Commission on Civil Disorders focused national attention not only on the riots themselves, but on working, educational, and living conditions of a substantial minority population in the United States. The fact that the report became a best seller is a testament to the interest shown by the general population to its reports and conclusions.

"Interest," however, is not the same as influence, and it is difficult to say whether the report had an actual impact on society. It certainly exposed abuses and discrimination. Retrospectives at both the 25th and 40th anniversaries have detailed changes since the "long hot summer" of rioting, looting, and killing. Whether these changes are a direct result of the report is open to debate. However, it is safe to conclude that the report will continue to have a lasting impact as an important look at life in America in the mid-to-late 1960s with implications for life today.

Larry Burriss

See also: Black Voters; Class Voting; Hispanic Voters

Further Reading

Farley, Reynolds. 2008. "The Kerner Commission Report Plus Four Decades: What Has Changed? What Has Not?" University of Michigan: Population Studies Center, September 22.
Harrington, Michael. 1972. *Other America: Poverty in the United States.* New York: Penguin Books.
Kerner Commission. 1968. *Report of the National Advisory Commission on Civil Disorders.* New York: Bantam Books.

Keynesianism

Keynesianism refers to a set of economic concepts developed by British economist John Maynard Keynes (1883–1946). These principles have been applied by the United States and other Western nations during times of economic recession as a means to stimulate demand for goods and services. Keynesianism is not universally accepted, especially by conservatives, as a sound basis for government fiscal policy. Nonetheless, massive federal borrowing to stimulate the economy during the Great Recession of 2008–2009 was employed during the presidential administrations of both Republican George W. Bush and Democrat Barack Obama. The Tea Party movement rose to prominence through its impassioned rejection of Keynesianism and the vast federal spending it inspired.

Keynes sought theories to explain business cycle fluctuations, such as the devastating global Great Depression that began with the Wall Street crash of 1929. He published *The General Theory of Employment, Interest and Money* in 1936. Keynes rejected neoclassical economics teaching that free markets, at least in the short term, would naturally lead to full employment as long as workers were not too aggressive in wage demands. Keynes also thought employment was tied to demand for goods and services, but he found that aggregate demand often is erratic, influenced by natural "boom and bust" business cycles. He advocated that government can and should intervene in these natural cycles, using fiscal and monetary policies to increase spending and make borrowing easier. His ideas became enormously popular among Western governments in the 1940s since they both offered an explanation for the Great Depression and gave a defense of government policies like the New Deal programs in the United States as a response to such devastating downturns.

Keynes is frequently credited as the most influential economist of the 20th century and an important source for macroeconomic theory. He was made a hereditary peer of the realm in 1946 and is often referred to as "Lord Keynes" since he was the first Baron Keynes of Tilton in England's Sussex County. But his theories eventually came under fire from American monetarist economists, including Milton Friedman, who doubted that Western nations overcame the Depression primarily through increased government spending. The best way to moderate boom and bust cycles, according to monetarist theory, is through varying the interest rates set through the Federal Reserve's Open Market Committee.

In contrast to monetarists, Presidents Bush and Obama decided they could not rely solely on actions by the Federal Reserve in the face of a banking liquidity crisis caused by a massive devaluation in housing prices, which caused millions of American homes almost overnight to be worth less than their mortgages. Unemployment was rising rapidly in what was immediately understood as the worst economic decline since the 1930s. Major banking, financial, and manufacturing institutions were in imminent danger of failing.

"That we are in the midst of crisis is now well understood," Obama said in 2009 during his first inaugural address. "Our economy is badly weakened, a consequence of greed and irresponsibility on the part of some, but also our collective failure to make hard choices and prepare the nation for a new age. Homes have been lost, jobs shed, businesses shuttered."

In such times, conservatives and liberals alike embrace Keynesian thinking. Bush approved the Emergency Economic Stabilization Act of 2008, passed in the final days of his administration, to authorize the U.S. Treasury to buy $700 billion worth of distressed financial instruments like mortgage-backed securities. Obama won congressional approval of the American Recovery and Reinvestment Act of 2009 to authorize even greater spending (usually estimated at more than $800 billion) to stimulate the economy through federal infrastructure investment, tax incentives, and increased unemployment benefits. Just as important to Keynesian theory, federal spending in general did not waiver under either president despite plummeting revenues.

The national debt stood at $5.6 trillion when George W. Bush took office in 2001. He enacted three rounds of federal tax cuts while combating two recessions, the first taking place in the first year of his administration, and while waging anti-terrorism wars in Afghanistan and Iraq. The debt surpassed $10 trillion when he left office in January of 2009. Obama somewhat increased the borrowing curve to cover stimulus costs and to maintain federal spending despite huge revenue declines. The debt surpassed $16 trillion in Obama's first four years in office.

Unemployment rose to a zenith of 10 percent of the workforce in October of 2009 and then declined at what seemed to be a snail's pace. Despite the massive rounds of spending and borrowing, the jobless rate dropped to just 7.9 percent by the end of Obama's first term. On the fifth anniversary of the passage of the stimulus bill, the unemployment rate had dropped to 6.6 percent, well above the traditional federal employment goal of unemployment rates not higher than 4 percent.

"The stimulus has turned out to be a classic case of big promises and big spending with little results," concluded House Speaker John A. Boehner, Ohio Republican. "Five years and hundreds of billions of dollars later, millions of families are still asking: 'Where are the jobs?'"

Public concern over the size of federal spending was probably the biggest reason for the smashing Democratic defeats in the 2010 off-year elections, one of the largest so-called wave elections in U.S. history. Republicans gained 63 seats in the House of Representatives, giving them control of that body. The GOP also picked up six seats in the Senate and made widespread gains in state house races, picking up 680 seats to give them control of 26 state legislatures, as well as control of 29 of the nation's 50 governorships.

But anger at stimulus spending abated and Obama was reelected in 2012. Economists and historians are still debating the legacy of one of history's largest applications of Keynesian theory. The editors of the *New York Times* concluded it was been a qualified success. "Put simply, it prevented a second recession that could have turned into a depression," they wrote on the fifth anniversary of the passage of the American Recovery and Reinvestment Act. "Government spending worked, helping millions of people who never realized it."

Thomas K. Hargrove

Further Reading

Keynes, John Maynard. 2007 (first published 1936). *The General Theory of Employment, Interest and Money.* Basingstoke, UK: Palgrave Macmillan.
Krugman, Paul. 2011. "Keynes Was Right." *The New York Times*, December 29.
Editorial Board. 2014. "What the Stimulus Accomplished." *The New York Times*, February 22.

Knowledge Gap

The knowledge gap refers to the unequal distribution of knowledge across various segments of society. The original knowledge gap hypothesis predicts that increases in media coverage of public affairs would result in the disproportionate distribution of knowledge across socioeconomic classes. Citizens with a higher socioeconomic status were expected to acquire information quicker than citizens in lower socioeconomic segments of society. This would leave some citizens with less overall knowledge about public affairs and create inequitable distributions of social power and privilege across society.

There are several reasons for the knowledge gap that relate to educational differences across citizen groups. Citizens with a higher socioeconomic status, which correlates with education, are more likely to expose themselves to information about public affairs since they perceive themselves to have a higher stake in society. Education also provides the cognitive ability to process and retain information, especially on complex issues relating to science, technology, and public health. Citizens in higher socioeconomic groups are also more likely to have contact with like-minded citizens in civic or community organizations who share an interest in public affairs. This leads to a greater dissemination of information within the social networks of people already holding an informational advantage. Finally, the knowledge gap may occur due to media companies targeting content to citizens in higher socioeconomic groups. This has the effect of exacerbating and reinforcing existing gaps in knowledge.

The knowledge gap is usually measured as differences in the depth of information on a topic, but gaps have also been found on the range of knowledge citizens possess across a variety of issues, general awareness of issues, and the ability of people to discuss topics in response to open-ended cues. These informational asymmetries have been found across a variety of topics such as political campaigns, energy policy, education policy, transportation policy, criminal justice policy, welfare, public housing, government finance, knowledge of world affairs such as the Persian Gulf War and the Palestinian-Israeli conflict, and general knowledge of political actors and processes. Knowledge gaps have also been found on public health issues such as HIV/AIDS, water fluoridation, cancer, and alcohol abuse.

There is also evidence that the knowledge gap extends beyond socioeconomic classes. Knowledge gaps have been found between men and women, voters and nonvoters, and users of different media, as well as across age cohorts, different levels of political interest, and different levels of education. Thus, it is more appropriate to speak of knowledge *gaps* than a single gap. However, some gaps arise for unique reasons. The gap between men and women can be attributed to women demonstrating risk aversive behavior when responding to questions about public affairs. Conformity to existing stereotypes, such as some groups being unintelligent, can lead members of those groups to underreport their knowledge of public affairs, a phenomenon known as stereotype threat.

The knowledge gap has important implications for political campaigns and voting. The goal of electoral campaigns is to disseminate information to voters regarding candidates and issues. Information on candidate traits, policy positions, and past performance can influence voter mobilization and vote choice. Yet campaign information may only reach citizens that already have a high interest in politics and are motivated to learn about new candidates or policy problems. Citizens with less interest in politics, usually those from lower socioeconomic classes, are less likely to expose themselves to campaign information. Thus, campaigns may fail at reaching all segments of the electorate. This can result in the most knowledgeable citizens making informed electoral choices that continue to promote their interests, while the least knowledgeable risk voting for a candidate that may not reflect their interests.

Some campaigns can reduce the knowledge gap. Longer campaigns, for instance, can diminish the knowledge gap as information has more time to reach more people. At some point, the most knowledgeable encounter a ceiling effect, where there is simply no more information for them to learn. The least knowledgeable voters will eventually obtain comparable levels of information as the campaign continually redistributes information. Campaigns with high levels of conflict surrounding salient issues have also been shown to have a more equitable distribution of knowledge across different segments of voters. There is also evidence that major campaign events, such as candidate debates or nomination conventions, can reduce the knowledge gap. However, even during lengthy campaigns, the knowledge gap may still persist on new or complex campaign issues.

There is a common belief that the development of new technologies and forms of media will reduce the knowledge gap. These are assumed to create an environment where information is accessible to everyone, yet the arrival of new technologies or media often enhances, rather than diminishes, the knowledge gap. The invention of the radio, for instance, did little to reduce the gap. Even though people in low socioeconomic groups listened to the radio more than people in high socioeconomic groups, they listened to more entertainment programs than serious news content. Newspapers have also been found to do very little in decreasing the gap, particularly since most readers already possess high levels of public affairs knowledge. Early television news broadcasts did make marginal gains in reducing the knowledge gap since access to news programming was high and the selection of non-news programming in the evening was low. Television news also presents information about public affairs using visual cues and sound bites, which is less cognitively demanding than listening to the radio or reading the newspaper. However, the rise of cable television and the Internet have increased programming options for viewers. These forms of new media have increased the knowledge gaps as people with less interest in public affairs consume more entertainment content and people with a high interest in public affairs take advantage of the larger number of options for political content. This suggests motivation to learn about public affairs is a key factor in contributing the to knowledge gap.

Mark Ramirez

Further Reading

Gaziano, Cecilie. 1997. "Forecast 2000. Widening Knowledge Gaps." *Journalism & Mass Communication Quarterly* 74(2): 237–264.

Holbrook, Thomas M. 2002. "Presidential Campaigns and the Knowledge Gap." *Political Communication* 19(4): 437–454.

Tichenor, P.J., G. A. Donohue, and C.N. Olien. 1970. "Mass Media Flow and Differential Growth in Knowledge." *Public Opinion Quarterly* 34(2): 159–170.

Koppel, Ted (1940–)

American television journalist Ted Koppel pioneered the late-night newscast and thus can be considered an important source of the 24-hour news cycle, a change in broadcast media delivery and news consumption habits that is still transforming the political process. Politicians and policy makers must accept that they govern in a time of instant coverage and analysis.

Koppel used the stage of network news' late-night offering to establish himself as broadcast journalism's premiere interviewer. The success of ABC's *Nightline* program can be linked to the poise, judgment, and sense of fairness of its host. Koppel was named host when the program premiered in March 1980. It evolved from ABC's late-night specials hosted by Frank Reynolds, "The Iran Crisis: America Held Hostage," covering the American hostages held in Iran. Koppel, as ABC's State Department correspondent at the time, received much air time during the specials and was the logical choice to fill in as host. Koppel became the permanent host of *Nightline* when Reynolds found doing both the evening news and the specials too taxing.

Koppel, a native of Lancashire, England, was born on February 8, 1940, and moved to the United States when he was a teenager. He holds degrees from Syracuse and Stanford Universities. ABC hired him in 1963, and he became part of incoming ABC News President Elmer Lower's efforts to identify and groom talent that could lift ABC to respectability in news. Koppel was 23 years of age when he was hired at ABC as a general assignment reporter. His previous professional experience was as an off-air writer and desk worker at a New York City radio news department. Koppel was ABC's chief diplomatic correspondent from 1971 to 1980. Prior to that, while Hong Kong bureau chief, he covered stories from the Pacific, including Australia and Vietnam. For two years, ending in 1977, he anchored the ABC *Saturday Night News*. When ABC News president Roone Arldege moved him out of that position, Koppel considered resigning.

Koppel's skillful work on *Nightline* brought him national attention, and he received acclaim from the critics for his direct, but fair, interviewing style. *Nightline* emerged from the Iran hostage specials to cover a wide range of issues, and Koppel demonstrated versatility with his insights on many subjects. The format of *Nightline* features an overview on an issue, followed by Koppel leading a discussion among spokespersons. He provided participants, frequently from opposing sides, the opportunity to make their points. Koppel is quick to point out inconsistencies or challenge a guest to substantiate a point.

Nightline provided late-night viewers with timely and in-depth coverage of the day's key issues. *Nightline* has proved that there was both viewer and advertiser support for a late-night news program. The program not only identified this important niche but displayed such quality in content and format that it has been a favorite of media critics ever since.

Much of *Nightline*'s success has hinged on the professionalism and credibility of Ted Koppel. An experienced diplomatic correspondent and expert interviewer, Koppel is known for treating guests with balance and fairness, yet he challenges them when he detects inconsistencies or unsubstantiated claims. *Nightline* evolved from ABC News's coverage of the 1979 American hostage crisis in Iran. ABC News president Roone Arledge aggressively programmed late-night updates, taking advantage of this event to demonstrate that ABC could best cover breaking stories.

The *Nightline* format usually consisted of a program introduction by Koppel, followed by a setup piece in mini-documentary style. The setup could be reported by a number of ABC's correspondents, but regular *Nightline* correspondents Chris Bury and Dave Marash generally handled those duties. The program frequently involved interviewees with opposing views on the particular subject, in joint discussion with Koppel. It is in these situations that Koppel shone. He allowed the guests appropriate opportunities to air their views and even argue with each other at times.

A key strength of *Nightline* was its ability to cover timely events and topics. When there was no particular breaking news, *Nightline* provided in-depth analysis and interpretation on a current issue. The program occasionally delved into feature coverage. With virtually no news competition in the late-night venue, *Nightline* could take risks to challenge the medium and its own format. *Nightline* has expanded its vision from time to time with a series of programs on a particular topic, or even with programs that allow for audience participation. Topics such as prison life, political struggle in South Africa, and race relations in America have been treated in series form. "America in Black and White" began as a five-part series in May 1996 and has continued on a periodic basis by providing new perspectives as needed.

Over the years, *Nightline* has been an outlet for virtually every major newsmaker of both domestic and international import. Significant guests on *Nightline* have included South Africa's Desmond Tutu, Libyan colonel Muammar Qaddafi, Israeli Prime Minister Shimon Peres, Vietnamese negotiator Le Due Tho, and former presidents Nixon, Carter, Ford, Reagan, and Bush. Since its founding in 1980, *Nightline* has been at the scene of every major historical worldwide event. *Nightline* provided in-depth coverage of the fall of the Iron Curtain, the unrest in Moscow, student demonstrations in Tiananmen Square, and the Middle East peace process.

On the national scene, *Nightline* tracked political campaigns, the economy, and social issues. The show has promptly covered late-breaking stories such as the explosion of TWA Flight 800 off the coast of Long Island. *Nightline* closely followed the Whitewater investigations, the O.J. Simpson trials, and the Unabomber case. Nightline has been praised consistently by media critics for its news judgment, fairness, and balance. The program has received numerous awards from the broadcast industry: *Nightline* has been recognized in the Peabody, Overseas Press Club, Emmy, and duPont-Columbia Awards competitions.

Jeffrey M. McCall

Further Reading

Bliss, Edward. 1991. *Now the News: The Story of Broadcast Journalism.* New York: Columbia University Press, 1991.

Koppel, Ted, and Kyle Gibson. 1996. *Nightline: History in the Making and the Making of Television.* Westminster, MD: Times Books.

Ku Klux Klan (KKK)

The Ku Klux Klan (KKK or the Klan) is a right-wing organization that focuses on white supremacy, anti-immigrant, and white nationalist views. The Klan—also referred to as the "Invisible Empire"—is known for using violence and terrorism to brutalize and intimidate blacks and other minorities to prevent them from exercising their civil rights. It is America's best-known and best-researched "hate group." Although somewhat subdued in the 21st century by civil lawsuits that sought recompense for Klan violence, today there are between 5,000 and 8,000 members active in at least 41 cities, according to the Southern Poverty Law Center. This movement is divided among dozens of separate organizations, often at odds with each other, that use the Klan name.

Members of the Klan wear robes and hoods to mask their identities and honor the ghosts of the Confederate dead, a pro-slavery stance. Original hoods and robes were in many colors (such as red) to look ghoulish, but Klan members are now known for their white regalia and cone-like hoods. The Klan believes it is exercising Christian morals and ideals and, since 1915, has burned the cross in ceremony, believing that the light of the cross burning represents the eternal knowledge that the Klan is trying to bring regarding white supremacy and the invasion of minorities in America.

The Ku Klux Klan's strength and influence have ebbed and flowed over time, generally categorized by three eras, although some scholars highlight four eras. The first era was from its formation in 1866 to 1875. The Klan was founded in Pulaski, Tennessee, as a purely social club for ex-Confederate soldiers and Confederate sympathizers. Members participated in "night rides" to frighten newly freed slaves. Reconstruction following the defeat of the South in the Civil War gave blacks the right to vote and lessened Southern power and autonomy, which aggravated and motivated many white men to join the Klan. Nathan Bedford Forrest, a former Confederate general, gained control over the early Klan, while night raids and terrorism against blacks spread across the South. In addition to night rides, the Klan would flog and lynch blacks, often conducting these violent incidents at night to both mask identities of Klan members and to add to the terrifying mystery of the group. Forrest, fearing that the group had gone too far with its violence, ordered the group disbanded and all organizational records destroyed. The Enforcement Act and Ku Klux Acts passed nationally in 1871 and 1872 made it a felony for two or more to conspire or go in disguise with the intent to deprive others of civil rights. These acts were successful in undermining the Klan, which disbanded largely by 1875.

The second era of the Klan was from approximately 1915 to 1945. The United States in the early 1900s saw increased immigration due to the Industrial Revolution, and numbers of Catholics, Jews, and other immigrants swelled, stirring white nationalist sentiment. Popular literature of the time framed the Klan as a heroic group of honorable men trying to maintain traditional American values, making the organization respectable in the eyes of some. The film *Birth of a Nation* fueled Klan membership, portraying the Klan as saviors of white women from aggressive black men. William Joseph Simmons, a Georgia preacher, officially reignited the Klan in Georgia in 1915. Simmons became the first Imperial Wizard of the Klan, formalizing the organization by writing down a constitution, glossary, and other governing documents.

The Klan marketed itself as a patriotic organization, using the slogan "America for Americans" while continuing to oppress and exclude minorities. In 1921 the Klan was investigated by Congress for financial mismanagement and corruption. The congressional hearings did not lead to any charges, and the increased attention increased Klan membership. Christian symbolism and the American flag were attractive symbols for recruitment. By 1935 there were over three million members nationwide. In the early 1930s the Women of the Ku Klux Klan were formed, since women were forbidden from joining the male-only Klan.

Second-era Klan members were highly visible, intimidating voters, organizing marches and economic boycotts against non-white businesses, influencing and endorsing political candidates, and even electing politicians that were open members of the organization. The Klan had influence over law enforcement members who were sympathetic to their actions and would ensure there were few or light consequences for violent acts. Klan influence under David Curtis Stevenson was especially powerful in Indiana, drawing 350,000 members into the organization and conspiring with elected officials. Stevenson's involvement in the rape, beating, and later death of a woman led to exposure of Klan ties to politicians and ultimately the downfall of the organization nationwide.

The third era of the Klan (from 1946 to the present) was fueled largely by opposition to the gains of the civil rights movement. This era also marked a change from a national structure to local control over Klan chapters of various names. The *Brown v. Board of Education* decision of 1954 ignited membership, and the Klan used this surge in interest to further organize violent acts. The cross burnings used in ceremony were placed on lawns of black families to terrorize them and prevent them from voting or exercising other rights. The Klan was involved in brutalizing the Freedom Riders; murdering voting rights activists Chaney, Schwerner, and Goodman in Mississippi; and bombing the 16th Street Baptist Church in Birmingham, Alabama, killing four black girls and drawing widespread criticism. As was common for the time, Klan members weren't convicted for their crimes by all-white, all-male juries who were sympathetic to the organization. The gains in the civil rights movement and the federal prosecution of Klan members led to its disintegration.

The 1970s saw Klan activity focused on "reverse discrimination" and immigration, led by David Duke. Duke was seen as a new face for the Klan, and he distanced himself from the robe and hood. The 1980s saw the Klan organizing paramilitary camps for its members, exchanging the white regalia for military-type outfits. The Southern Poverty Law Center (SPLC) successfully sued the United Klans of America for the murder of Michael Donald in 1987, bankrupting the organization and holding it responsible for the actions of its members. The SPLC, which tracks activities of hate groups, currently lists over 160 active Klan chapters nationally.

Sarah R. Young

Further Reading

Chalmers, D.M. 1987. *Hooded Americanism: The History of the Ku Klux Klan*. Durham, NC: Duke University Press.

Greenhaw, W. 2011. *Fighting the Devil in Dixie: How Civil Rights Activists Took on the Ku Klux Klan in Alabama*. Chicago: Lawrence Hill Books.

Newton, M. 1991. *The Ku Klux Klan: An Encyclopedia*. New York: Garland Publishing.

Newton, M. 2010. *The Ku Klux Klan in Mississippi: A History*. Jefferson, NC: McFarland & Co. Press.

Wade, W.C. 1987. *The Fiery Cross: The Ku Klux Klan in America*. New York: Simon and Schuster.

L

Laissez-faire (Free Market) Capitalism

Laissez-faire (pronounced lah ZEY fair) describes both a philosophy and an economic doctrine in which individual actions and economic affairs are free from outside interference, especially government interference. It is a French phrase that literally means "let do" but is usually translated as "allow people to do as they wish" or more simply "let them be." It is one of the major tensions in both historic and modern U.S. politics—the degree to which individuals, businesses, and large corporations are free from government oversight and regulation.

Modern-day laissez-faire proponents rarely use the phrase, preferring to describe themselves simply as advocates of a "free market." The phrase, according to economic legend, resulted from a 1681 meeting between French finance minister Jean-Baptiste Colbert and a group of prominent businessmen. When Colbert asked how the government could assist the nation's merchants, he was simply told, "Laissez-nous faire" or "let us be." The phrase was embraced by the French physiocrat movement, and its underlying philosophy was adopted by Scottish philosopher Adam Smith, widely regarded as the father of modern economics.

The United States struggled with laissez-faire issues even in its founding. The participants in the Constitutional Convention sought to fix the economic and monetary chaos created by the Articles of Confederation, which allowed so much latitude by state governments that national and even international commerce was threatened. Sole control over currency was given to the new federal government, which was largely financed through its power to levy national tariffs on imported goods.

The new United States almost immediately became embroiled in heated debates over the founding of a "Bank of the United States" proposed by the first Secretary of the Treasury, Alexander Hamilton, to the First Congress in 1790. Hamilton wanted the national bank to be a source of financial order for the new nation and a source of credit for the cash-starved federal government. It immediately drew opposition from two prominent Virginians: Secretary of State Thomas Jefferson and primary author of the Constitution James Madison. They argued a central bank was unconstitutional since it would centralize economic power into the hands of a small and decidedly non-Southern group of business interests.

The young nation struggled with the very idea of a central bank, allowing both the First Bank of the United States and a Second Bank of the United States to expire amid concerns that too much economic power was being entrusted to the federal government. The modern Federal Reserve Bank was created by the Federal Reserve Act of 1913 in response to the Panic of 1907 (also called the "bankers' panic" and the "knickerbocker crisis"), in which private bankers like J.P. Morgan became "lenders of last resort" to troubled financial institutions during an economic upheaval caused by a stock market crash the year before and by a nationwide recession.

Conservatives—and even many liberals—frequently voice concerns over how "the Fed" and other governmental agencies impact the economic freedoms of individuals and corporations. Tensions over the "free market" resonate throughout modern American politics.

Ronald Reagan equated free markets with freedom itself and considered the greatest threat to both to be from government regulation. "I hope we have once again reminded people that man is not free unless government is limited," he said repeatedly. "There's a clear cause and effect here that is as neat and predictable as a law of physics: as government expands, liberty contracts."

The issues raised by laissez-faire philosophy came to center stage during President Barack Obama's reelection campaign in 2012. Republicans lashed out at economic initiatives like Obama's American Recovery and Reinvestment Act of 2009, an $800 billion spending bill to stimulate the economy. That program represented "yet another made-in-Washington package of subsidies and spending to create temporary or artificial jobs," the GOP said in its party platform adopted that year. "Republicans will pursue free market policies that are the surest way to boost employment and create job growth and economic prosperity for all."

But Obama campaigned by blaming laissez-faire thinking as the one of the causes of the Great Recession. "Thanks to some of the same folks who are now running Congress, we had weak regulation, we had little oversight, and what did it get us? Insurance companies that jacked up people's premiums with impunity and denied care to patients who were sick, mortgage lenders that tricked families into buying homes they couldn't afford, a financial sector where irresponsibility and lack of basic oversight nearly destroyed our entire economy," Obama told a Kansas crowd in late 2011 during a meeting at Osawatomie High School. (Conservatives widely distributed complete texts of the speech as proof of Obama's anti-free-market philosophy.)

"There is a certain crowd in Washington who, for the last few decades, has said: 'Let's respond to this economic challenge with the same old tune. The market will take care of everything,' they tell us. 'If we just cut more regulations and cut more taxes—especially for the wealthy—our economy will grow stronger.' But here's the problem: It doesn't work. It has never worked. It didn't work when it was tried in the decade before the Great Depression. . . . And it didn't work when we tried it during the last decade. I mean, understand, it's not as if we haven't tried this theory," Obama said.

Conservatives reacted with genuine outrage at what they viewed as an assault on one of America's core values—commitment to the free market. "News flash to Washington politicians: you don't create jobs; the American people do," said Amy Kremer, chairman of the Tea Party Express, one of several organizations in the Tea Party movement. "In the private sector, ordinary Americans start businesses and hire people. All that is needed is that the government leaves our money in our pockets and gets out of the way, ending excessive and burdensome regulation."

The debate over just how much America embraces laissez-faire capitalism will certainly continue in future elections.

Thomas K. Hargrove

See also: Economic Stimulus Programs; Obama, Barack

Further Reading

Bernstein, Andrew. 2005. *The Capitalist Manifesto: The Historic, Economic and Philosophical Case for Laissez Faire.* Lanham, MD: University Press of America.
Obama, Barack. 2011. Speech to a Kansas audience assembled at Osawatomie High School. Complete text provided by the *Washington Post*, December 6. http://www.washingtonpost.com/politics/president-obamas-economic-speech-in-osawatomie-kans/2011/12/06/gIQAVhe6ZO_story.html. Accessed May 26, 2014.

Lasswell, Harold Dwight (1902–1978)

Harold Lasswell was a pioneer propaganda analyst and political scientist who wrote studies of power, the individual, and politics; propaganda; and political communication. But he is perhaps best known for his development of the policy sciences, a fusion of law, political science, sociology, and psychology into one discipline dealing with public choice and decision making.

Lasswell was born in Donnellson, Illinois; he received his Ph.D. in political science from the University of Chicago, where he taught (1922–1938). Later, he was director of war communications research at the Library of Congress (1939–1946), and he taught at Yale (1946–1971) and at the City University of New York (1971–1972). He was also codirector of the Policy Sciences Center in New York City.

Lasswell, who is often called the "father of propaganda study" in the United States, made important contributions toward the development of a comprehensive theory for analyzing propaganda. War propaganda during World War I was the basis for his doctoral dissertation, "Propaganda Technique in the [First] World War." He argued that propaganda is "the making of a deliberately one-sided statement to a mass audience" and concluded that the propagandist works in a specific culture in which strategies are circumscribed by media availability, the value norms of targeted audiences, and other preexisting constraints that are not universal in character.

In 1927, Lasswell taught one of the first college courses in public opinion and propaganda at the University of Chicago. Lasswell's work is now outdated, but in its time it influenced later propaganda studies, especially during the revisionist 1930s, yet few altered his conclusions. His communications formula—"who says what, in which channel, to whom, with what effect"—is still the starting point for most empirical studies.

During World War II, Lasswell analyzed propaganda for the Office of War Information and served as director of the War Communications Division of the Library of Congress, where he demonstrated how content analysis could be used to track international and domestic propaganda. In 1946, he became a professor of law at Yale, where he remained until 1972.

His books include *World Politics and Political Insecurity* (1935); *Propaganda and Dictatorship* (1936) with Harwood L. Childs; *World Revolutionary Propaganda* (1939) with Dorothy Blumenstock; *Public Opinion and British-American Unity* (1941); *Public Opinion in War and Peace* (1943); and *Power and Society: A Framework for Political Inquiry* (1950) with Abraham Kaplan; and propaganda bibliographies. He edited the three-volume *Propaganda and Communication in World History* (1979–1980) with Daniel Lerner and Hans Speier.

Martin J. Manning

Further Reading

Daugherty, William E. 1958. *Psychological Warfare Casebook*. Baltimore: Johns Hopkins University Press.
McDougall, Derek. 1984. *Harold D. Lasswell and the Study of International Relations*. Lanham, MD: University Press of America.

Law and Order

"Law and Order" became a political issue in the 1960s. It started out as a code word for segregation. The violations of law under focus were related to African Americans in the civil rights struggle—not going to the back of the bus, sitting in at segregated lunch counters, trying to register to vote, and holding demonstrations. Technically these were violations of the law in Southern states, and African Americans were arrested for doing things that white people did routinely. Police in Southern states often responded with excessive force against African Americans and also looked the other way when segregationists attacked African Americans.

Republican presidential candidates Barry Goldwater in 1964 and Richard Nixon in 1968 used Law and Order as campaign slogans. While they were not sympathetic to the civil rights movement, they were not racists. The purpose of the slogan was to attract Southern voters, to break up the Democrats' hold on the "Solid South." It was a successful tactic. Goldwater took Alabama, Georgia, Louisiana, Mississippi, and South Carolina in 1964. Nixon took only South Carolina in 1968, but George Wallace took the other four, and Nixon took all five in 1972. Law and Order was part of Nixon's Southern Strategy that produced significant Republican gains in Congress.

Several other issues in the 1960s fed into the Law and Order issue. Riots in big cities, beginning with Los Angeles in 1965 and peaking in 1968 with riots set off by the assassination of Martin Luther King Jr. fed the law. So did student protests over the Vietnam War. However, both were short-term phenomena, and even by the presidential campaign of 1972, Law and Order had faded as an issue. Another factor was the increase in use of illegal drugs. Also, the crime rate began to rise in the 1960s and continued to rise for 30 years.

Law and Order is not the political slogan it was 50 years ago. Astute political candidates recognized that Law and Order was a code word and instead spoke about crime and specific legal issues. This was illustrated markedly in the 1988 presidential campaign. In the summer of 1988 Michael Dukakis had a clear lead over George H.W. Bush. Then Bush supporters attacked Dukakis on prison furloughs when Dukakis was governor of Massachusetts and on Dukakis's opposition to the death penalty. The most remembered part of that campaign and one of the most remembered TV ads of any presidential campaign was the Willie Horton ad on cable television about a Massachusetts felon who committed rape and murder while he was out of prison on furlough. This emphasis on specific facets of crime worked for Bush as he defeated Dukakis easily. No presidential campaign since then has had crime as a major issue. It has, however, been a major issue in some local and state races.

Since the beginning of the 21st century, the crime rate has been rising again but has not reached the level of 1990, when violent crime was nearly twice as high as it is now. States responded to crime in the 1960s and 1970s by increasing jail sentences and creating mandatory sentences. The most extreme example of this was "three strikes and you're out" laws, now in force in 28 states. That the other 22 states did not have such laws reflects the extent to which crime is more a state issue than a national issue. It also reflects the wide variation in state crime rates. For example, the murder rate in Tennessee is five times what the murder rate is in Maine.

This toughening of sentencing has given the United States the highest incarceration rate in the world and serious overcrowding of prisons. There is some movement in the opposite direction. "Three strikes and you're out" laws have been modified in some states to include only serious crimes. U.S. Attorney General Eric Holder proposed reducing sentences for drug offenders in federal prisons, and the U.S. Sentencing Commission adopted reforms that went into effect in late 2014. However, these changes would reduce the population of federal prisons by only 6 percent. There is also some controversy about the death penalty, which is banned in 18 states despite the fact that a 2013 Gallup poll found that 61 percent of Americans think the death penalty is morally justified.

Polls also indicate that although public concern about crime has lessened, it is still substantial. That 2013 Gallup poll found 55 percent of Americans think crime is an extremely serious or very serious problem, and the fact is that the murder rate in the United States is three times what it is in Canada. This suggests that crime is still a viable political issue that we will hear about from some politicians.

Guido H. Stempel III

Further Reading

Dugan, Andrew. 2013. More Say Crime Is Serious Problem in U.S. Than Locally. The Gallup Poll. www.gallup.com/poll/165677/say-crime-serious-problem-locally.aspx. Accessed January 15, 2015.

Loo, Dennis D., and Grimes, Ruth-Ellen M. 2004. "Polls, Politics and Crime: The Law and Order Issue of the 1960s." *Western Criminology Review* 5(1): 50–67.

League of Women Voters

The League of Women Voters was formed in 1919, six months before the ratification of the 19th Amendment, which gave women the right to vote. It was created at the suggestion of

Carrie Chapman Catt, president of the National Woman Suffrage Association. While the League was set up to assure the voting rights of women, it extended its concerns to the voting rights of men and of minorities. It voted to admit men as members in 1973.

From the beginning the League was political but nonpartisan. The League promoted and lobbied for such issues as education, the right to vote, health care, civil rights, and rights of children. However, the League did not support or oppose candidates. The League sometimes finds itself in conflict with one of the parties when the League's position on an issue is contrary to that of a party. Currently that is the situation on voters' rights because the Republican Party favors voter ID requirements and restrictions on time and place of voting that the League opposes.

The League works to facilitate voting and protect the rights of voters. It tells voters where and how to register, what the requirements are for registering, and what the deadline is for registering. It informs voters of the places and times to vote. It works against gerrymandering and works to keep elections open and honest.

The League began as a group of state organizations but moved toward putting units in congressional districts. By 1924 there were League units in 342 of the 435 congressional districts. Currently there is the national League and leagues in each of the 50 states, the District of Columbia, Puerto Rico, and the Virgin Islands. There are leagues in 765 communities, and there are 140,000 members.

Local leagues have focused on informing voters. Voters guides are prepared and either printed or put online. Many newspapers bear the cost of printing the guides and include them as supplements in the paper. Short questionnaires are sent to all the candidates for local offices. State Leagues send questionnaires for state offices and distribute responses to the local leagues so they can include them in the local voters' guides. Responses are published as submitted, which makes the candidate, not the League, responsible for what is said.

Personal attacks are not permitted. Of course, it is up to the candidate whether or not to return the questionnaire, and many do not. It is often the case that one candidate for a given office is included in the voters' guide while his or her opponent is not. The League, however, is not required to have entries for all candidates. The questionnaire provides the opportunity for all to participate, but it is completely up to the candidate to take advantage of the opportunity.

Local leagues also sponsor debates that are open to the public, and many are broadcast on radio or television. All candidates are invited, but, as is the case with voters' guides, some candidates decline to participate. A typical format for debates is to allow each candidate to make a brief opening statement. Then a panel of journalists directs questions to the candidates. Candidates may also have the opportunity to make brief closing statements. The voters' guides and debates offer voters more information about the issues in elections than they get from local media in most instances.

The League sponsored debates between presidential debates in 1976, 1980, and 1984. This came about because of concerns that if the networks sponsored them the Equal Time provision in the regulations of the Federal Communications Commission might require that third-and fourth-party candidates be included. However, although the League of Women Voters was the sponsor, the networks provided facilities at no charge.

The League ended sponsorship in 1988 because of demands from candidates and the political parties that the League felt would make the debates a fraud. Issues included who would select the journalists for the panels at the debates and what follow-up questions would be allowed.

As it nears its 100th anniversary, the League is a respected force in informing the electorate and a major force in keeping our elections fair and open and in ensuring the right of citizens to vote.

Guido H. Stempel III

Further Reading

Maxwell, Kay J. 2007. "The League of Women Voters Through the Decades." League of Women Voters of Oregon. voteoregon.org/files/pdf/LWVThroughthedecades-april2007.pdf. Accessed January 15, 2015.

Libel

Libel is a civil or criminal wrong caused by a defendant's denigration or unfair criticism of a plaintiff. The law against libel has presented to the American system of freedom of expression some of its most momentous challenges, in attempts to balance the values of power, dignity, reputation, civility, and prosperity, on the one hand, with the values of liberty, equality, accountability, democracy, and truth on the other. The result is a compromised, complicated legal regime that frustrates ardent supporters of any of these values.

Libel law, which was invented partly to provide an alternative to dueling or other violence when one's honor was sullied, has prominent places in both private law and constitutional law in the United States. Common-law libel is a tort, a noncriminal legal wrong committed by a private party, such as an individual or organization, against another private party. (Government cannot be libeled, and government officials as accused libelers are generally protected by constitutional privilege.) The exact principles depend on the common-law jurisdiction where a case arises. In tort law, "defamation" may be the preferred term; libel is often called printed defamation while slander is oral defamation, a largely anachronistic distinction in the Internet age.

Defamation, according to its most basic definition, is a communication that harms a plaintiff's reputation, i.e., how other people regard the plaintiff. By establishing with "a preponderance of evidence" that the defamation was communicated, that the plaintiff was identified in the communication, that the communication was defamatory, and that the communication resulted in injury, the plaintiff may recover actual, punitive, special, and/or compensatory damages from the defendant. Common-law defenses that can completely defeat a libel plaintiff's case include the following:

- Truth. The defendant should prevail if the defamatory statement is shown to be true.
- Conditional or qualified privilege. The defendant may succeed if the publication was an accurate and fair representation of the content of a public record or proceeding of government.
- Fair comment. Common law shields even harsh commentary on the public offerings of film companies, restaurants, product manufacturers, and museums, among other sources of culture.

Criminal libel law has a notorious history. One branch proscribes seditious libel, defined as criticism of authority. During the colonial era, critics in England and America were deterred from, and severely punished for, expressing disrespect of religious, political, and royal persons and policies. A legendary example was the failed prosecution in 1735 of John Peter Zenger for publishing newspaper attacks on New York's royal governor. Seditious libel prosecutions faded in England and America, but the concept survived the ratification of the Constitution and the First Amendment. In the Sedition Act of 1798, the Federalist Congress provided for fines and prison sentences for criticism of the president and Congress. Twenty-five Republicans were arrested, 11 were tried, and 10 were convicted. Each was fined up to $1,000 and/or sentenced to up to 18 months of confinement. The Sedition Act expired in 1800, but Congress has subsequently enacted, and prosecutors have applied, other statutes punishing forms of dissent that civil rights groups argue should be protected by the First Amendment.

The second branch of criminal libel law, more common outside of the United States than inside and not part of federal law, has been enacted by states that want to criminalize insulting others. Sixteen states have such statutes, from which a trickle of mostly misdemeanor cases continues to flow. Noted journalists in the 19th and early 20th centuries served jail time and paid fines for editorially attacking their competitors and political opponents.

Although both civil and criminal libel law belongs to the states, the U.S. Supreme Court has been drawn into the issues because of their implications for freedom of speech and the press. Civil libel law was at the root of perhaps the most important First Amendment case the Court ever decided, *New York Times* v. *Sullivan* in 1964 when the Court, in dicta, compared civil libel law to seditious libel law, for the first time indicating that seditious libel law was incompatible with the First Amendment. The justices seemed unanimous in assuming that "although the Sedition Act was never tested in this Court, . . . the attack upon its validity has carried the day in the court of history." The Court feared that public officials as libel plaintiffs could use the civil court, as an instrument of government, to award amounts of damages that were so large as to harm critics of government even more than the fines and jail sentences in seditious libel laws. But the Court rejected an opportunity categorically to declare government officials' civil libel complaints to be unconstitutional.

Instead the Court decided that plaintiffs who can redress harm to their reputations in the marketplace of ideas should be disadvantaged compared to the majority of plaintiffs who have little ability to counteract defamation in the public media. In the Sullivan case and its progeny, the Court imposed on libel plaintiffs who are powerful government employees, famous public figures, and others who volunteer for public attention the "actual malice" rule, i.e., they must show with "clear and convincing evidence" that the defendant lied or was in "reckless disregard for the truth" in composing the allegedly libelous communication, a burden that was designed to be, and has turned out to be, exceedingly difficult to carry. Further, the Court has bestowed First Amendment protection upon libelous discussion of public affairs for its valued contributions to democratic deliberation.

Similarly, in three cases in the 1950s and 1960s, the Court did not rule criminal libel law unconstitutional. The justices seemed to tolerate criminal punishment for libel, suggesting that the actual-malice rule in criminal libel law was adequate to protect interests in freedom of expression.

The law of libel represents perhaps the best example of the application of First Amendment theory to the practical problems of freedom of expression. Weighty pronouncements about the importance of speech and press freedom to the democracy and the states' interests in respecting the reputations of individual citizens have been harmonized to create doctrines in an attempt to simultaneously protect political freedom and community stability.

Thomas A. Schwartz

Further Reading

Curtis Publishing Co., v. Butts, Associated Press v. Walker, 388 U.S. 130 (1967).
Garrison v. Louisiana, 379 U.S. 64 (1964).
Gertz v. Robert Welch, Inc., 418 U.S. 323 (1974).
Lewis, Anthony. 1991. *Make No Law: The Sullivan Case and the First Amendment*. New York: Random House.
New York Times v. Sullivan, 376 U.S. 254 (1964).

Liberal Voters

Less than a quarter of Americans identify themselves as politically liberal, although that self-identification has been slowly rising in recent years. The Gallup Poll reports that 23 percent of its respondents in 2013 said they are "liberal" in their political views, based upon telephone interviews with more than 18,000 adults conducted throughout that year. That figure was a modest but significant rise from 1992 when 17 percent said they consider themselves to be liberal.

Liberals tend to vote for Democratic Party candidates and are more likely than self-described conservatives or political moderates to come from racial and ethnic minority groups.

The meaning of liberalism or exactly what modern American liberals believe is even more difficult to define than the meaning of modern conservatism. There are, however, considerable historical sources for the broad movement that can be called liberalism. Just as Irish-born writer and politician Edmund Burke is often credited with being the intellectual father of conservatism in Great Britain, liberals look back fondly to the ideas espoused by English philosopher John Locke (1632–1704), whose theories of government had a profound influence upon the European Enlightenment and, particularly, the Founding Fathers of the American Revolution.

Locke—in his "Letters Concerning Toleration"—urged Europeans to adopt a philosophy of religious tolerance since it is not possible for people (and governments especially) to conclusively determine the truth among competing religions. The conflict between Roman Catholicism and the new theology of Protestantism led to considerable bloodshed in the 150 years before Locke's writing. Locke reasoned that government coercion in favor of any one religious view would prompt social disorder. He urged tolerance toward the natural diversity of ideas—a critical liberal notion.

More importantly, Locke believed humans were born with a natural right to "life, health, liberty or possessions"—a phrase that may have inspired Thomas Jefferson to espouse a right to "life, liberty and the pursuit of happiness" in the Declaration of Independence. As a consequence, Locke believed that governments must acknowledge the natural rights of the individual and must obtain "the consent of the governed" if they are to have legitimacy. Such thinking, of course, leads naturally to a rejection of monarchy, aristocracy, and class privilege—another liberal mainstay.

Liberalism enjoyed a robust history in the earliest days of the United States. Thomas Paine, author of the pro-revolutionary tract "Common Sense," was acknowledged as one of the world's leaders in radical liberal philosophy. Liberals generally called for curbs on central government powers and a commitment to individualism and the inherent rights of the individual. For the next 100 years, liberals in the United States and throughout Europe espoused support to acknowledge the rights of less empowered citizens: the poor, immigrants, women, and racial and ethnic minority groups. Liberalism did not always fit neatly into political party affiliations, however. Many liberals in the 1870s would have felt comfortable in the ranks of the Republican Party, which had just obtained, at tremendous cost, the freedom of America's black slaves.

Liberalism, because of its concerns for social welfare and its expectation that government acknowledge the rights of the politically and socially disadvantaged, in the late 19th century became associated with the rising economic movements of unionism, socialism and communism. Liberals, generally, called for toleration for these new economic ideas.

Liberalism in the United States came to political prominence and intellectual clarity as a result of the Great Depression, which began with the 1929 collapse of Wall Street and the rise of Democratic President Franklin Delano Roosevelt. The liberal response to the global economic collapse was an unprecedented, at least for the United States, reliance on federal economic intervention. Roosevelt embraced the theories of British economist John Maynard Keynes, who rejected traditional thinking that an unfettered marketplace would naturally achieve full employment. Keynes warned of economic "business cycles" that suffer damaging downturns, which can be mitigated through government intervention. Much of FDR's New Deal programs focused on Keynesian ideas of government spending to increase aggregate demand for goods and services during periods of economic bust. Roosevelt established a powerful political coalition of blue-collar workers, unions, unemployed persons, racial and ethnic minorities, and academics—all of whom were comfortable under a Democratic Party banner of liberalism since it espoused tolerance.

Under Roosevelt, American liberalism was firmly cemented to the notion that government intervention is an acceptable vehicle to ease human suffering. While accepting the Democratic presidential nomination for the first time in 1932, Roosevelt rejected critics who challenged that federal policies could undo the Great Depression. "While they prate of economic laws, men and women are starving. We must lay hold of the fact that economic laws are not made by nature. They are made by human beings," Roosevelt said.

The New Deal coalition dominated American national politics from 1932 through 1980, with only occasional lapses when Republicans Dwight Eisenhower and Richard Nixon won national elections with a brand of conservatism that seems mild today. This changed with the "conservative revolution" under Ronald Reagan, who assailed many fundamental liberal ideas about government. Reagan warned Americans they were suffering because government had become too big, too tax heavy, and too regulatory. Bill Clinton became the first two-term Democratic president after Reagan by espousing moderate ideas that often appealed to conservatives. But the political pendulum swung firmly to the left under two-term Democratic President Barack Obama, probably the most liberal president since Democrat Lyndon Johnson.

It's difficult to establish recent political goals of liberalism since the movement is so widely scattered among writers and philosophers. Nevertheless, there has been recent acknowledgement of the importance of the writings of Harvard University philosopher John Rawls (1921–2002) who wrote "A Theory of Justice" in 1971, which addressed the issue of "distributive justice" in how wealth is dispersed in U.S. society. He concluded that the "First Principle of Justice" is that "each person is to have an equal right to the most extensive basic liberty compatible with a similar liberty for others" while the "Second Principle" is that economic inequalities should be permitted only if "they are to be of the greatest benefit to the least-advantaged members of society." Rawls, during a time of rising political conservatism during the Reagan years, argued that society and government have fundamental obligations to serve "the least advantaged members of society."

Polls show that self-defined liberal voters generally support abortion rights for women, improved access to health insurance, gun control, greater acceptance for gay and lesbian rights including government-recognized same-sex marriage, increases in the federal mandatory minimum wage, decriminalization for personal use of marijuana, acceptance of euthanasia and doctor-assisted suicide, curbs on pollution to mitigate human-caused climate change, and a variety of policies under the umbrella of "economic justice" that, especially, call for equalization of pay between men and women.

Thomas K. Hargrove

Further Reading

Jones, Jeffrey M. 2014. "Liberal Self-Identification Edges Up to New High in 2013." January 10. Princeton, NJ: The Gallup Poll.

Rawls, John. 1999. *A Theory of Justice*. Rev. ed. Cambridge, MA: Belknap Press of Harvard University Press.

Ryan, Alan. 2012. *The Making of Modern Liberalism*. Princeton, NJ: Princeton University Press.

Libertarian Party

Members of the Libertarian Party espouse unregulated capitalism and individualism. Ayn Rand's novel *Atlas Shrugged* (1955) provides a unifying philosophy for the movement. Her anti-Christian brand of libertarianism attracted the anarchist wing of American conservatives, but it also appealed to former New Left elements. At a conference of the conservative Young Americans for Freedom (YAF) held in 1969, the libertarian wing of the group broke away and joined with left-wing libertarian groups to establish a new group, the Society for Individual Liberty. Murray Rothbard, one of the society's most prominent intellectuals and its spokesperson, described its credo in his book *For a New Liberty*. Under his influence and that of another leader, Jerome Tuccille, the libertarians started distancing themselves from the militant leftists.

Unhappiness with political affairs and the direction of the Nixon administration led to the formation of the Libertarian Party in the summer of 1971. On August 15, 1971, five disgruntled Republicans formed the party in David Nolan's apartment in Denver, Colorado.

Nolan was a writer for a small Denver advertising agency and a former member of the YAF. The cofounders were Hue Fritch, an anarchist; David Nelson, a college student; John James, a Denver architect; and Susan Nolan, wife of David Nolan. Nolan assumed the head of the new party on December 11, 1971.

The Libertarian Party positioned itself on the anarchist wing of the American political spectrum. Listed among its goals were the reduction of taxes, a decrease in government spending, the elimination of the Federal Reserve System, an end to all forms of censorship, the elimination of government intervention in labor relations, the abolition of the military draft, a repeal of the laws on the ownership of gold, a curtailment of laws on sexual conduct and drug use, and the end of all entangling foreign alliances. Leaders of the party attempted to win public office by promising to implement these goals, but their efforts had little success. They lacked corporate resources and an established party organization to win political power.

The party has been gaining political traction, both in the number of adherents who hold political office and in the votes received by its presidential candidates in national elections. The ticket of Gary Johnson and Jim Gray won more than 1.2 million votes in the 2012 General Election, roughly 1 percent of all votes cast. U.S. Rep. Ron Paul, a Texas Republican who ran as the Libertarian presidential candidate in 1988, drawing more than 430,000 votes, ran for the Republican presidential nomination in 2008 and 2012. Although Paul was never a serious challenge to the eventual GOP nominees, his candidacy was taken seriously and his Libertarian views enjoyed considerable attention among the news media and conservative voters.

Stephen E. Atkins and Thomas K. Hargrove

Further Reading

Diamond, Sara. 1995. *Roads to Dominion: Right-Wing Movements and Political Power in the United States.* New York: Guilford Press.
Ely, Jane. 2000. "At Very Least, Libertarians Excite Selves." *Houston Chronicle*, June 11, Outlook, p. 2.
Flynn, Adrianne. 1996. "Philosophy No Longer Burden to Libertarians." *Arizona Republic*, June 8, p. A1.
Goodman, Walter. 1984. "Libertarian Asking Less Government." *New York Times*, September 28, p. 2.
Sciacca, Joe. 1998. "The Naked Truth; Libertarians Have a Long Way to Go." *Boston Herald*, October 19.

Limbaugh, Rush (1951–)

Conservative American radio talk show host and commentator Rush Hudson Limbaugh III was born January 12, 1951, in Cape Girardeau, Missouri. He went on to become one of the highest paid media personalities in history, signing a contract in 2008 that paid $400 million through 2016. His three-hour daily national broadcast *The Rush Limbaugh Show* is the highest ranked talk-radio program in the United States.

Limbaugh became the symbol and the most visible practitioner of conservative talk radio, itself an influential political medium. Although many of his remarks became controversial over the years, prompting him sometimes to apologize, Limbaugh has been widely cited as an important voice for conservatism. Former President Ronald Reagan sent Limbaugh a letter in 1992 thanking him "for all you're doing to promote Republican and conservative principles" and calling Limbaugh "the Number One voice for conservatism in our country."

Limbaugh dropped out of college at Southeast Missouri State University to move to Pennsylvania in 1972 to pursue a career as a radio personality. He started as a disc jockey at the small WIXZ-AM station on a top-40 music show and soon moved to Pittsburgh's KQV-AM as an evening disc jockey in 1973. He was fired the following year and returned to Missouri, where he eventually became promotions director for the Kansas City Royals baseball team. He moved to Sacramento, California, in 1984 to replace Morton Downey Jr. as a talk show host on KFBK-AM.

Limbaugh's success was connected to two important movements in radio broadcasting. First, AM radio was in rapid decline in the 1980s since FM stations could carry music with much improved fidelity. But AM signals were more than sufficient for the human voice, prompting this medium to focus on news and commentary. Also, the Federal Communications Commission in 1987 repealed the Fairness Doctrine, which had previously required stations to provide free air time to opposing views after controversial opinions had been broadcast.

After gaining the ear of ABC Radio President Edward McLaughlin for his work in Sacramento, Limbaugh moved to New York City in 1988 to begin his national radio show on flagship station WABC. Relentlessly conservative, with a quick and flamboyant wit, Limbaugh quickly drew attention. Lew Grossberger wrote a 1990 *New York Times* feature called "The Rush Hours," in which he described Limbaugh's on-air style as "bouncing between earnest lecturer and political vaudevillian."

Limbaugh seems to covet an "I-can't-believe-he-just-said-that" reaction from his listeners. A few examples follow:

About pro-choice feminists: "A Feminazi is a woman to whom the most important thing in life is seeing to it that as many abortions as possible are performed. Their unspoken reasoning is quite simple. Abortion is the ultimate symbol of women's emancipation from the power and influence of men."

About the National Football League: "Look, let me put it to you this way: the NFL all too often looks like a game between the Bloods and the Crips without any weapons. There, I said it."

Speaking about Iraq War protests in 2003: "It's beyond me how anybody can look at these protestors and call them anything other than what they are: anti-American, anti-capitalist, pro-Marxist Communists."

About President Obama: "What he is talking about is the absorption of as much of the private sector by the U.S. government as possible, from the banking business, to the mortgage industry, the automobile business, to health care. I do not want the government in charge of all of these things. I don't want this to work. Okay, I'll send you a response, but I don't need 400 words. I need four: I hope he fails."

Limbaugh laid out his beliefs in great detail in two books, *The Way Things Ought to Be* in 1992 and *See, I Told You So* in 1993. Both quickly rose to number one on the *New York Times* best seller list. He experimented from 1992 to 1996 with a half-hour television show produced by Roger Ailes on the Fox network but eventually decided that radio was his preferred medium.

The Rush Limbaugh Show never wavered in its appeal to a niche audience of conservative white listeners who share his outrage at expansive government, political-correctness, and the Democratic Party. He repeatedly won the Marconi Radio Award for Syndicated Radio Personality of the Year given by the National Association of Broadcasters. He was inducted into the National Radio Hall of Fame in 1993. Limbaugh moved to Palm Beach, Florida, in 1996 and broadcasted his show from there.

Limbaugh has had several personal controversies. He faced criminal investigation for illegally obtaining the prescription drugs oxycodone and hydrocodone in 2003. After the investigation was reported in national tabloids, Limbaugh went on the air with a remarkable confession: "You know I have always tried to be honest with you and open about my life, so I need to tell you that part of what you have heard and read is correct. I am addicted to prescription pain medication." He said his addiction resulted from excruciating back pain following unsuccessful surgery.

The drug investigation continued for several years. He was arrested in 2006 on a Florida charge of "doctor shopping" to obtain pain killers from multiple physicians. He denied the charge but three years later agreed to pay $30,000 to defray the cost of the criminal investigation, to complete an 18-month period of therapy with his physician, and to submit to random drug testing.

Some of Limbaugh's comments brought withering national criticism. He called actor Michael J. Fox "shameless" for "moving all around and shaking" in a political TV ad Fox made advocating funding for stem cell research for Parkinson's disease. He said that Iraqi War veterans who returned to the United States to oppose the military occupation of Iraq are "phony soldiers." Limbaugh said Georgetown University law student Sandra Fluke was a "slut" and a "prostitute" after she testified before Congress urging that insurance coverage for contraceptives should be mandated by health care reforms. Limbaugh later apologized on his show for the remarks, apologies that Fluke rejected.

Limbaugh, who has married four times, has no children.

Thomas K. Hargrove

Further Reading

Chafets, Zev. 2010. *Rush Limbaugh: An Army of One*. New York: Sentinel.

Colford, Paul. 1993. *The Rush Limbaugh Story: Talent on Loan from God: An Unauthorized Biography*. New York: St Martin's Press.

Franken, Al. 1996. *Rush Limbaugh Is a Big Fat Idiot and Other Observations*. New York: Random House.

Limited Effects Model

The Limited Effects Model says that the main effect of mass media in political campaigns is to reinforce initial intentions of voters. The model is based on the following findings from a series of voting studies in the 1940s and 1950s:

- Voters' choices were based on religion, social class, and ethnic and family identi-
  fications rather than new information obtained from the media and other sources
  during the campaign.
- Very little conversion on political choices occurred during the campaign.
- Voter choices were reinforced by face-to-face interactions with like-minded individuals including families, friends, and coworkers.

Berelson et al. offered this conclusion regarding the limited effects model: "The usual
analogy between the voting 'decision' and the more or less carefully calculated decisions of
consumers or businessmen or courts . . . may be quite incorrect. For many voters political
preferences may better be considered analogous to cultural tastes—in music, literature, recreational activities, dress, ethics, speech, and social behavior. . . . Both have their origin in
ethnic, sectional, class, and family traditions. Both exhibit stability and resistance to change
for individuals but flexibility and adjustment over generations for the society as a whole.
Both seem to be matters of sentiment and disposition rather than 'reasoned preferences.'

"While both are responsive to changed conditions and unusual stimuli, they are relatively invulnerable to direct argumentation and vulnerable to indirect social influences.
Both are characterized more by faith than by conviction and by wishful expectation rather
than careful prediction of consequences" (pp. 310–311).

A number of researchers subsequently explained the limited effects model by analyzing three processes in message reception:

- Selective Exposure and Attention: Audiences are receptive to information supporting existing attitudes, beliefs, and behaviors, and avoid contradictory information
  to avoid dissonance, an uncomfortable cognitive state.
- Selective Perception: Perception is functionally selective; audiences interpret
  information to support existing attitudes, beliefs, and behaviors.
- Retention Selectivity: Audiences learn and remember supportive material more
  readily than contradictory material.

The limited effects model has been extended to account for an "activation" effect of
the mass media and other information sources on voter choices. According to the activation model, political campaigns and media information are important because they activate
"latent predispositions" (Finkel 1993, p. 4). Therefore, individual votes depend less on
attitude change than on activating long-term predispositions based on group memberships
and demographic characteristics, including race and pre-campaign party identification. In
this sense, the activation model supports the limited effects model: voters do not change
during a campaign; political information reinforces existing choices; and political information activates latent predispositions.

In a test of the activation model, Finkel found that race, pre-campaign party identification, and evaluations of incumbent performance accounted for over 80 percent of all
votes in the 1980 election. He also found that preconvention preferences of voters were
"extremely" stable.

The limited effects model has been reevaluated in light of recent developments:

- the increase in voters self-identifying as independent—potentially individuals who
  would be more susceptible to campaign influence

- a shift from attitude and behavioral change as media effects to other cognitive processes such as framing of issues and evaluations of the salience of issues
- a shift from studying voter choices as media effects to voter turnout, which could be more susceptible to media influence
- a shift from studying short-term media effects (e.g., during a campaign) to long-term effects.

Alexis Tan

Further Reading

Berelson, Bernard, Paul Lazarsfeld, and William N. McPhee. 1954. *Voting.* Chicago: University of Chicago Press.

Finle, Steven. 1993. "Reexamining the 'Minimal Effects' Model in Recent Presidential Campaigns." *The Journal of Politics* 55(1): 1–21.

Limited Government

The notion of limited government is at the foundation of much of American political thought. Henry David Thoreau began his essay "On the Duty of Civil Disobedience" with the famous phrase: "That government is best which governs least." The phrase has often been misattributed to Thomas Jefferson, the founder of the Democratic Party. However, the third president of the United States personally vacillated on the question of how much government is necessary. Jefferson wrote in 1782 that "great societies cannot exist without government." But shortly before his death, Jefferson wrote to a friend in 1824 that "we have more machinery of government than is necessary, too many parasites living on the labor of the industrious."

The idea of limited government, simultaneously contains elements of modern liberalism and conservatism, although in recent years it has become a mantra of American conservative thought. It began as a revolutionary notion of classical liberalism that challenged older doctrines of government like the divine right of kings, which taught that power naturally extends from individuals appointed by heaven to have sweeping authority over human affairs. Englishman John Locke, one of the most influential classical liberals, celebrated the individual and said that government can only derive its just powers from the consent of the governed. Adam Smith, in his seminal *The Wealth of Nations* published the same year that the United States declared its independence from Great Britain, called for limited government, an end to restrictive trade policies, and the elimination of royal monopolies. The individual, Smith argued, could be trusted to direct his own affairs wisely through the desire for personal profit. Government, however, often interferes with the natural tendency of enlightened self-interest, he said.

James Madison spelled out much of classical liberalism's philosophy of limited government when he presented the Bill of Rights to the first United States Congress in 1789. Those 10 amendments to the newly ratified Constitution set rigorous limits defining what government may not do to individual liberties. The last amendment even created a default clause so that "the powers not delegated to the United States by the Constitution, nor prohibited by it to the States, are reserved to the States respectively, or to the people."

The liberal notion of limited government was tested as the United States matured and faced new economic challenges. During the Progressive Era, laissez-faire economics seemed to threaten individual liberties. Late 19th and early 20th century liberals looked to government to check the growing excesses of multimillionaire capitalists and the so-called "robber barons" who dominated the Gilded Age. During the Great Depression, President Franklin D. Roosevelt's New Deal policies expanded the role of government much further to become an economic and social force to stem poverty and suffering.

Liberalism was changing as a result, wrote Eric Alterman, a senior fellow at the Center for American Progress. "Over the course of the 19th Century, the traditional or "classical" understanding of liberalism came to represent a kind of conservatism, as powerful institutions (including, primarily, corporations and trusts) found ways to constrict the freedom of individuals through the onerous working conditions of early industrial factories while at the same time paying tribute to the liberal virtues of self-reliance and freedom to choose one's own path to prosperity," Alterman said.

FDR, shortly before his death, outlined a "Second Bill of Rights" in 1944 that included rights to adequate food, clothing, recreation, education, decent homes, and protection from unfair competition and dominating monopolies at home or abroad.

It was in response to modern liberalism's embrace of strong interventionist government that the philosophy of limited government became a fundamental principal of modern conservatism. Ronald Reagan helped define and lead a "conservative revolution" in the 1980s under a maxim that classical liberals would have applauded: "As government expands, liberty contracts." And Reagan did so with humor when he summed up government's view of economics: "If it moves, tax it. If it keeps moving, regulate it. And if it stops moving, subsidize it."

But liberals never, really, abandoned their commitment to the ideal of limited government. Democratic President Bill Clinton extolled the politics of a Third Way, which acknowledged the importance of individual economic rights over powerful central governments. The biggest applause line Clinton ever received during a State of the Union Address was delivered on January 27, 1996, when both Republicans and Democrats rose to their feet for several minutes to clap loudly on the floor of the House of Representatives. "The era of big government is over," Clinton said. After the extended applause ended, the president continued, "But we can't go back to a time when our citizens were just left to fend for themselves."

The political tensions over how large the federal government should be, or what role it should play, will continue probably indefinitely even as Americans generally remain committed to the ideal that the best governments are limited.

Thomas K. Hargrove

Further Reading

Alterman, Eric, and Kevin Mattson. 2012. *The Cause: The Fight for American Liberalism from Franklin Roosevelt to Barack Obama*. New York: Viking.

Hudelson, Richard. 1999. *Modern Political Philosophy*. New York: M.E. Sharpe Inc.